977.5
McD

154897

McDonald.
History of the Irish in Wisconsin in the nineteenth century.

THE IRISH-AMERICANS

This is a volume in the Arno Press collection

THE IRISH-AMERICANS

Advisory Editor
Lawrence J. McCaffrey

Editorial Board
Margaret E. Conners
David N. Doyle
James P. Walsh

*See last pages of this volume
for a complete list of titles*

History of the Irish in Wisconsin
In the Nineteenth Century

Grace McDonald

ARNO PRESS

A New York Times Company

New York — 1976

Editorial Supervision: ANDREA HICKS

Reprint Edition 1976 by Arno Press Inc.

Copyright © 1954 by The Catholic University
of America Press, Inc.

Reprinted by permission of The Catholic
University of America Press and Grace McDonald

THE IRISH-AMERICANS
ISBN for complete set: 0-405-09317-9
See last pages of this volume for titles.

Manufactured in the United States of America

Library of Congress Cataloging in Publication Data

McDonald, Grace, 1917-
   History of the Irish in Wisconsin in the nineteenth century.

   (The Irish-Americans)
   Reprint of the author's thesis, Catholic University of America, published by the Catholic University of America Press, Washington.
   Bibliography: p.
   1. Irish Americans--Wisconsin--History.
2. Wisconsin--History. I. Title. II. Series.
[F590.I6M32 1976]   977.5'004'9162   76-6355
ISBN 0-405-09348-9

HISTORY OF THE IRISH IN WISCONSIN
IN THE NINETEENTH CENTURY

This dissertation was approved by Professor John T. Farrell, as director, and by Sister Marie Carolyn Klinkhamer, O.P., and the Reverend Henry J. Browne, as readers.

The Catholic University of America

History of the Irish in Wisconsin In the Nineteenth Century

A DISSERTATION

SUBMITTED TO THE FACULTY OF THE GRADUATE SCHOOL OF ARTS AND
SCIENCES OF THE CATHOLIC UNIVERSITY OF AMERICA IN
PARTIAL FULFILLMENT OF THE REQUIREMENTS FOR
THE DEGREE OF DOCTOR OF PHILOSOPHY

THE CATHOLIC UNIVERSITY OF AMERICA PRESS
WASHINGTON, D. C.
1954

Copyright 1954
THE CATHOLIC UNIVERSITY OF AMERICA PRESS, INC.

MURRAY AND HEISTER
WASHINGTON, D. C.

PRINTED BY
TIMES AND NEWS PUBLISHING CO.
GETTYSBURG, PA., U.S.A.

TABLE OF CONTENTS

	PAGE
LIST OF TABLES AND MAPS	vi
PREFACE	vii
ABBREVIATIONS USED IN FOOTNOTES	ix

CHAPTER

I. FACTORS INFLUENCING IRISH IMMIGRATION INTO WISCONSIN 1

II. LOCATION AND OCCUPATIONS OF THE IRISH IN SOUTHERN WISCONSIN 40

III. LOCATION AND OCCUPATIONS OF IRISHMEN IN CENTRAL AND NORTHERN WISCONSIN 86

IV. WISCONSIN IRISHMEN IN POLITICS, 1836-1866 124

V. WISCONSIN IRISHMEN IN POLITICS, 1866-1900 150

VI. THE RELIGIOUS AND SOCIAL LIFE OF WISCONSIN IRISHMEN 194

APPENDIX—TABLES OF IRISH POPULATION BY TOWNSHIPS 255

BIBLIOGRAPHY 299

INDEX 309

TABLES TO BE FOUND IN TEXT

TABLE		PAGE
1.	Irish Arrivals in the United States, 1841-1860	3
2.	Irish Arrivals in Milwaukee, 1879-1884	37
3.	Occupations of Irishmen in the City of Milwaukee, 1850 and 1860	53

LIST OF MAPS

MAP		PAGE
1.	Foreign-born Irish in Wisconsin, 1850	44
2.	Irish Families in Wisconsin, 1850	45
3.	Foreign-born Irish in Wisconsin, 1860	63
4.	Irish Families in Wisconsin, 1860	64

PREFACE

This study of the Irish in Wisconsin in the nineteenth century is an account of a minority national group within the state. Census data for the years 1840 to 1870 reveal that the Irish were the second largest foreign-born group in Wisconsin. Their entrance into the state generally preceded that of the Germans and paralleled it, but the Irish were gradually outnumbered. No effort prior to this study has been made to recount and evaluate the participation of this national group in the life of the state. Since Irish immigration into Wisconsin was not an isolated movement, but part of the great exodus of emigrants from Ireland to the United States, a brief summary of that larger movement is first given as a background. Throughout the study an attempt has been made to place the history of Wisconsin Irishmen into the broader scope of state and national history. This study is neither an endeavor to account for every Irishman who held a political office or who could claim some right to recognition, nor to satisfy the antiquarian or the genealogist's interest in specific Irish families.

The more important sources of information for this study are: the United States Manuscript Census for the years 1840 to 1870; newspapers, particularly the Boston *Pilot*, the Milwaukee *Catholic Citizen*, and the Milwaukee *Sentinel;* the papers of the Democratic state chairman, Wendell A. Anderson; letters of the Democratic state chairman, E. C. Wall, addressed to United States Senator William F. Vilas; and the papers of the Republican state chairmen, Elisha W. Keyes and Ellis B. Usher.

The writer wishes to acknowledge the courteous assistance received from the staff of the National Archives, of the Mullen Library at the Catholic University of America, of the manuscript and newspaper divisions of the Library of the State Historical Society of Wisconsin, and of the Milwaukee Public Library.

The research on this subject was begun at the suggestion of the late Professor Richard J. Purcell to whom the writer is greatly indebted. To Professor John T. Farrell under whose direction this study was completed the writer is deeply grateful; also to Sister Marie Carolyn Klinkhamer, O.P., and to the Reverend Henry J. Browne, who read the manuscript. Thanks are due Alice Smith and the Reverend Peter Leo Johnson who offered helpful criticism and suggestions; also to geographer Kenneth Bertrand. Finally, the writer expresses gratitude to her Superiors and the Franciscan Sisters of Perpetual Adoration for the opportunity of pursuing graduate work at the Catholic University of America.

ABBREVIATIONS USED IN FOOTNOTES

AAB—Archives of the Archdiocese of Baltimore
CUA—Catholic University of America, Department of Archives and Manuscripts
ADL—Archives of the Diocese of La Crosse
NA—National Archives, Washington, D. C.
ASRC—Archives of St. Rose Convent, La Crosse, Wisconsin
WSHS—State Historical Society of Wisconsin, Manuscript Division
AHR—American Historical Review
CHR—Catholic Historical Review
WMH—Wisconsin Magazine of History

CHAPTER I

FACTORS INFLUENCING IRISH IMMIGRATION INTO WISCONSIN

Immigration has been a vital factor in the historical development of the American republic. European immigrants and their descendants not only constituted the early American population but they continued to enter the United States throughout the nineteenth and into the twentieth century. These immigrants and their families occupied the various regions of the United States, helped to develop its vast resources, to frame its laws, and to shape its institutions. Significant within the influx of Europeans into American ports was the large immigration from the British Isles, particularly from Ireland.

During the great Atlantic migration of the nineteenth century Ireland ranked highest among five northern and western European countries in immigration to the United States for the twenty-year period from 1840-1859. It held second place during the decades from 1860-1869 and 1880-1889, and ranked third from 1870-1879.[1] Statistics show that during these same years there was an almost continuous influx of Irish immigrants into Wisconsin; therefore a study of Irish immigration into the state must be set into the general background of Irish immigration into the United States and of migration from the eastern United States into Wisconsin.

During the decade from 1831 to 1840 a conservative estimate places at 207,381 the number of Irish entering the United States. This figure is probably an understatement. Immigration records at the eastern ports were not efficiently kept at that time and arrivals through Canada were not recorded.[2] Conditions on both sides of the ocean combined to form the causes for this early nineteenth-

---

[1] Maurice R. Davie, *World Immigration with Special Reference to the United States* (New York: The Macmillan Company, 1946), p. 55.
[2] Frances Morehouse, "The Irish Migration of the Forties," *AHR*, XXXIII (April, 1928), 588-589.

century migration of the Irish to America. In Ireland a failure of the potato crop in 1831 caused many who had the necessary means to emigrate for America. Ships bringing corn to the hungry Irish carried back emigrants to the United States. An epidemic of the cholera in the 1830's also furnished motivation for emigration. Some of the evicted tenants, victims of the Irish land system and too poor to provide for their own transportation, were helped by their landlords with small sums sufficient to pay their passage.[3] Others left because of dissatisfaction with English rule which found expression in movements for Catholic emancipation, for repeal of political union with England, and in tithe agitation.[4] Reports of high wages, security, low taxes, expansive tracts of land, political and religious freedom, and social equality to be found in the United States in contrast with the reality of low wages, instability, high taxes, small farms, political, religious, and social oppression in Ireland were inducements too attractive to be resisted.

By the early 1840's, therefore, as Irish newspapers indicate, there was a steady outpouring of emigrants during the spring and summer months of each year.[5] In certain sections emigration had become the fashion and practically the sole topic of conversation, for it was reported, "people think of nothing else."[6] At times there was group migration of individuals from the same neighborhood, sometimes of a "family, consisting of twenty or thirty individuals,"[7] or even of a group of workers, such as the fifty woolen operatives who left from Wexford in September, 1841.[8]

---

[3] Boston *Pilot*, May 7, 1842; May 25, 1844. This latter reference mentions the tariff and corn laws as causes of alarm and hence of emigration. Morehouse, *loc. cit.*, pp. 579-592, elucidates the land system and evictions in Ireland.

[4] *Cf.* W. F. Adams, *Ireland and Irish Emigration to the New World from 1815 to the Famine* (New Haven: 1932), chap. iv; also, Boston *Pilot*, for items concerning repeal agitation.

[5] Boston *Pilot*, May 9, 1840, citing the Cork *Reporter;* May 7, June 11, 1842; May 25, 1844, citing the Kerry *Examiner;* June 8, 1844, and May 24, 1845, citing the *Derry Journal;* Racine *Advocate*, May 28, 1841, citing the Tuam *Herald*.

[6] Boston *Pilot*, May 24, 1845.

[7] *Ibid.*, May 9, 1840.

[8] *Ibid.*, September 11, 1841.

Hence, by 1845, when one of the worst potato famines ever to occur in Ireland brought on starvation and untold suffering, the stream of emigration from Ireland to the United States had already reached large-sized proportions. Alarmed and fearful of the future, thousands of Irishmen swelled the tide and by 1850 the number of Irish emigrants reached its peak. The number emigrating in 1847 more than doubled that of 1846. Of this surge, Marcus L. Hansen says:

> Probably few of those who decided on emigration in 1847 reasoned consciously regarding their state. Their impulse was merely to get away. A curse rested upon the land. Misfortunes had been great; they might become greater. "Poor Ireland's done," "The country's gone forever," "It can never again recover"—these were the expressions heard wherever emigrants congregated. Even in parts of the country which had escaped the severest blows the sentiment prevailed, for they feared their turn might come next.[9]

Statistics for the years 1841-1860 reveal the number of Irish arrivals in the United States:[10]

TABLE 1

Year	Number	Year	Number
1841	37,772	1851	221,253
1842	51,342	1852	159,548
1843	19,670	1853	162,649
1844	33,490	1854	101,606
1845	44,821	1855	49,627
1846	51,752	1856	54,349
1847	105,752	1857	54,361
1848	112,934	1858	26,873
1849	159,398	1859	35,216
1850	164,004	1860	48,637

[9] M. L. Hansen, *The Atlantic Migration, 1607-1860* (Cambridge: Harvard University Press, 1940), p. 249.

[10] Richard J. Purcell, "The Irish Immigrant, the Famine and the Irish-American," *The Irish Ecclesiastical Record,* Fifth Series, LXIX (October, 1947), 861-862. Morehouse, *loc. cit.,* pp. 590-591, after comparing the British and United States' official figures arrives at the following:

Year	Number	Year	Number
1846	92,484	1849	204,771
1847	196,224	1850	216,041
1848	173,744		

Carl Wittke, *We Who Built America* (New York: Prentice-Hall, 1940), p. 131, cites the numbers given by Morehouse.

Before 1847 the bulk of emigration was made up of the small but more substantial farmers, evicted tenants, and laborers. The earlier migration included Irishmen chiefly from the northern and western section while that during the 'forties and after was predominantly from the southern portion and therefore indicative of a larger number of Catholics.[11]

The famine years brought all types of Irishmen to American shores. For many there was the necessity of making a choice between starvation or emigration. Many used their last cent for the voyage; others obtained the amount by begging. Some landlords, afraid that the tenant would become a charge upon the estate, paid the passage. Between the years 1850-1860 many Irishmen in better economic circumstances left for the United States, because support of paupers in the workhouses and the functioning of the poor law proved to be a drain on their financial status which emigration alone could relieve. Even after conditions in Ireland improved, emigration continued. Propaganda and advertising still made emigration to the United States appear enticing and better wages in Ireland made it possible.[12] In the latter half of the 1850's, however, there was a decided decline in the number of Irish migrating to the United States. A revival of Know-Nothing activity caused bitter opposition toward foreigners, Irish Catholics in particular. During the panic of 1857 reports reached Ireland of low wages, unemployment, and a general economic depression in the midst of which foreigners were unable to compete with native-American labor. Conditions were more prosperous in Ireland and there were few left to emigrate. Most of those who did leave for America were sent for and aided by relatives and friends.[13]

Emigration agents and shipping companies throughout the nineteenth century were not slow to take advantage of the situation as is evidenced by the advertisements and propaganda appearing in circulars, pamphlets, emigration handbooks, and newspa-

---

[11] Adams, *op. cit.*, p. 222. Boston *Pilot,* May 9, 1840; May 7, June 11, 1842.
[12] Hansen, *op. cit.*, pp. 280-283.
[13] *Ibid.*, pp. 281, 302-305; Purcell, *loc. cit.*, p. 865.

pers. Adams states that for every notice of British North America in the Irish press there were at least three of the United States.[14] These often played on anti-British sentiment and glorified the United States: the British colonist in America, "the cords of oppression being pulled too tightly," had "snapped the connection and established the simplest, most democratic and happiest republic" in the world. No rents, light taxes, the right to vote, fertile soil, ownership of land, thousands of navigable rivers "crowded with packets and barges of all sizes"—all of this the United States offered, but above all, freedom from persecution. "It is not to be wondered at . . . that men should crowd into it . . . from Ireland, the most oppressed and persecuted" country of all.[15] Besides such glowing accounts, letters from relatives and friends who had already made the voyage across the Atlantic told with enthusiasm of favorable conditions and possibilities of advancement.

Sums of money were sent by Irishmen in the United States to relatives and friends in Ireland either to better their condition in the homeland or to provide for their transportation to America. Brokers and shipping companies took advantage of this latter plan and either offered to secure exchange of the money or accepted prepaid passages.[16] Employers desiring cheap labor also provided sums for the passage of artisans and laborers.[17] Promises of good wages and steady employment were important incentives to many.[18]

Not even the Civil War stopped the influx of Irish immigrants. At this time young men especially were emigrating and upon

---

[14] Adams, *op. cit.*, p. 179. *Cf.* also, the Boston *Pilot,* March 3, 1838, citing the Dublin *Review;* October 23, 1841.

[15] Boston *Pilot,* July 17, 1841, citing the Dublin *Pilot.*

[16] Adams, *op. cit.*, pp. 180-182, says that two leading shipping agents at Belfast reported in 1834 that one-third of their passages to the United States was paid in America. The Boston *Pilot,* June 28, 1856, stated that sums remitted to Ireland from the American emigrants since 1848 amounted to £8,393,000. *Ibid.,* January 24, 1852, notes that remittances sent by relatives during 1850 were reported to total £957,000.

[17] Wittke, *op. cit.,* p. 131.

[18] Adams, *op. cit.,* p. 177.

arrival in the United States were persuaded to serve in the Union army. Britain accused the United States more than once during the war of having federal recruiting agents at work in Ireland. Tickets for free passage to America were distributed in Ireland according to a letter William West, American acting-consul in Dublin, addressed to the Secretary of State, William H. Seward, in 1864. West also wrote that many Irishmen had requested free passage to America, chiefly to join the army. How many tickets were distributed is not known.[19]

Various causes contributed to the continuous emigration of Irishmen after the Civil War. Because Ireland's slow industrial progress and weak agricultural economy provided no hope of advancement to the young men and women in their native country, they looked instead to America, the advertised land of opportunity. Emigration among the Irish youth had become almost a tradition. By the Irish Church Act, 1869, and the Land Act of 1870 Irish tenants had made gains in their attempts for security, but in 1879 the failure of the potato crop, which was accompanied by a deficiency in other crops, once more forcefully reminded the tenant farmer in Ireland of his precarious position. This accounts for the increased emigration in 1880 and in the years immediately following.[20] It was reported:

> ... the thoughts and longing hopes of thousands of Irishmen are turned to the United States as a haven of refuge and are fixed thereupon not only because of the famine, so-called, but by reason of the current political agitations which have to a certain extent transferred the discussion of the "Irish Question" to American soil.[21]

Looking for positive causes of Irish emigration during the post Civil War period John Elliott Cairns in 1873 listed the following:

---

[19] William D'Arcy, *The Fenian Movement in the United States: 1858-1886* (Washington, D. C.: Catholic University of America Press, 1947), pp. 61-63.

[20] Franklin E. Fitzpatrick, "The Irish Immigration into New York from 1865-1880" (Unpublished Master's thesis, Catholic University of America, 1948), pp. 3-9.

[21] *Ibid.*, p. 15, citing report of E. P. Brooks, U. S. Consul at Cork.

popular education which supplied the motive; steam and free trade which, furnishing the means for the expansion of industry and commerce, could not but facilitate emigration; progress of colonization, for the modern emigrant to America was entering a well-ordered society and emigration became less repulsive as colonization extended.[22]

Just as European immigration into the United States was a continual movement in varying degrees of intensity throughout the nineteenth century, so migration from the East to the West within the United States did not occur suddenly but was a steady, although uneven, flow. The years of the heaviest immigration into the United States were also the years of the largest migration to Wisconsin and other western states. The total immigration into the United States during the twenty-year period from 1830 to 1849 was approximately 1,400,000, while that during the six-year period from 1849-1855 alone totaled more than 2,000,000.[23] In the remaining years before 1860 the number of immigrants declined. During practically the same period, from 1831-1860, the population growth of Wisconsin was phenomenal. By 1830 there were only 3,245 inhabitants in the state. Returns from the 1836 territorial census revealed a total population of 11,036; in 1840, 30,945; in 1842, 46,678; and in 1846, 155,277. The official returns from the 1850 and 1860 census records indicated totals of 305,191 and 775,881 respectively. These statistics, therefore, show an increase between 1830 and 1840 of 27,700; between 1840 and 1850 of 274,246; and between 1851 and 1860 of 470,690, making a total increase of 773,636 persons in thirty years.

To some extent, therefore, as the foreign element moved into the eastern ports of the United States and diffused itself throughout New York and the New England States especially, many of the natives of these states were seeking new homes on the western frontier and in Wisconsin. As one report put it:

> The emigration to Wisconsin at the present time is said to be rapid beyond all precedent. There are whole

---

[22] John E. Cairnes, *Political Essays* (London, 1873), pp. 146-147.
[23] Joseph Schafer, *Four Wisconsin Counties, Prairie and Forest* (Madison: State Historical Society of Wisconsin, 1927), p. 85.

sections of the country that are now thickly settled that a few months ago were entirely uninhabited.[24]

Statistics from the Federal census of 1850 reveal the extent of this large migration to Wisconsin from the eastern states. About 135,000 of the total population of 305,191 were individuals born within the United States, but outside of Wisconsin.[25] The 1860 census discloses a Yankee population in the state of approximately 251,000 with about 120,000 of these from New York; 54,000 from the six New England states; 21,000 from Pennsylvania; and 42,000 from the four older states of the Old Northwest. The remaining number can be accounted as coming from New Jersey and from the southern states and the area west of the Mississippi River.[26]

Within this surging mass of newcomers into Wisconsin were many Irishmen. Although among the foreign-born group in Wisconsin, the Germans ranked first in 1850 and in 1860 with totals of 38,064 and 123,879 respectively, it is significant that the Irish ranked second with 21,043 and 49,961 or in a proportion of 6.9 per cent to the total population of Wisconsin in 1850, and approximately 6.4 per cent in 1860.[27] In 1850 persons from the British Isles were the most numerous of the foreign element in the state. The Irish led within this group at the same time making up 19.7 per cent of the total foreign-born population.

[24] Boston *Pilot*, July 19, 1845. Milwaukee *Sentinel*, May 23, 1850; May 29, 1850, reports the number of passengers who arrived within a week at Sheboygan as 691; at Milwaukee, 2,321. These two reports combined with arrivals in Racine and Kenosha and other ports bring the total for a week to about 4,000 persons.

[25] J. D. B. DeBow, *Statistical View of the United States: Compendium of the Seventh Census of 1850*, XX, 46. According to the 1850 census, of those born in the United States outside of Wisconsin, 68,595 were born in New York; 10,157 in Vermont; 6,285 in Massachusetts; 4,125 in Connecticut; 3,252 in Maine; 2,520 in New Hampshire, and 690 in Rhode Island. Approximately 10,000 each were born in Ohio and Pennsylvania.

[26] W. F. Raney, *Wisconsin, A Story of Progress* (New York: Prentice-Hall, 1940), p. 138.

[27] Schafer, *op. cit.*, p. 85. The Germans maintained their lead among the foreign-born in Wisconsin but after 1870 the Irish number declined, giving way to the Norwegian element which ranked second in 1880 and 1890.

What attracted so large a population to Wisconsin? In the mid-forties when the peopling of Wisconsin had become what has been termed a psychological movement, Wisconsin was still a territory but one actively agitating for statehood. With the exception of the two years after its organization into a territory in 1836, when it included Iowa, Minnesota, and parts of the Dakotas and Michigan, Wisconsin Territory extended over practically its present boundaries. Statehood was achieved in 1848.

The state was accessible through two important waterways: the Great Lakes linking it with the Northeast, and the Mississippi River on the west connecting it with the Ohio Valley and the East, and with St. Louis and New Orleans in the South. Immigrants also could gain entrance into the state by means of overland routes opened by the teamsters between Milwaukee and the lead mining region of the southwest. The Black Hawk War of 1832 had successfully removed the Indian from southern Wisconsin, the area the white man had staked out for his country. The territory offered a favorable climate, productive soil, mineral wealth, woodlands, and prairies. It held out opportunities for immediate employment in the lead mines of the southwest, in railroad construction, in the Fox-Wisconsin River improvement project, and in the lumber camps opening in the extensive woodlands. Milwaukee, Racine, and Southport (Kenosha) were prosperous ports, and a railroad was being built across the state. Farmers were induced to seek immediate and permanent settlement in the rich lands in the south and also north and west of the Fox-Wisconsin waterway because of the liberal land policy and the state's freedom from public debt. Banks were already incorporated at Mineral Point, Milwaukee, and Dubuque. The educational system of the territory had advanced upward to include a free high school by 1846 and the foundations of Beloit, Carroll, and Lawrence colleges by 1847. The religious progress of the territory was evidenced in the organization by Catholics of the Milwaukee Diocese in 1843. Protestant missionaries were also active and an Episcopalian seminary had been founded at Nashotah in 1841.

That numerous groups of foreign immigrants disembarking at

eastern ports continued their journey by proceeding westward immediately is particularly true of the German and Scandinavian elements, but not true of the Irish. These latter usually remained at least for some time in the East as laborers and artisans, crowding the cities and laboring on public works; or they gradually worked their way westward while employed in building railroads and canals or performing farm labor.

This settling of the Irish in the East and the later migration of a comparatively small portion of them to the West is a fact revealed by contemporary writing, by the 1850 Federal census returns, and also by a study of the biographical facts of a sample of 150 Irish farmers and professional men who entered Wisconsin between 1830 and 1860. As early as 1848 a letter published in various newspapers in praise of Wisconsin expressed satisfaction that the attention of enterprising and industrious Irishmen was being directed to the state:

> You are now indicating to Irish immigrants that course, which alone can conduct them to honorable independence and comfort. Too long have Irishmen remained crowded together in cities and along our seaboard, overcompeting with each other in laborious and ill-recompensed occupations. Let them now seek the free air of the West....[28]

Further contemporary evidence that the Irish remained for some time in the East is contained in the report of Herman Haertl, emigration commissioner of Wisconsin in 1853:

> If it be true that the Irish emigration is near as extensive as the German, the reason why comparatively so few of them appeared at the office is ... that the greater portion arrive with but limited means, and are therefore induced to seize upon the first work offered them for subsistence, which, indeed, is abundantly furnished by railroads and other important enterprises.... The Irish-

---

[28] *Milwaukee Sentinel*, October 11, 1848, citing a letter in the New York *Tribune*. Letter dated, September 22, 1848, addressed to Thomas Mooney, and signed by H. H. Van Amringe.

man, also, is more inclined than the German to a residence in large cities.[29]

Frederick W. Stone, Wisconsin Commissioner of Emigration in 1854, reiterated this fact when he wrote that the Irish, chiefly because of insufficient funds, remained in the eastern states working as laborers before going West.[30]

The 1850 Federal manuscript census affords evidence that in most instances in the case of Irish-born heads of families at least one or more of the children of that family were born in other states or in some cases, in Canada.[31] Using the 1850 census, a Wisconsin historian made a study of the place of nativity of the oldest child in 184 Irish families having American-born children. These families resided in the towns of Cedarburg and Saukville in Ozaukee County (part of Washington County in 1850). The study revealed that

> one-half of those families had lived in other states before coming to Wisconsin, and that the oldest children born in other states averaged more than three times the age of those born in this state. The conclusion is that among the pioneer Irish settlers of Wisconsin a heavy proportion were seasoned denizens of the United States, familiar with American social ways and political institutions.[32]

The tabulation of biographical data on 150 Irish-born farmers, business men and professionals, from about 25 different counties, reveals that of this group the average length of time spent in other states before migration to Wisconsin is 7 years, the number of years' residence in other states for each individual rang-

---

[29] *Annual Report of the Emigration Commissioner of the State of Wisconsin for the Year 1853* (Madison: Beriah Brown, 1854), p. 6.
[30] WSHS, Executive Records, Immigration, Box 1: Extracts from Quarterly Report of Emigrant Commissioners, New York, August 1, 1854.
[31] NA, Manuscript Division, Seventh Census of the United States.
[32] Schafer, *op. cit.*, p. 88. While the census records reveal this as true of the Irish, they also indicate that it is not true of the other foreign-born groups.

ing from 1 to 40 years. A list of the states represented discloses New York and Massachusetts[33] in the lead followed by Maine, Vermont, Rhode Island, New Jersey, Pennsylvania, Ohio, Missouri, Illinois, Michigan, and Louisiana. A number had spent time in more than one state and some in Canada.[34]

Regarding the migration of Irish into Wisconsin from Canada definite numbers are not available. A report made by the emigration agent at Hamilton, Canada West, concerning the number of English and Irish arrivals for the period from January 1 to July 1, 1857, reads as follows:[35]

```
Total arrived at Hamilton since January 1 ........ 21,982
Total left for the United States ................. 19,432
Remaining in Canada .............................. 2,550
```

The Hamilton *Spectator* "regretted that large numbers still push

---

[33] Boston *Pilot*, April 15, 1854, contains a communication from Wisconsin which mentions that many Irish farmers had settled around Newburg (Washington County) from Boston, Lowell, Taunton, and Roxbury, Massachusetts.

[34]

States Resided in before Entering Wisconsin	Number of Irish	States Resided in before Entering Wisconsin	Number of Irish
New York	50	Ohio	14
Massachusetts	19	Illinois	10
Pennsylvania	9	New Orleans	5
Vermont	6	Missouri	5
Maine	5	Michigan	4
New Jersey	5	Canada	16
Rhode Island	2		

These Irish-born immigrants to Wisconsin entered the United States sometime between 1813-1858 and entered Wisconsin between the years 1840-1859. They represented every county of Ireland.

[35] Cited in the Boston *Pilot*, July 25, 1857. During this month of June, 1857, the number of English and Irish emigrants arriving at Hamilton was 9,414, of whom 2,193 remained in the country.

their way on to the Western States, very few, in proportion to the numbers arriving, remaining in this province."³⁶ The 1850 and 1860 manuscript census returns indicate that, particularly in the then more northern counties, rather large numbers of Irish came through Canada. In Brown County some Irish families had as many as six children born in Canada, while others had three and some one, indicating that the length of their stay varied greatly.

Any attempt to account for the movement of Irish into the West, and into Wisconsin in particular, will reveal that such migration confirms the prevailing economic generalization that more intensive westward migration occurred during periods of relative prosperity.³⁷ Since every group moving West needed money to finance both journey and settlement, the time of depression was not likely to produce much migration, especially not to unsettled areas where hard work, inconvenience, and no definite assurance of improving their condition existed. An exception to this general trend was a number of early Irish settlers in Milwaukee who had been employees in the mills of Fall River, Massachusetts, and who had joined the westward migrants after the mills were forced to close because of the panic of 1837.³⁸

In 1837, moreover, the East was not so crowded as it was to be during the 'forties and 'fifties; hence, during the former period there was less reason for migration westward than later and there were actually fewer foreign immigrants to swell the ranks of the Yankees moving west. Later, hard times in Ireland, especially during the late 1840's and early 1850's, occurred simultaneously with prosperity in America; advertising of the advantages of migration increased; immigrants moved in and the Yankees moved on; both natives and foreigners who already possessed moderate means sought prospects of furthering their economic independence by progressing westward to Wisconsin where land was cheap and

---

[36] *Ibid.*, July 25, 1857.

[37] Robert E. Riegel, *America Moves West* (New York: Henry Holt and Company, 1947), p. 189.

[38] H. J. Desmond, "Early Irish Settlers in Milwaukee," *WMH,* XIII (June, 1930), 367.

plentiful and where taxation, relatively speaking, was non-existent.[39]

One of the factors which induced Irishmen to move West was the appearance of articles in eastern newspapers concerning emigration to Wisconsin as early as the 1840's, along with letters from Irishmen urging others of their nationality to take advantage of the opportunities which Wisconsin afforded them. One such letter estimated the number of Wisconsin Catholics in 1845 at 25,000 and maintained that "for industry perseverance and respectability, [they] will compare with a like number of their fellow citizens of native or foreign origin. . . . Wisconsin is the country for our Irish emigrant population with small means, who intend to settle on land."[40] Thomas Mooney, an educated Irishman who wrote a history of Ireland, worked for an Irish emigrant society, and traveled as far west as Wisconsin, contributed articles to the Boston *Pilot* which were a means of inducing many of his countrymen to emigrate to Wisconsin, especially to Washington and Ozaukee Counties.[41]

Wisconsin newspapers themselves helped to advertise Wisconsin. Under the heading, "A Word to Emigrants," the Watertown *Chronicle* propagandized the agricultural prospects within a radius

---

[39] The *Wisconsin Standard*, May 5, 1849, citing contemporary opinion stated: "The heavy emigration and foreigners' ability to live more cheaply force the easterner to move West and turn to farming." Cf. also, G. P. Garrison, *Westward Extension, 1841-1850*, Vol. XVII of *The American Nation: A History*, ed. A. B. Hart (28 vols.; New York: Harper and Brothers, 1904-1918), chap. i.

[40] Boston *Pilot*, March 29, 1845. The Reverend Patrick O'Kelley, first resident priest in Milwaukee, described the advantages Wisconsin offered to settlers in the Milwaukee *Courier*, March 9, 1842. His letter, dated January 23, 1842, was addressed to the editor of the New York's *Freeman's Journal* and was an answer to a request sent the *Courier* by the Irish Emigrant Society of New York. Cf. Milwaukee *Courier*, June 16, 1841.

[41] *Ibid.*, January 22, 1848; February 5, 1848. Cf. also, August 13, 1842, letter of Daniel Fitzsimmons of Prairieville (now Waukesha), dated June 12, 1842; March 29, 1845, letter of Richard Murphy of Milwaukee, dated, March 4, 1845. Issues dated September 20, 1845; March 27, 1852; June 25, 1853; December 3, 1853; January 7, 1854; June 7, 1856; July 29, 1859, all contain letters from various parts of Wisconsin.

of twenty to thirty miles, declaring that their possibilities were not to be equaled, that water power existed in abundance, that the climate was mild and all was conducive to health and prosperity.[42] The phrase, "Fifty years' labor in New England or twenty years' toil in Ohio are not equal in their results to five industrious years in Wisconsin," was often seen in newspapers in Wisconsin and in the East.[43] Advertisements for farm hands, for mechanics and day laborers were written with more optimism than actual circumstances warranted, as the following statements indicate: "Ten thousand could find work in the state—$12 to $20 a month and board through the summer"; "Laborers are wanted in the St. Croix Valley. Five hundred men might hire out on farms in the valley. Mechanics are also in demand."[44] The Boston *Pilot* invited information concerning employment for laborers in the West,[45] and in 1864, a Wisconsin newspaper, after quoting a letter describing unemployment in Ireland, commented:

> The man who wrote these lines, however unskilled a laborer he may be, if he stood on our shores, would be ten times the man he is. As a volunteer or farm-hand he would be sought for. His wife could earn six shillings a day in Madison. The contractors on the peninsular railroad to Marquette would pay him 14 shillings daily until he was enticed away by miners who are discovering Californias in our northern wilderness. If he be a skilled worker, his wages would be proportionately greater.[46]

As private letters from Irishmen to their relatives and friends brought immigrants to the eastern ports, so correspondence from Irishmen in Wisconsin to relatives in Ireland and the East, sometimes substantiated with funds, resulted in the latters' migration to particular places within the state. A few of many such instances

---

[42] Cited by the Milwaukee *Sentinel*, April 26, 1851.
[43] The Racine *Advocate*, April 9, 1856, citing the Cincinnati *Gazette*, August 7, 1855.
[44] *Ibid.*, April 2, 1855; April 29, 1857; also, April 15, 1857.
[45] Boston *Pilot*, November 28, 1857. February 28, 1857, contains a letter from A. Kearnan, Watertown, Wisconsin, denying the need for laborers.
[46] Madison *Wisconsin State Journal*, June 6, 1864.

may be cited: the McKernan family who were influenced by their half brother, Felix, a successful school teacher near New Diggings;[47] John Skelly and wife who after a seven years' residence in Connecticut chose Chippewa Falls at the urging of relatives;[48] the Dunne families who settled at Prairie du Chien;[49] and John Rooney and Patrick Jennings at Chippewa Falls.[50] In order to assure himself of locating among friends, Patrick Walsh, who had emigrated to New York in 1845, some years later inserted an advertisement in a New York paper, probably the *Freeman's Journal,* stating that he desired to settle in Wisconsin among Irishmen from County Kildare. A copy of the paper reached a man named Troy, a native of Kildare, who had settled in Kildare Township in Juneau County. He answered the advertisement and urged Walsh to begin his trek westward at once. This Walsh did.[51]

Kinship and friendship also could be instrumental in drawing Irishmen to a given locality. The settlement in Mount Hope Township, Grant County, popularly known as Irish Ridge, is typical. The first Irish-born settler was Michael McNamee, native of Monaghan County, who had been in Potosi, Wisconsin, previous to taking up land on Irish Ridge where he became a land speculator in 1847. He influenced Michael Callan, his cousin, and Thomas Garvey, also natives of County Monaghan, to follow his example. John Beers, a native of Cork who settled first in Cassville, Grant County, was induced by William Whitesides to settle at Mount Hope as was Peter Trainor, also of County Monaghan. As a veteran of the Mexican War, Peter possessed a soldier's deed to the land. This Trainor was responsible for the arrival of his cousin, James Trainor, and Owen McEntee, both natives of

---

[47] Interview with Sue Conley, Eau Claire, Wisconsin, August 22, 1950.
[48] *Diamond Jubilee Souvenir and History of Notre Dame Church, Chippewa Falls, Wisconsin, 1856-1931* (Chippewa Falls, Wisconsin: The Chippewa Printery, n.d.), p. 134.
[49] P. L. Scanlan, *Prairie du Chien: French, British, American* (Menasha, Wisconsin: George Banta Publishing Company, 1937), p. 209.
[50] *Diamond Jubilee Souvenir and History of Notre Dame Church, Chippewa Falls, Wisconsin, 1856-1931,* pp. 131, 120.
[51] Information obtained from Richard Walsh, Lyndon Station, Wisconsin, grandson of Patrick Walsh.

County Monaghan. James Trainor's wife was the twin of William Collins whom she induced to come to the Ridge. John Collins, Patrick Conley, and Michael Hanley also followed James Trainor. James Nagle and Patrick Rooney moved in from Patch Grove, the adjoining township. The latter influenced Patrick Coyne who had come through Patch Grove from County Sligo, and he in turn persuaded a relative, Daniel Roseman, native of Galway, to follow him. John Stack, of Waterford, had married a sister of John Roseman and in 1858 came to the Ridge. In much the same way through various ties of marriage, blood, or friendship came Henry Cull, Peter and Patrick Morgan, Hugh Quinn, John Murphy, Arthur Murphy, and John Woods, all in the 1850's.[52]

Through an incident which seemed mere chance a stream of native Irishmen began to flow into Irish Ridge from Vermont. One Mathew Walsh and his family left Castleton, Vermont, in the spring of 1854 and arrived at Galena, Illinois, where they stopped temporarily. Walsh left his family to search for land. Having crossed over into Iowa he returned by way of Prairie du Chien where, as he was leaving the village, he met Michael McNamee who told him of the Irish settlement on the Ridge and directed him to it. Others from Vermont followed Walsh to Irish Ridge: in 1855 and 1856, James O'Brien, James Mulrooney, John Morissey, Thomas O'Shaughnessy, Patrick and Thomas Carmody, Thomas Culkin, Darby Mulrooney, and Thomas Corcoran. Following these in 1857 and 1858 came John Scanlan, Thomas Hanley, Edward Brennan, Thomas and John Mulrooney, Edward Dunn, Michael and William Keating. Thus the Ridge became an Irish settlement not by organized immigration but rather through personal influence—one Irishman bringing others and they in turn drawing more. Practically no one in the group had come directly from Ireland to the Ridge, and the majority from 1850 to 1858 had first settled in Vermont.[53]

Some Irish settlements were more definitely the result of group migration, not from Ireland, but from the East. The Irish in

---

[52] Peter L. Scanlan, "A Bit of Local History," unpublished manuscript in Scanlan Papers. *WSHS*, pp. 4-12.
[53] *Ibid.*, pp. 11-16, 25.

Almond and Buena Vista Townships, Portage County, were originally a group of about twenty families from the powder mills near Wilmington, Delaware, who, led by George McMulkins, popular Irish foreman in the mills, migrated in the late 1850's to Wisconsin.[54] About 1854, Jonas Tower, an iron manufacturer from New York, found quantities of iron ore in the western part of Sauk County now called Ironton. Tower persuaded some of his former employees, many of them Irish Catholics, to settle there.[55]

Of the Irish who originally located in the East some had found themselves direct objects of intolerance and bigotry before moving on by stages to Wisconsin. A group who landed in Boston when that city was seething with intolerance against Irish Catholics was attacked by a mob in the streets. A few among them found somewhat less antagonism in New York, but were mobbed again in Philadelphia. In Virginia they were well treated while working on the Baltimore and Ohio Railroad; nevertheless, from there they migrated to Wisconsin.[56]

Although letters, personal influence, and ill treatment provided the motivation for some immigrants to Wisconsin, Irishmen and others were also notified of the excellence of the state by means of pamphlets, emigrant guides, and histories of the state. One of the earliest of these was John B. Newhall's, *The British Emigrant's "Handbook" and Guide to the United States of America, Particularly Illinois, Iowa and Wisconsin,* published in London, in 1844 for the benefit of emigrants from the British Isles, as the title signifies. Another, *The Emigrants' Handbook and Guide,* by Samuel Freeman, published in Milwaukee in 1851, was "compiled for the use of emigrants from eastern United States and for emigrants on this side of the Atlantic, upon arrival in the Ports of the United States, especially from Great Britain and

---

[54] Harry Heming (ed.), *The Catholic Church in Wisconsin* (Milwaukee: 1895-1898), p. 677.

[55] *Ibid.*, p. 789.

[56] Letter of Edward J. Dempsey to the writer, Oshkosh, Wisconsin, August 27, 1951. Dempsey's maternal grandparents were among this group.

Ireland."[57] In addition to presenting Wisconsin as a haven "to the middle working classes, especially the farmers and farm laborers of Great Britain and Ireland," the writer offered advice to the emigrant regarding the best means of travel, standard routes, and other enlightening information. Donald McLeod, in his *History of Wiskonsan, from Its First Discovery to the Present Period*, entices the Irish:

> Above Van Buren is another town called Dublin. This as the name portends is an Irish settlement. There are many Irish in the territory. They are a peaceable, hardworking, industrious class of citizens, are republicans to the very core, and generally members of the Catholic Temperance Association.[58]

Early in Wisconsin history, in 1846, before the attainment of statehood, the Wisconsin Historical Society was founded and among the reasons for the publication of its *Wisconsin Historical Collections* in durable form was included that of attracting immigrants.

It would prove highly useful to the State, by furnishing reliable materials for historians and other writers,

---

[57] S. Freeman, *The Emigrants' Handbook and Guide* (Milwaukee: Sentinel and Gazette Power Press, 1851), p. 5.

[58] Donald McLeod, *History of Wiskonsan, from Its First Discovery to the Present Period* (Buffalo: Steel's Press, 1846), p. 233. Other early histories and guides were: J. B. Grinnell (Oculus), *The Home of the Badgers, or A Sketch of the Early History of Wisconsin* (Milwaukee: Wilshire and Co., 1855); J. W. Hunt, *Wisconsin Gazetteer containing the Names, Location, and Advantages of the Counties, Cities, Towns, Villages, Post Offices, and Settlements, together with a Description of the Lakes, Water Courses, Prairies, and Public Localities, in the State of Wisconsin* (Madison: Beriah Brown, 1853). The Boston *Pilot*, January 17, 1852, advertised Daniel Curtis's *Western Portraiture and Emigrants Guide, a Description of Wisconsin, Illinois and Iowa with Remarks on Minnesota and other Territories*, as a "pretty and useful book of three hundred and fifty-one pages and an accurate map of the States and Territories described." John Gregory's *Industrial Resources of Wisconsin*, published in 1853, gained wide circulation, especially among the Irish, and contributed to the promotion of the settlement of Wisconsin.

at home and abroad, by thus disseminating a correct knowledge of the history and progress of our towns and counties, render our State more favorably known abroad, and more especially direct the attention of an intelligent class of emigrants and capitalists to our borders.[59]

Officially, also, Wisconsin was alert to the possibilities of advancing the interests of the state as is evident from the passage of a bill by the state legislature in 1852 to establish an emigrant agency in New York.[60] It is interesting and significant that while the bill was being discussed in the Assembly, David McKee of Potosi, Grant County, moved to amend it by requiring that the agent reside in "Cork, in the county of Limerick, in the State of Ireland."[61] The amendment was not passed, for the population of Wisconsin was already at that time too heterogeneous to warrant a display of favoritism to the Irish. G. W. Van Steenwyck was appointed Wisconsin's first State Commissioner of Emigration. With headquarters in New York he took up the duties assigned by the law which had created his office, namely, to keep the usual business hours customary in New York; to distribute free literature in various languages to the immigrants, giving them information regarding the state; to protect them from imposition; and to report the number of immigrants sent to the state, their nationality, and occupations.[62]

The Wisconsin State Emigrant Agency opened its offices on June 3, 1852; pamphlets were distributed on immigrant vessels, in hotels and taverns; some were sent to European countries to influence those embarking for America; and advertisements were placed in German, Dutch, English, and Irish newspapers in this country and in Europe. Advice was given personally to the immigrant and he was urged to proceed to Wisconsin. The agency

---

[59] *Wisconsin Historical Collections* (1854), II, 15-16. Hereafter cited as *Collections*. The date usually given for the establishment of the society was 1848, but Peter L. Johnson, Wisconsin historian, discovered the actual date to be 1846. *Cf. WMH*, XXVI (September, 1942), pp. 72-78.

[60] Madison *Wisconsin Argus*, April 8, 12, 14, 17, 1852.

[61] *Ibid.*, April 12, 1852.

[62] Boston *Pilot*, July 23, 1853, letter from John A. Byrne, the Irishman connected with the Wisconsin agency.

performed a valuable service in opposing "sharks" who felt safe in defrauding the immigrant traveling to a region so far inland as Wisconsin. The estimate of foreign immigrants entering Wisconsin reported by the agency for the year 1853 included approximately 4,000 to 5,000 from Ireland; 16,000 to 18,000 from Germany; 3,000 to 4,000 from Norway; and 2,000 to 3,000 from other countries.[63]

In order to increase the efficiency of the emigration agency the agent employed an Irishman, a German, and an American who were "to make the necessary impressions on the newly arrived."[64] John A. Byrne, the Irishman, was employed by the commissioner as his assistant.[65] In attempting to insert notices and advertisements into the Boston *Pilot*, Byrne probably achieved greater publicity for Wisconsin than he had originally hoped for. The editor of the *Pilot* had warned settlers who were approached by the Wisconsin agency to "look before they leap," and had spoken disparagingly concerning the type of material sent him by Byrne.[66] The latter defended himself and cleverly acquiesced to the *Pilot's* advice, maintaining that the material and counsel which disseminated from his office was such that the Irish immigrant would not only profit by "looking," but also, by "leaping."[67] Byrne proved to be efficient in the agency, but found that the greater portion of Irishmen with whom he came in contact lacked

---

[63] T. C. Blegen, "The Competition of the Northwestern States for Immigrants," *WMH*, III (September, 1919), 6.

[64] Boston *Pilot*, July 2, 1853.

[65] *Annual Report of the Emigration Commissioner of the State of Wisconsin for the Year 1853* (Madison, 1854), p. 3.

[66] Boston *Pilot*, June 25, 1853.

[67] *Ibid.*, July 23, 1853. Boston *Pilot* generally seemed to favor western emigration for the Irish. Defense of its policy appeared, May 31, 1847: "P. Q., Berlin, Wisconsin. Your letter contains nothing more than what has time and again appeared in our columns. The *Pilot*, has done more for the settlement of the Irish Catholics at the West, for the past twenty years, than all the spouters and wind-bags in the country. Thousands are now in good circumstances at the West, who have gone there from information received in our columns. We have always encouraged emigration to the West, and shall continue to do so in that way which is most conducive to the interests of Western settlers."

sufficient funds to continue their journey immediately to Wisconsin.[68]

Further Wisconsin legislation in the interests of immigration was enacted in 1853. A law was passed which authorized the governor to appoint a traveling agent who was to move continually between Wisconsin and New York from May 1 to December 1,

> ... to see that correct representations be made in eastern papers of our Wisconsin's great natural resources, advantages, and privileges, and brilliant prospects for the future; and to use every honorable means in his power to induce emigrants to come to this state.[69]

Thomas J. Townsend, the first traveling agent to be appointed, reported in December that the prejudice which had been prevalent in the East when he took his duties had greatly diminished through his efforts.[70]

A branch office of the emigration agency was established in Quebec in 1854 for a six-month period commencing on May 1. Political opposition, however, had arisen against the agency and accusations of corruption and inefficiency were made. The office had become a kind of political reward, the appointee often being one who, regardless of qualifications, was appointed for political reasons. Opposed also by the Nativists, the office was abolished by the state legislature in 1855. According to the Racine *Advocate*, at least twenty thousand more persons had emigrated to Wisconsin than would have if the agency had not existed.[71] Among these were numerous Irishmen.

Although it is difficult to ascertain to what extent Irish veterans of the Mexican War took advantage of land grants offered them by Congress, it is certain that some settled on such grants in Wisconsin. An instance in point is that of Patrick O'Connor, a native of County Limerick and a farmer in New York, who

---

[68] *Annual Report of the Emigration Commissioner, 1853*, pp. 3, 6.
[69] *General Acts of Wisconsin* (1853), chap. 56.
[70] T. C. Blegen, *op. cit.*, p. 7. Townsend traveled 42,000 miles during 1853 and inserted notices in about 900 newspapers on Wisconsin.
[71] Racine *Advocate*, January 29, 1856.

enlisted in the United States Army and was stationed for a time at Fort Atkinson, Iowa Territory. After active service and ultimate discharge, he obtained his one hundred sixty acre land grant at the Mineral Point land office.[72] It was owing to a Scotch-Irish Mexican War veteran with his own grant and one bought from a fellow soldier that the group of settlers from Knockahollet, County Antrim, emigrated to Exeter, Green County, Wisconsin.[73]

Besides the work of government agencies in promoting immigration and protecting the immigrant, emigration societies in New York and Philadelphia (1841), in Boston (1842), and in other cities were organized by naturalized Irish leaders.[74] As expressed at the charter meeting of the Irish Emigrant Society in New York the aims of the society would, if carried out, do away with all the evils concomitant with Irish emigration. As a positive program the society aimed "to advance the temporal interests, and to promote in every possible way the moral worth and social respectability of the Irish emigrant."[75]

As a means of carrying out its endeavors the society planned to post correspondents in the principal seaports of Ireland, at Liverpool in England, at ports in the United States and at points in the interior of this country which offered the best prospects for employment. According to their own reports these societies were a means of aid and support to a number of Irish newcomers.

---

[72] NA, Veteran Pension Records, MSC 2994. Dominick Devaney, native of County Sligo, discharged at Pittsburgh at the close of the Mexican War, settled at Montello, Wisconsin, in 1849. George Hall, veteran of the war, entered 160 acres in the town of Akan, Richland County. Cf. *History of Crawford and Richland Counties* (Springfield, Illinois: Union Publishing Co., 1884), p. 972. Peter Trainor, as mentioned previously, held a soldier's deed to his land on Irish Ridge, Mount Hope, Wisconsin.

[73] E. M. Wallace, "Early Farmers in Exeter," *WMH*, VIII (June, 1925), 415-422. *Infra*, p. 71.

[74] Boston *Pilot*, April 17, July 15, 1841; December 31, 1842. The Boston Society of the 1840's never flourished very well owing to a lack of cooperation and insufficient funds. Cf. Boston *Pilot*, June 20, 1844 and June 21, 1845. Societies had been established in New York, Philadelphia, and Baltimore as early as 1817-18, but their existence had not been permanent. Cf. Purcell, *loc. cit.*, p. 854; Hansen, *op. cit.*, p. 93.

[75] Boston *Pilot*, April 17, 1841.

The New York society reported for the year 1845 that it had obtained employment for 2,680 emigrants and that during a five-month period from May to October, of the 15,508 Irish arrivals, 7,215 proceeded to the interior to settle on land, while 2,681 went to their friends in the country, leaving but 5,412 to seek employment in the city.[76] Plans were being contemplated in Milwaukee to form an association auxiliary to the New York society and thus to provide continuous aid to the Irish immigrant who had been directed to Wisconsin from the port of New York.[77] No evidence has been found that such an organization was actually effected. In 1855 the Irish Aid Society of Boston was founded to aid in transporting Irish laborers to the western states. In its first annual report the society could account for 125 persons sent West.[78]

Irishmen at home had also attempted to aid the emigrants by setting up the Catholic Emigration Society in 1843 for the purpose of giving advice to the Irish who wished to emigrate to America and to safeguard them from the fraudulent practices of agents in the English and Irish ports. One of their most important aims was to buy land, centering attention on Wisconsin, but

---

[76] *Ibid.*, June 6, 1846.

[77] *Ibid.*, March 29, 1845, Richard Murphy of Milwaukee, in a letter dated, March 4, 1845. The issue of March 31, 1849, contains a letter from Dr. James Johnson, M.D., prominent Irish leader in Milwaukee, suggesting that the approximate sum of $30,000 in the hands of the Irish Executive Committee of New York, since it consisted mainly of the contributions of Irish in the United States, be used to benefit them according to the following plan. With the $30,000, 300 land warrants could be purchased at $100 each, which in Wisconsin would purchase 48,000 acres of the finest land in the world. The land could then be divided into farms of 40 acres each, which would make 12,000 farms to be sold to actual settlers at the government price of ten shillings the acre or $50 for 40 acres. The society was to benefit through interest. He felt that the relatively high wages at that time would insure the payment of the principal and interest. Johnson's evaluation of the shilling is incorrect. According to his calculations the shilling was worth $.12½, but as far as the writer has been able to determine, the shilling's actual value was approximately $.24 1/3.

[78] Boston *Pilot*, May 24, 1856. This society also was seriously hampered because of lack of funds.

including the states of Illinois, Iowa, Ohio, Michigan, and Minnesota, and to supply priests from Ireland for these proposed settlements. It was hoped that after working for the society for three years, poor settlers would be able to pay the cost of their transportation and at the same time acquire title to ten acres of land.[79] Although the project had been inaugurated under the patronage of Daniel O'Connell and other Irish leaders, including churchmen, nothing came of it. The *Freeman's Journal* expressed doubt concerning the possibility of successfully carrying out the purpose but regarded Wisconsin "as a judicious selection, as there were churches and Irish priests in this sparsely settled agricultural region."[80] It seems that this plan, as Henry Browne points out, was the closest thing to what Archbishop John Hughes later referred to as

> one of my early dreams in which I imagined that I might associate a number of worthy gentlemen in an undertaking from motives of pure philanthropy—motives of Irish patriotism, I may call it or at least a love of my country—to buy ten or twenty thousand acres of land in what is now called Wisconsin and that they should dispose of those acres in small lots to emigrants, that is, to those who should know how to use the axe and even the plow in this country; to have always cabins in advance for those who might come, and still keep it working regularly, so as to bear its own expenses.[81]

With somewhat greater success the Irish National Emigration Society, active in the 1840's, converted its aims into practical efforts by setting up offices in the cities in the United States. John Gregory, a native of County Kerry, president of the College of Civil Engineering, Mining and Agriculture in Dublin, and sec-

---

[79] *Ibid.*, April 28, 1843. *Cf.* also, Adams, *op. cit.*, p. 223. Henry J. Browne, "Archbishop Hughes and Western Colonization," *CHR*, XXXVI (October, 1950), 257-285. R. J. Purcell, "The Irish Emigrant Society of New York," *Studies*, XXVII (December, 1938), 583-599.
[80] New York *Freeman's Journal*, May 6, 1843.
[81] Browne, *loc. cit.*, p. 262, quoting John R. G. Hassard, *Life of the Most Reverend John Hughes, First Archbishop of New York* (New York: D. Appleton and Co., 1866), p. 393.

retary of the Irish National Emigration Society, arriving in Milwaukee in the latter capacity in 1849, furthered Irish emigration to Wisconsin by his labors for the society and by his publication, *Industrial Resources of Wisconsin,* which gained wide circulation.[82] Another agent of the society, D. G. Power, also a civil engineer, set up offices in Milwaukee in 1849 and by 1852 was advertising that he was "grateful to his countrymen for their liberal support" and that "his increasing business has induced him to offer greater facilities . . . for the Forwarding of Passengers from any part of the Old Country. . . ." The Boston *Pilot* vouched for his honesty and integrity. It seems that by this time he had set up his own passenger business.[83]

The Irish Pioneer Emigration Fund was likewise instituted in Ireland during the 1840's. It proposed to improve the condition of indigent families in the poorest districts of Ireland by assisting one member of each family to emigrate to the United States or Canada. This assistance was to be directed principally to young women selected because of their excellence of character and industrious habits. Back of this plan was the expectation that persons so assisted would prosper and ultimately send for or help their families financially. Gentlemen of England, including Lord Palmerston, Viscount Canning, the Lord Lieutenant of Ireland, and also prominent Americans and churchmen, allowed their names to be used in support of this organization and contributed funds for the achievement of its objectives. Within eight years the number of persons actually assisted to emigrate from Ireland to this country amounted to about four hundred, most of them having been selected from the counties of Louth and Clare. Among these were forty-five young Irish ladies who, in 1857, found homes in Janesville, Rock County, Wisconsin, thanks to the efforts of Vere Foster, active manager of the society, who had made personal contacts with clergymen and other interested parties in the mid-West during the winter of 1856-1857.[84]

---

[82] J. G. Gregory, editor, *Southeastern Wisconsin: A History of Old Milwaukee County* (4 vols.; Chicago: The S. J. Clarke Publishing Co., 1932), III, 276.

[83] Milwaukee *Sentinel,* August 22, 1849; Boston *Pilot,* March 13, 1852.

[84] Boston *Pilot,* June 20, 1857; Racine *Advocate,* June 24, 1857.

The interest of Catholic clergymen in the welfare of the immigrants is evident also in the part which some of them played in the Irish Immigrant Aid Convention of 1856 held in Buffalo for the purpose of organizing colonization through planned settlements of Irish immigrants in the western sections of the United States and in Canada.[85] Although this movement failed, principally because of the opposition of Archbishop John Hughes of New York, other Irish colonization movements were undertaken, chiefly the Irish Catholic Colonization Association with its attempted organization in 1869, its successful organization in 1879, and subsequent work under the guidance of Bishop John Lancaster Spalding of Peoria.[86] Irishmen in Wisconsin were active in these national attempts to help their countrymen settle in the West and also in local endeavors to the same end. Three delegates had planned to attend the Buffalo Convention, but because of their inability to do so a meeting was held in Waukesha on April 7 and a Society to Promote Western Colonization was formed.[87]

The Reverend James Caussé, laboring among the Irish in Mineral Point in the lead mining region, supported the Irish colonization cause. In answer to the *American Celt's* accusation that the clergy of the West were slow in offering their opinion, he insisted that his experience among the Irish proved them to be zealous and faithful, that he favored Irish colonization in the West, and that he felt committees should be organized in the East and West which could promote the common cause. Father Caussé was sure that the Reverend Samuel Mazzuchelli, O.P., long a missionary in southern Wisconsin, Iowa, and Illinois, would cooperate. Mazzuchelli was then pastor of the Irish congregation at Benton which was also in the lead mining region.[88]

Ten years after the Buffalo Convention, in January, 1866, an

---

[85] For the Buffalo Convention and its aftermath, see Sister Mary Gilbert Kelly, *Catholic Immigrant Colonization Projects in the United States, 1815-1860* (New York: The United States Catholic Historical Society, 1939), pp. 210-269. Cf. Browne, loc. cit., for a re-evaluation of Hughes' role.
[86] Cf. Sister Mary Evangela Henthorne, *The Irish Catholic Colonization Association of the United States* (Champaign, Illinois: 1932), pp. 34-59.
[87] Kelly, op. cit., p. 244.
[88] *American Celt*, March 17, 1855. Kelly, op. cit., pp. 221-222.

Irish Emigration Aid Society was organized in Madison for the purpose of encouraging unemployed laborers of the large eastern metropolitan areas and natives of Ireland to migrate to Wisconsin. Dillon O'Brien of St. Paul was called in at the preliminary organizational meeting because of his experiences with a similar society in Minnesota. To achieve its aims the Wisconsin society planned to furnish information concerning the soil and natural resources of the state, the kind of labor needed in the different localities, and any other information pertinent to enabling an Irishman "whose capital is principally strength and industry, to make an intelligent choice" of a desirable place for settlement. John A. Byrne, formerly connected with the Wisconsin emigration agency in New York, was elected president. General J. M. Lynch, who later was an active delegate to the St. Louis Convention in 1869, was elected to the vice-presidency, while John Reynolds, Madison city treasurer, became secretary, and John H. Slavan of the Farmers' Bank, Madison, was chosen treasurer.[89] Evidence that anything was accomplished by this society is lacking. These attempts to organize Irishmen in Wisconsin indicate, however, that Irish leaders in the state were alert to the promotion of organized Irish migration, a movement which was developing through the efforts of prominent Irishmen in the United States.

As a matter of fact, in 1869, when William J. Onahan of Chicago and Dillon O'Brien of St. Paul, through the St. Patrick's Society of Chicago, called for a convention to organize a National Immigrant Aid Association, Wisconsin Irishmen took an active part. Edward O'Neill, then mayor of Milwaukee, had become interested in the work of the emigrant societies and, accompanied by Andrew Mullen and two others, attended a meeting of the society in St. Paul in January of that year.[90] In reporting the meeting, the *Northwestern Chronicle* contended that Andrew Mullen had suggested Chicago as the place for a National Irish Emigration Convention and also that Milwaukee had waived claim to the con-

---

[89] Milwaukee *Sentinel*, January 22 and 29, 1866; Milwaukee *News*, January 28, 1866; Madison *State Journal*, January 26, 1866.
[90] Milwaukee *Sentinel*, January 20, 1869.

vention in favor of Chicago.[91] Despite this fact, St. Louis was chosen and, when Irishmen were called together in Milwaukee to elect delegates to the proposed convention, Mayor O'Neill, Andrew Mullen, and John O'Connor were chosen to represent Milwaukee.[92] Total Wisconsin representation amounted to twelve Irishmen, and the committee on organization contained two Wisconsin men among others.[93] O'Neill was appointed president of the convention and Onahan secretary.[94] The organization professed to encourage and aid Irish immigrants financially so they could proceed from their place of arrival to the agricultural districts of the West. To keep the society free from speculation, it was neither to buy nor own any land. Rather, the society was to bring the emigrant and his family to land which could be entered without a large initial investment, or to agricultural districts where employment could be obtained. The initial meeting was considered a success and actual organization left to a committee. A petition requesting a charter from Congress was prepared but, pending action by the national legislature, the Wisconsin members obtained a charter from the State Legislature. It was under this charter that the association organized. A meeting of the incorporators was held in Chicago on June 30, 1870. Enough of them were present to take the necessary initiatory steps. They adopted a resolution to open books of subscription to the capital stock of the company on August 1, 1870, in Chicago, Milwaukee, Madison, New Orleans, St. Louis, St. Paul, Memphis, Omaha, Iowa City, Vicksburg, in Lawrence, Kansas, and in Olympia, Washington Territory. The office in Milwaukee was under the direction of Andrew Mullen and John O'Connor; that in Madison under John Reynolds.[95] When the aggregate of 20,000 shares would be reached, the next meeting of the incorporators was to take place in Chicago for the purpose of designating a day for the election of directors. It seems that this point was never reached in the formation of the organization, hence its early demise.

---

[91] St. Paul *Northwestern Chronicle,* March 6, 1869.
[92] Milwaukee *Sentinel,* September 15 and 20, 1869.
[93] St. Paul *Northwestern Chronicle,* October 9 and 30, 1869.
[94] Milwaukee *Sentinel,* October 7, 1869; Henthorne, *op. cit.,* p. 34.
[95] St. Paul *Northwestern Chronicle,* July 23, 1870.

In 1879, again through the efforts and determination of O'Brien and Onahan, a national convention was called to meet in Chicago, March 17. This time, owing to better organization and cooperation, the convention succeeded in its purpose and the Irish Catholic Colonization Association of the United States was founded. An executive board of seven bishops and seven laymen was created and Archbishop John Ireland's colonization plan was adopted. Wisconsin was again represented and John Lawler of Prairie du Chien became a member of the executive board.[96] In other respects Wisconsin did not figure greatly in the achievements of the society which was instrumental in founding colonies in Minnesota, Nebraska, and Arkansas. One of the chief difficulties, as with all of the Irish immigrant aid societies, was the inability to collect sufficient funds. This society had achieved at least moderate success when it was dissolved in 1891.[97]

Although Wisconsin Irish leaders promoted and were involved in the workings of these emigrant aid and colonization societies,

---

[96] Henthorne, *op. cit.*, pp. 36-42; Milwaukee *Sentinel*, March 20 and December 22, 1879. Sister M. Sevina Pahorezki, *The Social and Political Activities of William James Onahan* (Washington, D. C.: The Catholic University of America Press, 1942), p. 91, describes the plan: "The Association, following Archbishop Ireland's plan of colonization, was to build an emigrant-house, or temporary shelter, a church, and a priest's residence in each colony, and in certain cases, advance money to plow twenty to thirty acres on each farm, the average price being about two dollars an acre. It would also erect a cottage on each farm at a cost of from $150 to $200. The farm with these improvements was to be sold to the settlers on an installment basis, the Association securing itself from loss by retaining the title until the final payment. Only railroad lands were to be purchased. . . . In this way the Association could resell on time at a much higher rate than it had paid, and yet give the colonists exceptionally favorable conditions, besides the social and religious privileges which it would secure to them. The terms of the sale to the colonists would provide the payment of fifty dollars down as earnest money. The interest payment on the principal would be due after the second year. The payment of the principal provided for annual installments—running generally five years—until the complete sum should be paid. Finally . . . the Association was to draw a rate of 6 per cent interest for every hundred dollars invested, so that the business was not only safe but profitable as well."

[97] Henthorne, *op. cit.*, p. 59.

the fact remains that Irish immigration into Wisconsin was not greatly increased, particularly after 1860. If reports of the local societies organized in Madison and Waukesha were available, perhaps they would reveal some little influence on Irish immigration into the state. It is not really known, however, whether these societies actually functioned after being organized. The reasons for this are also unknown but it is probable that insufficient financial backing, as in the case of so many like attempts, was the chief cause of their failure.

The differences of purpose in the immigrant aid societies before and after 1860 demonstrate the change in evils which they were designed to counteract and correct. Prior to 1860 the emphasis was on improving conditions aboard immigrant ships, protecting the immigrant from being defrauded of all he had upon his arrival, and helping him to find employment. Some few were sent West. After the Civil War, the emphasis was on colonization and placing the urban Irishman on land in the western states.

During the earlier period the emigrants, immediately before departure and after arrival, were often made the dupes of unscrupulous agents, runners, "Jackalls," and "Landsharks who prowled around the wharves and depots of the ports in search of their prey."[98] Laws passed in England and the United States to protect the emigrant were commonly evaded with the connivance and even with participation in the spoils on the part of port officials.[99]

Nor were these the only evils and sufferings endured by those crossing the sea. The passage took from three to six weeks or more. The bulk of Irishmen, provided with their own food and bedding and frequently with but a few articles of furniture, trav-

---

[98] Boston *Pilot*, September 25, 1841; June 25, July 16, 1842; July 29, 1843; March 2, 1844; June 14, 1845; January 8, April 15, 1848. The cost of passage from Liverpool to New York, according to advertisements in the Boston *Pilot* and the Madison *Enquirer*, amounted to about four or five dollars. In *The Emigrants' Manual* (Edinburgh, 1851), and the Boston *Pilot*, prices from 1851-1859 ranged from about £3 steerage to £20 cabin passage with cheaper but less comfortable passage from Irish ports. Sometimes it cost the emigrant less to cross the ocean than to travel inland to Wisconsin from an Atlantic port.

[99] Boston *Pilot*, February 11, 1843; March 2, 1844.

eled steerage in overcrowded ships. Lack of sanitation, impure water, and spoiled food often brought illnesses, such as cholera and typhoid fever, which claimed many victims especially among the women and children. Storms not only aroused terror among the seasick passengers but also caused some ships to spring leaks and others to sink with heavy loss of life. Often there were instances of highhandedness and even cruelty toward emigrants on the part of the captain and members of the crew.[100] Although numerous complaints were made concerning ill-treatment on board ship, not all reports were bad. At times acknowledgments of fair and kind treatment signed by the passengers were tendered the captain and crew.[101] By the 1850's there was some improvement in conditions as a result of the efforts of the emigration societies, better and more efficiently enforced regulations, and increased interest on the part of clergymen.[102] Furthermore, after 1855, the decline in the number of passengers caused shipping companies to offer better accommodations in order to make ocean travel more attractive.[103]

Irish and other immigrants used various routes and modes of travel to reach Wisconsin. During the 1840's and 1850's the most common procedure was travel by railroad to Albany and Buffalo followed by steamboat travel on the Great Lakes.[104] Boats to

[100] Instances of hardship and evils on board ship are described in the memoirs and poem of Lizzie Emerson whose parents from Ireland settled in Town of Lake, Milwaukee County, Wisconsin; also in the Boston *Pilot*, January 15, 1849; December 3, 1853. The issue of March 17, 1849, mentions a voyage in which forty passengers out of 400 died of cholera. For general treatment see M. L. Hansen, *The Immigrant in American History* (Cambridge: Harvard University Press, 1940), chap. ii; Wittke, *op. cit.*, chap. vii.

[101] Boston *Pilot*, July 31, 1841.

[102] Hansen, *The Atlantic Migration*, p. 300; Purcell, "The Irish Immigrant, the Famine and the Irish-American," *loc. cit.*, p. 863; Boston *Pilot*, April 24, 1852; June 20, 1857.

[103] Hansen, *The Atlantic Migration*, p. 300.

[104] Freeman, *op. cit.*, p. 88. For accounts of individual Irishmen traveling this route see *Biographical Review of Dane County, Wisconsin* (Chicago: Biographical Review Publishing Co., 1893), p. 227; *Commemorative Biographical Record of the West Shore of Green Bay, Wisconsin* (Chicago: J. H. Beers Co., 1896), p. 185; *Commemorative Biographical Record of the Upper Wisconsin Counties* (Chicago: J. H. Beers Co., 1895), p. 327.

Factors Influencing Irish Immigration into Wisconsin 33

Wisconsin passed over the Great Lakes touching, among other ports, Cleveland, Detroit, and finally the Wisconsin ports of Manitowoc, Sheboygan, Milwaukee, Racine, and Kenosha. The distance from Buffalo to Manitowoc was recorded as 846 miles and to Kenosha, 954 miles. The trip from Buffalo to Detroit by steamboat could be made in two days, while that to Milwaukee and other Wisconsin ports on Lake Michigan took up to five days or more.[105] A class of vessels called "propellers," large-sized schooners with a small steam engine in the hold for use in head winds and calms, became popular and carried freight and passengers at a cheaper rate than the larger steamers.[106]

Shipping companies advertised fair treatment for their clients along with information concerning any part of the western country. In 1843 the price to Milwaukee by way of the Great Lakes was about ten dollars, twice the amount the steerage passenger had paid for his trip across the Atlantic.[107] In some cases the same steamship company that brought the emigrant from Europe also handled his transportation West, while some lake steamers contracted to convey a certain number of passengers during the season.[108] By 1852 railroad service as far as Chicago was advertised, Milwaukee not being linked by railroad with Chicago until 1855. Three lines out of Milwaukee reached westward as did the short lines later extending from Sheboygan, Kenosha, and Racine. By 1860 Milwaukee was connected with Waukesha and Madison, and with Prairie du Chien and La Crosse on the Mississippi River.[109]

Many of the emigrants from the East who entered Wisconsin over its southern border made their way through Pennsylvania, Ohio, Indiana, and Illinois in prairie schooners and wagons drawn by oxen or horses. The long journey was perilous and replete

---

[105] Freeman, *op. cit.*, pp. 88–89.
[106] *Ibid.*, p. 89; Boston *Pilot,* January 22, 1848.
[107] Boston *Pilot,* August 27, 1842; January 13, 1844; January 24, 1846; New York *Freeman's Journal,* July 8, 1843.
[108] Milwaukee *Sentinel,* May 7, 1851.
[109] Raney, *op. cit.*, pp. 183–185; Boston *Pilot,* June 16, 1855.

with hardships. There were others who came up the Mississippi River from St. Louis or New Orleans as Peter Scanlan testifies.[110] This was a common means of entry into the lead mining region and the western portion of the state.

Upon arrival at a Wisconsin port or railroad station, the immigrant proceeded to his destination on foot, by stage, by team and wagon, or by means of a combination of these modes of travel. Irishmen arriving in Chicago were known to walk to the lead region in about a week; others made the trip in three days by stage at an expense of about ten dollars.[111]

If the immigrant Irishman survived the voyage across the Atlantic Ocean, he was not thereby assured of a like fortune on his journey inland. Some of the danger to his life was caused by inhuman treatment of second-class passengers on the railroads.

> Those who are able to pay their fare on the first-class cars, I would caution not to go on the "emigrant" train. Here the poor emigrants are huddled into those loathsome, suffocating cars like so many cattle, without any accommodation, but benches to sit on, no place to lie down or rest, but remain in that position day and night, at a slow motion with freight trains for nearly a week between New York and Chicago. Many died of Cholera on these trains last year.[112]

Accidents often resulted in injury or death. An emigrant train on the Michigan Central Railroad near Chicago collided with a Southern Michigan train, killing and injuring passengers, a number of whom were Irishmen bound for Wisconsin.[113] A steamboat, the "Shamrock," carrying English, Scotch, and Irish emi-

---

[110] Scanlan, *op. cit.*, p. 10.

[111] Boston *Pilot*, January 22, 1848; *History of Crawford and Richland Counties*, p. 977; *Biographical Review of Dane County*, p. 227; *Commemorative Biographical Record of Upper Wisconsin Counties*, p. 327; L. Kessinger, *History of Buffalo County, Wisconsin* (Alma, Wisconsin: 1888), p. 592; H. S. Hubbell, *History of Dodge County* (2 vols.; Chicago: The S. J. Clarke Publishing Co., 1913), II, 306.

[112] Boston *Pilot*, June 16, 1855; also the issue of July 8, 1853.

[113] Racine *Advocate*, May 8, 1854.

Factors Influencing Irish Immigration into Wisconsin 35

grants never reached its destination because of a boiler explosion. About half of the passengers lost their lives.[114]

Those Irishmen who entered Wisconsin with migrants from the south by way of the Mississippi often found deplorable conditions on the river boats which were crowded beyond capacity. Cholera broke out and more than one emigrant was buried on the banks of the river. Steamboat companies were accused of gambling with human life.[115]

Frauds practiced on immigrants were not confined to the ocean ports on either side of the Atlantic but many Irishmen were also victims of dishonesty and injustice perpetrated by shipping agents and officers of ships on the Great Lakes as well as by railroad agents and train conductors. A number of Irishmen so treated aired their complaints and warned their fellow Irishmen through the columns of the Boston *Pilot*.[116] The following account is typical of what frequently happened. A group of Irish mechanics, five adults and one child direct from Ireland, having landed in New York on September 22, 1849, bought tickets through to Milwaukee for which they paid $43.87 with the assurance that these tickets covered railroad fare to Buffalo and second class cabin fare on the Lakes. Contrary to this arrangement the group was compelled to board a canal boat at Albany, to pay $14.52 for their luggage, to pay for berths in a small cabin shared with nine other persons, and to buy the water they used. After this nine day trip from Albany to Buffalo the company was charged an additional seven dollars for cabin accommodations on the Lakes.[117] Resistance on the part of the immigrants was futile, for this was the proposition: pay the amount charged or remain where you

---

[114] Madison *Wiskonsan Enquirer*, August 4, 1842.

[115] George Forrester, editor, *Historical and Biographical Album of the Chippewa Valley, Wisconsin* (Chicago: A. Warner, 1891-92), II, 521. Boston *Pilot*, June 9, 1849; January 22, 1848. The ten-day trip from New Orleans to southwestern Wisconsin cost about $9.

[116] Boston *Pilot*, September 16, 1843; July 29, 1884; June 21, 1845; July 14, 1855; May 13, 1848.

[117] Milwaukee *Sentinel*, October 13, 1849. The editor stated that this group of Irishmen called at his office and related their experiences.

are. Choice of the latter would have meant loss of the original amount invested in the through ticket.

With increased legislation and stricter enforcement of existing laws on the part of the United States and British governments, with the introduction of steam, increased speed, and generally a better class of emigrants, conditions aboard ship on the whole were improved, although much was left to be desired in steerage accommodations. The Board of Commissioners of Emigration of the State of New York was successful in lessening the fraud and impositions practiced on the new arrivals.[118]

Although a large immigration into Wisconsin continued after 1860, the number of Irishmen was steadily declining. The only statistics available are those contained in the reports of the commissioner and board of immigration. In 1869, for example, during the seven months from May to November, only 50 Irishmen among 14,576 immigrants are recorded as having entered Wisconsin through Milwaukee. No records were kept of arrivals on the Misissippi or of those through Canada or by way of Green Bay, Manitowoc, and other Lake ports.[119] Reports for the years 1879 to 1884 are shown in Table 2.[120]

The state revived its former interest in attracting immigrants, and in 1867 a board of immigration was established consisting of the governor, secretary of state, and six others.[121] The members served without compensation. A committee of three in each county was appointed by the governor to secure names of relatives and friends of the people residing in each county. These names were to constitute a mailing list and thus facilitate the distribution of

---

[118] Fitzpatrick, *op. cit.*, chap. ii, deals with the improved conditions of the later migration. Fitzpatrick concludes that the Irishmen arriving during this period were not inclined to remain in the eastern cities as had previously been the case. This is principally due to the fact that they were of a better class financially than the earlier immigrant. More of them, also, probably had a definite destination in mind where friends and relatives were already located.

[119] Milwaukee *Sentinel,* May and June, 1869, reports of Major Fuchs, state immigration agent.

[120] *Biennial Report of the Board of Immigration of the State of Wisconsin* (Milwaukee: Burdick and Armitage, 1885), p. 9, is the source.

[121] *General Laws of Wisconsin* (1867), chap. 126. *Cf.* Blegen, *loc. cit.*, p. 11.

TABLE 2
IRISH ARRIVALS IN MILWAUKEE, 1879-1884

Year	Total No. of Immigrants	Total No. from Ireland
1879	4,781	66
1880	15,681	178
1881	25,769	173
1882	31,758	221
1883	27,230	156
1884	23,632	187

the literature which the board had published.[122] The official pamphlet was compiled by Increase A. Lapham and translated into various languages.[123]

In 1871 the board of immigration was replaced by a commissioner of emigration who was to reside in Milwaukee as a local agent. County committees were to help the commissioner as in the board system. The distribution of literature continued to be the chief activity aside from cooperation with the United States Bureau of Immigration Office and attempts to get reduced fares for the immigrants on railroads. The office of commissioner of immigration was abolished in 1875 and activity ceased until 1879 when a board was again set up.[124] This board was active until 1901 when it went out of existence. Throughout the latter half of the nineteenth century, state promotion of immigration placed emphasis on the German and Norwegian nationalities. There was usually an Irishman on the board, J. W. Carney of Fond du Lac serving from 1868-1870, but very few Irishmen served on the county committees.[125]

---

[122] *Ibid.*, pp. 11-12. In 1868 the membership of the board expanded to eight and the appropriation was increased from $2,000 to $3,000. To assist the immigrants an agent was placed in Milwaukee and one in Chicago four months of the year.

[123] The pamphlet was entitled *Statistics: Exhibiting the History, Climate and Productions of the State of Wisconsin* (Madison, Wisconsin: Atwood and Culver, 1870). There were several editions, the first one in 1867.

[124] Blegen, *loc. cit.*, pp. 20-22.

[125] WSHS, Executive Records, Immigration, Box 1, letter of J. W. Carney to Governor Lucius Fairchild, Fond du Lac, Wisconsin, March 24, 1868.

Accusations of political partisanship and favoritism had been made against the board and commissioners of immigration, not without cause.[126] Party loyalty was an important factor in obtaining an appointment even on the county level. Edmund Sweeney, one of those rare Irish Republicans, in 1867 acknowledged his willingness to accept a position as a member of the State Board of Immigration, stating:

> . . . political reasons require me to do so [.] it comes in good time [.] it will be a stopper on the mouths of Democrats who are always saying Republicans would only use the Irish for selfish purposes and forget them when offices were to be given.[127]

The *Catholic Citizen,* Irish Catholic weekly of Milwaukee, questioned the Board's efficacy and suggested that attention be directed to other nationalities besides the German.[128] The *Catholic Sentinel,* edited by Arthur Gough, an Irishman in Chippewa Falls, later charged the legislature with organizing an immigrant board "to make places for dilapidated members of the party," and accused the governor of discriminating against the Irish.

> We fail to see the name of a man on his list from that nation which gave America the greatest number of immigrants, and whose blood and brain and muscle are found in two-thirds of all the masterminds and sturdy workers of the Union. That nation whose lusty sons dug our canals, built our railroads and manned our vessels, whose influence made Boston, New York and Chicago what they are, has no representative on Governor Upham's immigrant commission. No Irish need apply to him for place or position. He wants none but Norwegians

---

[126] *Ibid.* Answers from editors of newspapers, county clerks, and others sent in response to Governor Fairchild's request of July 22, 1867, for suggestions for county assistants to the board of immigration almost invariably insisted on the importance of the nominee's faithfulness to the Republican party. Since Irishmen were predominantly Democrats, few Irish names were suggested.

[127] *Ibid.,* Edward Sweeney to Governor L. Fairchild, Watertown, Wisconsin, April 22, 1867.

[128] *Catholic Citizen,* April 12, 1879.

to people the houseless wilds of Marathon and Marshfield.[129]

By 1899 the *Catholic Sentinel* was advising Irish Catholics not to emigrate to the United States because they would be the objects of mistreatment, discrimination, and bigotry.[130]

As far as Wisconsin was concerned there existed little need for the warning. Irish immigrants after 1870 numbered very few; some entered the northern sections of the state as these became more densely populated. Actually, beginning in 1870, the total number of Irish-born in Wisconsin had declined. Not a sufficient number arrived to replace those who had died or migrated from the state.

As has been pointed out, the heaviest Irish immigration into Wisconsin was concentrated between the years 1850-1860. This is likewise true of Irish immigration into the United States, and the causes of that immigration in both instances parallel each other. Obviously, the causes which had their roots in Ireland were the same, whether the emigrant was just migrating to the United States or whether he had Wisconsin definitely as his goal. Where the Irishman had already done the former, Wisconsin, because of various types of influences, became for him and many of his companions the second and final objective. Wisconsin never became, however, a center for organized Irish colonization. Prior to 1860, when the state's efforts to attract immigrants were directed as much to the Irish as to the other nationalities, and the Irish were by far the majority among the immigrants entering the United States, a shortage of funds and other factors prevented many of them from reaching Wisconsin. After 1860, when Irish colonization programs were being carried out, the state of Wisconsin was applying its efforts to attract German and Norwegian settlers.

Despite the lack of organized Irish immigration into the state, however, Irishmen frequently did settle in groups in the rural areas and in sections of Milwaukee and other Wisconsin cities. It is logical, therefore, to answer these two questions next: Where did the Irish locate within the state, and what were their occupations?

---
[129] *Catholic Sentinel*, May 23, 1895.
[130] *Ibid.*, May 11, 1899.

CHAPTER II

LOCATION AND OCCUPATIONS OF THE IRISH IN SOUTHERN WISCONSIN

As late as 1820 the trading and military posts of Green Bay and Prairie du Chien were the only centers of settlement in the present state of Wisconsin, each counting a population of about 500. A wave of immigration, however, into the southwestern portion of the future state, where lead mines had been discovered, occurred between 1820 and 1850. Simultaneously during the 1830's and 1840's the population growth of southeastern Wisconsin began to rival and even surpass that of the lead region.[1] Lead mining, cheap lands for agriculture, the demand for labor, and accessibility caused this part of Wisconsin to be settled first. The portion of the state just north of this southernmost section was peopled chiefly by agricultural settlers during the latter half of the nineteenth century. Agriculture, lumbering, and work connected with iron mining drew immigrants into the extensive northern regions of Wisconsin chiefly after 1870 and into the twentieth century. As late as 1896 the newly formed board of immigration was making extensive efforts to attract immigrants to northern Wisconsin. In large measure because of geographical factors this extreme northern section has never compared with the southern portion of the state in population or density of settlement.

Following the general pattern of settlement in Wisconsin Irish immigration likewise began in the 1820's with the ingress of immigrants into the lead mining region, which in Wisconsin proper included the present counties of Grant, Iowa, Lafayette, and the western edge of Dane and Green Counties—the most southwest section of southern Wisconsin. The Indians had been mining the

---

[1] *Wisconsin, A Guide to the Badger State,* compiled by Workers of the Writers' Program of the Work Projects Administration in the State of Wisconsin (American Guide Series; New York: Duell, Sloan and Pearce, 1941), p. 46.

lead for more than a century and the first white men to do so were the Indian traders. Now adventurous settlers who had already pushed their way into the southern United States came up the Mississippi River and by 1828 most of the worthwhile "diggings" had been discovered. Gradually the population increased with the arrival of immigrants chiefly from the eastern states and the British Isles.[2]

The exact number of Irishmen among these earliest lead miners is impossible to determine, but in the 1836 territorial census at least one-tenth of the names are Irish among the approximately 1,000 heads of families listed for Iowa County.[3] The location of some of these earliest Irish arrivals is designated on an 1829 map of the lead region. Murphy's residence and furnace were located in the present town of Benton, Lafayette County; Kirkpatrick's furnace in the town of Dodgeville; and Keho's Diggings in the town of Linden, Iowa County.[4] The Murphy brothers, Dennis

---

[2] Raney, *op. cit.*, pp. 89-91. For more detailed information on the lead region *cf.* Joseph Schafer, *The Wisconsin Lead Region* (Wisconsin Domesday Book, General Series, III; Madison: State Historical Society of Wisconsin, 1932); Orin G. Libby, "Significance of the Lead and Shot Trade in Early Wisconsin History," *Collections,* XIII (1895), 293-334; "Chronicle of the Helena Shot Tower," *ibid.,* pp. 354-374; Reuben G. Thwaites, "Notes on Early Lead Mining in the Fever (or Galena) River Region," *ibid.,* pp. 271-292; John A. Wilgus, "The Century Old Lead Region in Early Wisconsin History," *WMH,* X (June, 1927), 401-410.

[3] Reuben G. Thwaites, "The Territorial Census for 1836," *Collections,* XIII (1895), 257-270. This article contains a brief history and explanation of the census and then lists the "heads of families" in alphabetical order according to the four counties: Crawford, Brown, Iowa, and Milwaukee. Iowa County then included the territory south of the Wisconsin River, the present Grant, Iowa, Lafayette, and Green Counties, and the western portion of Dane. Some names not included in those considered for the 100 Irish given above may, of course, have been Irish and some of those counted may have been of Irish descent but not Irish-born.

[4] R. W. Chandler, "Map of the United States' Lead Mines on the Upper Mississippi River, 1829," *Collections,* XI (1888), 400. The 1840 Manuscript Federal Census lists Francis Kirkpatrick in Iowa County with a household of seven persons, five employed in mining. NA, Cartographic Records, Original map accompanying D. F. Owen's "Geological Survey of the Wisconsin Lead Mining Region," shows the location of two Kirkpatrick furnaces

and James, from County Wexford, were prominent in the locality and the first permanent settlers in the town of Benton. Dennis is considered the founder of the village of Benton which he surveyed and laid out in 1844.[5] Although Morgan Keogh (Keho on the 1829 map) and Patrick O'Meara were the first to settle in the town of Linden, its population soon became predominantly English and Welsh.[6] Irish settlers were among the earliest in the town of Willow Springs also,[7] while in Iowa County John Burns and his family were the first to locate permanently in the town of Clyde in the spring of 1845. They were followed by Michael Murphy, John Doherty, and Thomas Gorman among others, thus forming the nucleus of an Irish settlement which continued to grow through the 1850's.[8] Dublin, an Irish settlement, had been

---

and one residence. The residence is marked, "S. Kirkpatrick." John G. Gregory, "Old Crawford County," *Southwestern Wisconsin: A History of Old Crawford County*, ed. by J. G. Gregory (Chicago: The S. J. Clarke Publishing Co., 1932), I, 53, tells of a certain Kirkpatrick in the town of Dodgeville who reported in the summer of 1837 that after three years of labor he had completed an excavation which cost 12,000 dollars. He had by 1837 taken out 600,000 pounds of ore which brought him a sum of 5,000 dollars above the cost of the work. *Ibid.*, p. 52, states that at the Irish Diggings, a mile north of Shullsburg, a "lucky strike" was made in 1834 by a man named Doyle, "who in a short space of two years, and with only the most primitive means at his command raised five million pounds of lead ore, worth at the time something like three hundred thousand dollars." Doyle is said to have been "the hero of the hour" throughout the country and to have traveled about spending his money lavishly. Finally, he became addicted to drink and "in reduced circumstances, returned to the diggings and died neglected in a cabin near the spot from which he had extracted his squandered wealth." This was probably the same man listed in the 1836 Territorial Census as "Patrick Doile" and in the 1840 Federal Census, "Patrick Doyle," with a household of three employed in mining.

[5] The Madison *Argus*, April 7, 1846. Thomas D'Arcy McGee, *Irish Settlers in North America* (Boston, 1852), p. 184, wrote that the town of Benton was almost exclusively Irish and that its founder represented his county in the State Senate.

[6] *History of Iowa County, Wisconsin* (Chicago: Western Historical Company, 1881), p. 807.

[7] *History of Lafayette County, Wisconsin* (Chicago: Western Historical Company, 1881), p. 629.

[8] *History of Iowa County, Wisconsin*, p. 790.

formed before 1829 about a mile north of the village of Shullsburg and adjoining the rather extensive Irish Diggings.[9]

Irish immigration steadily increased and by 1846 Donald McLeod, after visiting the lead region, reported that many Irish had settled there.[10] More specifically, the 1850 Federal census recorded more than 3,000 Irishmen[11] in the three most important lead mining counties with approximately three-fifths of these located in Lafayette County, especially in the towns of Benton and New Diggings, Shullsburg and Willow Springs.[12] Most of the foreign-born of the region were from England and Ireland.[13] Locations having the heaviest concentrations of population also had the most Irishmen. These concentrations centered around the lead diggings rather than in scattered agricultural areas and the proportion of Irishmen grouped within them was greater than for any other single nationality.[14] Statistics on the percentage of Irish families in the areas of heavy concentration indicate that, although the number of unmarried male adventurers was high, most of the Irishmen located in the lead region were by 1850 settled there with their families.[15]

As shown on the map, page 45, the concentration of Irish in the lead region in 1850 formed a broken band, the lower portion of which rested in southwestern Lafayette County with a small

---

[9] Chandler, *loc. cit.*, p. 400; McLeod, *op. cit.*, p. 232; Wilgus, *loc. cit.*, p. 405, map; *History of Lafayette County, Wisconsin*, p. 657. Dublin became a part of Shullsburg. *Cf.* Charles Scanlan, "History of the Irish in Wisconsin," *Journal of the American Irish Historical Society*, XIII (1914), 250.

[10] McLeod, *op. cit.*, p. 233.

[11] All statistics on the Irish in this study for the years 1850 and 1860 were obtained by the writer from the manuscript census records at the National Archives, Washington, D. C. Irishmen entered Wisconsin chiefly between 1840 and 1860, hence the value of data derived from the census records of those years. The 1840 census does not record nationality.

[12] The words township and town are used interchangeably in this study. The term town is not used to designate a village, settlement, or small city.

[13] Schafer, *The Wisconsin Lead Region*, p. 45.

[14] Mary J. Read, "A Population Study of the Driftless Hill Land during the Pioneer Period, 1832-1860" (unpublished Ph.D. dissertation, University of Wisconsin, 1941), p. 182.

[15] *Cf.* Appendix, pp. 255-257, Tables 4, 5, 6.

WISCONSIN
FOREIGN-BORN IRISH
1850

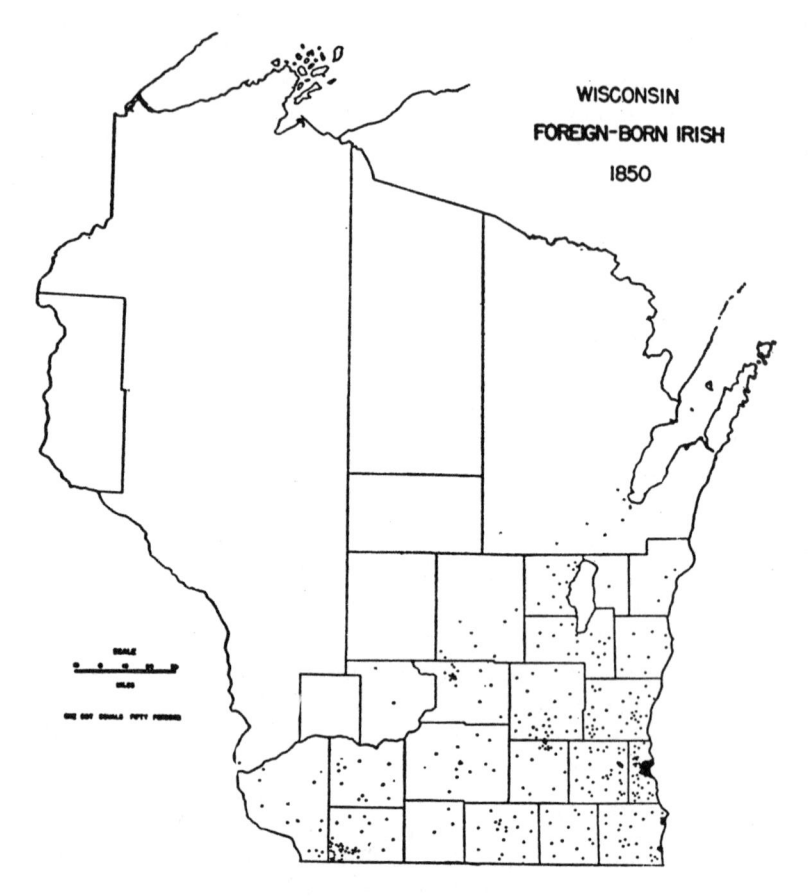

section in Grant County, then extending northeastward through Lafayette and Iowa Counties. In 1860 the general contour of that band was much the same only that it had lengthened, widened, and become more dense, indicating a growing Irish population.

The census returns for each decade of the nineteenth century after 1870 indicate a steady decrease in the population of the three counties of the lead region and also in the numbers of Irish-born inhabitants. The Mineral Point land office was closed in 1865, an indication that settlement in this section of Wisconsin had been practically complete. For statistical purposes, therefore, the census returns for this region which indicate the numbers of foreign-

WISCONSIN
IRISH FAMILIES
1850

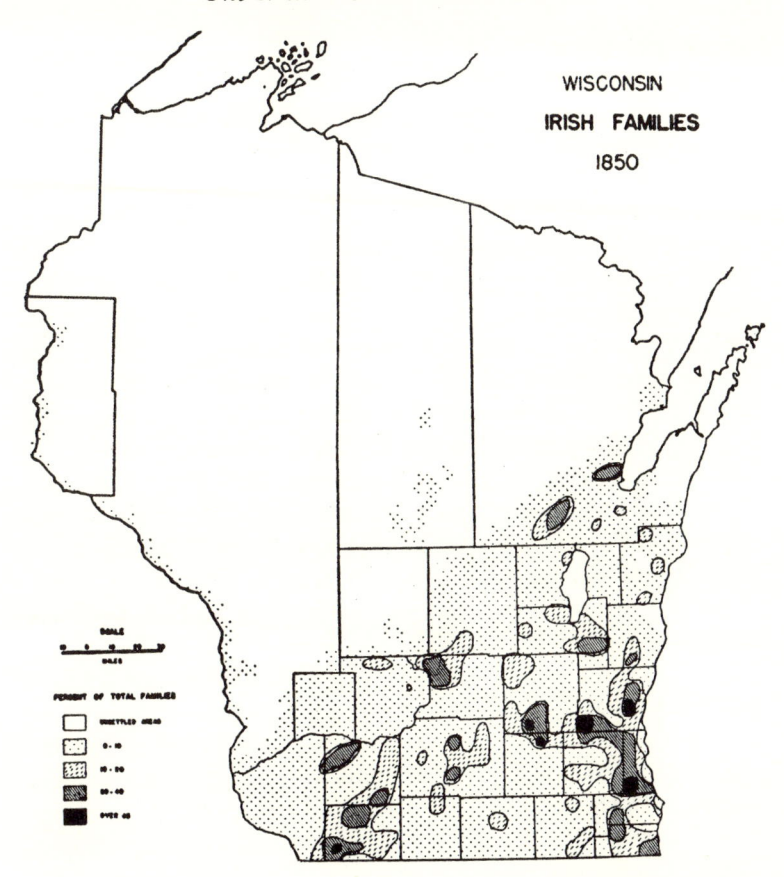

born Irishmen are not of particular value after 1870 because once immigration has reached its height, the term Irishmen must include the American-born children of Irish-born parents and, before the passing of the century, also the third and in some instances the fourth generations.[16]

Localities that had been designated as Irish in 1850 and 1860, because of the Irish-born immigrants who settled there, were still

---

[16] Frederick L. Holmes (ed.), *Wisconsin: Stability, Progress, Beauty* (5 vols.; Chicago: The Lewis Publishing Co., 1946), I, 357, maintains that by 1850 "the Irish, like the English and the Scotch, had so long been incorporated into the basic elements of the American race that the effort to discriminate between a native Irishman and a native Irish-American was largely academic."

considered such in 1890 although it was now the second and the third generations that made up the population. For example, the towns of Benton, Darlington, Gratiot, Kendall, Seymour, Shullsburg, and Willow Springs of Lafayette County, were listed by a county clerk in 1889 as predominantly Irish, while the remaining towns of the county were recorded as predominantly American, German, or Norwegian with smaller proportions of Irish.[17]

From what parts of Ireland did these Irish who located in the lead mining region emigrate? The answer to this question is difficult to ascertain. Many settlers of Benton, Lafayette County, were from Sligo and Monaghan, but practically all the counties of Ireland were represented. Tombstones in the old church cemetery at Shullsburg record the counties of Galway, Wexford, Donegal, Limerick, Wicklow, Monaghan, Kilkenny, Tipperary, Cork, Tyrone, Queens, Waterford, and Kerry. The last two were together the original homes of as many Irishmen as all of the other named counties combined. The Irish who settled in Mount Hope Township, Grant County, especially on Irish Ridge, were natives of the counties of Kildare, Kilkenny, Queens, Cork, Limerick, Waterford, Armagh, Down, Monaghan, Sligo, Leitrim, Galway, Mayo, and Roscommon.[18] An agricultural community of about 150 Irish families in Adams Township, Green County, adjoining Argyle Township, Lafayette County, can be cited as a similar example. In the old church cemetery are the graves of Irishmen from West Meath, Tipperary, Sligo, Limerick, Waterford, Mayo, Cavan, and Dublin. An old Irish burial ground just outside Monroe, Green County, practically duplicates the preceding findings, with at least twelve counties represented. These localities seem to

---

[17] WSHS, Manuscript Division, John S. Roeseler Papers, 1888-1890, report of S. Vickens, County Clerk, Darlington, Wisconsin, December 21, 1889. Roeseler, in making a study of nationalities in Wisconsin, sent out a questionnaire to school superintendents, teachers, county officials, pastors of religious denominations, and others. The information returned to Roeseler by these individuals varied greatly in length and value of content. Two questions of importance here were: What nationality is predominant? Are other nationalities represented to any extent, and what is their approximate proportion to the predominant nationality?

[18] P. L. Scanlan, "A Bit of Local History," pp. 23 and 24.

be typical of the rest of the lead mining region and of Wisconsin for that matter. The Irish gradually entered southwestern Wisconsin through a period of a little more than twenty years and they were quite generally representative of most of the counties of Ireland, with one or more Irish counties contributing a slightly heavier proportion in some localities.

From 1820 to 1847, mining in the lead region was the object of "almost everyone's enterprise, anxiety, and labor."[19] Agriculture was considered a secondary pursuit. In October, 1834, however, the Mineral Point land office had been opened for the sale of the agricultural lands in the region and by 1847 the reserved mining lands were being sold since agriculture had begun to take its place along with mining as an important industry. Nevertheless, in 1850 the chief occupation among the Irishmen in the locality still was mining or some phase of work connected with the mining process. Most of the Irishmen who were not engaged in mining were farmers.

It has been seen that agriculture in 1847 had begun to supersede mining in importance in the lead mining region; at least a larger proportion of the population had begun to engage in farming than was occupied in the mines. This was owing to the fact that the mining rush had subsided, that the more worthwhile diggings were being consolidated and controlled by mining companies, that reserved mining lands had been sold for agricultural purposes, and that by 1860 many of the miners had moved on to the more glittering prospects of gold in California, or to the copper deposits in the Lake Superior region. This trend toward farming as a means of livelihood did not noticeably affect the Irish population until sometime between 1850 and 1860. With Irish miners turning to agriculture and more Irish immigrants entering the region, the number of Irish farmers by 1860 had increased greatly in each county, while the number of miners had decreased.[20] Numerically the Irish farmers in Iowa County during the 1850-

---

[19] Boston *Pilot*, January 22, 1848, Thomas Mooney to the editor, New Diggings, Wisconsin, December 8, 1847.

[20] Miners in the lead region in 1860 totaled 2,400; Irish miners numbered about 360, or 15 per cent.

1860 period increased fourfold; in Grant County, tripled; and in Lafayette County, more than doubled. If farm laborers are to be included in the totals of Irishmen engaged in agriculture, the increases are even greater.[21]

Just what kind of work Irishmen were engaged in as laborers is difficult to determine although it seems reasonable to conclude that most of these were a part of the mining industry. In 1860 the only ones categorized were four railroad laborers.

Writing of the miners in 1847, Thomas Mooney said:

> Some of them are rich, but the majority are not beyond the condition of the common laborer, for the majority spend their lives hunting for mineral without finding any; and spend all their time and money in the enterprise. For the one that gets a prize, there are at least ninety-nine that get nothing. Yet they all work on under a species of infatuation—and when broken down and utterly ruined in means they deliberately hire themselves out at a dollar a day as helpers where mines are worked, and when, by working a few months, they get again into the possession of provision, they return to the search for mineral with as much freshness and buoyancy as if they had just begun the enterprise.[22]

Not all Irishmen in the lead region were miners, farmers, or common laborers, although these three groups far outnumbered those engaged in other occupations. Usually residing in the villages near the diggings were Irishmen engaged in occupations that would classify as professional, managerial, or clerical work-

---

[21] Farm laborers were not enumerated in the 1850 census, but in 1860 there are 220 Irish farm laborers listed for the three lead mining counties. It is difficult to ascertain whether these were hired men or were working without pay on their fathers' farms.

[22] Boston *Pilot*, January 22, 1848, Letter of Thomas Mooney, *loc. cit.* The 1850 and 1860 census returns do not provide distinctions within the general category of miners. Some of those listed as miners were undoubtedly mine owners and managers, while many were probably laborers within the mines. Then too, in the early days it was often the case that the owner of a mine was also laborer. The amount of real and personal estate which is recorded would be an indication of the miner's status.

ers, as wholesale or retail traders, craftsmen, operatives, or service workers. Eight per cent could be thus classified in 1850 and only seven per cent in 1860.

The settlement of the lead mining region along with its political and economic growth decisively influenced the development of Wisconsin. The lead miners had obtained the removal of the Winnebago, Fox, and Sauk tribes and had demanded the surveying of southern Wisconsin by the United States government. Not only because of the presence of the miners but also on account of their prosperity and influence, Wisconsin was created a territory by Congress in 1836.[23] Moreover, the lead and shot trade opened routes from the mines in the southwest to Milwaukee, Racine, and Southport (now Kenosha), the most southeastern section of southern Wisconsin. From these ports the lead was shipped eastward over the Great Lakes, thus opening the way for immigrants from the East and attracting the attention of merchants and capitalists to the territory and to the possibility of profitably building lines of transportation and communication between Lake Michigan and the Mississippi River.[24] Of great importance to the immigrants between 1840 and 1850 were the overland routes formed by the teamsters in the late 1830's. More than a hundred, sometimes as many as two hundred, teams were constantly plying between Milwaukee and Mineral Point hauling lead and often returning with the freight and baggage of the immigrants at cheap rates.[25] Without these paths traced by the teamsters the immigrants would have been delayed, possibly for several years, in penetrating the regions between the lake ports and the lead mines.[26]

The southeastern corner of the state thus opened to immigrants comprised an extended Milwaukee County in which in 1836 the territorial census revealed a population of approximately 2,890. The majority of these settlers was located along the lake

---

[23] Joseph Schafer, *The Winnebago-Horicon Basin, A Type Study in Western History* (Wisconsin Domesday Book, General Series, IV; Madison: State Historical Society of Wisconsin, 1937), 77.
[24] Libby, *loc. cit.*, p. 334.
[25] Milwaukee *Enquirer*, August 11, 1842.
[26] Libby, *loc. cit.*, p. 334.

shore in Milwaukee, Racine, and Southport.[27] By 1840 Milwaukee County had been cut down to include the present counties of Milwaukee and Waukesha but the population within this reduced area had reached 5,600. Four hundred and fifty-one family heads were American or English and 51 clearly Irish.[28] The population increase in Milwaukee County during the two decades 1840-1860 was phenomenal. There were in 1850 approximately 31,000 inhabitants of which 4,350 were Irish-born and in 1860 the Irish-born totaled over 5,300 among a population of approximately 62,500.

Milwaukee, the most important of the lake ports, was in the early 1830's merely a fur-trading post. Solomon Juneau, one of the first to settle there, saw that the site held promise for the future and with three others shared the land on which was built the city of Milwaukee. The location of this city within the borders of Milwaukee County created a situation that was hardly comparable to that existing in any of the other Wisconsin counties, because no other city expanded as rapidly in area and population as did Milwaukee. It early passed through the stages of a settlement and bustling frontier village to become by the turn of the century the only Wisconsin center ranking among the fifty largest cities of the United States.[29] Milwaukee's location and importance

---

[27] Thwaites, "The Territorial Census for 1836," *loc. cit.*, pp. 266, 251, map.
[28] Schafer, *Four Wisconsin Counties,* p. 81. Schafer arrived at these numbers by counting Irish names. The place of birth is not recorded in the 1840 census. This increase between 1836 and 1840 is greater than at first appears, because Milwaukee County had been cut down to eliminate Rock, Walworth, Racine, Kenosha, Jefferson, Dodge, Washington, Ozaukee, and eastern Dane Counties. The portion directly south of Milwaukee became Racine.
[29] Boston *Pilot,* September 16, 1843, letter from "An Emigrant," Milwaukee, Wisconsin Territory, August 21, 1843, is a contemporary description of the transition: "Milwaukie [sic] is built upon a very uneven tract of land, at the south of Milwaukie river, and is known by three separate districts, viz.: Juneau, Kilburn and Walker's Point, division. The number of buildings erected here this season, and now going up, cannot be short of five hundred. The principal street is Water Street, very pleasantly bordering the bank of Milwaukie River. The stores on this street are mostly constructed with arcades and imposing fronts. There are also many respectable hotels, taverns and boarding houses kept on this street. Huron Street, which runs from

as a lake port rendered it possible for many Irish immigrants upon arrival in Wisconsin to remain in the city. In a sense Milwaukee was a counterpart in miniature of New York City. As New York was the chief port of entry into the United States, so Milwaukee held that position in respect to Wisconsin. Many Irishmen remained in New York as laborers, some later moved westward onto the land. Much the same is true for Milwaukee. Irishmen in the Empire City ultimately became a political factor to contend with in the Democratic party machine and many of them worked their way into the professions. As will be seen this occurred also in Milwaukee where Irish democrats could not be ignored in the politics of the city even after the state was in Whig and Republican hands and although their countrymen were a minority in the population of the city.

In 1850 the population of Milwaukee was two-thirds that of the entire population of the county.[30] Irishmen were 14 per cent of the county's population; those in Milwaukee were 15 per cent of the city's population. In 1850 about 70 per cent of the Irish in Milwaukee County resided in Milwaukee itself and in 1860 about 80 per cent lived in the city. While the Irish-born population of the city increased during the 1850-1860 decade, that in the rural section of the county decreased. Where these rural Irishmen went

---

Water Street to the Pier, has many buildings, chiefly built since last April. The Eastern Hotel stands on this street, which was erected this summer by an enterprising Irishman. There are many fine public houses in Milwaukie, and one in particular, the Milwaukie House on Michigan Street, at the foot of which street stands the 'light house.' There are several Protestant Churches in Milwaukie, of all denominations, and a small Catholic Church, a parochial house, a school-house, and an academy. Society here seems to be a thorough mixture, but two-thirds of the people appear to be foreigners. There has been great emigration into this Territory this summer, and it is expected that there will be an overflowing number coming out early in the fall. There is plenty of room for them here, and as good land as in the world. . . . In walking through this town, it presents to the eye and to the ear one entire carpenter's shop, with men at work on the new buildings."

[30] The names of a number of Wisconsin counties are identical with the names of towns, villages, or cities within the county; therefore, whenever such a name appears in this study the absence of any other designation ordinarily indicates the municipality.

is difficult to determine, but it is probable that some entered the city and others moved to farms farther west.[31]

The Irishmen gradually filled in the southern section of the city east of the Milwaukee River, the third ward, where in 1860 Irish families made up 60 per cent of the total number of families.[32] Thirty-seven per cent of all the Milwaukee Irishmen made their homes in the third ward, 19 per cent were located in the fourth ward, 17 per cent in the first, and smaller percentages resided in the remaining six wards.

The towns of Wauwatosa, Greenfield, Franklin, and Granville had relatively large concentrations of Irishmen in 1850 and 1860, although in Greenfield and Franklin the number had decreased by 1860. A number of Irish Catholic families had already settled within about twelve miles of Milwaukee in 1840 where they were described as "peaceably cultivating rich well-timbered land which was their own."[33] The Irishmen in the towns outside of Milwaukee were predominantly farmers except in Wauwatosa where laborers outnumbered the agriculturists. Three-fourths of the laborers in the county were located in Milwaukee itself in 1850 and about seven-eighths in 1860.[34] Most of the Irish craftsmen were carpenters and shoemakers while many Irishmen were employed as draymen and not a few as sailors on the Great Lakes.

The city of Milwaukee, being the most heavily populated area in Wisconsin, had in comparison to the rest of the state a proportionately large number of laborers. In 1850 much of the state was still unsettled and the portions west of Milwaukee were definitely rural frontier sections where men were clearing forests, breaking land, and commencing to farm. Hence, in 1850, while there were 3,200 Irish laborers in Wisconsin, 625, or one-fifth, lived in the city of Milwaukee, one-fourth in the county of Mil-

---

[31] Schafer, *Four Wisconsin Counties,* p. 102.

[32] *Cf.* Appendix, p. 257, Table 7.

[33] Boston *Pilot,* September 12, 1840, letter from a correspondent of the *Catholic Advocate.* This was the Irish settlement at Greenfield.

[34] Table 3, p. 53

TABLE 3

OCCUPATIONS OF IRISHMEN IN THE CITY OF MILWAUKEE, 1850 AND 1860*

Classification	1850	1860
Professional and semi-professional workers	20	20
Farmers and farm managers	20	5
Proprietors, managers, and officials, except farm	55	100
Clerical, sales, and kindred workers	30	70
Craftsmen, foremen, and kindred workers	260	465
Operatives, and kindred workers	85	200
Protective service workers	5	30
Service workers, except domestic and protective	25	45
Laborers, except farm and mine	630	735

*This classification is based on that used in the 1940 Federal Census. Certain adaptations had to be made, such as substituting draymen and teamsters for truckers. The census of 1840 also listed the two following classes not given here: domestic service workers, farm laborers and foremen. There were none of the latter in the city of Milwaukee in 1850 and 1860 and the former were all women in the 1860 census. The 1850 census did not list domestics nor certain other occupations for women.

waukee.[35] As the rest of Wisconsin developed, however, railroads were built across the state, public works' projects got underway, some few villages grew into cities, and as a matter of course the number of laborers in the state increased. By 1860 there were almost 6,200 Irish laborers in Wisconsin with only about one-eighth of these located in the city and county of Milwaukee.

Occupations of women in Milwaukee in 1860 other than that of housewife included domestic work, dressmaking, millinery, laundering, teaching, and nursing. More than 450 Irish women, most of them young, were hired into families as domestics. About half of these Irish maids were employed in the seventh ward, the better residential part of town.

[35] The number, 625, is derived from counting only those designated as "laborers" in the manuscript census. The number, 630, in Table 3 includes, according to the 1940 classification, 5 fishermen. Stephen Klopfer, "The First Conferences of the Society of St. Vincent De Paul in Milwaukee," *Salesianum*, XXIX (April, 1934), 30-32, lists the charter members, all Irish, of the Vincentian societies in two Milwaukee parishes—St. John's Cathedral and St. Gall's. Approximately fifty names are listed for each society with the members' occupations. Very few professional men are in the two groups. The list compares favorably with the classification in Table 3.

After 1860 the Irish-born population of Milwaukee County gradually decreased. This decline may be attributed to the decrease in Irish immigration, to the tendency of many of the early Irish settlers to move from one location to another, to the completion of settlement of the area signified here as in the lead region by the closing of the land office in 1865, but even more so to the *Lady Elgin* disaster in 1860. This catastrophe was the direct cause of the death of more than 300 Milwaukee Irishmen.[36]

The story of the ill-fated *Lady Elgin* has its background in a long controversy over the constitutionality and enforcement of the Fugitive Slave Law, which was defied by the Republicans then in power in the state. The incident involved a runaway slave, Joshua Glover, who had been captured in 1854, then was aided in his escape from Federal authorities by radical abolitionists.[37] Public opinion had been greatly aroused in the state and politicians argued the issue. Consequently, when Governor Alexander W. Randall, states'-rights Republican, asked Garrett Barry, the captain of the Union Guards of Milwaukee, Irish Democrats to a man, what they would do in case their Company were called upon to support the state against the Federal government, Barry maintained that they would uphold the authority of the Federal government. The military company's arms which had been furnished by the state were seized, Barry's commission as captain was revoked, and the company was ordered to disband.[38]

Undaunted, the Union Guards planned to raise funds for the procurement of arms by sponsoring an excursion trip by boat from Milwaukee to Chicago where Stephen Douglas was to speak at a Democratic rally on September 7. The *Lady Elgin* was chartered and with some 400 passengers, chiefly young Irish men and women, reached Chicago; but on the return trip late in the night of September 7-8 in the rain and fog just off the bluffs at Winnetka, Illinois, the excursion boat was rammed by a lumber-freighted schooner, the *Augusta*. The *Lady Elgin* sank

---

[36] Milwaukee *Sentinel*, September 10, 11, 13, 14, 1860.
[37] Cf. *infra*, p. 140, n. 42.
[38] Milwaukee *Sentinel*, March 4, 9, 12, 13, 1860.

and all but ninety-five of her passengers were drowned.[39] This September 8, 1860, marked the beginning of a decline in the Irish population of Milwaukee.[40]

Although the Irish-born declined numerically, Irish-Americans increased throughout the century in number and influence. Practically every movement or organization that was considered Irish included in its ranks promoters and members who were Irish-American, that is, Americans born of Irish parents and descendants of native Irishmen. Children with only one parent Irish-born were not only sympathizers and active promoters of Irish movements but were frequently more enthusiastic in their support than native Irishmen themselves. A little Irish blood often went a long way. Near the turn of the century Irish-Americans to the second generation along with the Irish-born numbered approximately 12,900 in Milwaukee.[41] An estimate for 1890 based on the

[39] *Ibid.*, September 10, 11, 13, 14, 1860. C. M. Scanlan, *The Lady Elgin Disaster, September 8, 1860* (Milwaukee, 1928), gives the entire account. *Cf.* also, Milo M. Quaife, *Lake Michigan* (Indianapolis: The Bobbs-Merrill Co., 1944), pp. 258-261. Frances M. Stover, "The Schooner That Sank the Lady Elgin," *WMH*, VII (September, 1923), 30-40, writes the history of the schooner *Augusta*. When relatives and friends of the Irishmen who had lost their lives heard that the *Augusta,* repaired and renamed *Colonel Cook,* had docked in Milwaukee some time after the accident, they plotted to destroy the "murder ship." Quick action on the part of the *Augusta's* owners, however, prevented this from happening.

[40] C. M. Scanlan, *The Lady Elgin Disaster,* p. 5, claims that "As the Irish in Milwaukee seemed to be in the ascendancy at that time, that accident forever pushed them into the background, there, as most of the people lost were young Irishmen and Irishwomen. Also, it had a tendency to put Milwaukee back at least twenty years and to permit Chicago a boost." The cholera epidemics of the 1850's were considered to be factors in the crippling of Milwaukee's growth along with the *Lady Elgin* disaster.

[41] Department of the Interior, Census Office, *Report on Population of the United States at the Eleventh Census: 1890* (Washington: Government Printing Office, 1895), pp. 710, 716, 722, 726, 728. Irish-born in the city of Milwaukee totaled 3,436; Americans having both parents Irish-born, 6,154; native Americans having one parent Irish-born, one foreign-born (not Irish), 1,198; total, 12,889. Census tables also give the total number of white persons having Irish-born parents and parents of mixed nationality with one Irish-born, but these would include Irish-born children. The numbers given here, therefore, are more accurate since Irish-born children are included in the first figure.

1885 state census returns places the combined total of Irish-born and Irish-Americans of Milwaukee County at 15,000, or 8 per cent of the population.[42]

Racine and Kenosha, also lake ports and counties, developed south of Milwaukee and simultaneously with it, although not proportionately in population. This most southeastern section of Wisconsin, Racine County, in 1840, had a population totaling 3,475.[43] Kenosha County, carved from Racine in 1850, had in that year a total population of 10,735 while Racine totaled 15,000. In the former, Irishmen led the foreign contingent, but in the latter the Irish-born were outnumbered by the Germans. In 1850 a little less than half of the Irishmen in Kenosha County were residents of the city of Kenosha.[44] There was a greater discrepancy between Racine's rural and urban Irish, however, where about 60 per cent were located in the rural towns and the rest resided in the city of Racine.[45] The city of Kenosha did not grow as rapidly as Racine and ceased to attract Irish laborers; hence, the Irish in Kenosha between 1850 and 1860 decreased while the rural group increased slightly. In Racine County, however, after 1850 the trend was towards an increased urban population; about 50 per cent of the Irish in the county were rural. Outside of Kenosha city, the towns of Brighton, Pleasant Prairie, and Salem each had an appreciable number of Irishmen; Dover and Caledonia were the most pronouncedly Irish towns in Racine County.

As the years after 1860 and again after 1870 had seen a decline in the Irish-born population in the lead region and in Milwaukee County so the number of Irish-born in Kenosha and Racine Counties decreased. Irish immigration into the region had decreased,

---

[42] Milwaukee *Catholic Citizen*, March 1, 1890. The Irish-born total for Milwaukee County in 1885 was 3,755. The computation was made as follows: 3,755 multiplied by 3.3 (the multiplicand justified by the Federal census of 1880) with seven-tenths added by way of allowance for the difference of ten years.

[43] Schafer, *Four Wisconsin Counties*, p. 81, in attempting to determine the nationality of these early settlers, concluded that 643 family head names were Anglo-Saxon, while of 40 others, 22 were Irish.

[44] *Cf.* Appendix, p. 258, Table 8.

[45] *Cf.* Appendix, p. 258, Table 9.

all of the unimproved land in these two counties had been taken up, Germans were moving in, and some of the Irish migrated to other counties or to other states.[46] Kenosha County, outdistanced by Racine already in 1860, not only ceased to grow between 1860 and 1880, but actually decreased in population.

Counties west of the lake ports through which teamsters had cut paths to the lead region were Waukesha, Walworth, Rock, Green, Jefferson, and Dane. All of these except Green and the western portion of Dane belonged to the original Milwaukee County and were included as such in the 1836 census. Early immigrants into Green and Dane Counties were chiefly an overflow from the lead region. The southwestern corner of Dane County and the western edge of Green had some mines and either one had to be crossed in order to transport lead to Milwaukee or the other lake ports. The order of settlement in these counties, east to west, is indicated by the population of each in 1840: Walworth, Rock, Green, Jefferson, and Dane.[47] Settlement between 1840 and 1850 went on at a rapid pace and by 1860 Waukesha, Walworth, and Rock Counties had practically reached their peaks while Dane, Jefferson, and Green with large increases also, continued to make significant gains after 1860. According to their Irish population in 1850 these counties ranked as follows: Waukesha, Rock, Jefferson, Walworth, Dane, and Green.[48]

The area which became Waukesha County was easily reached from Milwaukee and immigrants soon entered lands for permanent settlement. Irishmen were among these early pioneers. One Wisconsin historian found a number of the land entries in present Waukesha County bearing Irish names in the towns of Muskego, New Berlin, and Brookfield.[49] Irishmen had also located

---

[46] Schafer, *Four Wisconsin Counties,* pp. 101-103, discusses these facts in comparison with Milwaukee and Ozaukee Counties.

[47] Waukesha was still a part of Milwaukee County in 1840. The two counties had a combined population of 5,605.

[48] *Cf.* Appendix, pp. 259-264, Tables 10, 11, 12, 13, 14, 15.

[49] J. H. A. Lacher, "Waukesha County," *Southeastern Wisconsin: A History of Old Milwaukee County,* ed. by J. G. Gregory (Chicago: The S. J. Clarke Publishing Co., 1932), II, 985.

in Pewaukee, Genesee, Mukwonago, and Menomonee Townships before 1842.[50] By 1850 the Irish was the largest foreign-born group in Waukesha County. Most of the early Irish settlers were Catholics from the southern provinces of Ireland, although a few were Protestant families from Ulster and from southern Ireland.[51] Notwithstanding the fact that the town of Menomonee is claimed to have been settled originally by the Irish, Americans moved in and as early as 1844 the Germans began to purchase land for farms with the result that certain sections became populated entirely by this nationality.[52] The town of New Berlin, as the name indicates, was also settled by the Germans, but had, nevertheless, a number of Irishmen among its first inhabitants.[53]

On the northern border of Waukesha County, Merton became one of the most Irish towns of the county. The boundary which separated Merton from Erin Township in Washington County was for all practical purposes non-existent for this Irish settlement extending into the town of Erin. The first settlers, practically all from Killarney, entered the region in September, 1842: John Beston, William Courtney, Thomas Fitzgerald, Jeremiah Flynn, Michael and Patrick Gallaher, John Grady, James Keneally, John Kinney, James and John Lynch, Bernard McConville, William McGrath, William Mountain, James Murphy, Andrew, John, and Michael Shields, John Sullivan, John and Peter Whelan.[54]

The settlement or village of Monches is located just south of the county border in the town of Merton. Many of the settlers located north of the village in the town of Erin and some in Merton. Local tradition provides four reasons why so large a group of Irishmen passed up level fertile land on their way from Milwaukee for this hilly and rocky locality. The first explanation is

---

[50] Boston *Pilot,* August 13, 1842, Daniel Fitzsimmons to the editor, Prairieville [Waukesha], Wisconsin Territory, June 12, 1842.

[51] Lacher, *loc. cit.,* p. 985.

[52] *The History of Waukesha County, Wisconsin* (Chicago: Western Historical Company, 1880), p. 755.

[53] Lacher, *loc. cit.,* p. 957.

[54] Lincoln F. Whelan, "'Them's They' the Story of Monches, Wisconsin," *WMH,* XXIV (September, 1940), 41; Heming, *op. cit.,* p. 475. The Shields family was from County Roscommon, Ireland.

that a sharp-witted, "blarney-tongued" fellow Irishman and land agent, Michael Lynch, "for a small fee directed the destinies and blinded these immigrants to the merits of other localities."[55] Michael Lynch himself, however, bought four sections within Erin township between 1841 and 1845 which were patented to him in 1848.[56] He may have seen some merits in the locality or he may have been just speculating. Another reason for their choice is laid to the fact that these Irishmen connected the level lands with the undesirable lowlands and bogs of their native country. As they later said: "We didn't come half way across the continent to be 'bogtrotters!'" Moreover, being from the mountainous region around Killarney, they were at home among the verdant forested hills, the valleys, and nearby lakes.[57] And finally, when they heard of plans being made for construction of the Milwaukee and Rock River Canal under government subsidy and control, the Irishmen with a kind of innate suspicion and fear of the government sought to be far removed from the canal. Hence their settlement farther north.[58] The village of Monches was originally called O'Connellsville in honor of the Irish statesman, Daniel O'Connell. In the spring of 1848, however, when a post office was created there the name was changed to Monches.[59]

Brookfield Township was conspicuous in 1850 for the aggregation of approximately 250 Irish laborers, the majority of whom were employed by an Irish contractor, Redmond O'Gary, in the construction of the Milwaukee and Mississippi Railroad. This railroad company, the first actually to build in Wisconsin, was

---

[55] Whelan, *loc. cit.,* p. 41.

[56] NA, Land Grant Records.

[57] Whelan, *loc. cit.,* p. 42.

[58] *Ibid.* The most logical reason is undoubtedly the first. The group of Irishmen relied on the direction of a fellow countryman who had preceded them to Wisconsin. Although Lynch had bought a section in November, 1841, this is not proof that he had seen or ever visited the locality. Lynch did not survey that township.

[59] *Ibid.*, p. 44. A meeting of the citizens was called to nominate a postmaster. Inclement weather kept most of the men at home. The Swiss miller and two Britishers composed the attendance at the meeting, nominated one of the Britishers postmaster, and voted to change the name of the village

originally chartered in 1847 as the Milwaukee and Waukesha.[60] On September 28, 1849, contracts for the construction of the road from Milwaukee to Waukesha were awarded to five contractors, each to construct certain sections. Four of these bore Irish names: Thomas Murray, Redmond O'Gary, Henry Darcey, and M. L. O'Connor.[61] The railroad also extended west from Brookfield through Pewaukee, Delafield, and Oconomowoc. The last two in comparison with many of the other towns of Waukesha County did not have large Irish populations. The town and village of Oconomowoc, however, had 200 Irishmen, Irish families constituting about 17 per cent of the total number of families.

The presence of so many railroad laborers in the town of Brookfield in 1850 made the total number of laborers in Waukesha County greater than the number of farmers, about 500 to 400. This laboring force, however, represented a fluid element of the population. The Irish railroad construction gang had already, October 1, 1850, dispersed because of the failure of their employers to pay them.[62] In 1860, therefore, the number of laborers was greatly reduced. There were about 200 laborers in comparison with more than 500 farmers and 140 farm laborers.

---

to Monches. These men who had braved a storm to attend the meeting faced another when their deed became known to the Irishmen. Nevertheless, the name, Monches, was kept. Monches was the name of an Indian, part Potawatomi and part Chippewa, who was buried on a hill overlooking Monches.

[60] Raney, *op. cit.*, p. 179.

[61] Milwaukee *Sentinel,* September 29, 1849, December 7, 1849, citing the Watertown *Chronicle.* O'Connor built the plank road from Watertown to Oconomowoc, which job he finished about December 3, 1849. At the end of this job he set out with his crew of 60 or 70 laborers to start work on the Milwaukee and Waukesha Railroad. O'Gary was definitely Irish-born according to the manuscript census of 1850 where he is listed for the Town of Brookfield, Waukesha County.

[62] NA, Manuscript Census, 1850, XX. The assistant marshal in Brookfield noted on the bottom of one of the pages that these men had been at work for months, but owing to some failure in the pay they had left. He obtained their names and birthplaces from the roll of their employer. Lacher, *loc. cit.*, p. 946, and Schafer, *A History of Agriculture in Wisconsin*, p. 51, mention the presence of these Irish laborers in Brookfield. Schafer notes that they were a transient group.

The railroad to Waukesha began train service in February, 1851. From then until 1860 iron rails slowly began to penetrate to the interior of the state and they reached the Mississippi River at Prairie du Chien, 1856, and La Crosse, 1858. A contemporary Irishman described the progress:

> They [the people of Wisconsin] are also dashing ahead with railroads, which give employment to such laborers as are not employed at farming. One railroad is to run from Chicago along through all the towns and cities on the west shore of Lake Michigan, passing through Milwaukie and on northward; besides these are two leaving Milwaukie, another goes to Green Bay; another to Fond-du-Lac; another to Prairie Lacrosse [sic], on the Mississippi, near Minnesota; another road for Watertown, to be finished in July next. The Milwaukie and Mississippi Railroad has seventy miles in operation, and intends to continue on. Another road is from Racene [sic] to Janesville, and other from Kenosha to Belloit [sic], and thence through the Leadmines, west of the Mississippi. Thus in a few years, instead of the "Corduroy Railroads," we can run through the various parts of the state on a good Iron Trail.[63]

Eight hundred and ninety-one miles of railway were in operation by 1860. The trans-state routes passed north of the lead region however, and the branch line from Janesville westward stopped short at Monroe in Green County. A line ran south from Mineral Point but did not come in contact with any of the railroads leading to one of the lake ports. This by-passing of the lead region was indicative of its decline in Wisconsin's economy.

Within the ten-year period, 1850-1860, railroads penetrated the interior of the state. Waukesha County which was the first to welcome the iron monster had the largest Irish population in 1850 but the smallest increase in numbers of Irishmen of the five southeastern counties between 1850 and 1860. Along with Wau-

---

[63] Boston *Pilot,* January 7, 1854, Edward Gillin to editor, Janesville, Wisconsin, December 3, 1853.

kesha the other counties were hosts to railroad construction gangs and to railroad men between 1850 and 1860. During this time not only did these counties experience large increases of population but the Irish element trebled in some and increased 500 per cent in others. The coming of the railroad undoubtedly was one cause of this increase.[64]

Walworth County, south of Waukesha and one of the most densely populated counties in 1850, did not have a very large aggregation of Irishmen in any single town. By 1860, however, the number of Irish-born had tripled, but were still only 8 per cent of the total. The increase was concentrated especially in those towns and villages through which the railroad had been built. The road from Racine to Beloit in the late 1850's passed through Elk Horn Village, Lyons (then Hudson), Geneva, Delavan, and Darien townships, leaving along the road increased numbers of Irishmen, Irish laborers, and railroad workers of various kinds.[65] Significantly, the percentage of Irish-born and of Irish families grew larger in these townships and Irish laborers slightly outnumbered the farmers. The city of Whitewater, containing 'the largest concentration of Irishmen in the county grew rapidly after the railroad from Waukesha to Janesville extended through it.

From Whitewater the road reached into Rock County through the town of Milton to Janesville. In 1850 the more than 900 Irishmen of Rock County had been scattered throughout the townships and were only 4 per cent of the total number of inhabitants. The heaviest concentrations of Irishmen were in Janesville and Beloit. With the coming of the railroad the Irish population of the county rose to more than 3,300, an increase of

---

[64] The number of Irishmen tripled in Walworth County and more than tripled in Rock. The increase was five-fold in Green and Dane Counties. Jefferson County showed the smallest increase; the Irish total did not even double.

[65] Many of the Irishmen in Elk Horn Village were from the provinces of Munster and Leinster, Ireland. The first settlers had arrived in 1841. *Cf.* WSHS, Roeseler Papers, Report of James Nicholas, pastor of Catholic Church, Elkhorn, Wisconsin, February 8, 1891. Irishmen constituted the largest foreign-born group in the towns of Sugar Creek and Whitewater (exclusive of the city) in 1860 and 1870.

WISCONSIN
FOREIGN-BORN IRISH
1860

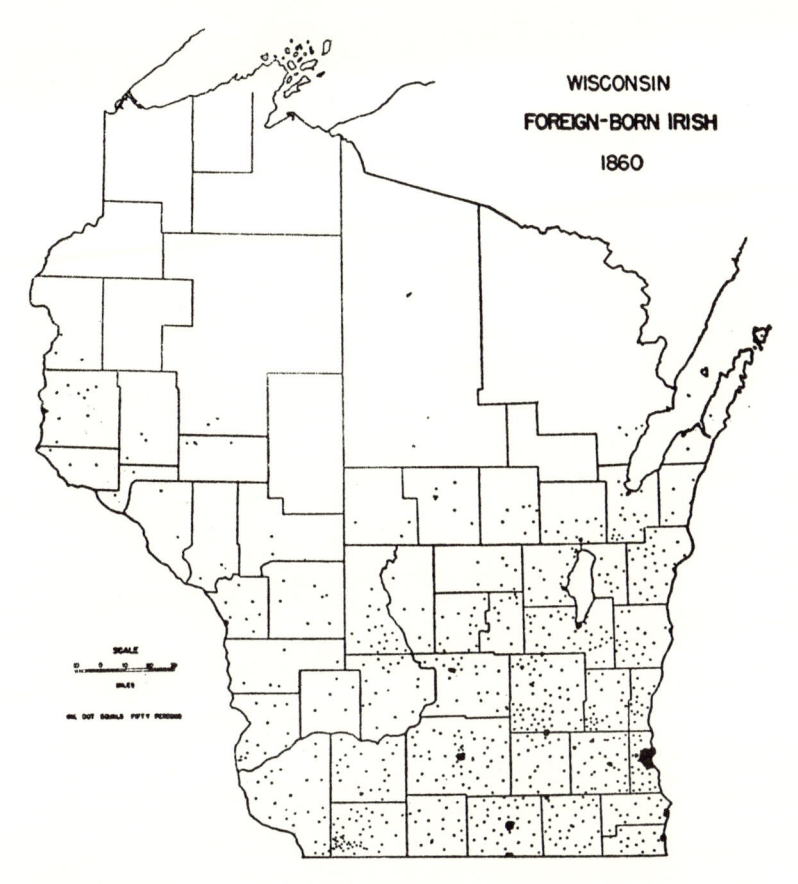

about 264 per cent. In 1860 Rock County ranked second to Milwaukee County in the total number of Irish-born inhabitants.

Moreover, Rock County probably had more miles of railroad track within its borders by 1860 than any other Wisconsin county.[66]

---

[66] The road from Racine to Beloit entered the county on the southeast and from Beloit extended to Evansville. The Milwaukee-Mississippi entered through the northeast and branched off through Milton and Edgerton into Dane County. It also ran a branch into Janesville. The Chicago and Northwestern, then called the Chicago, St. Paul and Fond du Lac, came from the north through Jefferson County, crossed the northern border into Milton Junction and to Janesville. Another road extended west to Monroe from Janesville.

WISCONSIN
IRISH FAMILIES
1860

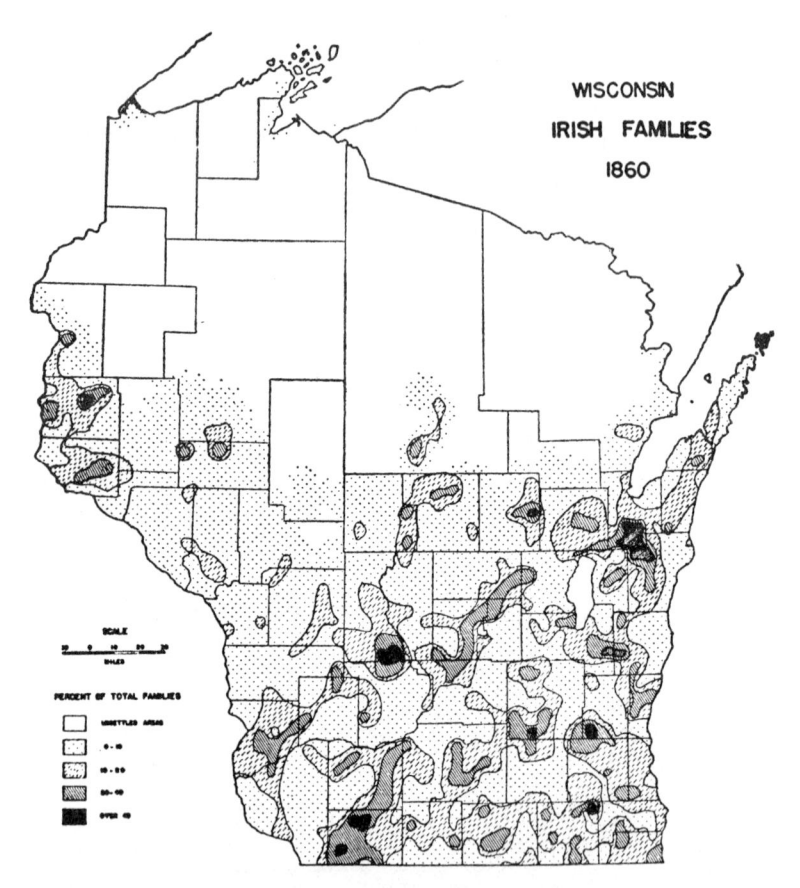

The Milwaukee-Mississippi was being constructed through Milton by Irish labor in the fall of 1852. It was reported:

> Milton is at present alive with the Engineers, Contractors, and Paddys, all acting their various parts towards the completion of the Road, which it is confidently expected will be completed to Janesville this fall, they have begun this week on the branch from this place to Janesville and if no unforseen [sic] delay occurs, I doubt not but their expectations will be realized, at any rate there is no moral doubt but it will reach here.[67]

[67] WSHS, Benjamin Densmore Papers, 1845-57, James Fraser to Benjamin Densmore, Milton, Wisconsin, September 1, 1852.

The railroad did reach Janesville, but not until January, 1853.[68] Before that date the census of 1850 had recorded almost 100 Irish laborers in the city and a large proportion of the not too numerous Irish population of the towns of Harmony, Milton, and Johnstown was also listed as such. Irish laborers outnumbered farmers in Rock County in 1850, 300 to 180.[69] By December, 1853, Janesville was described as a rapidly growing city, "where two trains of railroad cars run daily" and where another railroad was being constructed from Chicago and on up the Rock River valley.[70]

---

[68] Boston *Pilot*, June 25, 1853, T. J. in letter to the editor, Janesville, June 2, 1853, wrote: "Janesville is the name of a city but lately incorporated, and on account of its future Rail-roads there is no doubt that it may be in time, the second city in the State. It contains at present, 5,000 inhabitants, it is on the Rock River, and surrounded by a most beautiful and fertile country, its waterpower alone should make it of great advantage, aside from its advantages by the Rail-road, one which is already completed from here to Milwaukie, and several others are now about being finished. The Rock River Valley Railroad when completed, will place us in direct communication with Chicago and New York, and the Southern Wisconsin, with Dubuque and Galena, so that you will perceive that this city, which five years ago, was a mere village, will at some future day, be of great importance." The Rock River Valley Railroad became the Chicago and Northwestern Railway. The Southern Wisconsin reached its terminus in Monroe, Green County, 1857. That year the panic and railroad failures halted much of the railroad building.

[69] Labor had been attracted to Janesville by the building of a dam three miles north of the city in 1849 and the presence of sawmills, woolen and flour mills, carriage factories, and brickyards, while the work of building the city also required labor. *Cf.* Orrin Guernsey and Josiah F. Willard, *History of Rock County and Transactions of the Rock County Agricultural Society and Mechanics' Institute* (Janesville, Wisconsin: Wm. M. Doty and Brother, 1856). In Johnstown an asylum was built during 1849-1850. The twenty unmarried Irish laborers recorded in the census may have been engaged in its construction.

[70] Boston *Pilot*, January 7, 1854, Edward Gillin to the editor, Janesville, Wisconsin, December 3, 1853. In 1854 this road was completed from Fond du Lac to Janesville; in 1859 it reached Oshkosh. Fond du Lac and Oshkosh were rivals for the lumber trade.

With the construction of railroads through Rock County up until 1860 and after, Irish laborers more than doubled their numbers. Forty-two per cent of them were located in the city of Janesville, 19 per cent in Beloit township, and 11 per cent in the town of Milton. There is no doubt that the majority of Irish laborers in Milton was occupied with railroad construction because at least 50 were designated in the 1860 manuscript census as such. Thirty-eight of these were listed as one group. It is not surprising to find so many railroad laborers because even prior to 1860 Milton Junction had two different lines crossing through it. Janesville became a railroad center in the state for handling freight second only to Milwaukee. The first Janesville depot and roundhouse were built in 1853. In 1878 there were eight arrivals and departures at the passenger depots and by 1887 the combined freight traffic of the two roads reached 80 trains daily. Consequently, after the roads had been built there was plenty of railroad work to retain Irish laborers in the city. The majority of Irishmen, especially laborers, took up residence in Janesville's fourth ward.[71] In 1860 the Irish population of Janesville which exceeded 1,200 was 16 per cent of the total population and Irish families reached 27 per cent. Occupations aside from laborers varied as in other cities where there were large numbers of Irishmen: a few men in the professions, larger numbers engaged in crafts, and some handling managerial or proprietary jobs.

According to the 1850 manuscript census there were about 30 young Irish girls working in homes as domestic servants although they were not designated as such. These were usually recorded as the last member of a family group and, of course, as not having the same surname as the rest of the family. In 1857, through the Irish Emigrant Fund at least 45 Irish girls had been transported from Ireland to Janesville with the intention of having them employed in homes as domestics.[72] The 1860 census lists and specifically designates approximately 160 Irish girls thus employed.

---

[71] The fourth ward contained about 665 of the city's 1,200 Irish-born inhabitants. The second ward had 240.
[72] *Supra*, p. 26.

Quite generally, in the towns of Rock County except in Milton and Fulton, and in the cities of Janesville and Beloit, the number of Irish farmers exceeded the number of laborers. The predominantly agricultural townships of Rock, Porter, and Plymouth ranked in percentage of Irish families next to Janesville in 1860. The town of Lima during the 1840's and 1850's became home to a number of Scotch-Irish Presbyterians from the freehold town of Ballymacombs, Parish of Ballyscullion, County Londonderry, and from County Antrim.[73] Roley Godfrey and William Galloway as young men founded settlements in the town of Lima, Rock County, and Koshkonong, Jefferson County. The Godfrey settlement in Lima grew with the ingress of immigrants from County Antrim: James Boyd, Frank McWhinney, the Kyles, the Harrises, McCarneys, Barclays, Glasses, and McNamees; the Dales, Burnsides, Londens, and Lees.[74] Godfrey was generous in finding work for many of the newcomers and when young men wanted to send for a prospective bride he advanced the necessary sum. He then took the young girl into his home upon her arrival where she worked as a domestic until her marriage.[75]

Galloway settled on a farm in Koshkonong Township, Jefferson County, which is contiguous to the town of Lima, Rock County. His letters to relatives back home encouraged emigration and he helped the newcomers get started by offering them work until they were settled. During the 1840's came the Lees, McQuillens, Seawrights, Steeles, Armstrongs, Dixons, Galloways, Grahams, Kyles, McIntires, MacMillins, McCords, and Vances.[76] By 1850 there were eighteen Irish families in Koshkonong all engaged in agriculture.

In 1859 the Minnesota and Fond du Lac Railroad was completed from Janesville through Jefferson County to Minnesota Junction. The laying of the last rail took place about one and one-half miles south of the village of Jefferson where the Irish

---

[73] Anna Adams Dickie, "Scotch-Irish Presbyterian Settlers in Southern Wisconsin," *WMH*, XXXI (March, 1948), 291.

[74] *Ibid.*, p. 295.

[75] *Ibid.*, p. 294.

[76] *Ibid.*, pp. 294-295.

labor gangs from north and south met.[77] With Irish laborers employed on the road, Koshkonong township's Irish population by 1860 had increased to 44 families; 33 of the Irishmen were listed in the 1860 census as laborers, only 8 farmers and 11 farm laborers remaining from among those listed in 1850. Railroad labor also absorbed the energy of most of the male Irishmen in the town of Jefferson bordering Koshkonong on the north, although the Irish population constituted only 4 per cent of the total in 1860 and consisted of about 30 families.

The most prominent and the largest concentration of Irish-born population in Jefferson County was located in Watertown. The first settlers were Irishmen who took up land in 1835 and 1836. James and Patrick Rogan were among the first to arrive. In 1842 Daniel Fitzsimmons wrote:

> There are also some Irish families residing at Watertown in Jefferson County on Rock River; their names are Rogans and Crangle; Rogans is the principal proprietor of that town, and he intends to have a Catholic Church built there shortly.[78]

The Irish population of Watertown Township decreased by half between 1850 and 1860 because of a boundary adjustment between the townships of Watertown and Milford. In the village the number of Irish-born more than doubled. This Irish accretion in the village was probably occasioned by the removal of some Irish farmers into the village as German immigrants moved on to the land.

Watertown provided the junction for two railroads: the Milwaukee, Watertown and Baraboo passing through on its way westward to Sun Prairie and, after 1860, to Madison; the Minnesota and Fond du Lac crossing from north to south on its way from Fond du Lac to Janesville. Because of this a number of railroad workers lived in the city in 1860 of whom two section

---

[77] Craig Rice, "Jefferson County," *Southeastern Wisconsin,* II, 820, citing L. B. Caswell of Fort Atkinson, Wisconsin.

[78] Boston *Pilot,* August 13, 1842, Daniel Fitzsimmons to editor, Prairieville, Wisconsin Territory, June 12, 1842.

masters and one locomotive engineer were Irishmen. Irish laborers outnumbered those working in other occupations. Gradually the German element increased in Watertown and in the surrounding townships until by 1890 the German population of Watertown was larger than the Irish. Nevertheless the Irish and Irish-Americans remained a strong and influential element.[79]

As mentioned previously, the attempt to extend the southern Wisconsin Railroad across the state from Janesville was successful only as far as Monroe, Green County, in 1858. This county in 1850 was sparsely populated. In a sense it neither belonged wholly to the lead region, although it contained a few mines, nor to the southeastern counties, for it was located within the original Iowa County boundaries. By 1870 Green County had increased in population to the extent of being only a little less populous than Waukesha and Walworth. With lead miners settling down to agriculture and with the coming of the railroad between 1850 and 1860, the population of the county increased about 130 per cent and the Irish population by more than 400 per cent. Irishmen who built the road through Green County did not generally settle along the route but moved to other locations.

The towns of Green County which had no direct connection with the railroad but which became the location for Irish agricultural settlements were Adams and Exeter. The former, located on the western border of Green County, was on the edge of the lead region and contained several mines. One of the first settlers, Michael Crotty, came to Adams Township from County Sligo, Ireland, in 1842. Since he had no means to enter land he worked in the mine owned by Jonas Shook.[80] He also went to Wiota, Lafayette County, and was employed in the mines until he had sufficient money to buy a farm in Adams Township. He then sent for his wife and family and continued to divide his time and labor

---

[79] WSHS, Roeseler Papers, Report of H. Kampshroer, Pastor of Catholic Church, Watertown, Wisconsin, February 10, 1890.

[80] The mine run by Jonas Shook was the most prominent. Two Irishmen, Patrick Ryan and Patrick Egan, were also working a mine in Adams Township. Cf. Loyola J. Murphy, "Green County," *Southwestern Wisconsin: A History of Old Crawford County*, I, 656.

between mining and farming until he could manage a living by farming alone. By 1876 Crotty had become one of the most important stock raisers in Adams and owned 560 acres of land, the largest farm in the town of Adams. Most of the settlers in the town were Irish although there were also many Norwegians and a few Germans. The Irish grouped themselves in and around the valley through which flowed Dougherty Creek, named after an Irish Indian trader from the town of Exeter. A sawmill had been built on the creek sometime prior to 1846 and wild ducks in large numbers made the mill pond a frequent resting place. The name "Duck Puddle," given the pond and surrounding locality, was reversed somehow to Puddle Duck and before long corrupted into Puddle Dock.[81] The Irish families, constituting 30 per cent of the families in the town of Adams in 1860, became prosperous farmers. A list of the owners of the largest farms in the township, from 160 to 560 acres, dated 1876, is composed almost entirely of Irishmen.[82] When the present Catholic Church at Puddle Dock was built in 1902, the congregation numbered approximately 150 Irish and Irish-American families.[83]

A second Irish agricultural community developed in the town of Exeter in the north central section of the county. Already in 1831 John Dougherty had established an Indian trading post in the locality. When the Black Hawk War broke out in 1832 Dougherty left his post only to return after the fighting to work in the mines and buy a furnace. In 1835 he sold the furnace to another Irishman, William Collins, and a man named Kemp. From then on the diggings in that locality were known as the Kemp and Collins' Diggings.[84] Michael and Thomas Welsh, Irish immigrants, also located in the region, building their cabins where the village of Exeter is now. Tom and his wife, "Mother Welsh,"

---

[81] Helen M. Bingham, *History of Green County, Wisconsin* (Milwaukee: Burdick and Armitage, 1877), p. 160; Murphy, *loc. cit.*, p. 755.

[82] Bingham, *op. cit.*, p. 165.

[83] A plaque in the vestibule of the church listing the donors who built it consists of approximately 150 Irish names. The only name not Irish is German.

[84] Bingham, *op. cit.*, p. 71.

kept a tavern there.[85] In 1849 the immigration of Scotch-Irish settlers from Knockahollet, County Antrim, began with the arrival of John Lynn and his wife. Lynn had decided on the location at the close of the Mexican War, when as a veteran he had obtained a land grant, visited the location, and then returned to Ireland to get his wife and urge his friends and relatives to follow. Knockahollet was practically depopulated as the Lynns, Moors, Hughys, Wallaces, and Cains all followed John Lynn to America.[86] The exodus did not take-place all at once, but individual families set out as soon as they had succeeded in laying aside the price of a farm and sufficient money for the expense of the journey. Others emigrated to New York and after earning enough to reach Exeter, Wisconsin, set out on their journey west.

As in other Wisconsin counties, at least a part of the increase of Irish population in Dane County apparently was connected with the advance of the railroad which cut a diagonal through the county from the southeast to the northwest corner by 1860.[87] Some of the Irish farmers who had located in Dane County during the 1850-1860 decade had preceded the railroad but others had been laborers on the road before taking up farming. The towns containing the heaviest concentrations of Irishmen ordinarily were those through which the railroad passed and each of these contained large percentages of Irish laborers in contrast to the number of farmers and other workers.[88]

---

[85] *Ibid.*, p. 73.

[86] Wallace, *loc. cit.*, 415-422, writes of this settlement of Scotch-Irish farmers.

[87] The Milwaukee and Mississippi Railroad transversed the towns of Albion, Dunkirk, Pleasant Springs, Blooming Grove, Madison, Middleton, Cross Plains, Black Earth, and Mazomanie. The seven villages through which the road passed were Stoughton, located in Dunkirk, McFarland in Dunn, Madison, Middleton, Cross Plains, Black Earth, and Mazomanie in towns bearing the same names. Here again, of the towns through which the railroad passed those containing villages with railroad stations had the larger Irish populations and preponderance of Irish laborers. Regarding the latter, Dunn and Cross Plains are exceptions.

[88] In the town and city of Madison in 1860 Irish laborers composed 68 per cent of all the employed male Irishmèn. In Westport, just north of Madison, and in Fitchburg south of it, both with large concentrations and a

Although Irishmen were scattered throughout practically all of the towns of Dane County, heavier concentrations in 1860 were centered in Madison and the adjacent towns of Westport on the north, Fitchburg and Dunn to the south, with an extension northeastward into Cottage Grove. These townships with the city of Madison contained over half of the Irish-born inhabitants of Dane County.[89]

Madison, the capital of the state and the fourth largest city of Wisconsin in 1860, was the home of approximately one-third of the county's Irishmen.[90] More than two-thirds of these were located in the first and fourth wards of the city. Forty-four per cent of the families in the fourth ward and 28 per cent in the first ward were Irish; in the second and third wards 13 per cent and 11 per cent of the families were Irish. Thus an average of 24 per cent of the city's families were Irish, 3 per cent less than in Janesville.

In the town of Westport more than one-third of the families were Irish in 1860. The first men to locate in the town were Louis Montandon, a Frenchman, and Edward Boyles, an Irishman, who settled there in 1845. In their log cabin they endured the privations and experiences of many of the early pioneers: forest clearing, rail splitting, breaking the land, traveling long distances on foot to gristmills, and undergoing adventures with the Indians and wild animals. It is said that they barricaded the door some nights to keep out the wolves. Some American families became their neighbors in 1846 in addition to a number of Irish families from Westport, County Mayo, Ireland: the O'Malleys, Collinses, Fitzgibbons, and Ruddys. During 1849 and 1850 settlers from Kilkenny and other parts of Ireland penetrated the central and western parts of the town. Among these were Mathew

---

high percentage of Irish-born inhabitants, more than half of the Irish working men were laborers. That same year Mazomanie had twice as many Irish laborers as Irishmen engaged in all other occupations combined, and in Sun Prairie the occupations were divided about evenly between laborers and a combination of all other occupations.

[89] *Cf.* p. 63, map.
[90] In size Milwaukee ranked first, Racine second, and Janesville third.

Roach, P. R. Tierney, J. Welsh, William and Lawrence O'Keefe, Martin Reed, and others.[91]

The name Westport was for some years "synonymous with that of O'Malley."[92] Michael O'Malley, the first of that family to settle in Westport had, in addition to two daughters, eight sons to perpetuate the name. He was not only one of the first, but also one of the most influential of the settlers. It was through him in 1849, when the town was carved from Vienna Township, that it received the name Westport.[93] Since the Irish element was not only numerically strong, but also influential, there was little difficulty in getting the name accepted. The first town meeting was held in Michael O'Malley's house. He was elected town chairman with John Collins and Louis Montandon assisting him as supervisors.[94] Bordering Westport on the east is the town of Burke named for the Irish-born statesman, Edmund Burke.[95] Some of the first settlers were Irish and they probably influenced the choice of name, although the Irish population never reached large proportions.

West of Burke are the towns of Sun Prairie and Medina which, with Cottage Grove, form a triangle in eastern Dane County that in 1860 contained about 320 Irishmen. Within this area farmers outnumbered laborers, although Sun Prairie contained more laborers than the other two towns together. The reason for this lay in the fact that the Milwaukee and Baraboo Valley Railroad, built from Brookfield to Watertown in 1855, was completed from the latter point to Sun Prairie in 1857. Its extension was checked by

---

[91] Albert O. Barton, "Dane County," *Southwestern Wisconsin*, II, 1107-1109.

[92] *Ibid.*, p. 1107.

[93] Frederick Cassidy, *The Place-Names of Dane County, Wisconsin* (Greensboro, North Carolina: American Dialect Society, 1947), p. 243.

[94] E. L. Noyes, "Westport and Village of Waunakee," *Madison, Dane County and Surrounding Towns; Being a History and Guide* (Madison: Wm. J. Park and Co., 1877), p. 301. Prominence of the O'Malleys is evident from the offices they received as a result of the first town meeting. Thomas O'Malley was elected town clerk and Martin O'Malley a constable.

[95] Cassidy, *op. cit.*, p. 82. The village of Burke is located within the town; Burke Creek rises within the town's borders and a school is named Burke Station School.

the railroad debacle of 1856 and 1857 and by the outbreak of the Civil War a few years later.[96] Sun Prairie thus remained the terminus for more than ten years and as such it became a bustling village and grain shipping center for the surrounding area.

Natives of Ireland had arrived in Fitchburg already in 1843. Among these were the Reverend William Fox, a Protestant clergyman; Doctor William H. Fox; George Fox; the Reverend Matthew Fox, also a Protestant clergyman, and John and George Keenan.[97] By 1860 Irish families were 30 per cent of the total. Irish Catholics had built a church in 1856 on property donated by Brian McGlynn.

In the western portion of the county the township of Cross Plains contained a distinctly Irish settlement west of Pine Bluff in the southern portion of the town. The group consisted of about forty Irish Catholic families all engaged in agriculture. Most of these, including many Murphy families, Farrells, Donahues, Caseys, Dunns, and others, had migrated to this locality between 1850 and 1860.[98] Just west of the town of Cross Plains, Vermont Township also contained a settlement of Irish farmers, nearly all from the Counties of Cork and Limerick.[99]

Irishmen in Mazomanie, the most northwestern town of Dane County, had come from different parts of Ireland, but Counties Cork, Claire, and Donegal were particularly well represented.[100]

---

[96] Barton, *loc. cit.*, p. 1099. The railroad scandal in 1856 involved a large number of the people's representatives at Madison. The La Crosse and Milwaukee Railroad Company bribed the state legislature, the governor, and three other state officials in order to obtain a land grant worth $36,615,000. The stocks and bonds distributed among thirteen senators amounted to $175,000; those given to thirty-nine of the assemblymen totaled $355,000; the reward of the three state officials was valued at $30,000, and the governor's share amounted to $50,000. With the panic of 1857 the railroads collapsed. Campbell et al. (eds.), *op. cit.*, pp. 66-71.

[97] Barton, *loc. cit.*, p. 1078.

[98] *Ibid.*, p. 1103. Boston *Pilot*, March 8, 1856, lists subscribers from Pine Bluff, Wisconsin, for the year 1856. The names tally with those given by Barton.

[99] Barton, *loc. cit.*, p. 1124. *WSHS*, Roeseler Papers, Report of P. J. Jones, Catholic pastor, Mazomanie, Wisconsin, October 31, 1889.

[100] *Ibid.*

They were mainly engaged in railroad labor in 1860. From here the Milwaukee and Mississippi Road entered Iowa County on its last lap to Prairie du Chien.

Irish settlement in each of the foregoing counties of southeastern Wisconsin followed a generally similar pattern. Some Irish immigrants were among the first pioneers in these counties. Many influenced relatives and friends to follow them. Between 1850 and 1860 Irishmen built railroads into the region; as described by a contemporary: "hard working, brawny Irishmen, strangers imported with no other interest than to shovel dirt, build the track and lay the rails for others to use and enjoy."[101] Some who had worked on railroad construction as a means of earning sufficient funds for the purchase of a farm or to finance their start in some business settled on farms or in cities and villages along the road. They usually located near others of their own nationality. Some remained in the wake of the railroad construction as section masters, section hands, and station agents.

Railroading often had a way of becoming an almost hereditary occupation in some families. It is a tradition in Janesville that the first generation of Irishmen built the road and worked in railroad crews as section hands. Desiring something better for their sons they helped and encouraged them to get into positions of higher rank as firemen, engineers, and brakemen. These in turn provided for their sons' education and encouraged them to work for advancement into office jobs and executive positions.[102]

Not all of the railroad laborers, however, settled down to farming, railroading, or some other occupation within the southeastern section of the state. For, although these counties experienced an increase in population in varying degrees until the end of the century, they simultaneously experienced a decrease in the number of Irish-born inhabitants.[103] This decline in the Irish-born

---

[101] Craig, *loc. cit.*, p. 820, citing L. B. Caswell.

[102] Interview with Maurice J. McCarthy, Janesville, Wisconsin, August 12, 1951. McCarthy, a locomotive engineer, has been in the employ of the Chicago, Milwaukee, St. Paul and Pacific Railroad for more than fifty years.

[103] The population of Green and Jefferson Counties dropped in 1880 and although there was an increase in 1890, the totals did not again reach that of 1870.

population continued steadily throughout the rest of the century. By 1890 each county, in comparison with the others, ranked in regard to Irish-born population as it had in 1860, with the exception of Jefferson which fell to the second last place. Reasons for the decrease of Irish population in Milwaukee, Racine, and Kenosha hold also in these counties.[104] Another cause lies in the fact that comparatively large numbers of Irish laborers composed a migratory element of the population. The greatest railroad development in Wisconsin occurred after the Civil War. In 1867 there were only 1,030 miles of track, most of it located in the southeast.[105] Irish labor had been predominant in laying these first miles. As the railroads and other public works in the western and northern sections of the state were being constructed after 1865, Irish laborers moved into the region with the construction gangs which were no longer, however, so exclusively Irish. Furthermore, railroads and lumbermen in the northern pineries were not only advertising for labor but were also pointing out the advantages of settlement in northern Wisconsin. Hence, some of the Irish settlers went north and worked as laborers and lumbermen until able to procure land for settlement.

North of Milwaukee, Waukesha, Jefferson, and Dane Counties are Ozaukee, Washington, Dodge, and Columbia. These predominantly agricultural counties were also part of the Old Milwaukee County of 1836.[106] Dodge and Washington Counties, created before 1840, were at that time sparsely settled having populations of 67 and 343 respectively. By 1850 Washington had grown to 19,485 and Dodge to 19,138, while Columbia contained a population of only 9,565. Irishmen in these counties had been among the first settlers as elsewhere and by 1860 Dodge County ranked fourth in Irish population among the counties of Wisconsin.[107]

---

[104] *Supra,* pp. 56-57.

[105] Raney, *op. cit.,* p. 180.

[106] Part of Columbia had belonged to Old Milwaukee County.

[107] The only location entitled to the rank of "city" in Dodge County in 1860 was Beaver Dam with a population of 2,765; of these, 175 were Irish-born. For statistics on the Irish in these counties *cf.* Appendix, pp. 265-267, Tables 16, 17, 18, 19.

In Dodge County, 1860, the Irish led the foreign contingent in 9 out of the 24 towns: Chester, Clyman, Elba, Emmet, Fox Lake, Oak Grove, Portland, Shields, and Trenton.[108] By 1870, however, the large German gains had reduced this lead to three towns: Chester, Elba, and Trenton. In Shields by 1870 the numbers of German and Irish families were practically the same. The German population of Dodge County was located mainly in the more densely wooded eastern section of the county, the Irish in the western half.[109] Using the 1850 census as a basis of comparison, Schafer noted that English, Irish, and Canadians, chose the open-land towns. The Irish, especially, in the towns of Emmet, Shields, Elba, and Clyman, had lived in the eastern states or Canada, frequently from seven to fifteen years, before settling in Dodge County in the late 1840's and early 1850's. Schafer concluded from this that the Irish either had entered that region soon enough to obtain the open lands at government price in competition with Americans from the East, or had first earned sufficient funds in the East and then upon arrival were able to buy lands from speculators or private owners.[110]

About 40 per cent of Dodge County's Irish population was concentrated in the southwestern portion of the county.[111] The boundaries of the towns of Shields and Portland are contiguous to Watertown and Milford townships in Jefferson County. Furthermore, the city of Watertown extends into both Dodge and Jefferson Counties. Thus it can be seen that despite the political boundaries this agglomeration of Irishmen had much in common: nationality, settlement, religion, and quite generally, social and economic position.

Moreover, Irishmen who had located in Watertown advertised the merits of the locality, and when other Irishmen arrived they were directed by the surveyor to the towns north and west of

---

[108] The basis for this count was families. The number of foreign families other than Irish was obtained from Schafer, *Winnebago-Horicon Basin*, pp. 317 and 318, tables.

[109] *Ibid.*, p. 143.

[110] *Ibid.*, pp. 144-145.

[111] This 40 per cent was specifically located in the towns of Elba, Lowell, Clyman, Emmet, Shields, and Portland.

Watertown.[112] These would be in the first place, Emmet and Shields, but also the other towns of southwestern Dodge County. Emmet and Shields were long known as Irish townships because of the dominant influence of the Irish. Instigated by Patrick Mahoney, one of the first settlers, the Irish population named the former town in honor of the Irish patriot, Robert Emmet.[113] The town of Shields was named for General James Shields, a native Irishman who was active in Irish colonization work and who at various times represented three different states in the United States Senate.[114]

Other towns with comparatively large Irish populations were Hubbard, Oak Grove, Chester, Beaver Dam, Fox Lake, Trenton, and Ashippun. The railroad passed through all of these towns with the exception of Trenton and Ashippun; hence, the large numbers of Irish laborers in comparison with farmers, especially in Beaver Dam and Fox Lake; also in Oak Grove and Hubbard, where Minnesota Junction and Horicon were the centers for these Irish laborers. Railroad constructors throughout the county before 1860 relied mainly on Irish labor and as in other counties Irishmen settled in large numbers in several of the towns through which they had built the road.[115] The temporary residential status of the railroad laborers was realistically indicated by the census taker who wrote the word "shanty" to indicate the value of their real estate. A further indication of their insecurity was the entire lack of any personal estate.

West of Dodge County and north of Dane lay the region which in 1846 was to become Columbia County. In its northwestern section the future Columbia County had been intersected by the boundaries of the four old Wisconsin counties: Iowa, Milwaukee, Crawford, and Brown. Just east of this point were located Fort

---

[112] William F. Whyte, "Chronicle of Early Watertown," *WMH*, IV (March, 1921), 311. The surveyor, Judson Prentice, told this to Whyte. He also maintained that he distributed the German immigrants east of Watertown and the Americans south.

[113] John Kelley, "Dodge County," *Southeastern Wisconsin*, II, 1013.

[114] *Ibid.*, p. 1023. *Cf.* also, *History of Dodge County, Wisconsin* (Chicago: Western Historical Co., 1880), p. 405.

[115] Schafer, *Winnebago-Horicon Basin*, p. 158.

Winnebago, established in 1828, and the place of portage between the Fox and Wisconsin Rivers. Attempts to make these rivers a single navigable waterway from Green Bay and the Great Lakes to the Mississippi River at Prairie du Chien were not only an integral part of Wisconsin's economic and political history, but also important factors in the settlement and development of the lands along the waterway. Talk of the Fox River improvement and portage canal had begun as early as 1828; the project was publicly launched in Wisconsin in 1836, and land sales in the lower Fox River Valley at that time demonstrated speculators' interest. Not until 1846, however, after repeated appeals to Congress, could the final steps be taken for commencing the actual construction work.[116]

As part of the project, the construction of the Portage canal hastened the settlement of Columbia County, particularly the region around Fort Winnebago, now Portage. A letter of an Irishman written in the late winter of 1852 describes the place:

> Having got beyond the boundary of civilization in the Far West, I send you a hurried scrap. I will first try your geographical knowledge. . . . You may ransack all the charts, maps, atlasses [sic], and geographies in Boston, and not be able to find Goudgeville. . . .
> About two years ago a canal was commenced here at Fort Winnebago to join the Fox and Wisconsin rivers. At the head of this canal a town sprang up in a few days, with the rapidity of a mushroom. It being in the Indian reserve, and the lands not of course in market, every one claimed a lot for himself, built on it, and lives on it without having paid the government a cent. They have changed its name from Goudgeville to Portage City. It bids fair to be a place of considerable importance, being situated at the junction of the Fox and Wisconsin Rivers, the navigation of both will soon be completed. Boats can run from the Mississippi up the Wisconsin

---

[116] Schafer, *The Winnebago-Horicon Basin*, pp. 77-131. In 1836 the Wisconsin territorial governor, Henry Dodge, in his first message to the territorial council urged among other projects the Fox River improvement and portage canal; hence, this date for the public launching of the project in Wisconsin.

River to this place, and will shortly be able to pass down the Fox River to Lake Winnebago, thence to Green Bay, and into the great Western Lakes. It is thought that this land will come into market next summer, when each settler will purchase his own lot, and have a permanent residence. The country north and west from here has been Indian land, the aborigines have moved off, further westward, leaving room for the white man to fill up this vacant ground. It is claimed for some miles back already, as any man can go and claim 160 acres until it comes into market. I am told there are some good locations in it, and other parts are rather sandy, and overgrown with green pine trees, not a good prospect for farming in the pinery. It is rather far north, winter sets in early, and spring is long in making its appearance.[117]

Fort Winnebago village and township, scene of this activity, contained approximately 500 Irishmen in 1850 who constituted nearly one-third of its total population and more than one-half of the Irish population of the entire county. Of these Irishmen more than 200 were employed as laborers, one as a civil engineer, and one as a "contractor on public works." By 1860 the population of Portage (formerly the village of Fort Winnebago) had increased sufficiently to give it the status of a city, but the Irish population had remained approximately the same. The Irish laborers in the city after 1855 were engaged rather in railroad work than river improvement since in 1856 the Milwaukee and Mississippi Railroad on its way to La Crosse had been completed through the county to Portage.

The only other localities in Columbia County that had fairly large concentrations of Irishmen in 1860 were the towns of Lewiston and Columbus, town and village. Farmers were predominant in the former, farmers and laborers about equal in the latter. Columbus, however, was different in that a railroad contractor, baggageman, night watch, section master, and newsboy were all

---

[117] Boston *Pilot*, March 7, 1852, "Western Pioneer" [probably Edward Gillin] to the Editor, Goudgeville [Portage], Wisconsin, March 1, 1852. That settlers did occupy the lands north of Portage is evidenced in the 1850 manuscript census for Marquette County in the portion west of the Fox River called Indian Lands. The population was 2,864; 200 of these were Irishmen, about 60 Irish families engaged in farming.

native Irishmen. During the decade between 1850 and 1860 the number of laborers dwindled, while immigration of Irishmen combined with the settlement of laborers on the land practically doubled the number of Irishmen engaged in agriculture in the county.

Thus Irishmen in Columbia County had pioneered first as laborers on public works and then they settled on the land. In Washington, the county east of Dodge, this was not the case. In the early 1840's the southwestern corner of Washington County was settled by a group of Irish immigrants who had not been attracted to the locality as laborers, but rather with the intention of settling on the land. These Irishmen located chiefly in what became Erin Township and were an integral part of the Irish migration to and settlement of Monches in Merton Township, Waukesha County. These two townships, Merton and Erin, offer another instance of the grouping of Irishmen within a given area regardless of county and town boundaries. Erin, whose early history is identical with that of Monches, was the most Irish agricultural town in Wisconsin in 1850 and 1860.[118]

One-third of the Irish population of Washington County was located in Erin Township. In addition to the first Monches settlers already named there were the Ryans, Daleys, Welches, Donahues, McCormicks, McLoughlins, and others who entered the town. By 1846 the land in the town had all been taken.[119] The group of Irish settlers in the southern section of the town around Monches was chiefly from Killarney, County Kerry, while most of those in the northern part around Thompson had emigrated from other parts of the same county. Because of this the village of Thompson locally was called Kerry. Although local differences and bickering occurred between the "Kerry crowd," those from parts of Kerry other than Killarney, and the "Killarney crowd," the two groups professed the same religious and political faith and displayed a united front when it came to naming the town.[120]

[118] *Supra*, p. 58 f., for Monches, town of Merton, Waukesha County. For statistics on the town of Erin *cf*. Appendix, p. 265, Table 16.
[119] Carl Quickert, "Washington County," *Southeastern Wisconsin*, II, 1101.
[120] Whelan, *loc. cit.*, pp. 47-48; *History of Washington and Ozaukee Counties, Wisconsin* (Chicago: Western Historical Co., 1881), pp. 323-324, 730-732; Quickert, *loc. cit.*, pp. 1100, 1133. *Cf*. Peter Leo Johnson, *Stuffed*

Although the two villages in this Irish settlement do not bear Irish names, three lakes perpetuate the memory of the early settlers: Malloy, Murphy, and McConville Lakes. Erin Township kept its Irish complexion throughout the century: ". . . it is today [1881] as purely Irish in its population, as purely Catholic in its religion, as any town in old Ireland itself."[121]

Irishmen were scattered throughout the rest of the towns in Washington County with slight concentrations in the northern townships of Farmington and Wayne. Both in 1850 and 1860 Irishmen in Washington, as in Dodge County, were cultivating the land. The proportion of farmers to laborers was even greater in Washington County than in Dodge.

In 1853 the seven most eastern townships of Washington County were severed from it to form Ozaukee County.[122] This county was smaller in area and population than either Dodge or Washington. Sixty per cent of the Irish within its borders were located in Cedarburg and Saukville Townships engaged chiefly in tilling the land. An Irish settlement called New Dublin had flourished in 1850 just southeast of the locality which became the village of Cedarburg. The name was later changed to Hamilton and with the gradual migration of the Irish away from this location Hamilton declined.[123]

Unlike any of the other counties of southwestern and southeastern Wisconsin, Ozaukee's Irish population had decreased during the ten-year period after 1850. The decline between 1860 and 1870, however, was much greater. In comparison with other counties the percentage of decrease was large because the original number of Irish-born inhabitants was smaller. Dodge and Washington Counties both experienced a similar diminution in the size

---

Saddlebags, The Life of Martin Kundig, Priest, 1805-1879 (Milwaukee: Bruce Publishing Co., 1942), p. 216. Father Kundig presided at the town meeting which had been called for the purpose of naming the town. When the name "Erin" was proposed it was adopted by unanimous approval.

[121] *History of Washington and Ozaukee Counties, Wisconsin*, p. 324.

[122] In this study the two counties are being treated separately for 1850.

[123] J. G. Gregory, "Ozaukee County," *Southeastern Wisconsin*, II, 1225. The Irish in Saukville Township were located around their parish church, St. Finbar's, built in 1850.

of their Irish populations between 1860 and 1870. Dodge lost almost 800 and Washington County slightly more than 450.

Several causes contributed to this decrease in the number of Irishmen. First, the Irish were a "fluid population element." After migrating to Wisconsin, as has been previously noted, they often moved from one county to another and sometimes to a different state.[124] Secondly, many of the Irish were not willing to endure all of the hardships concurrent with forest clearing; hence, they moved about in search of lands amenable to more immediate possibilities of farming. When social conditions in an environment, regardless of other difficulties, were compatible with their way of living, however, some "bent to the task, slashed, grubbed, broke up new land, extending their fields as rapidly as the best workers of any other derivation."[125] Thirdly, population studies reveal that where the German element penetrated in ever increasing numbers not only the percentage but the actual number of Irishmen decreased. The process seems to have occurred sooner in Ozaukee County than elsewhere. In all of the counties it was gradual and came about not so much as an actual removal of the original Irish settlers but rather because of their failure to keep the farm within the family. As Whyte pointed out concerning the townships of Emmet and Shields in Dodge County, the sons and daughters in many instances did not remain on the homestead. The "peaceful penetration" of the Teuton gradually crowded out the Celt, not only in the two townships mentioned, but also in every township surrounding the city of Watertown.[126] The town of Elba may be included among these latter. Schafer uses it as an example of the German penetration:

> The town of Elba, prevailingly Irish in its foreign element, had no German family in 1850 and only 31 in 1860, while there were 113 Irish. But by 1870, though the Irish had decreased to 82 families, the Germans had increased to 62. The American contingent, also, had declined slightly. The Germans, in a word, were in the as-

---

[124] Schafer, *Four Wisconsin Counties*, p. 102.
[125] *Ibid.*, p. 103.
[126] Whyte, *loc. cit.*, p. 311.

cendant almost everywhere, displacing Yankees and Irish, who were more restless, by buying their farms or other properties and facilitating their emigration to the farther west or to the cities.[127]

By 1890 the process was still going on, according to a report on the national complexion of Cedarburg, Ozaukee County, and Jackson, Washington County, which stated that most of the immigrants originally had come from Ireland, but that they were rapidly being replaced by the Germans.[128] The population of the town of Oak Grove was undergoing a like change. The southern part of the town had been settled quite heavily by Irishmen, who also were gradually being crowded out by the Germans.[129]

Irishmen had entered the southern portion of the state as lead miners, railroad builders, laborers, and craftsmen of various kinds, and as farmers. There was a definite and close relationship between their location and occupations. As mining waned in the southwest Irish miners took to agriculture and after railroads were completed westward and northward Irish laborers settled on the land among others of their own nationality or found jobs in the villages and growing cities living in the wards most populously Irish. Numerous Irishmen entered the state for the purpose of taking up land and settling on farms. The majority were engaged in agriculture. Statistically by 1860 most Wisconsin Irishmen classi-

---

[127] Schafer, *Winnebago-Horicon Basin*, p. 163. He also adds: "Germans were destined to become mobile, too, but as yet they were the most sedentary of the several immigrant groups."

[128] WSHS, Roeseler Papers, Report of F. Ryan, Catholic priest, Cedarburg, Wisconsin, February 27, 1890.

[129] WSHS, Roeseler Papers, Report of W. T. Rambusch, Juneau, Wisconsin, March 15, 1889. Rambusch states that the Irish were, however, giving way to the Germans more slowly than the Americans were. This agrees with Schafer, "Editorial Comment," *WMH*, X (March, 1927), 329, who says that a typical series for Wisconsin settlement would be: a) Yankees and some Irish Catholics; b) "gradual displacement of the Yankees by the later Irish arrivals and the increasingly large influx of Germans" (1840-1860); c) "the disappearance of nearly all Yankee and Irish families and the racial unification of the community as German, with the survival of influences derived from the other stocks."

fied as farmer or laborer, but in the villages and cities a fair proportion were engaged in some craft, in professional and managerial positions, as wholesale and retail traders, and in a variety of other occupations.

Settlement in this southernmost section of Wisconsin was practically completed in 1860 and although most of the counties just north of Ozaukee, Washington, and Dodge are located in the southern half of Wisconsin, settlement there usually was not completed until after 1870. This is true also of the extreme western counties of the state. Some of these counties, moreover, developed along with the Fox River improvement and the lumbering industry, hence for the purposes of this study the northeastern and extreme western sections of southern Wisconsin can best be linked with the study of the northern half of the state.

CHAPTER III

LOCATION AND OCCUPATIONS OF IRISHMEN IN CENTRAL AND NORTHERN WISCONSIN

Settlement of the upper three-fourths of the state of Wisconsin was not generally completed until the last forty years of the nineteenth century and into the twentieth. The northernmost counties were the last to be settled. In the southern part of this region, that is, in the counties just north of those studied in the previous chapter and extending across the central portion of the state, settlement had practically reached completion by 1870. This portion of the state, the old Brown County of 1836, was ultimately divided into fifteen counties.[1] As the population of these counties increased, the number of Irishmen within their borders was also augmented.

Generally these counties were peopled originally by homesteaders interested in living on the land. Settlement was aided by the construction of two railroad lines into the region: the Chicago and Northwestern reaching the city of Fond du Lac in 1854 and Oshkosh, Winnebago County, in 1859; and the Milwaukee and Mississippi, passing through Ripon and terminating in Berlin, Green Lake County, in 1857. Work on the Fox River improvement directly affected the settlement and development of Brown, Outagamie, and Winnebago Counties, through which the Fox River flowed. Settlement in the counties a little north and west of the Fox River also probably received some impetus from the Fox River improvement insofar as laborers on the improvement project ultimately settled within their borders, but lumbering was more important in their development. All of these factors which influenced the settlement of this section of Wisconsin likewise definitely induced Irish immigration into the region.

Irishmen in Fond du Lac County were scattered throughout the

---

[1] The fifteen counties are: Brown, Winnebago, Fond du Lac, Calumet. Sheboygan, Manitowoc, Marquette, Kewaunee, Door, Outagamie, Green Lake Waupaca, Waushara, Shawano, and Oconto.

townships with the heaviest concentrations in Eden and Osceola which achieved the reputation of being Irish towns.[2] In 1860 foreign families predominated in twelve of Fond du Lac's twenty-one towns and the Irish led in four of these: Eden, Osceola, Eldorado, and Empire.[3] In nine towns American families were predominant but the Irish led the foreign contingent in six, Byron, Fond du Lac, Metomen, Waupun, Ripon, and Springvale.[4] Moreover, approximately two-thirds of the Irishmen were located in the western half of the county.[5]

During the 1860-1870 decade Irishmen continued to migrate into Fond du Lac County particularly into Eden and Osceola Townships and into the city of Fond du Lac. Other small increases occurred in the towns already containing a number of Irish inhabitants. The Irish population of the city of Fond du Lac was concentrated in the fourth ward where, in 1870, Irish families were 23 per cent of the total number of families. Irishmen in the city of Fond du Lac were engaged in the same types of work as in other Wisconsin cities. Laborers were in the majority, craftsmen were quite numerous, and there were several professional men, a few merchants and grocers, some railroad employees, a city marshal, and a justice of the peace.

From a statistical point of view then, the general status of Irishmen in Fond du Lac County resembled that in some of the other predominantly agricultural counties. Irishmen first entered these counties to locate on farms not heavily timbered. Later the railroad, sawmills, and public works provided labor for incoming Irishmen, causing an increase in the percentage of Irish laborers in comparison with Irish farmers.

East of Fond du Lac lies Sheboygan County with Lake Mich-

---

[2] Schafer, *The Winnebago-Horicon Basin*, p. 156. *Cf.* Appendix, Table 20.
[3] *Ibid.*, p. 157.
[4] *Ibid.*, pp. 159-160. The Germans led the foreign group in two predominantly American towns and the English in one. In three of the predominantly foreign towns which were heavily timbered the Germans led the foreign contingent by large majorities. Irishmen were most numerously located in the towns of Ripon, Osceola, Eden, Eldorado, Fond du Lac (exclusive of the city), Byron, Forest, Springvale, Empire, and Taycheedah.
[5] *Cf.* p. 63, map.

igan as its eastern boundary.[6] Mitchell, the town having the largest Irish population of the towns in Sheboygan in 1860 is contiguous to Osceola, the most Irish town of Fond du Lac. By 1860 approximately two-thirds of the Irishmen of Sheboygan County lived in the townships composing the western half of the county; hence, the bulk of each county's (Fond du Lac's and Sheboygan's) Irish population was adjacent to the other. In the town of Mitchell Irishmen were one-fourth of the population and Irish families constituted more than half of the total number of families settled within the town. These Irish-born settlers had apparently filtered in at different times, although the first group of settlers had formed a colony in New York before emigrating to this region.[7] Mitchell was originally a part of Lyndon and had been named Olio. In 1851 the name was altered to Mitchell in honor of John Mitchell, the Irish patriot.[8] A number of rural Irish communities surrounded Catholic parishes and missions in the towns of Mitchell, Sherman, Lyndon, Lima, and Holland: St. Mary's, Cascade, in the town of Lyndon; its mission, St. Michael's in the town of Mitchell; and St. Patrick's near Adell in Sherman Township, which drew Irish parishioners from the town of Holland. Surrounding and separating these groups of Irishmen were German and Luxemburger Catholics, Dutch Reformed Hollanders, and German Lutherans.

Irishmen were urged to settle in Sheboygan by T. N. James who, with O. O'Sullivan, offered to give advice and direction to any Irishman arriving there. James likened the climate to that of Ireland—a land flowing with milk and honey—and maintained that there was work for all who wanted it.[9] A very small percentage of the entire population of the town and city of Sheboygan was Irish. These were engaged as laborers, craftsmen, seamen, fishermen, and boarding house proprietors. One was county treasurer and one was a justice of the peace. An Irish

[6] *Cf.* Appendix, p. 272, Table 25.

[7] Carl Zillier, *History of Sheboygan County, Wisconsin, Past and Present* (Chicago: The S. J. Clarke Publishing Co., 1912), I, 268.

[8] Gustave W. Buchen, *Historic Sheboygan County* (1944), pp. 302-304.

[9] Boston *Pilot,* June 2, 1849, T. N. James to the editor.

railroad conductor and engineer are reminders that the railroad from Sheboygan had been completed westward to Plymouth by 1860. In 1850 and 1860 the Irishmen in Sheboygan County were definitely an agricultural population.

Manitowoc County's Irish-born population was also chiefly rural and not grouped in adjoining townships in one part of the county but in heavier concentrations in Manitowoc town and city, in Franklin, Maple Grove, Liberty, and Cato townships, with somewhat smaller, but significant groups in Cooperstown and Meeme.[10] The city of Manitowoc held less than one-tenth of the Irish-born inhabitants of the county. Most of these were found in the second ward where they constituted 17 per cent of the families. The majority were laborers but a number were engaged in some phase of the lumbering industry. Two were designated in the 1860 census as lumbermen, one a shingle purchaser, another a shingle inspector, and one an engineer in a mill. Some of the Irish laborers were probably working in lumber mills.

In northern Manitowoc County the towns of Franklin, Maple Grove, and Cato were early settled by Irishmen, especially Franklin where more than half of the families were Irish. In Cato the Irish were surrounded by Norwegians and in Maple Grove Germans were numerous. Southwest of the city of Manitowoc there was an aggregation of Irishmen called Meeme settlement, which included portions of Meeme, Liberty, and Newton townships. This concentration of Irishmen, often referred to as "Irish settlement," consisted of an entirely rural Irish population centered about a Catholic church.[11] The towns of Newton and Meeme were both more German than Irish, the former being one of the most distinctively German towns of Wisconsin.[12] But Meeme's northern section was almost exclusively Irish and with the south-

---

[10] *Cf.* Appendix, p. 270, Table 23.
[11] Louis Falge (ed.), *History of Manitowoc County, Wisconsin* (Chicago: Goodspeed Historical Association, n.d.), I, 39; Ralph G. Plumb, *A History of Manitowoc County, Wisconsin* (Manitowoc: Brandt Printing Co., 1904), p. 34; W. A. Titus, "Meeme, A Frontier Settlement That Developed Strong Men," *WMH*, IV (March, 1921), 281-286.
[12] Schafer, *A History of Agriculture in Wisconsin*, p. 54.

ern portion of Liberty and the southwest section of Newton composed the Irish settlement. The first settlers in Meeme were Irish and among them were Dennis Nagle, Peter and Henry Mulholland, J. Doolan, Patrick O'Shea, and the Taugher family.

Calumet, west of Manitowoc, along with Kewaunee and Door Counties extending into the Door Peninsula were quite sparsely populated in 1850 and 1860. Although the Irish population was likewise small there was, besides scattered groups of Irishmen, at least one heavier concentration of them in each county. In the town of Chilton, Calumet County, one-fourth of the families was Irish.[13] In Rantoul Township, where the Irish were most numerous, Irish families evidently had come directly to Wisconsin or were young Irish-born couples married after their arrival, for all of the children had been born either in Ireland or in Wisconsin. The Irish populations of Rantoul and Chilton increased slightly between 1860 and 1870. The largest group of Irishmen in Kewaunee County was located in the town of Franklin, where the 40 Irish families were one-third of the families in the town.[14] Washington Island just off the tip of the mainland of Door County was the only locality within the county containing an appreciable number of Irishmen.[15] Approximately one-third of the families were Irish, the majority of these being fishermen. In the other parts of Door County the few Irishmen were chiefly engaged in farming.

West and north of Lake Winnebago lay the three counties, Winnebago, Outagamie, and Brown, which had direct contact with the Fox River improvement, for most of the work on the project was expended on the lower Fox between Green Bay and Menasha. In 1836 construction on the dam and locks at De Pere had begun, but the bulk of the construction work on dams, locks, and canals farther up the river did not take place until 1849 and the succeeding years when the dams and locks at Kaukauna, Appleton, Neenah, and Menasha were built.[16]

---

[13] *Cf.* Appendix, p. 269, Table 22.
[14] *Cf.* Appendix, p. 269, Table 21.
[15] *Cf.* Appendix, p. 271, Table 24.
[16] It was probably some of the early construction work in this region that Jackson Kemper, Episcopalian Bishop, was referring to when on his way south from Green Bay he wrote in his diary, August 13, 1838, that he and

Contractors relied heavily on Irish labor here as at the Portage Canal in Columbia County. In 1850 over 100 of the 190 Irishmen at Neenah were engaged as laborers when the construction work was underway. At Kaukauna in 1850 Irish laborers numbered 40. Work on the improvement project at this point was still in progress in the middle 1850's and many Irishmen with intentions to settle on farms in one of the three surrounding counties first earned the price of a few acres by working on the Fox River improvement.[17]

Chiefly because of the Irish laboring group in Winnebago County in 1850, Irishmen were the largest foreign-born group.[18] By 1860 the laborers had largely dispersed and a number of Irishmen had located in each township. In the towns of Poygan, Menasha, and Nepeuskun, where American families predominated, Irish families led the foreign-born group. The number of Irish families in Poygan increased during the decade after 1860 and it retained the reputation of being an Irish town. Practically five-eighths

---

his company met Morgan, who "had 7 irishmen in company on their way to dig the Portage canal at 16^{00} per mo. . . . He carried their packs—and they helped him in difficulties—and talked to him." *Cf.* Jackson Kemper, "A trip Through Wisconsin in 1838," WMH, VIII (March, 1925), 443.

[17] Publius V. Lawson (ed.), *History of Winnebago County, Wisconsin, Its Cities, Towns, Resources, People* (Chicago: C. F. Cooper and Co., 1908), II, 746. *Cf. Commemorative Biographical Record of the West Shore of Green Bay, Wisconsin*, cites at least seven such instances in which Irish-born immigrants first worked on the improvement project. Thomas Finnerty worked for two summers at Kaukauna on the river improvement and after that settled with his father and family in Holland Township. *Cf. ibid.*, p. 72. Patrick and Bernard Finnegan worked on the canal in the early 1850's before taking up farming. *Cf. ibid.*, p. 185. Cornelius Dougherty, in 1854 or 1855, labored on the Kaukauna canal and after saving thirty dollars bought land in Glenmore Township, Brown County. *Cf. ibid.*, p. 325. After migrating from the East and traveling up the Fox River to Kaukauna with his family in 1851, Hugh Finnegan worked for several years on the canal. *Cf. ibid.*, p. 332. Patrick Bailey brought his family as far as Green Bay in 1854 and leaving them there he went on to Kaukauna to earn money for the purchase of land. *Cf. ibid.*, p. 342. Similarly, Thomas Lawlor in 1852 located his family in West De Pere while he earned sufficient funds as a laborer on the improvement at Kaukauna. *Cf. ibid.*, p. 420.

[18] *Cf.* Appendix, p. 274, Table 27.

of the Irish population of Winnebago County could be found in the three towns of Menasha, Neenah, and Oshkosh (including the city of Oshkosh), all bordering Lake Winnebago on the northwest. In the entire county in 1850 only about 70 Irishmen had been engaged in farming, but by 1860 the number had almost tripled while the Irish laboring group had decreased.

The eight southernmost towns in Outagamie County surrounding the Fox River improvement contained all but 40 of the county's Irishmen in 1860.[19] The towns of Freedom, Greenville, and Kaukauna together had approximately 300. Although a number of Irishmen were engaged in tending the locks, the majority were engaged in agricultural pursuits by 1860.

The towns of Holland, Wrightstown, Rockland, Glenmore, Morrison, and the city of Green Bay, containing eighty per cent of the Irishmen of Brown County, completed the semi-circle of Irish settlement which had been given its original impetus by the Fox River improvement.[20] Although the town of Holland, as its name implies, was first settled by eleven Dutch families in 1848 and organized in the spring of 1854, Irishmen had begun to enter the town during the 1850's in increasingly large numbers.[21] More than two-thirds of the town's families were Irish by 1860 and 1870. Askeaton, named for a town of Ireland in the county of Limerick, was the center of the Irish settlement and the location of the Catholic church. Some of the immigrants had come through Canada, particularly those arriving after 1860.

Although the Irishmen in Wrightstown, north of Holland, and in the town of Morrison were fewer in number than in Holland

---

[19] *Cf.* Appendix, p. 273, Table 26.
[20] *Cf.* Appendix, p. 275, Table 28.
[21] *History of Northern Wisconsin* (Chicago: The Western Historical Co., 1881), p. 109. Early Irish settlers in the town of Holland were the families of James, John, and Michael Brick, John Burns, James and John Carroll, Mathew Cleary, Patrick Colwell, John Conroy, Charles Coughlin, Patrick and John Fox, Patrick Hobbins, John Holloway, Barney, Michael, and Peter Hart, John Hayes, Michael Keating, Dennis Mack, John and Patrick Meehan, Patrick McQueen, Richard and Will Powers, James, John, and Michael Setright, John Sheehan, James and Maurice Summers, and John Wall.

Township, they constituted a significant proportion of the population. The area embraced by Rockland Township, carved from De Pere in 1856, was chosen for settlement by James Hobbins in 1850 and Stephen Joyce in 1855, the first Irish families in the town.[22] Other Irishmen followed and by 1860 Irish families were almost half the population of the township. East of Rockland in Glenmore Township, which was also cut from De Pere in 1856, the Irish element predominated.[23] The majority of Irishmen in Brown County were engaged in agriculture. Most of those employed in other occupations resided in the northern section of the city of Green Bay.[24]

Waupaca and Waushara Counties, west of the area surrounding Lake Winnebago, were about equally populated in 1860 and the number of Irish-born inhabitants in each was likewise approximately the same. Irishmen in Waushara, however, had begun to decline numerically after 1860 while both the general and Irish populations of Waupaca underwent substantial increase. More than one-half of the Irish-born population of the county in 1860 were situated in three townships on the eastern border: Bear Creek, Lebanon, and Mukwa.[25] The most Irish was Lebanon which retained its reputation as an Irish town throughout the century. The village of Northport, located in Mukwa Township near the Lebanon-Mukwa boundary was originally an Irish settlement and in 1856 it was reported that most of the settlers in the vicinity had up to that time been Irish, but that New Englanders were replacing them.[26] Waushara County, south of Waupaca, had numbers of Irishmen scattered throughout the county with slightly heavier concentrations in the three towns forming the southeastern corner: Poysippi, Aurora, and Warren.[27] Agri-

---

[22] *Ibid.*, p. 109.
[23] *Ibid.*
[24] It is interesting to note that in 1850 at Fort Howard, later part of Green Bay, one of the army officers and 33 of the soldiers were native Irishmen.
[25] *Cf.* Appendix, p. 276, Table 29.
[26] A. J. Lawson, "New London and Surrounding Country," *Collections,* III (1856), 483.
[27] *Cf.* Appendix, p. 277, Table 30.

culture was the chief occupation of Irishmen in both counties in 1860.

Marquette and Green Lake Counties are located directly south of Waushara. The Fox River flowing north from Columbia County winds through these two counties on its way to the Lake Winnebago region. Before 1860 Marquette and Green Lake were combined under the name of Marquette which in 1840 had a population of only 18. A decade later this number had increased to 8,640. Of the 380 Irishmen in 1850 approximately 140 were located in the future Green Lake County.[28] In 1860 Green Lake, although covering a smaller area, counted a larger population than Marquette and kept that lead throughout the century. Marquette's sandy soil and the large areas of swamp land precluded a heavy settlement. Over half of the Irishmen who had entered Marquette County before 1850 were located in the portion west of the Fox River then called Indian Lands and constituting the bulk of what actually remained of Marquette County after Green Lake had been carved from it in 1858. Towns nearest the Fox River showed the heaviest concentrations of Irishmen. Neshkoro and Shields with comparatively small Irish populations in 1860 were nevertheless one-fourth Irish according to a count of families while larger numbers of Irishmen resided in Montello, Buffalo, and Douglas Townships. Four hundred and seventy-five of the 645 Irishmen of the county were located in these five townships in 1860. Most of them were farmers. As in Winnebago, Outagamie, and Brown Counties Irish immigrants had first worked on the Fox River improvement before settling on farms, so some of the Irish settlers in Marquette County had first worked on the canal at Portage.[29] Seneca and St. Marie Townships in Green Lake County border the town of Neshkoro in Marquette County and like it were not heavily populated, but Irish families were one-third of the total. Berlin, town and village, terminus of the Milwaukee and Mississippi Railroad, contained the largest concentration of Irishmen in the county.

In the western half of Wisconsin the old Crawford County of

---
[28] *Cf.* Appendix, p. 278-279, Tables 31 and 32.
[29] *Supra*, p. 80, n. 117.

1836 extended from the Wisconsin River on the south well into northern Wisconsin. By 1840 this region had been divided into four counties, all only sparsely populated: Crawford, Portage, St. Croix, and Sauk. The area covered by each of these varied greatly and by 1850 two additional counties had been carved from the old: Richland and Adams.

Sauk, Richland, and Crawford are the southernmost counties located in this area. Sauk had a population of 4,370 in 1850, Richland only 900, and Crawford extending north to the Buffalo River was the most heavily populated with 2,500 inhabitants. Very few Irishmen had made their way so far west. Approximately 100 had reached Sauk County, only 4 had settled in Richland, and 70 had located in Crawford. Practically all of these were located on farms excepting those in the northern Black River district where a few Irishmen were engaged in lumbering and one was occupied as a shingle maker.

The years immediately following the mid-century saw western Wisconsin penetrated by the railroads, but Sauk and Richland were not touched by them. The road to Prairie du Chien was built along the valley south of the Wisconsin River, crossing to the northern bank at Wauzeka and running through a few miles of Crawford County until it reached Prairie du Chien on the Mississippi River. On the other hand, the railroad to La Crosse followed a course north of these three counties. Statistics for Sauk, Richland, and Crawford Counties between 1850 and 1860, nevertheless, demonstrate large increases in their predominantly rural populations, each continuing to grow throughout the remainder of the century. By 1870 the number of Irish-born inhabitants in each of these counties had reached its peak and practically all of them were as a matter of course engaged in farming.

Although Irishmen were scattered throughout the townships of Sauk County, rather large settlements were located in the towns of Bear Creek, Dellona, and Winfield.[30] The latter two townships on the northern border of Sauk County are adjacent to each other and to Seven Mile Creek (contiguous to Kildare) and Lyndon

---

[30] *Cf.* Appendix, p. 282, Table 35.

Townships in Juneau County, both of which contained large concentrations of Irish-born inhabitants. Irishmen were among the first settlers in Dellona and Winfield. Patrick Hickey located within the present boundaries of Dellona in 1845 when Sauk County was part of Dane. He was joined by Peter Haskin, Patrick Mulligan, James Slaven, John Timlin, and S. J. Seymour who formed the nucleus of a settlement consisting of fifty Irish-born farmers by 1860.[31]

Another distinctly Irish settlement was located in the northern part of Bear Creek Township in the southwestern corner of the county. Here, too, Irish-born immigrants were among the first settlers in that section of the county. In 1853 John O'Meara and another Irish settler entered the town with their families. Patrick Shea, Patrick Donohoe, Patrick and Michael O'Neil, James Quinn, Peter Welsh, Michael Conly, John Lahey, Thomas Carney, Thomas Murray, William Rooney, and others came in 1854, pioneers of the Irish settlement which was ultimately named Loreto.[32] Some of these early Irish settlers had worked on the railroad in and near Madison before taking up land in Bear Creek Township.[33] The old cemetery on Marble Ridge which is

---

[31] *History of Sauk County, Wisconsin* (Chicago: Western Historical Co., 1880), p. 623. J. G. Gregory, "Sauk County," *Southwestern Wisconsin*, II, 1171.

[32] Heming, *op. cit.*, p. 825. A handwritten manuscript, "History and Record of Noteworthy Events of St. Patrick's Church, Marble Ridge, Sauk County, Wisconsin" (1891) by Stephen Duren, the pastor at Loreto, 1889-1891, was found in the rectory of the church. Evidently, Heming derived his material either directly from this manuscript or through one of the pastors succeeding Duren who had access to the manuscript. *Cf.* also, *History of Sauk County, Wisconsin*, p. 670; Gregory, "Sauk County," *loc. cit.*, p. 1177. The Irish settler with John O'Meara was an O'Brien. None of the sources gives his first name or is he listed in the 1860 Federal manuscript census.

[33] Duren, *op. cit.*, p. 5. History of *Sauk County*, p. 821, relates that Andrew Dwyer, native of County Clare, emigrated to America in 1852 and to Delafield, Wisconsin, in 1854. Later he moved to Pewaukee, Wisconsin, and worked as a railroad agent until he finally settled in Bear Creek Township in 1866. Dwyer is also a good example of the Irishman who moved from one state to another and from one county to another before finally locating permanently.

located at the site of the first church is a memorial to the Irish pioneers of Loreto. Tombstones indicate Irishmen native to Counties Mayo, Clare, Limerick, Galway, Tipperary, Donegal, Wexford, Tyrone, and Kerry. Loreto was one of those Irish agricultural communities of successful farmers who remained relatively shut off from the rest of the world clinging to their Irish traditions and customs.

It was also in Sauk County that a manufacturer, Jonas Tower, established a settlement in the town of Ironton in 1854. Among the group of iron workers who migrated with him from New York was a number of Irishmen who constituted the nucleus for the parish of St. Michael.[34]

Settlement in Richland, the second southern county of old Crawford, not only progressed slowly, but its population never attained large proportions. In 1870 the number of Irish-born inhabitants reached 430 and remained at that figure until 1880. Small concentrations of Irishmen in 1860 were located in the towns of Akan, Henrietta, Marshall, and Westford.[35] By 1890 the Irish reportedly approximated one-half of the population in Westford Township, one-fourth in the adjacent town of Henrietta, and one-fifth in the town of Rockbridge.[36]

In Crawford County, 1860, Irishmen constituted 9 per cent of the population.[37] Crawford like Richland never became heavily populated and was settled even more slowly. The number of Irish-born immigrants located in Crawford County, however, compared to that in Richland, was three times as great in 1860 and more than twice as great in 1870. Prairie du Chien, village and town, had already become the central location for Irishmen in 1850 since about 50 of the 70 Irishmen in Crawford County had situated there. In 1836 Patrick Quinn was the only Irish-born inhabitant in Prairie du Chien but some time before 1840 Joseph Dunn ar-

---

[34] *Supra*, p. 18.
[35] *Cf.* Appendix, p. 281, Table 34.
[36] WSHS, Roeseler Papers, Report of J. W. Fowler, Richland Center, Wisconsin, December 28, 1889.
[37] *Cf.* Appendix, p. 280, Table 33.

rived and many of his relatives followed.[38] Edward Hughes, John Cummins, John McClure, and Barnaby Dunn, Irishmen who are reported to have been in service at Fort Crawford, upon expiration of their enlistment some time before 1850 settled in the town of Prairie du Chien.[39] With the coming of the Milwaukee and Mississippi Railroad in the spring of 1857 a large number of Irishmen located at Prairie du Chien and, according to Peter L. Scanlan, they soon exceeded the number of native Americans.[40] By 1860 the Irishmen definitely were the largest foreign-born group. The Germans ranked a close second and by 1870 surpassed the Irishmen.

The town of Eastman, bordering Prairie du Chien on the north was, with a smaller Irish population, more Irish than its southern neighbor. Among those who arrived in the 1850's were James Malone, James Ryan, John Cragan, John Smith, James Foley, Thomas Burton, Peter Casey, Michael Maloney, Daniel McNamara, and James Lenehan.

The town of Clayton was originally settled in the middle 1850's by several Irishmen: Robert Welch, Matthew Ryan, Henry, John, and Morris Murphy, Peter and Lawrence Gaffney, Martin and Patrick Garrity, and others.[41] These grouped around St. Philip settlement and a Catholic church of the same name.[42] Irish set-

---

[38] Peter L. Scanlan, *Prairie du Chien: French, British, American* (Menasha, Wisconsin: George Banta Publishing Co., 1937), p. 209.

[39] WSHS, Roeseler Papers, Report of James Degnan, pastor of Catholic Church, Wauzeka, Wisconsin, April 4, 1889. All of these are listed in the 1850 census. John Cummins, however, is the only one whose military record can be traced completely through muster rolls and entrance papers. Edward Hughes and John McClure are found enlisted but there is no record of their having been stationed at Fort Crawford. No military record for Barnaby Dunn was found. NA, AGO, Division of Old Records.

[40] P. Scanlan, *Prairie du Chien: French, British, American*, p. 209.

[41] J. S. Earl and J. P. Evans, "Crawford County," *Southwestern Wisconsin*, p. 363; *History of Crawford and Richland Counties, Wisconsin*, pp. 574-76.

[42] Heming, *op. cit.*, p. 864. The land for the Catholic church and cemetery had been donated by Gaffney and Garrity. Before the church was built Philip Murphy died and since he was the first to be buried in the cemetery the parish was named St. Philip.

tlers who gradually entered the town were from all parts of Ireland, those from the province of Connaught in the majority.[43] By 1870 one-fourth of the town's families were Irish and in 1890 the Norwegians and Irish were the predominant nationalities within the township.[44]

In the town of Marietta, just north of Wauzeka, Irishmen were estimated to be the second largest group in 1890. Americans were predominant, but the Irish were almost as numerous.[45] Among the first settlers in the town of Seneca was the Robert Garvey family who emigrated from northern Ireland and after locating in Seneca engaged in farming and the mercantile business.[46] Other native Irishmen joined them and during the ten years after 1860 the Irish population increased considerably. By this time only improved land in the town was available. An Irish-born immigrant, Edward McNamara, who migrated to Seneca from Newark, Ohio, in 1870 can be cited as a typical Irishman, moving from one place to another and finally locating among others of his nationality.[47] He felt that location in the town of Seneca among

---

[43] WSHS, Roeseler Papers, report of B. P. Connolly, Catholic priest, Soldiers Grove, Wisconsin, March 17, 1890.

[44] WSHS, Roeseler Papers, Report of C. E. Alder, Prairie du Chien, Wisconsin, February 6, 1890. Alder, County Clerk, reported that the Norwegian nationality was predominant in the town of Clayton and that the Irish were 90 per cent of the remaining nationalities. B. P. Connolly, the pastor at St. Philip within the township, however, maintained that the Irish were predominant and the Norwegians next in line; that the ratio was 1 to 3. The *History of Crawford and Richland Counties, Wisconsin*, p. 575, backs up Connolly's estimate when it states that the inhabitants of the town of Clayton "are [1884] an industrious class of people, a large percentage of which are of Irish descent, with some Norwegians, and a few Americans."

[45] WSHS, Roeseler Papers, Report of C. E. Alder.

[46] WSHS, Roeseler Papers, Report of James Degnan, Wauzeka, Wisconsin, April 4, 1889.

[47] Edward McNamara, letter to his daughter, Sister Anna Maria, Seneca, Wisconsin, 1871. The original of this letter and others by Edward McNamara are in the possession of Mayme McNamara, Prairie du Chien, Wisconsin. According to Catherine Lenehan, Seneca, Wisconsin, granddaughter of Edward McNamara, the family moved from Newark, Ohio, to Seneca in 1871. The family saw the ruins of Chicago after the great fire on their way to Wisconsin. The letter must have been written in the fall of the year, 1871. In

his countrymen would be a means of providing for his sons' future. Edward McNamara's sons and those of his Irish neighbors did remain on their fathers' farms or located in the neighborhood and intermarried within the township or chose Irish partners from surrounding towns. Because of this the Irish nationality in 1890 was still predominant in Seneca.[48]

North of Crawford, Sauk, and Richland Counties are the counties of Adams, Vernon, Juneau, Monroe, La Crosse, Trempealeau, Buffalo, Pepin, Pierce, and St. Croix. Of these, Juneau and St. Croix not only contained the largest number of Irishmen but the largest percentage also. Irish-born inhabitants of St. Croix County in 1860 were 12 per cent of the population and in Juneau County they constituted 11 per cent. Irish families in each of these two counties amounted to 22 per cent of the total number of families.

At the other extreme among the counties within this group Adams and Vernon had small Irish populations in comparison with the other counties and contained no single heavy concentration of Irishmen. A partial explanation of this may be that neither of these counties had direct contact with the railroad or other public works. In 1860 the largest aggregation of Irishmen in Adams County was 55, located in the town of New Haven.[49] About 10 families in addition to this Irish group were situated in the adjoining town of Dell Prairie. They had arrived between 1852 and 1860, most of them having worked as common laborers in the East before migrating to Wisconsin. These two townships in Adams County were considered the only ones having significant

---

the letter McNamara described the journey from Ohio to Seneca and explained that he paid 2,500 dollars down on the farm remaining 500 dollars in debt. As could be expected he had to invest in equipment and live stock: a wagon and a plow, a team of horses, and three cows. Their share of the crop that fall amounted to 105 bushels of oats, 52 of wheat, 30 of apples and 20 or 30 bushels of potatoes. The corn he estimated would amount to 200 bushels when husked. McNamara was enthusiastic about his wife's happiness in the new location and he felt that the region around Seneca was "a very healthy country." A second of McNamara's letters is dated November 19, 1871, which repeats some of the information and adds more.

[48] WSHS, Roeseler Papers, Report of C. E. Alder.
[49] *Cf.* Appendix, p. 283, Table 36.

numbers of Irishmen in 1890.[50] The heaviest concentrations of Irish-born in Vernon County were located in Franklin and Greenwood Townships.[51]

Juneau, Monroe, and La Crosse Counties are crossed by the Milwaukee and Mississippi Railroad and owe much of their Irish population to this fact. Some of the Irishmen residing in Juneau County also had labored on the Portage Canal or had worked with a lumbering crew in the woods before choosing a site for permanent settlement.[52] Almost three-fifths of the Irish-born population of Juneau County in 1860 was located in the four southwestern townships: Seven Mile Creek, Lyndon, Kildare, and Lemonweir.[53] Irish immigrants had located in Seven Mile Creek and Kildare in the years 1849, 1850, and 1851. Among these earliest settlers were William Taylor, Maurice and James Havey, Patrick Doyle, William Green, Peter and Patrick Smith, John Leonard, James Casey, Patrick Hayes, and John Murray.[54] Nearness to the Portage Canal and the construction of the railroad through Lyndon, Lemonweir, and Lisbon were factors in augmenting the Irish population in these towns. Although each town had a few Irish laborers, in 1860, most of the Irishmen were engaged in farming. After the railroad intersected the southeastern section of the county, 1857, the villages of Lyndon Station and Mauston became centers for marketing and the sites for Catholic churches.[55] Railroad construction also drew Irish laborers

---

[50] WSHS, Roeseler Papers, Report of C. A. Cady, March 7, 1889. The foreign population of the town of New Haven was about evenly divided between the Irish and Norwegians.

[51] *Cf.* Appendix, p. 289, Table 43.

[52] J. G. Gregory and Thomas J. Cunningham, editors, *West Central Wisconsin: A History* (Indianapolis: S. J. Clarke Publishing Co., 1933), I, 414. For example, John Smith worked at Portage and then located in the town of Lindina. Robert Doyle did both, canal work and lumbering, before settling in the southeastern corner of the town of Lemonweir, Juneau County.

[53] *Cf.* Appendix, p. 285, Table 38.

[54] Heming, *op. cit.*, p. 823, gives the family names of these individuals. First names were obtained from the 1860 Federal manuscript census.

[55] The Catholic church serving the Lyndon area had been located on section five, Kildare Township, but was moved to Lyndon as a more central location. *Cf.* Heming, *op. cit.*, p. 824.

to Lisbon and Necedah townships farther north,[56] while farming attracted Irishmen to the town of Plymouth.[57]

The most significant increases in Irish-born population between 1860 and 1870 in Juneau County occurred in the largely Irish towns of Lyndon, Kildare, and Seven Mile Creek. The majority of these Irishmen in Juneau County had settled down to farming by 1860, but because of the railroad the group of laborers was quite large.

The Milwaukee and Mississippi Railroad intersected only the southern half of Juneau County and after cutting through the town of Orange entered Monroe County. Monroe's greatest increase in population occurred between 1860 and 1870. This is true also of the number of Irishmen.[58] In 1860 the towns of Tomah, Greenfield, and Sparta led in Irish population with comparatively small concentrations. Although the increase in the Irish-born population of Monroe County was significant between 1860 and 1870, the concentrations of Irishmen remained small. Four towns in the southeast corner of the county, Clifton, Glendale, Wilton, and Wellington, experienced some increase as did four towns which the railroad transversed: Tomah, Greenfield, Lafayette, and Sparta. Not until 1880, however, did the number of Irishmen in Monroe County reach its peak. Whereas the Irishmen in the southern section of the county were chiefly farmers, those along the railroad were doing "work on the railroad tracks." In Sparta a number of Irish laborers was also employed in the grist mill and at other forms of common labor.

La Crosse County, bordering Monroe on the west, extended to the Mississippi River where the city of La Crosse in 1860 constituted the largest center of population in western Wisconsin. It is the only county west of Dane in 1860 in which Irish laborers

---

[56] Twelve Irish laborers were living in one boarding house in the town of Lisbon and 5 in another. These were probably in the village of New Lisbon, a railroad village which developed as a freight yard and a center where east and west bound passenger trains meet the northbound.

[57] In 1889 the town was reported as predominantly Irish. *Cf.* WSHS, Roeseler Papers, report of H. Ninnemann, Pastor of the Evangelical Association of North America, Elroy, Wisconsin.

[58] *Cf.* Appendix, p. 286, Table 39.

outnumbered farmers. In comparison to Dane numerically, Irishmen were only a very small group, but the disparity between the number of Irish laborers and farmers was much greater.[59] The completion of the Milwaukee and Mississippi Railroad to La Crosse in 1858 was an important factor in the location of Irishmen within the county and the development of the city of La Crosse on the banks of the Mississippi at the mouth of the Black River was another. Irishmen in comparatively small numbers were situated in the towns along the railroad as laborers. Roughly, about two-fifths of the Irishmen in the county were living in these towns and two-fifths were located in the city of La Crosse.

The rest of the counties of western Wisconsin are situated up the Mississippi River from La Crosse to Prescott, Pierce County, and then along the St. Croix River. They are: Trempealeau, Buffalo, Pepin, Pierce, and St. Croix. Each of these counties was quite sparsely settled in 1860 and continued to experience growth in population throughout the rest of the century.

Trempealeau contained only slightly more than 100 Irishmen in 1860 and about 90 of these were located in the towns of Gale and Trempealeau of which Ettrick was then still a part.[60] July 30, 1860, a post office was established in the midst of this Irish settlement and was given the name Armagh, but on September 20 the name was changed to Ettrick through the influence of John Cance, a native of Scotland and the first postmaster.[61] After 1860

---

[59] In 1850 Irish laborers outnumbered farmers in Columbia County, which is west of Dane County, but that was reversed in 1860. Eight young men, native Irishmen, were listed in the 1860 census among a group of laborers and raftsmen in a boarding house. These men and others at the end of the list had no occupations designated, neither was there notice of the fact that they were unemployed. They were probably laborers or raftsmen, also. For statistics on the Irish population in La Crosse County cf. Appendix, p. 284, Table 37.

[60] Cf. Appendix, p. 289, Table 44.

[61] The information concerning the first naming of the post office was obtained from Clara Sheehy, Ettrick, Wisconsin, December 12, 1951. Cance was an admirer and avid reader of the works of Sir Walter Scott. He named the town for Ettrick, a forest in Scotland described in Scott's *Marmion*. Cf. Franklyn Curtiss-Wedge and E. D. Pierce (eds.), *History of Trempealeau County, Wisconsin* (Chicago: H. C. Cooper, Jr., and Co., 1917), p. 271. Early

Irish settlers chose five different sites in the county but the bulk of them located in the town of Ettrick around Ettrick settlement and Beaver Creek. spreading into Gale, Arcadia, and Trempealeau Townships. In the town of Ettrick toward the end of the century Irishmen were outnumbered by the Norwegians. By 1890 the predominant national character of the town was judged to be almost two-thirds Norwegian and one-third Irish, with a sprinkling of Scotch and American.[62]

West of Trempealeau in Buffalo County, a small Irish population was located in the towns of Glencoe, Naples, Waumandee, and Maxville in 1860.[63] These small centers of Irish-born settlers except that in Naples grew to larger concentrations in 1870 and 1880. In Glencoe by 1870 one-third of the families was Irish. These were situated in what became known as Irish Valley located in the town of Glencoe and extending into Waumandee.[64]

---

settlers in the region included among others, John and Dennis Mahoney, John and Daniel Kennedy, Thomas and Andrew Beirne, Peter and Timothy Dufficy, Daniel Nefficy, Patrick McCormick, Michael Connolly, James Quinn, James McLaughlin, Peter, Hugh, and Thomas Crogan, Timothy Lane, Edward Reilly, Owen, Thomas, and Patrick Mulligan, Michael McGillindy, James McCarthy, Sylvester McAvoy, Thomas and Michael Cullity, Thomas and Darby Whalen, John Harmon, James and John Corcoran, Thomas, Patrick, and John Wall, John, James, and Richard Cantlon, Thomas Sheehy, Daniel Cahill and Bernhard Brady, Maurice Casey, James Larkin, James Dolan, John Beirne, John Hunt, Thomas Roach, John Dolan, Thomas Shaw. Irish veterans of the Civil War who located at Ettrick were Peter Hoff, Patrick and Walter Wall, John O'Neil, Michael Hoy, John O'Brien, Daniel McGillindy, and Daniel Cullity. *Cf.* John C. Gaveney, "Irish in the County," *History of Trempealeau County, Wisconsin,* pp. 143-150; Clara Sheehy, letter to writer, Ettrick, Wisconsin.

[62] WSHS, Roeseler Papers, Report of William L. Cummings, County Superintendent of Schools, Blair, Wisconsin, February 21, 1889; report of E. N. Trowbridge, County Clerk, Whitehall, Wisconsin, December 18, 1889. The list of postmasters who served from 1860 to the 1930's is indicative of the national strains: John Cance, native of Scotland, Iver Pederson, James E. McCarthy, Nels T. Nelson, John B. Corcoran, Eric J. Brovold, Mrs. Clara M. Johnson, Leonard P. Sheehy.

[63] *Cf.* Appendix, p. 287, Table 40.

[64] Lawrence Kessinger, *History of Buffalo County, Wisconsin* (Alma, Wisconsin, 1888), p. 415. Kessinger lists early Irish settlers and their first location: Patrick Mulcare, 1855, and Michael J. Cashel, 1857, in Glencoe;

In 1888 an estimate by the historian of Buffalo County, Lawrence Kessinger, placed the number of Irishmen within the county as follows: Glencoe Township, 267; towns of Waumandee and Maxville, each 200; Canton and Mondovi Townships, each 100.[65]

Pepin County, although smaller in area than Buffalo County, also had about the same number of Irish-born inhabitants in 1860 the majority of whom were located in the towns of Pepin and Waubeek.[66] This Irish population did not grow but was soon surrounded by German, Norwegian, and Swedish settlers. In 1860, three Irishmen were hands in a sawmill among seventy-seven natives of Germany, Norway, Switzerland, and the United States.

The Irishmen of Pierce County in 1860 were scattered throughout the townships with small concentrations in the village of Prescott and in the towns of River Falls and Pleasant Valley.[67] By 1870 a little more than 40 per cent of the 51 families in El Paso Township were Irish and by 1890 El Paso was the only township in Pierce County considered to be predominantly Irish.[68]

St. Croix, the most northern county of this section of western Wisconsin, also became the most Irish county of western Wisconsin in 1870 and 1880. St. Croix County, which in 1850 comprised the present counties of St. Croix, Pierce, and Polk and included small portions of Barron and Burnett, contained a total population of 625, of whom 30 were Irish-born.[69] Among these were seven farmers, eight lumbermen, three sawyers, and seven craftsmen. In the decade after 1850 the population of the county, cut down to its present size, had increased more than eight times

---

Peter Tierney, 1855, and Mathias Waters, 1854, in Waumandee; Barney McDonough, 1856, and Thomas Fox, 1857, in Maxville; John Callahan, 1856, in Naples.

[65] WSHS, Roeseler Papers, Manuscript map made by L. Kessinger and submitted to Roeseler, September, 1888.

[66] *Cf.* Appendix, p. 288, Table 42.

[67] *Cf.* Appendix, p. 288, Table 41. Pleasant Valley in 1860 was divided to form the towns of Maiden Rock, Salem, and Union.

[68] WSHS, Roeseler Papers, Report of J. B. Benson, County Clerk, Ellsworth, Wisconsin, December 20, 1889.

[69] *Cf.* Appendix, p. 290, Table 45.

and the Irish population grew to be twenty-one times larger than in 1850.

It is said that Michael Lynch, a surveyor in Janesville, informed a number of Irishmen of the fertility of farm lands in St. Croix County and as a result, John Casey and James, Michael, and Thomas McNamara went north and entered upon land in the county in 1854. Patrick Ring and others followed soon after.[70] A group of Irishmen emigrated from Dane County to the town of Pleasant Valley, St. Croix County, in the spring of 1855. These Irish immigrants had left Ireland at various times prior to 1850, had located for some time in Connecticut, and between 1852 and 1855 had met again in Dane County locating near Madison. The group was composed of Lawrence Hawkins, his two sons-in-law, Patrick Shields and Michael Caffrey with their wives and families; two married sons with their families, and his eight other children; also, the James K. McLaughlin family. From Dane County they journeyed overland in wagons drawn by oxen and horses, blazing new trails and fording streams and rivers. These pioneers settled on heavily wooded lands in the present town of Pleasant Valley. The locality came to be known as "Hawkins Settlement."[71] Also, Irishmen had been imported in 1854 or 1855 as laborers for the construction of the Superior and Bayfield Railroad. A colony of them located in Hudson and when the work was suspended because of the railroad failures in 1857 many of the Irish laborers settled in the towns of the county, particularly in Erin Prairie and Emerald, which were to become so predominantly Irish.[72]

In 1860, 87 per cent of the families in the town of Erin (formerly called Erin Prairie) were natives of Ireland.[73] By 1870

---

[70] *History of Northern Wisconsin*, p. 965.

[71] S. N. Hawkins, *The Hawkins Settlement, St. Croix County, Wisconsin, June 4, 1855* (1914); Catharine Kinney, "History of Some Incidents of My Ancestors" (Unpublished manuscript, 1951). The original of this manuscript is in the hands of its author who resides in Hudson, Wisconsin. Catharine Kinney is the granddaughter of James K. McLaughlin.

[72] Genevieve E. C. Day, *Hudson in the Early Days* (Hudson, Wisconsin, 1932), p. 38. *Cf.* also, M. J. Read, *op. cit.*, p. 255.

[73] Erin then embraced part of Emerald Township.

Erin's 170 Irish families constituted 94 per cent of the families within the town and in the town of Emerald Irish families were 69 per cent of the total. By 1870 St. Joseph, Cylon, Richmond, and Warren Townships also had fairly large proportions of Irish families although the total populations and number of Irishmen were small.

The town and village of Hudson contained almost 100 Irish families in 1860 but by 1870 the number of Irishmen in Hudson had decreased considerably.

Except in Hudson, Irishmen throughout the county were situated on the land. By 1870 there were 200 Irish farmers in the town of Erin alone. An editorial correspondent of the *Northwestern Chronicle* found that since he could not afford a trip to Ireland a visit to Erin Prairie proved to be "the next best thing."

> The prosperity the Irish settlers on this prairie—and there are none others—have attained to within a few years, is wonderful, indeed, and refutes so thoroughly the ignorant and too frequently malicious slanderers—who taking some barroom loafer as a model, judge the Irish people from this low standard—that I have felt proud and happy to listen to many a settler's story of early trials and ultimate success.
>
> Twelve years ago the first Irish settlers came into Erin Prairie with little or no capital, but brave hearts and strong arms; now the Irish have not alone possessed themselves of every acre of this fine prairie for six miles square, but they have spread out into the townships of Emerald, on the east, Hamond [sic] on the south, Warren, southwest, Richmond, west, and Star Prairie, north.
>
> In most instances the Irish who moved from Erin Prairie into those other townships bought improved farms, for which they paid from twenty to thirty dollars an acre; they did not go in quest of better land than they had where they first settled, for it would be impossible to find such; but, in order to have room to farm on a larger scale and they got ready purchasers in their neighbors, who remained, and were also anxious to enlarge their farms.[74]

---

[74] St. Paul *Northwestern Chronicle*, December 21, 1867.

By the year 1890 Erin Prairie was still almost exclusively Irish. Emerald Township had retained its Irish predominance but the Germans were on the increase. Richmond, Stanton, and St. Joseph were also predominantly Irish, while in Hammond, Kinnickinnic and Warren, Americans predominated and the Irish ranked second. In Warren Township the number of Irish was reportedly increasing. Throughout St. Croix County, but particularly in the town of Cady and even more so in Springfield Township, Irishmen from Canada were quite numerous.[75]

A glance over the part of Wisconsin discussed this far reveals that by 1860 the Irish-born population had reached its apex in the counties south and east of the Wisconsin River as far north as the northern boundaries of Adams, Waushara, and Manitowoc Counties, and including La Crosse, but excluding Fond du Lac, Winnebago, and Calumet. The number of Irish-born inhabitants in this region in 1860 totaled 37,190, almost three-fourths of the Irish-born population of Wisconsin, and within the area native Irishmen decreased numerically after 1860. By 1870 the number of Irish-born had reached its peak in each of the following counties: Kewaunee, Brown, Oconto; Calumet, Fond du Lac, Winnebago, and Waupaca; Juneau, Sauk, Richland, Crawford, and Vernon; Trempealeau, Buffalo, and Pepin. These counties in that year contained 11,500 native Irishmen or 4 per cent of their population. The bulk of Irishmen within these two areas was occupied in agricultural pursuits but general population growth in the northern section of Wisconsin was probably influenced more by the lumbering industry than any other factor.

Lumbering and sawmill activities were carried on in Wisconsin from the 1830's into the twentieth century. Pine lands necessary to the lumbering industry were located chiefly in that part of Wisconsin which would fall north of a line drawn from the northern border of Ozaukee County on Lake Michigan to Prescott, the point where the St. Croix River flows into the Mississippi River. Seven distinct lumbering areas developed within this region. The most eastern and first to be exploited formed a tri-

---

[75] WSHS, Roeseler Papers, Report of Charles Lewiston, County Clerk, Hudson, Wisconsin, January 14, 1890.

angle extending from the tip of the Door Peninsula along Lake Michigan to the northern border of Ozaukee County and west to Lake Winnebago. A second region lay west of Green Bay in Brown, Oconto, and Marinette Counties. The remaining five areas of lumbering activity lay in the basin of the Wolf River which joins the Fox near Oshkosh and along the Wisconsin, Black, Chippewa, and St. Croix Rivers which flow into the Mississippi River. Each of these sections was exploited from the south northward; those east of the Wisconsin River, except in their extreme northern regions, were the first to be exhausted. This was primarily due to the accessibility of Chicago and Milwaukee as markets, to the early extension of the railroad to Fond du Lac and Oshkosh, and the opportunity to supply Watertown, Janesville, Beloit and other locations in the Rock River Valley with lumber.[76]

Lumbering with its accompanying manufactures absorbed the energies of some Irishmen. The phases of the lumbering industry which furnished them with employment were in some instances specifically recorded by the census taker in the terms lumber merchant, sawyer, mill hand, or raftsman. Frequently, however, the designation was no more specific than "lumberman" which, unless the value of real and personal estate indicated otherwise, might mean anything from one who worked in a logging camp to the manager of a lumber company. Likewise, the term laborer was used often with no specification of the type of labor that was being expended. Some of the Irish laborers in Oshkosh and Fond du Lac, for example, were most probably employed in the sawmills and shingle factories. Winneconne was one of the chief sawmill towns on the Wolf River and in 1850 the census recorded one Irish-born lumberman among six from the East and twenty

---

[76] For detailed information on lumbering in Wisconsin see Robert F. Fries, *Empire in Pine: The Story of Lumbering in Wisconsin, 1830-1900* (Madison: State Historical Society of Wisconsin, 1951); George B. Engberg, "Labor in the Lake States Lumber Industry, 1830-1930" (Unpublished Ph.D. dissertation, University of Minnesota, 1949). For a brief summary of lumbering in the state cf. Raney, *op. cit.*, pp. 198-215. Schafer, *The Winnebago-Horicon Basin* devotes chapters fifteen and sixteen to Fond du Lac and Oshkosh in which he stresses the importance of the lumbering industry in their development.

Irish-born laborers. No doubt these laborers were employed in the sawmills.[77]

Lumbering, particularly before the industry was revolutionized by the advent of the railroads, provided seasonal employment. Laborers rotated from logging in winter camps to spring and summer work in the sawmills, in the driving and rafting of logs, on farms, or on railroad construction.[78] Usually the laboring force in camps and mills was drawn chiefly from the surrounding areas. Farmers, however, provided the largest source for part-time work. Many of them in clearing their land took the logs they had cut during the winter to the sawmills and subsisted on the money thus earned until their farm had begun to produce.[79] Others worked in lumber camps during the winter while farm work was at a minimum and returned in time for spring plowing. Still others, and Irishmen among them, engaged in lumbering within a given area until that industry began to decline, or until they had sufficient money to purchase a farm or to go into business.[80] Milwaukee and smaller cities also furnished employees for the industry from their labor forces.

---

[77] By 1860 lumbering activity in Winneconne had declined. Oshkosh had absorbed much of it. The Irish population of Winneconne had decreased from 90 in 1850 to 40 in 1860; Irish laborers from 20 to 3.

[78] Engberg, *op. cit.*, pp. 29, 30, 33; Fries, *op. cit.*, pp. 204-206. *Biographical History of Clark and Jackson Counties, Wisconsin* (Chicago: The Lewis Publishing Co., 1891), p. 266, gives an account of Patrick H. Sheehan, a son of Irish emigrants to Canada West, who arrived in La Crosse, 1864, and worked in the lumbering camps during the winter months. In the summer he drove logs. He alternated this way for about thirty-six years before ultimately taking up farming in Clark County.

[79] Engberg, *op. cit.*, pp. 28-33.

[80] Specific examples of individual Irishmen of whom this is true are: Thomas Reynolds and John Leigh described in *Commemorative Biographical Record of the West Shore of Green Bay*, pp. 494, 504; Martin Neville, who worked in logging camp near Neillsville during the winter and then purchased a farm in Clark County, cf. *History of Clark and Jackson Counties, Wisconsin*, p. 325; Joseph Norton, Thomas Delaney, Luke Killoren, Bartholomew Drury, all of whom turned to farming after having spent a number of years in some phase of lumbering, described in *History of Northern Wisconsin*, pp. 149, 151, 752; Arthur Gough, James Nolan, John L. Rooney, and Michael Hogan of the Chippewa Falls region, described in *Diamond Jubilee History of Notre Dame Church*, pp. 135, 117, 129, 115.

Because of this inter-occupational flow, statistics for the number of men employed in the lumbering industry are at best only rough estimates. According to the census of 1850 a total of 75 native Irishmen was engaged in some phase of lumbering. By 1860 the number had increased to 310, of whom about 200 were listed as mill hands. The number of Irishmen engaged in the lumbering industry in Wisconsin remained fairly constant after 1860; approximately 350 were thus employed in 1870, 390 in 1880, and 330 in 1890, but because of the constancy of the number of Irishmen and the increase in numbers of men employed, the percentage decreased from 5 per cent in 1870 to 2 per cent in 1890.[81] In 1880, according to the Federal census, there was a total of 3,810 workers in the woods, 147 of whom were Irish.[82] Irish-born sawmill operatives the same year numbered 239.

Although the Irish were outnumbered by Americans, Canadians, Scandinavians, and Germans in the lumber industry, they were prominent in some sections and camps or mills. In the town of Stiles, Oconto County, according to the manuscript census of 1860, John Leigh, an Irish-born immigrant, was owner of a sawmill, Irishmen were in charge of two lumber camps, and 40 Irish laborers were working among Germans, Belgians, and Canadians in Eldred and Balcomb's Mill.[83] An Irish mill owner, two

---

[81] Engberg, *op. cit.*, pp. 54, 55, 58. The inaccuracy of the census figures is discussed by Engberg. Comparisons from one year to the next are inaccurate because there is a difference in the classification of lumbermen; for some individuals lumbering was a dual occupation and their main occupation was listed, not lumbering; some were not engaged in the industry when the census was taken, since it was a seasonal occupation. In the manufacturing section of the census report, statistics are also given, but these usually err because the reports contain part-time workers who considered some other occupation their principal one.

[82] Fries, *op. cit.*, p. 204. The numbers which Fries takes from the census are as follows: 1,805 American, 915 British-American, 473 Scandinavian, 275 German, 147 Irish, 106 other countries, and 89 British.

[83] *Commemorative Biographical Record of West Shore of Green Bay*, p. 504, gives a biography of John Leigh, native of Ireland, who lived first in Maine when he came to America. In 1850 he migrated to Berlin, Wisconsin, and in 1852 to Stiles Township, Oconto County, making the journey on the river by canoe. He was employed in a sawmill which after three years he purchased. He engaged in lumbering until his mill burned in 1878.

lumbermen, and approximately 50 Irish-born laborers were engaged by the lumbering industry in the town of Oconto, the same county. Isaac Stephenson's "lumber establishment" employed 30 Irishmen among men of other nationalities. In some sections of Oconto County, therefore, around 1860, Irishmen were employed in rather large numbers by the lumbering industry.[84]

In Brown County Irish-born lumbermen numbered 15 in 1850. Eleven of these were located in the northern town of Suamico which had a total population of 172. Twenty-three of these were Irishmen. Only 14 families had settled there, 3 of which were Irish farmers. The remainder of the Irish population was engaged in lumbering. Besides the 11 lumbermen there were a sawyer, 2 carpenters and joiners, and one laborer. Marinette in 1850 belonged to Brown County and had 2 Irish-born lumbermen and 14 laborers. Thirteen Irishmen in the town of Billington, later in Outagamie County, made up one-fifth of the small population. Two of the Irishmen were lumbermen, but by 1860 the Irish population was engaged solely in agriculture. In the late 1850's Brown County was the leading shingle market in the United States but during the 1860's lumbering began to decline and by the middle 1870's the forests of the county had been practically depleted.

Lumbering in the upper Wisconsin River Valley gave impetus to the formation and ultimate settlement of Portage, Wood, and Marathon Counties. The Irish-born population of these counties did not increase significantly after 1860. Scattered throughout Portage County, moreover, Irishmen were chiefly farmers. Thirty-five per cent of the county's Irishmen in 1860 were located in the towns of Hull, Sharon, and Lanark.[85] Thirty-six per cent, the largest concentration of Irish-born in the county, was centered at Stevens Point. One Irishman wrote in the mid-fifties:

> I will inform you a little about this part of the country. We have as good markets here as there are in the east

---

[84] In contrast, F. B. Gardner's mill in Pensaukee Township, Oconto County, employed one Irish-born laborer among numerous Germans, Belgians, Norwegians, and Canadians; Ogden's mill in Peshtigo Township employed 5 Irishmen among Germans, Belgians, and Canadians. For statistics on Irish population in Oconto County cf. Appendix, p. 291, Table 46.

[85] Cf. Appendix, p. 292, Table 49.

for farming productions; . . . There is plenty of Government land here yet, and there are more Irish farmers around this neighborhood than in any other part of the country [Portage County].[86]

The Irish-born inhabitants of Wood County were located in four townships: Grand Rapids, Saratoga, Centralia, and Rudolph.[87] Although some Irishmen were farmers, the emphasis especially in Grand Rapids and Centralia was rather on unskilled labor and some phase of lumbering. The Irish laborers may have been employed by the lumber industry in which the Irish were definitely represented by three lumbermen, a sawyer, a teamster, two river pilots, and three raftsmen.

In Marathon County in 1860 the heaviest concentration of Irishmen was located in the town of Mosinee where 16 Irish families constituted one-fourth of the township's families.[88] These Irishmen composed the nucleus of the later formed town of Emmet, contiguous to the western border of Mosinee, and which in 1890 was still considered an Irish town.[89] Cleveland Township adjoining Emmet on the west contained an aggregation of Irishmen known locally as "Irish settlement." Irish immigrants had begun to settle there already in the late 1850's.[90]

Within the three counties of Portage, Wood, and Marathon 153 Irishmen were engaged in farming, 94 were laborers, and 27 were employed in some phase of the lumbering industry. It is highly probable that some of the Irish laborers and farmers also constituted a portion of the part-time force employed in the woods and sawmills. The counties of Lincoln, Oneida, and Vilas, north of Marathon contained a total of only 132 Irishmen as late as

---

[86] Boston *Pilot,* June 7, 1856, Thomas Welsh to the editor, Stevens Point, Wisconsin, May 14, 1856.
[87] *Cf.* Appendix, p. 291, Table 47.
[88] *Cf.* Appendix, p. 292, Table 48.
[89] WSHS, Roeseler Papers, Report of John W. Miller, Clerk, Wausau, Wisconsin, December 16, 1889.
[90] *Ibid.;* Gregory and Cunningham, *op. cit.,* II, 503.

1890. That year in Oneida the villages of Minocqua and Eagle River were estimated to be 50 and 30 per cent Irish respectively.[91]

The lumbering region immediately west of the Wisconsin River was located in the basin of the Black River, a stream about 140 miles long and flowing into the Mississippi River at La Crosse. Taylor, Clark, and Jackson Counties lie in its course. In 1839 a sawmill was erected at Black River Falls in Jackson County; the three O'Neill brothers, James, Henry, and Alexander, of Irish descent, came to the valley in 1839 and in 1845 settled at Neillsville, Clark County. By 1850 there were approximately 500 to 600 men on the Black River. Population growth, however, in the three counties was very slow. In each county the small number of Irishmen had reached its peak by 1880; Jackson with 190, Clark with 100, and Taylor with a mere 35. Forty Irishmen, two-fifths of all the Irish-born inhabitants of Jackson County, 1860, were located chiefly in the town of Albion and the village of Black River Falls.[92] Among these, seven were laborers, three were lumbermen, two were mill hands, one a carpenter, and one a saloon keeper. Thirty-one Irishmen, chiefly farmers, in the towns of Manchester and Irving formed the beginnings of what became slightly larger Irish settlements by 1880. Clark County contained only 14 Irish-born inhabitants in 1860 who were located in the towns of Pine Valley and Weston.[93] James and Samuel McKinley, who managed two logging camps in the late 1850's, like the O'Neill brothers, were not natives of Ireland, but were of Irish descent. This is true of other settlers in Jackson and Clark Counties; numbers of them had entered the region through Canada.[94]

The basin of the Chippewa River and its tributaries west of the Black River covers an area equal to about one-sixth of the

---

[91] WSHS, Roeseler Papers, Report of E. S. Shepard, Register of Deeds and Deputy County Surveyor, Rhinelander, Wisconsin, May 22, 1889. Vilas County was formed in 1893 from Oneida. Eagle River is now located in Vilas County. The 1900 Federal census records 49 Irish-born inhabitants in Vilas.

[92] Cf. Appendix, p. 293, Table 50.

[93] Cf. Appendix, p. 294, Table 52. The village of Neillsville was located in the town of Pine Valley.

[94] Gregory and Cunningham, op. cit., I, 181–182, 224.

state of Wisconsin. The river originates in Ashland County and flows into the Mississippi River at the lower end of Lake Pepin. The Flambeau, Jump, Yellow, and Eau Claire Rivers on the east and the Red Cedar on the west are the Chippewa's largest tributaries. The counties drained by these waterways and which developed chiefly through the importance of the lumber industry are Eau Claire, Chippewa, Dunn, and Barron; Sawyer, carved from Chippewa and Ashland Counties in 1883 and Rusk, taken from Chippewa in 1901.

Logging and sawmill operations began on the Chippewa in 1836 and centered at Chippewa Falls. By 1850 Eau Claire, situated about twelve miles below Chippewa Falls where the Eau Claire enters the Chippewa River, had developed a thriving lumbering industry. Eau Claire by 1890 was the site for five prosperous lumber companies in addition to a number of smaller firms. Irishmen in the four counties of this region were more numerous than in the Black River Valley. There were 565 in Eau Claire by 1880 and 250 in Dunn. By 1890 Chippewa County contained 500 and Barron County (Dallas in 1860) only 115.

Although lumbering usually was not a cause of migration into Wisconsin and ranked second in importance to land as a natural resource, nevertheless it seems to have been the chief factor in drawing people to Chippewa Falls and the surrounding territory. The Irish and a number of Scotch-Irish families followed the French to the Chippewa Valley, many of them coming through Canada and some by way of the New England States.[95] The 1850 census indicates a few Irishmen engaged in the lumbering industry, 3 as lumbermen, one as a raftsman, one a shingle maker, and 36 as laborers among a total of 52 Irish-born inhabitants. The 1860 census, however, is not so revealing unless one concludes that at least some of the 35 laborers were engaged in lumbering. Individual biographies of Irish-born residents of Chippewa Falls give evidence that this nationality was represented

---

[95] Gregory and Cunningham, *op. cit.*, II, 873. Charles M. Scanlan, "History of the Irish in Wisconsin," *loc. cit.*, pp. 238-239. For statistics on the Irish population *cf.* Appendix, p. 294, Table 53.

Irishmen in Central and Northern Wisconsin

in the industry.[96] Although Irishmen were a minority, nevertheless record books, contracts, and correspondence reveal their presence as laborers in logging camps, on construction projects, in sawmills, as raftsmen, and as managers of logging camps.[97]

The number of Irishmen in Chippewa County continued to increase after 1860, the largest gain, 315, occurring between 1860 and 1870. Eighty-three per cent of this increase centered in Chippewa Falls and the towns surrounding it: Wheaton, Lafayette, Anson, and Eagle Point. In 1870 the 140 Irish-born residents of Chippewa Falls constituted one-third of the total Irish population of the county. Seventy-five were laborers, at least 20 of whom were working in the Union Lumber Company's sawmill; 4 were raft pilots and Irish craftsmen numbered 12. In the town of Lafayette where approximately 80 Irishmen were located there were 10 Irish-born farmers and about 20 sawmill laborers among 170 Norwegians and Canadians. A sawmill proprietor and two log drivers were also Irish-born.

Eau Claire County's Irish population in 1860 was located almost entirely in the western half of the county.[98] Thirty-five of them were farmers, 10 farm laborers, and 10 craftsmen, while there were 4 sawyers and more than 40 laborers in the lumbering industry. In 1870, also, approximately 90 per cent of the Irish-born inhabitants of Eau Claire County were situated in the western portion of the county. Within this area seventy-five Irishmen were employed in some phase of the lumbering industry: 40 in the sawmills, 30 on the river, and the remaining as lumbermen and loggers. Nearly 60 Irishmen were working on railroad construction under three Irish contractors.

Mill work in Dunn County on the Red Cedar and Eau Galle Rivers in 1860 employed almost 90 Irishmen.[99] In the town of Menomonie there were over 300 mill laborers of whom 55 were

---

[96] *Diamond Jubilee Souvenir and History of Notre Dame Church, Chippewa Falls, Wisconsin, 1856-1931*, pp. 115-116, 117, 129, 130-131, 135-136, 145, contains biographies of Michael Hogan, James Nolan, John L. Rooney, Bartholomew and John Rooney, Arthur Gough, and Patrick M. Agnew.

[97] Eau Claire Public Library, Bartlett Collection.

[98] *Cf.* Appendix, p. 293, Table 51.

[99] *Cf.* Appendix, p. 295, Table 54.

Irishmen in Central and Northern Wisconsin 117

Irish-born and the others were chiefly Norwegian, German, and French. It is interesting to note that among these Irish mill hands none was listed in the 1860 census with wife and family and therefore were evidently unmarried men. Of the 40 Irish-born inhabitants in the town of Eau Galle 20 were mill laborers. As in the town of Menomonie the majority of these were unmarried men. Sawyer and Washburn Counties, created in 1883, north of the Chippewa region had by 1890 Irish populations of only 24 and 20 respectively.

The most western lumbering region lay in the valley of the St. Croix River. Here on the Minnesota-Wisconsin border, men of the former state took the lead in developing the lumber industry. The counties most affected were Polk, St. Croix, Pierce, Douglas, and Ashland.

Polk County north of St. Croix never had a large Irish population. Eighty Irish-born inhabitants in 1860 within a population of 1,400 had increased by about 45 in twenty years. St. Croix Falls was the chief sawmill center within the county and contained 45 Irishmen. In the town of St. Croix Falls the Irishmen were engaged in farming, not lumbering, unless the latter was for them a part-time occupation. The one Irish-born lumberman in the county, however, was located here. A few Irish families had located in each of the towns of Osceola and Farmington by 1860 and aside from two carpenters all were farmers.

Pierce County's Irish-born inhabitants in 1860 were also chiefly engaged in farming, although some few were doing work in connection with the lumbering industry as millhands, sawyers, and raftsmen. The most northern of the counties along the St. Croix River is Burnett whose population by 1880 totaled 3,140. Fifty of these were Irish-born. By 1890 only six Irish-born inhabitants remained.

Lumbering continued to be one of the most important industries in the state until the turn of the century. The Weyerhauser interests gained control during the last twenty years of the 1800's, finally exhausting the Chippewa region by 1910.

Douglas, Bayfield, and Ashland, the most northwestern counties in Wisconsin, were very sparsely populated in 1860 with only a few Irishmen in each.[100] By 1890 Irishmen numbered 330 in Douglas, 100 in Bayfield, and 540 in Ashland.[101] The population of Bayfield almost doubled during the last ten years of the century while that in Douglas more than doubled. The number of Irishmen in Douglas County also more than doubled but in Bayfield only increased by about 40. Ashland's Irish-born population declined by more than 300 during the decade after 1890, but more than 100 of these were located in Iron County, carved from Ashland in 1893. In Douglas County, 630 of the 685 Irish-born inhabitants were located in the city of Superior in 1900. They had been drawn to the city chiefly to work at the ore docks.

Although in Wisconsin until after 1900 the lumber industry is credited with having employed more laborers than any other single industry it is difficult to ascertain, at least in 1860, whether this applies to the Irish-born inhabitants of the state. Fries estimates that lumbering used the labor of over 2,000 workers in 1860.[102] This comparison excludes agricultural laborers who numbered 31,472 in 1860 among whom were more than 2,400 Irish-born. Native Irishmen employed as millhands numbered approximately 200, and so did Irish-born laborers who were specifically termed "railroad laborers" in the census.[103] There is little doubt that both numbers are short of the actual figures because the assistant marshals frequently were not specific in indicating the type of labor in which individuals were engaged. Knowledge of the industrial activity in a locality often must be used to ascertain in what industry the labor was being expended. Use of this method does not produce accurate results but merely a rough estimate. The mining industry in 1860 employed 360 Irishmen. This number

---

[100] Bayfield was called La Pointe in 1860. Ashland included Iron County until 1893.

[101] *Cf.* Appendix, pp. 296-297, Tables 57, 58, 59.

[102] Fries, *op. cit.*, p. 206.

[103] These 200 railroad laborers were actually employed in railroad work, not in the construction of new railroads. This is evident from the fact that only small numbers of laborers are designated as such in the 1860 census and usually were located where the railroad had already been built. These 200 railroad laborers do not include Irishmen in positions on the road, such as section masters, engineers, station agents, and conductors.

does not include the teamsters or laborers in the region who were probably employed by the mining industry but not specifically designated as such in the census which also does not distinguish between mine owners and laborers within the mines.

Agriculture, however, was the most important industry of the state. By 1850 lead mining had begun to give way to farming and the settlement of the state progressing westward and northward was chiefly agricultural. Like mining in the southwest lumbering became an important natural resource in the north, but it never superseded agriculture.

Likewise, more Irishmen were engaged in agriculture than in any other industry. In 1850, Irish-born farmers in Wisconsin numbered approximately 4,400. By 1860 agriculture had become the occupation of approximately 12,900 Irish-born settlers in the state; 10,500 were owners or proprietors of farms and 2,400 were engaged as farm laborers. The increase of Irishmen in agriculture was much greater numerically and proportionately during these ten years than that among common laborers who numbered 3,200 in 1850 and totaled about 6,200 in 1860. About 200 railroad laborers and approximately the same number of millhands are included in this total. The decline of the mining industry is indicated by the decrease in Irish miners from 670 to 360.

It is generally stated that Irish immigrants into the United States flocked to the cities. This is true of most of those who entered before the Civil War. They usually were compelled to seek employment within or near the port of entry because of their immediate poverty. A recent study, however, by analysis of New York City's vital statistics, refutes this supposition in connection with the Irish immigration after the Civil War.[104] It seems that force of circumstances, therefore, was the most important reason for so many urban Irishmen. Those who migrated westward, especially to Wisconsin, did not, as a matter of course, settle in the cities.

There are several reasons for this. During the twenty years between 1840 and 1860, when the heaviest Irish immigration occurred into Wisconsin, there were few locations which merited

---

[104] Fitzpatrick, *op. cit.*

the title of city. Hence, the urban population of the state was small.[105] In 1850 Milwaukee, Racine, Kenosha, Janesville, and Sheboygan were the only cities of Wisconsin and by 1860 there were 13 whose population totaled 104,861, or 14 per cent of the entire population within the state.[106] Since cities were few there was less opportunity for Irish immigrants to locate in them.

Secondly, many of the Irish immigrants had worked their way West or had depleted their meager funds by the time they had arrived in Wisconsin. Although a portion of these located in the cities, they found that the number of laborers often exceeded the demand. Many, therefore, were forced to find work in sawmills or lumber camps, or on such projects as railroad construction and river improvement in order to maintain themselves and finally save sufficient money to settle on the land. These laborers were usually not found in the cities of 1850 and 1860, for railroads were built across the vast expanses of sparsely settled agricultural areas. Frequently it would be there that the assistant marshal in taking the census found them. Neither were sawmills usually located in cities in those early years, nor did work on the Fox River improvement draw Irishmen to urban areas.

A third reason for the location of Irishmen outside the urban areas is attributed to the fact that many of them migrated with the definite purpose of taking up farming. Not only did many of them undergo the hardships of clearing and breaking the land

---

[105] A city may be defined as a municipal corporation within a definite area having a population of 2,500 or more.

[106] The total population of these five cities of 1850 was 34,477, or 11 per cent of the total population of the state. The population of Sheboygan and Janesville as part of this total includes the entire population of the towns of Sheboygan and Janesville in 1850, but the small population outside the city probably was not large enough to cause too great a change in the total. The 11 per cent, therefore, may be a little larger than actually was the case. Regardless of this fact, the purpose is served. The incorporation of these municipalities of 1850 and 1860 was not verified, but merely the population total is taken into consideration.

The cities of Wisconsin in 1860 were: Beaver Dam, Fond du Lac, Janesville, Kenosha, La Crosse, Madison, Manitowoc, Milwaukee, Oshkosh, Racine, Sheboygan, Watertown, and Whitewater.

immediately after their arrival, but others worked on public improvement projects only as long as necessary to earn sufficient funds to invest in farm lands.

Approximately 4,400 native Irishmen, or 21 per cent of the total Irish population of the state, were located in the five cities of Wisconsin in 1850. Ten years later slightly more than 9,700, or 19 per cent, were found in the urban centers. These figures indicate an increase in urban Irish population of a little more than 120 per cent during the ten years. Since the number of urban Irish-born inhabitants in Wisconsin in 1850 and 1860 totaled 21 and 19 per cents of the Irish population respectively, rural Irishmen necessarily constituted 79 and 81 per cent for the two enumerations. Although the number of urban Irishmen increased, their proportion in comparison to the total number of Irishmen had decreased, while the opposite is true of rural Irishmen. Moreover, the total percentage of increase in the Irish-born population, 138 per cent, is greater than the per cent of increase among urban Irishmen. Again, the opposite is true regarding a comparison between the percentage of increase in the total number of Irish-born and in the number of rural Irish-born inhabitants. For the latter there was between 1850 and 1860 an increase of 142 per cent. These statistics indicate that at least during the 1850-1860 decade there was not a trend toward the cities among the Irish-born population.

A numerical comparison of urban Irish with the rural would be more meaningful if the numbers were divided on the basis of rural-farm population and rural-nonfarm. This distinction cannot be made accurately because the recording of census data by the assistant marshals for 1850 and 1860 was not uniform. Some census takers indicated the location of inhabitants by town, village, and city, but many did not indicate location specifically. Hence, the rural-nonfarm population cannot be accurately determined.[107]

---

[107] Rural-nonfarm population is defined in the census as all persons living outside cities or other incorporated places having 2,500 inhabitants or more who do not live on farms.

Occupational statistics, however, can furnish a basis for comparison of the Irish rural-farm population with rural non-farm and urban. Such a comparison takes for granted that practically all craftsmen and those not occupied in the agricultural industry were located in the cities or in villages and settlements serving the farming communities. In 1860, Irish-born farmers and farm laborers totaled about 12,900, while Irish-born laborers, miners, and men engaged in other occupations approximated 9,500. These figures also reveal that the Irish-born population of Wisconsin was located chiefly in the rural areas of the state.

Finally, it might be well to take note of the fact that, although Irish immigrants moved into Wisconsin gradually and were scattered throughout every portion of the state in varying degrees of density, nevertheless in certain instances they did form definitely Irish communities. In some areas only one or two Irish families were located in a given town, or Irish families within a town were scattered among settlers of other nationalities. The usual pattern, however, consists of groups of Irishmen concentrated within a township, or within a given portion of a township, with these townships often adjacent to one another and located within a definite portion of a county. Moreover, not only the largest numbers of Irishmen, but also the greatest percentage were situated in southern Wisconsin. In 1860 the counties in which Irish-born inhabitants had reached their highest numbers contained 37,190 Irishmen, or 7 per cent of the population of those counties. The area of Wisconsin in which the number of Irish-born had reached its peak in 1870 contained in that year 11,500, or 4 per cent of the total population. The counties in which the Irish-born had attained their highest total by 1880 numbered 5,860 Irishmen, or 3 per cent of the total number of inhabitants of the area in that year; while Irishmen in the region which reached its highest Irish total in 1890 numbered only 2,290 Irishmen, or 2 per cent.[108]

Although this comparatively small and scattered Irish population belonged chiefly to the agricultural and laboring classes,

---

[108] The population total of each of these areas in the given year is: 1860 group, 554,461; 1870 group, 261,240; 1880 group, 229,151; 1890 group, 142,044.

Irishmen did exert some influence on life in Wisconsin. At times this was a positive and aggressive influence occasioned by the direct action of some Irishmen or group of Irishmen. At other times, however, outside forces acted upon the Irish as a group for the purpose of obtaining some specific reaction. As will be seen this was particularly true of the Wisconsin Irishmen's participation in the political life of the state.

CHAPTER IV

WISCONSIN IRISHMEN IN POLITICS, 1836-1866

The population of Wisconsin included not only a large foreign-born element, but also the numerous progeny of these immigrant groups. "Hyphenated Americans" frequently retained the traditional political allegiance of their parents and were approached by politicians as national groups. This is true of the Irishmen in Wisconsin. Moreover, they were to some extent an influence on Wisconsin politics, but in numerous instances their participation in political activity was largely controlled or maneuvered by the politicians of the state. At no time in the history of Wisconsin was the Irish population alone the predominant or decisive factor in a given political situation. This statement applies to politics on a state, not local, level.[1]

Prior to 1836 political activity in the future state of Wisconsin centered chiefly about the election of representatives to the legislative council of Michigan Territory. Following this meager beginning, participation in politics on the part of the people increased considerably after 1836 when Wisconsin itself acquired territorial status. National political influence was reflected in appointments to the governorship: a Democratic president meant

---

[1] There is no completely satisfactory, penetrating analysis of politics in Wisconsin aside from the period of the 1870's covered by Herman J. Deutsch, "Political Forces in Wisconsin 1871-1881" (Unpublished Ph.D. dissertation, University of Wisconsin, 1929), much of which is published in a series of articles, "Yankee-Teuton Rivalry in Wisconsin Politics of the Seventies," *loc. cit.*, 262-282; (June, 1931), 403-418; "Disintegrating Forces in Wisconsin Politics of the Early Seventies," *WMH*, XV (December, 1931), 168-181; (March, 1932), 282-296; (June, 1932), 391-411; "Carpenter and the Senatorial Election of 1875 in Wisconsin," *WMH*, XVI (September, 1932), 26-46. Other sources relied on for this summary are: Alexander M. Thomson, *A Political History of Wisconsin* (Milwaukee: C. N. Caspar Co., 1902); Ralph G. Plumb, *Badger Politics, 1836-1930* (Manitowoc: Brandt Printing Co., 1930); Raney, *op. cit.*; Henry C. Campbell *et al.* (eds.), *Wisconsin in Three Centuries* (4 vols.; New York: The Century History Co., 1906).

a Democratic governor, and the only Whig administration between 1836 and 1848 occurred during the four years after 1840.[2]

Political activity within the territory was confined chiefly to the election of the congressional delegate and members of the legislature which consisted of a council of thirteen and a house of representatives of twenty-six members. Local issues and individual personalities, not parties, usually decided these elections. Democrats predominated in the territorial legislature throughout its existence, for the earlier settlers were for the most part Jacksonian Democrats. Strict party lines, however, were non-existent, since the Whigs and Democrats did not perfect local party organizations within the territory until 1841. The foreign immigrants, principally Irish and German, who increased the population in the lake region and southern Wisconsin, swelled the ranks of the Democratic party, while the influx of Yankees from the East caused the Whig party's increase in numbers and power.[3]

---

[2] The first territorial governor of Wisconsin was Henry Dodge, a friend of President Andrew Jackson and a Democrat from the lead region. He was governor until 1841, when the Whig president, John Tyler, appointed James Duane Doty of Green Bay, who held the office until September, 1844. Nathaniel F. Tallmadge, a United States Senator from New York, was appointed and served the ensuing nine months, but was replaced by Dodge in 1845 when a Democratic president returned to the White House.

[3] The earliest German immigrants to Wisconsin were Catholics, Lutherans, members of the German Reformed Church, and *Dreissiger Liberals*. These last were intellectuals, men of the professions, journalists, and the spearhead of any political action on the part of the German nationality in Wisconsin. These first Germans in Wisconsin became staunch Democrats practically having been driven into the party by Whig anti-foreign attacks. The German revolutionists known as forty-eighters arrived in Wisconsin during the 1840-1860 period and were at first welcomed by the Dreissiger and other Germans. These forty-eighters had visions of a German Republic, or at least a German state, but when in 1854 their hopes were shattered they sought admission into the new Republican party just being organized. In support of the abolition cause the older Wisconsin Germans had deserted the Democratic fold for the Free Soil party, but when in 1853 this political group in Wisconsin became more interested in temperance than in abolition the Germans returned to the Democratic standard. The German forty-eighters, on the other hand, hating Irish Catholics and favoring abolition succeeded after great difficulty in

Many of the Irishmen had joined the Democrats in the East and as such were welcomed by the local party organization. These natives of Ireland were suspicious of the Whigs whom they considered synonymous with the Nativist element and whose very name connoted an English background of unhappy memory. As an immigrant to Wisconsin from the Emerald Isle himself asserted, "an Irishman in America has the predisposition to be a Democrat."[4]

Whig anti-foreignism during agitation for statehood caused the German and Irish residents of Milwaukee to unite in a meeting,

---

getting a German delegation into the meeting which organized the Republican party. In the convention the three German delegates were appointed to the central and other committees. With this encouragement from the Republicans and under the leadership of Bernard Domschke, a radical journalist, the forty-eighters entered the Republican party *en masse*. At no time prior to 1860 was there a general defection of other Germans from the Democratic banner, for temperance and Know-Nothingism within the Republican party repulsed them. Moreover, the anti-clerical forty-eighters were completely obnoxious to the Catholics and Lutherans. These German forty-eighters were not strong party men because they formed the Jeffersonian Republican wing. The only bond between the two party elements was abolition. In Wisconsin when Carl Schurz was defeated for lieutenant-governor in 1857, the German wing turned against the administration and accused the native Americans in the party of Know-Nothingism. The Germans demanded that the natives support the nomination of Schurz for governor in 1859 as a sign that they rejected Know-Nothingism; in this the forty-eighters were unsuccessful. The breach between the two wings was partly bridged when Schurz was sent as a delegate to the national Republican convention of 1860 in Chicago. Wisconsin was, therefore, an exception to the general pattern in other states of the Northwest whose German population generally enlisted under the Republican banner after the Democrats deserted the foreigners in the Kansas-Nebraska Bill. *Wisconsin in Three Centuries*, p. 92, states: "The ascendancy of the Republican party in Wisconsin began when the Germans began to cut adrift from the Democratic Party." This occurred around 1860 and after. For the German participation in Wisconsin cf. Sister M. Hedwigis Overmoehle, "The Anti-Clerical Activities of the Forty-Eighters in Wisconsin 1848-1860" (Unpublished Ph.D. dissertation, St. Louis University, 1941); Ernst Bruncken, "Germans in Wisconsin Politics until the Rise of the Republican Party," *Parkman Club Papers* (Milwaukee, 1896); "Political Activity of Wisconsin Germans 1854-1860," *Proceedings*, XVI (1902), 190-211.

[4] Milwaukee *Sentinel*, October 31, 1846, letter to the editor from "An Irishman."

in December, 1843, with Dr. Francis Huebschmann and John White, respectively German and Irish-born immigrants, acting as joint chairmen, and Richard Murphy and C. J. Kern secretaries. This and a subsequent gathering formed petitions to the territorial legislature requesting that body for liberal suffrage legislation which would give foreigners the right to vote on the question of statehood and for delegates to the constitutional convention. As a result the legislature passed a law in 1844 granting this limited suffrage to all white male inhabitants over twenty-one years of age who had resided three months in the territory. In 1845 because of reaction to this liberal extension of suffrage the legislature increased the residence requirement to six months and exacted a declaration of intention to become a citizen from those wishing to vote and not already naturalized.[5] This liberal measure passed by a Democratic legislature was later embodied in the constitution by a Democratic controlled convention with the consequence that the foreign element felt indebted to that party and became its loyal supporters. Schafer asserts that the Democrats could not have retained control in the first state and national elections but for this enfranchisement of non-naturalized aliens.[6]

Irishmen themselves were urging their fellow countrymen,

> sons of "Erin's Green Isle," to lose not one minute, but go and declare their intentions to become citizens of these United States, and then, according to law, they will be entitled to a vote at the coming struggle at the next town meeting, and for delegates to form a state constitution.[7]

Irishmen not only showed their capacity for political action but politicians early demonstrated facility in taking advantage of this capability. Immigrants from Ireland represented constituencies in each territorial legislature and politicians cultivated the Irish with

---

[5] Bruncken, "The Germans in Wisconsin Politics," *loc. cit.,* pp. 225-238. *Cf.* also, Bayrd Still, *Milwaukee: The History of a City* (Madison: State Historical Society of Wisconsin, 1938), pp. 76-77.

[6] Schafer, *The Lead Region,* p. 86.

[7] Milwaukee *Courier,* March 25, 1846, in *Collections,* XXVI (1917), 216-217.

patronage.[8] This is shown in the distribution of school fund loans between 1848 and 1853 which were granted largely as political favors depending upon the influence of the recipients. Irishmen, who were about 7 per cent of the state's population, received thirty-four, or 13.5 per cent, of all the loans granted. Germans, on the other hand, composed 12.5 per cent of the total population but received only six, or 2.3 per cent of the loans. It is significant that these loans were obtained by the borrowers directly through members of the legislature and state officers. As Schafer concludes:

> It is well known that the Germans of this early period were politically quiescent and tractable; they were not yet trained to active participation in politics and, in a word, did not "count" politically. With the Irish the case was exactly reversed. They were so alert, vigorous, and insistent, so class conscious withal, that it was worth while for politicians to take special pains to conciliate their support.[9]

This effort of politicians to seek Irish patronage was also in evidence at the time delegates to the first and second constitutional conventions and members of the first state legislature were being elected in 1846, 1847, and 1848. Much of the discussion centered around the foreign vote with the two parties accusing each other of attempts to control it. The Whigs conceded that the German and Irish immigrants were "arrayed in mass on the

---

[8] Louise P. Kellogg, "The Story of Wisconsin to 1848," *loc. cit.* (March, 1920), p. 316; Thomson, *op. cit.*, p. 24, states that in the first territorial legislature there were three Irishmen in both bodies and that the council purged itself of any taint of Nativism by electing Henry S. Baird, a native Irishman, to the position of president. Madison *Wisconsin Argus*, February 2, 1847, listed the members of that legislature. Among them were the secretary of the council, Thomas McHugh, an Irish-born lawyer from Delavan, Walworth County; and in the lower house: Timothy Burns, a farmer from Mineral Point, Iowa County; Hugh McFarlane, a lumber merchant of Fort Winnebago, Portage County (now Columbia); and Andrew Sullivan, a farmer from Milwaukee.

[9] Schafer, "Wisconsin's Farm Loan Law, 1849-1863," *Proceedings* (1920), p. 189.

Locofoco side," but they attributed this allegiance to the all out efforts made by the Locofocos to deceive the foreigners into believing that the Whigs were inimical to their rights and interests.[10] When the election of delegates had resulted in a majority of Democrats, the Whigs challenged the methods of their opponents:

> In almost every county the whole aim and effort of the Locofoco leaders and presses was to induce the immigrants to band together as Germans, Irishmen, or Englishmen and vote in mass for what they were told was the Democratic ticket.[11]

Another specific challenge of Locofoco methods was made by a Whig contesting John O'Connor's seat in the second constitutional convention in behalf of William S. Hamilton. He wrote:

> He [Hamilton] has had considerable difficulty in getting the illegal voters, who are principally Irish, to come forward and testify. The Loco leaders in Layfayette [County] have done everything in their power to prevent him from getting his proofs.[12]

The Whigs, moreover, were forced to admit that the Democrats had been successful in getting the German and Irish vote.[13] In their turn the Democrats taunted the Whigs for alienating the

---

[10] Milwaukee *Sentinel,* August 24, 1846, in *Collections,* XXVI (1917), 190-192.

[11] *Ibid.,* September 8, 1846, p. 202.

[12] WSHS, John H. Tweedy Papers, Charles Bracken to Tweedy, Mineral Point, January 4, 1848. Hamilton did not succeed in ousting O'Connor. J. H. Lockwood to Tweedy, Prairie du Chien, February 17, 1848, and Allen Barber to Tweedy, Lancaster, May 23, 1848, complained that the Democrats defeated the Whigs in their counties, Crawford and Grant, with the foreign vote by distributing small offices strategically. Barber maintained that the "Whigs have been sadly defeated in Wisconsin by the foreign Catholic vote." In 1848 Catholic immigrants in Wisconsin were about equally divided between German and Irish. In 1846 Adelbert Inama, Premonstratensian missionary, estimated the Irish Catholics were in the majority. *Cf.* Inama to *Katholischen Blätter* of Tyrol, Prairie du Sac, W. T., February 6, 1846, *WMH,* XII (September, 1928), 85.

[13] Milwaukee *Sentinel,* September 28, 1846, in *Collections,* XXVI, p. 203.

foreign vote by their support of nativism and opposition to a liberal suffrage law. They charged that the Whigs before the election had solicited the vote of "the 'generous Irish' and the 'honest German'" but when the election was over they were ready to damn these immigrants.[14]

Seven Irishmen were elected to the first constitutional convention and five to the second, although Irish Democrats had been complaining that they were used for their votes but discriminated against in caucus and rejected for office.[15] In the conventions, however, the Irishmen were not conspicuous as a solid block representing Irish opinion. It was said of E. G. Ryan, one of the most prominent and active members of the first convention, that "he can hardly be considered as an Irishman as he never identified himself with them since he came to our territory."[16] The committee on education, schools, and school funds in the first convention contained five members of whom three, including the chairman, were Irish-born. The provisions regarding education were not strongly debated and became part of the constitution almost as they were formulated in committee.

Consequently it would be almost impossible to speak of an Irish viewpoint or stand on any issue before the two conventions with the exception of the suffrage question and possibly that of homestead exemption.[17] Irishmen were agreed on a liberal suffrage

---

[14] Madison *Wisconsin Democrat,* October 3, 1846, in *Collections,* XXVI (1917), 410-411; Madison *Wisconsin Argus,* October 6, 1846, in *Collections,* XXVI (1917), 489-491.

[15] Horace A. Tenney and D. Atwood, *Memorial Record of the Fathers of Wisconsin* (Madison: David Atwood, 1880), pp. 21, 22.

[16] Milwaukee *Sentinel,* September 5, 1846, letter to editor signed "Semper Paratus," in *Collections,* XXVI, 198. Ryan was chiefly responsible for the much debated banking article in the first constitution. He was chairman of the committee on banking and a member of the judiciary and education committees in the first convention. He was not elected to the second convention.

[17] Milwaukee *Courier,* March 25, 1846, in *Collections,* XXVI (1917), 215-217; August 19, 1846, pp. 221-225, letter of Daniel Fitzsimmons to the editor, Milwaukee, August 10, 1846; September 2, 1846, pp. 226-230, letter of "D" to the editor, Bark River, Waukesha County. The chief basis for differences in the constitutional conventions was the political and economic rivalry which

clause, but opposed to the Whig proposition of Negro suffrage in contrast to five years' residence and naturalization required for foreigners.[18]

> It is hoped that Wisconsin will be no less liberal towards foreigners than the general government has heretofore been. Shall the Irishman be restrained from voting merely because, according to the notions of some, he votes with the wrong party?[19]

During the second convention the issue upon which a distinctly but only partially representative Irish opinion appeared was the principle of homestead exemption. The first constitution had provided that a homestead not exceeding forty acres in the country, or property worth $1,000 in a village, was exempt from forced sale to satisfy a debt. Most of the debate centered not on whether the principle of exemption was to be embodied in the constitution but in which section it should be placed, how much it should embrace, and whether or not it should be submitted to the people separately from the constitution. The committee burdened with creating the exemption article and several members of the convention, including John L. Doran, Irish-born

---

had developed during the 1840's between the commercial interests of the lake region and the mining and agricultural interests of the remainder of the state. This was apparent in the debates of the two constitutional conventions particularly over banking, homestead and debtors' exemption, property rights of married women, an elective judiciary, and suffrage. Democrats in control of the convention split into conservative and radical groups over the banking provisions and other issues. They therefore failed to achieve ratification of the first constitution. A second convention was called which met from December 15, 1847, to February 2, 1848. This second convention, also containing a Democratic majority, framed a constitution providing for an elective judiciary, embodying a liberal suffrage provision, and providing for a referendum vote on the bank issue. The principle of homestead exemption was expressed with provision made for future legislation on the subject. With ratification of this second constitution by the people, Wisconsin emerged from territorial status to statehood on May 29, 1848.

[18] Milwaukee *Courier*, September 2, 1846, in *Collections*, XXVI, 226.

[19] Platteville *Independent American*, August 14, 1846, in *Collections*, XXVI, 321.

delegate from Milwaukee, argued that the matter was a legislative one and that if the declaration of the principle itself should not be left to the legislature, at least the details concerning it should be.[20] During the debate Charles H. Larrabee, delegate from Dodge County, appealed to "the representatives . . . from oppressed and downtrodden Ireland," asking them,

> whether in that unhappy country the principle of exemption has not been monopolized by the highborn, and titled, and the noble. What has been the effect of this monopoly? The people have been oppressed, broken down, ruined. The people now ask to come in and partake of this principle. They ask of us to give them a portion of ground on God's footstool which they can claim as their own, and not be liable to lose it through the insidious snares of monopolists or by the executions of bankers and usurers. They ask that their homestead may be secured to them and their families.[21]

Doran in answer maintained that although many in Milwaukee favored an exemption article the vast majority including the Irish were against it.

> He had consulted with his own countrymen [the Irish] in his intercourse with them and found they were almost universally opposed to it. Those who were poor said it would ruin their credit. They could not get an article without the cash down or a mortgage upon their houses or, if they had none, the security of some responsible friend. Those in better circumstances, merchants and business men, said it would ruin their trade—that it would compel them to be so rigid as to be ruinous upon all business, or else it would place them at the mercy of every scoundrel who might get their goods into his possession.[22]

Garrett Fitzgerald, a native Irishman and farmer also from Milwaukee County, not only opposed inserting the exemption

---

[20] *Journal and Debates of the Constitutional Convention of 1847-1848* in *Collections*, XXIX (1928), 287-288, 295-297.

[21] *Ibid.*, p. 771.

[22] *Ibid.*, p. 771.

article into the constitution but also objected to leaving it to the vote of the people. He considered the principle of exemption wrong as did Doran, and when the convention was told that Irishmen, who had endured the very evils exemption was designed to prevent, ought to favor the principle, Fitzgerald insisted:

> It would operate against the poor, who might wish to borrow or get credit, and he was satisfied the country did not need it, nor ask it. . . . His countrymen never had asked for any law which would enable them to evade the payment of their just debts. They wanted no such assistance; they were willing to pay.[23]

Both Doran and Fitzgerald adhered to their stand in later debate, but in presenting an "Irish" opposition to homestead exemption they were actually stating the opinion of but one group of their fellow-citizens, the city dwellers, laborers, craftsmen, and small business men. The rural Irish as such were not represented in the convention. Two of the three delegates from Washington County, however, were Irishmen; hence the rather large group of Irish farmers in that county might be considered as having been represented. But these two delegates, Patrick Pentony and James Fagan, never entered the debate on exemption and their vote varied where that subject was involved. It seems that they did not oppose the principle of exemption, but they did prefer leaving the matter to the future state legislature. If the convictions of the rural Irishman had been made known there is little doubt that he would have been on the side of the other agricultural homesteaders, who generally favored the principle. One seems justified in concluding that in this instance geographic and economic considerations made the appeal to national prejudice futile.

This cannot be said, however, of the appeal made to Irish pa-

---

[23] *Ibid.*, pp. 797–798. Fitzgerald was answering Abram Vanderpoel, a native American of Dutch ancestry, who was delegate from Jefferson County and, therefore, representing agricultural interests. He, like Larrabee, had appealed to the Irishmen. It should be noted that in the course of research for this study the writer was unsuccessful in attempting to discover a method for determining the response of Irishmen to political matters according to regions within the state.

triotism by the politicians in the state legislature four years later. With the Irish vote in mind the preponderantly Democratic legislature passed a joint resolution expressing sympathy for the imprisoned Irish patriots, John Mitchell, Smith O'Brien, and T. Francis Meagher, and requesting the president of the United States to use his influence with the English government to have these men and their associates released and allowed to return to their homes or to emigrate to the United States. The Whig governor, Leonard J. Farwell, vetoed the resolution insisting that he sympathized with its aim but objected to this clause in its preamble: "with no stain or dishonor to their names, except what English law makes such, that is the loving of their native land."[24] When the Assembly passed a second resolution stating that they agreed with the stand the governor took in his veto message, the senate returned the resolution with an amendment to the effect that the governor was interfering with the free expression of the legislature in a manner not warranted by his constitutional powers. The assembly subsequently passed a resolution similar to the first one but without the obnoxious clause. In this resolution the senate did not concur.[25] The Whig organs immediately defended Farwell's action and quoted Irish members of the legislature in his behalf.[26] M. R. Keegan of Fort Winnebago was quoted as saying that he felt the governor was not anti-Irish, but that the words of the resolution merely stated what is true and "England ought to be told the truth. She would respect us for doing so; she needs us as a friend and would therefore take notice."[27]

Both Whig and Democratic newspapers made much of this appeal to Irish patriotism. As a result, the campaign of the 1852 election in some of its aspects demonstrated an increasing interest in the Irish vote on the part of politicians.[28] Whig papers, espe-

[24] Milwaukee *Sentinel,* January 29, 30, 31, 1852.

[25] *Journal of the Assembly of the State of Wisconsin* (1852), pp. 76, 114, 119, 132, 141, 145.

[26] Milwaukee *Sentinel,* February 2 and 5, 1852.

[27] *Ibid.,* February 9, 1952.

[28] The decline of the Democratic party in Wisconsin had by this time begun, but quite naturally, the change from Democratic to Whig and ultimately to Republican control was not accomplished without a great deal of turmoil

cially in Irish communities, made overtures to the Irish-born inhabitants on the grounds that Franklin Pierce opposed a protective tariff, while all the great Irish leaders favored it as a means of cutting into English profits on American trade.[29] They were also busy refuting the Democrats' charges that General Winfield Scott, the Whig candidate, had given orders during the recent war in these words: "You are instructed not to enlist foreigners, for the battalion of St. Patrick has taught us that foreigners cannot be trusted."[30]

As a positive propaganda effort the Whigs published in their newspapers what they designated as a private letter from a "sterling Irish patriot" of Wisconsin to an old friend in New York City.

> I intend giving Scott and Graham a plumper next month. Nearly all the Irishmen in this section [Southern Wisconsin] will do likewise, and ... nearly all our countrymen in the broad West will do the same. All honest men must feel rejoiced at such a result, for hitherto we were set down as the rank and file of the "great demo-

---

and struggle. With the Democratic party divided over constitutional issues in 1847, the combined Liberty and Whig parties had been successful in sending a Whig to Congress as territorial delegate. Then in 1848 the Liberty party had merged with the Free Soilers and, although Wisconsin had cast a majority in the national election for Lewis Cass, the Democratic presidential candidate, the third party movement had drawn to Martin Van Buren slightly more than one-fourth of the votes of the state. The Whigs had continued to make gains and with the Free Soilers' vote had elected a Whig governor in 1851 but not a majority to the legislature. By 1852 many of the Free Soilers had returned to the regular Democratic ranks. In that year Wisconsin gave over half of its popular vote to Franklin Pierce and the Free Democrats' strength had dwindled to 13 per cent of the popular vote. This election was also significant because, with the exception of Cleveland's victory in 1892, it marked the last national election of the century that polled a Democratic majority in Wisconsin. For an account of the Free Soilers in Wisconsin *cf.* Theodore C. Smith, "The Free Soil Party in Wisconsin," *Proceedings* (1894), pp. 97-161.

[29] Janesville *Gazette*, October 30, 1852. The editor quotes Daniel O'Connell, John Costigan, T. Francis Meagher, Thomas Devin Reilly, and a Dublin paper, all showing their definitely pro-tariff stand.

[30] *Ibid.,* October 23, 1852.

cratic (over the left) party" who were to do all the voting, give and receive all the skullcracking, and perform all the scavenger work of that party, until we began to be looked upon by it as its hereditary supporters, so much so latterly its leaders hardly took the trouble of drilling us. They have adjutants enough among us since they learned how matters stand, but they are a day after the fair.[31]

Results of the election show that this converted Whig had miscalculated.

The gubernatorial election of the next year, 1853, was fought mainly on the temperance issue, a matter not likely to draw the foreign vote from the Democratic party.[32] The Free Soilers and discontented Whigs espoused the cause of temperance in opposition to the Democrats. The latter were victorious over the Free Soilers by a comparatively small margin while the old-line Whigs trailed with a few thousand votes.[33]

The Germans were politically vocal in opposition to prohibition legislation and license laws. On the other hand, although the move for total abstinence among some Irish Catholics gained momentum until it was to take on the proportions of a crusade after 1870, it never seriously determined voting habits. Total abstinence societies were usually the result of the independent efforts of individ-

---

[31] *Ibid.,* October 30, 1852; Milwaukee *Sentinel,* October 25, 1852.

[32] The temperance issue had entered Wisconsin politics from its earliest days and was attributed to the large Puritan element within the state's population. In 1849 the state legislature had passed a law requiring of liquor vendors a bond of $1,000. The foreign element of the population, particularly the Germans, opposed temperance legislation. In 1851 the law of 1849 and subsequent legislation was repealed and in its stead a law requiring of liquor vendors a license of $100 and bond of $500 was passed. *Cf.* Schafer, "Prohibition in Early Wisconsin," *WMH,* VIII (March, 1925), 281-299.

[33] The old Whig party never revived after this election. Rather, the Free Soilers, Whigs, and disgruntled Democrats combined to form the Republican Party on Free Soil principles, organization being effected in Wisconsin in July, 1854. In November of the same year this recently organized party elected two of the three Congressmen from Wisconsin and the following February the legislature chose for the first time a Republican as United States Senator.

ual Irish priests within their own congregations. There is no evidence that the beginnings of total abstinence among Irishmen in Wisconsin were in any way connected with the temperance movement which early (1849) achieved legislation favorable to its objectives. The Reverend Patrick O'Kelley of Milwaukee, who organized a Catholic Total Abstinence Society in his Irish congregation as early as 1841, had made it clear that Catholics did not condemn as sinful the use of alcoholic beverages and that,

> Total abstinence societies established in the Catholic Church are by no means grounded on the principle of the unlawfulness of the use of liquors, or alcoholic drinks, but on the ground of the expedience of suppressing the use of them. This is a matter of caution about which men differ as to how far it should be exercised.[34]

The Whigs, defeated on the temperance issue in the 1853 gubernatorial election, two years later capitalized on the accusation that Democratic opposition to prohibition was used to draw the Irish and German vote.

> Indeed, a Milwaukee Barstowite boasted that they would, if necessary, drench the State in lager beer and whiskey, adding that the one *would buy the Dutch and the other the Irish.*[35]

After the middle 'fifties, Irish loyalty to the Democratic party was substantially strengthened because of the Nativist and Know-Nothing activities sponsored by the Republican party. Nativism, however, was not so openly active in Wisconsin as in many other parts of the United States. The violence of eastern Nativists was not duplicated in the state, but charges were reiterated that popery

---

[34] Milwaukee *Sentinel,* May 18, 1841.
[35] *Ibid.,* August 27, 1855, citing the Madison *Patriot.* The latter, a Democratic organ, unfavorable to Barstow's nomination, charged that of forty-five delegates in the Democratic state convention not more than ten were Americans. "We do not make this statement from any wish to disparage the foreigners who were members, but mention this to show that all the capital Barstow has got, is barreled up in lager beer and whiskey."

would soon rule the Mississippi region and that the pope was ready and willing by a *coup d'etat* to become governor of Wisconsin or president of the United States.[36] In an attack upon the Catholics, the Reverend J. M. Clark, chaplain of the legislature of Wisconsin Territory, as early as 1843 alarmingly reported that the western states were divided into ten dioceses with three hundred priests and more than fifty educational institutions.[37]

Anti-foreignism had been identified with the Whig party before 1854 and, since the Democratic party continued to hold most of the foreign element, Republicans were identified with and accused of sheltering Nativists and Know-Nothings.[38] Republicans, making rapid gains after their inception in 1854, attracted the German forty-eighter political refugees to their ranks. That these anti-clerical German liberals had no other interests in common with Republicans than abolition and anti-clericalism was clearly stated by Bernard Domschke, their leader, who wrote: "Slavery and religion is the platform of the Democrats. How well the two harmonize; a slavery both mental and physical."[39] Deceiving them-

---

[36] Boston *Pilot*, February 22, 1845, quoting a sermon preached in the Congregational Church in Milwaukee. Racine *Advocate*, May 12, 1852; July 17, 1854.

[37] New York *Freeman's Journal* citing the *Catholic Herald*, July 22, 1843.

[38] In 1855 the American party became active in the state elections and claimed a large number of lodges within the state. Because of the many foreigners in Wisconsin, however, both parties considered the outright espousal of Know-Nothingism tantamount to political annihilation. Since the American party did not nominate a ticket, the Democrats and Republicans accused each other of harboring the Know-Nothings within their parties. The American party in Wisconsin declined after 1855 and never again figured prominently in a state election. Cf. Schafer, "Know-Nothingism in Wisconsin," WMH, VIII (September, 1924), 12-21. The exact strength of the Know-Nothings in Wisconsin is not known, but the party was a menace to Democrats and Republicans. During the campaign the Milwaukee *American*, the Know-Nothing organ, declared their party, the American, would support the Republican ticket and the day after the elections claimed that if the Republicans were victorious it was because of Know-Nothing support. The election resulted in a dispute. The first count gave victory to William A. Barstow, the Democratic candidate, by 157 votes; the second count gave it to Coles Bashford, the Republican, by a very narrow margin.

[39] Milwaukee *Atlas*, April 18, 1857, cited by Overmoehle, *op. cit.*, p. 196.

selves into believing that the anti-foreignism of the Know-Nothings in the party was not directed against themselves, the forty-eighters supported and abetted the party's anti-Catholic propaganda and its attacks upon religion. When formation of a separate political party was being considered by the Germans as an antidote to the Know-Nothing anti-foreignism, Domschke fought the idea on the grounds that such a move would unite the forty-eighters with the hated Irish Catholics. He asserted:

> The idea of forming a union of foreigners against Nativism is wholly wrong and destroys the possibility of any influence on our part; it would drive us into a union with the Irishmen, those American Croats. In our struggle we are not concerned with nationality, but with principles; we are for liberty and against union with Irishmen, who stand nearer barbarism and brutality than civilization and humanity. The Irish are our natural enemies, not because they are Irishmen, but because they are the truest guards of Popery.[40]

The charge of Know-Nothingism was used effectively against the Republicans in subsequent years in order to hold the Irish and non-forty-eighter Germans to their Democratic allegiance. Schafer observes that,

> of the various political forces operative in this state, which enabled the Democratic party to weather the storms of the Civil War and come out so nearly victorious in 1876, doubtless the purely negative force of "Nativism," influencing the loyalty of foreigners to the Democracy, was the most important.[41]

Shortly before the Civil War the questions of slavery and states' rights were brought forcibly before the people in Wisconsin's runaway slave case similar to that which evoked the Dred Scott de-

---

[40] Bruncken, "Political Activities of the Wisconsin Germans," *loc. cit.*, p. 197, citing the Manitowoc Wisconsin *Demokrat*, August 17, 1854.
[41] *Ibid.*, p. 21.

cision.[42] Under the leadership of Governor Alexander W. Randall, the Republicans in power, advocating states' rights on the issue, defied the Federal authorities. Wisconsin courts, including the state Supreme Court, upheld their defiance and declared the Fugitive Slave Act void and unconstitutional.

The position of Wisconsin Irishmen regarding the case was represented in the stand taken by Captain Garrett Barry and the Union Guards who, as has been seen, were loyal to the Federal government. Because of their attitude toward the case and their adherence to the Democratic party, the Irish were accused of being pro-slavery, but when the Civil War broke out they pledged their loyalty to the North.[43]

This does not mean that Irishmen as Democrats were not critical in their attitude toward the Republican administration and the conduct of the war. American and Irish Democrats were instrumental in instigating the opposition expressed in the German Democratic press. Although among the foreign element the Germans were strongest in their resistance to the draft, some Irishmen in the rural areas of the lake counties and southwestern region also resisted.[44] In Milwaukee, where feeling ran high and

---

[42] The case involved a Negro slave, Joshua Glover who, having escaped from his master in Missouri in 1852, was found in 1854 working in a mill in Racine. Glover was arrested on March 10 and taken to the Milwaukee county jail. In Racine, an abolitionist center, a public meeting declared the Fugitive Slave Act repealed, and one hundred men went to Milwaukee by boat to release the runaway slave. In Milwaukee Sherman M. Booth had been rousing the citizens who mobbed the jail and effected Glover's escape. The Federal authorities instituted proceedings against Booth, but were constantly thwarted by the Wisconsin courts. By March, 1859, Booth had been arrested three times by the Federal authorities only to have been released defiantly as many times by the state. In March, 1860, Booth was rearrested and finally pardoned in March, 1861, by President Buchanan. Vroman Mason, "The Fugitive Slave Law in Wisconsin," *Proceedings* (1895), pp. 117-144.

[43] Milwaukee *Sentinel,* March 13, 1860. For Barry and the Union Guards cf. *supra,* p. 54.

[44] Schafer, *Four Wisconsin Counties,* p. 162, cites Edward G. Ryan's "Address to the People, by the Democracy of Wisconsin, September 3, 1862," as an example of the critical attitude of the Irish. Ryan later became chief justice of the Wisconsin Supreme Court, 1874-1880.

their loyalty was being challenged, the Irish held one of their mass meetings in 1862. The resolutions and stirring speeches of prominent Milwaukee Irishmen left no doubt concerning their motives. They might criticize the Republican administration, but their loyalty to the Northern cause could not be questioned. Was not the South basing its hopes on English assistance? To them the rebellion was the resurrected spirit of the British aristocracy which had been laid out a corpse at the Revolution. "This rebellion is England, but it is not England open armed, but England in her own masked, assassin, slimy, serpentine character."[45]

Wisconsin Irishmen were among the first to enter the Union army. With J. O'Rourke as captain the Montgomery Guards of Milwaukee, one hundred strong, formed part of the famous Iron Brigade.[46] Irish action also resulted in the formation of an Irish regiment, the Wisconsin Seventeenth, in the spring of 1862.[47] John L. Doran of Milwaukee was appointed colonel and the Mulligan Guards of Kenosha under Captain Hugh McDermott was the first company to go into camp near Madison. Inability of the governor to pay the troops before they left Camp Randall for St. Louis, Missouri, caused trouble, but finally the regiment reached the South and acquitted itself well in battle.[48]

---

[45] Milwaukee *Sentinel*, August 12, 1862.
[46] *Catholic Citizen*, December 13, 1919.
[47] The companies which formed the Wisconsin Seventeenth were: Mulligan Guards of Kenosha, Corcoran Guards of Sheboygan, Emmett Guards of Dodge, French Mountaineers of Brown, Doran Guards of Outagamie, Watertown Infantry of Jefferson, Sauk County Union Guards, Jackson Guards of Juneau County, Fond du Lac Guards, Harvey Guards of Dodge, Oconto Rifles of Oconto, Peep O'Day Boys of Racine, and Milwaukee Badgers of Milwaukee. *Cf. WSHS, Correspondence of Wisconsin Volunteers, 1861-1865*, VI, 25.
[48] William De Loss Love, *Wisconsin in the War of the Rebellion: A History of All Regiments and Batteries the State Has Sent to the Field* (Chicago: Church and Goodman, 1866), pp. 493-516, 595, 644, 649, 653, 657, 699, 717, 731, 735, 959, 964, 984-986. A few days after its organization the seventeenth regiment was ordered to move from Camp Randall to St. Louis. A portion of the regiment refused to entrain because they had not been paid their wages. They became insubordinate and roamed the streets of Madison with their knapsacks and guns causing some anxiety to the inhabitants. Help

The formation of the Irish regiment served to stimulate a group consciousness among the Irishmen of the state which was not existent prior to this time. Irishmen in local areas had maintained a certain national consciousness, but they were so scattered throughout Wisconsin that there was little *esprit de corps* on a state level, politically or otherwise. Irishmen in the seventeenth regiment met their fellow-citizens from other parts of the state and besides the bond of nationality, closer ties of comradeship were formed through the mutual suffering of hardships and danger in a common cause. As a result the Irish of the state became politically more self-conscious, thus precipitating a more united action on their part when the Fenian movement roused their Irish ire against England and their political ire against those who stood in the way of their success.

At the close of the Civil War in 1865 when Fenian leaders in the United States felt that circumstances pointed to the opportune time for their proposed invasion of Canada, Wisconsin Irishmen joined the cause. Anti-British sentiment in the United States was high and the several hundred thousand Irish-born and Irish-American soldiers discharged from the victorious Northern army were already drilled and trained.[49] Efforts on the part of the national leaders to organize Irish military companies and circles of the Fenian Brotherhood throughout the states had been felt in Milwaukee as early as 1859.[50] Information on Fenian activity in these early days is scarce, but that there was some participation in the movement is evidenced by the fact that in 1863 Jeremiah Quinn, head of the Fenians in Milwaukee, called a meeting to elect delegates to the first Fenian convention which met in Chicago on

---

from Chicago and Milwaukee resulted in forcing the troops to leave. Practically all of the regiment was Irish excepting the company from Oconto and Green Bay called the French Mountaineers. Some Americans, Germans, and Indians were also among the regiment's recruits. For the thirteen companies and their captains *cf.* WSHS, Correspondence of Wisconsin Volunteers, *loc. cit.* This source is a series of volumes containing newspaper accounts and letters appearing in newspapers from the men of the various regiments.

[49] D'Arcy, *op. cit.*, pp. 61-64.
[50] *Ibid.*, pp. 15, 16.

November 3, 1863.[51] Wisconsin Irishmen took an active part in the convention's proceedings and Jeremiah Quinn was appointed state Centre, the principal executive position on a state level.[52] Fenian leaders and organizers visited Milwaukee and other parts of the state during the years 1864 and 1865. By March, 1866, the Wisconsin Fenians were boasting twenty "circles" with more than 6,000 members.[53] The Brotherhood in Milwaukee reflected the dissension in the national ranks when in March the Sweeney Circle was organized which endorsed the William R. Roberts faction. E. D. Burke became its president. The Wolf Tone Circle under Jeremiah Quinn remained loyal to the John O'Mahony group.[54] Wisconsin Irishmen contributed money and men to the cause,[55] and when Canada was invaded in early June, 1866, armed Wisconsin Fenians were heading for Milwaukee and Chicago. The first Wisconsin Irish regiment to arrive in Chicago reportedly numbered 811 men under the command of Colonel John Delahunt, a Civil War veteran of the Wisconsin Irish regiment.[56]

---

[51] Milwaukee *Sentinel*, October 27, 1863. *Cf.* also, B. J. Blied, *Catholics and the Civil War* (Milwaukee, 1945), p. 136, n. 22.

[52] Boston *Pilot*, November 21, 1863. Daniel Carmody was elected third vice-president of the organization and Bartholomew O'Neill acted as Wisconsin representative on the Committee on Constitution and By-laws.

[53] Milwaukee *Sentinel*, March 15, 1866; Madison *Capitol*, March 20, 1866; Baraboo *Republic*, March 21, 1866. Research reveals that by the time the attack on Canada in the summer of 1866 took place Fenian circles had been organized in at least the following places: Whitewater, Milwaukee (2 circles), Fond du Lac, Stevens Point, Baraboo, Beaver Dam, Watertown, Racine, Manitowoc, Appleton, Oshkosh, Madison, Portage, La Crosse, Sparta, Janesville, Waukesha, Muskego, Horicon, Prairie du Chien, Green Bay, and Oconto. Fenian Sisterhoods were also organized.

[54] Milwaukee *News*, January 25, February 2, March 16, 1866.

[55] CUA, O'Mahony Papers, a bond book and a number of incomplete accounts indicate bonds purchased and dues paid by Wisconsin Fenians. *Cf.* also, Milwaukee *Daily Wisconsin*, June 4 and 5, 1866; Milwaukee *News*, March 7, June 5, 1866; Milwaukee *Sentinel*, March 27, June 4, June 6, 1866; Fond du Lac *Commonwealth*, March 7, 1866; Appleton *Crescent*, April 21, 1866; Watertown *Democrat*, May 10, 1866; Waukesha *Plaindealer*, May 15, 1866.

[56] Milwaukee *Daily Wisconsin*, June 8, 1866; Waukesha *Plaindealer*, June 12, 1866.

On the international front Fenian affairs caused some difficulty to British and American diplomats besides contributing to the complexity of politics within the United States. Instead of supporting their cause or at least remaining neutral, on June 6 President Andrew Johnson ordered the hostilities to cease and had the leaders arrested. The Republican Congress attempted to make the most of the situation politically. Offering pro-Fenian resolutions in Congress and relegating them to committees became the political sport of the day. D'Arcy points out that the first real test of the determination of a large bloc of congressmen to espouse Fenianism for political ends came on March 27, 1867, when Cadwallader C. Washburn, representative from Wisconsin, presented an amendment to a resolution sympathizing with the efforts of the people of Ireland. Washburn's proposed amendment stated:

> Resolved, That in sympathizing with the people of Ireland we deem it proper to declare our belief that the present Fenian movement must prove entirely abortive in bringing relief to that country, and that any encouragement to that movement by resolutions, unaccompanied by force, can only result in involving brave, enthusiastic and patriotic Irishmen in difficulties from which their brethren are powerless to extricate them.[57]

The amendment was rejected. As D'Arcy points out: "Politicians looking for Irish support at the next election were not going to lose that support by casting a slur on the Brotherhood." Moreover, passage of the resolution would have brought matters to a head as far as the friends of the Fenians were concerned. They would either have to supply them with arms or stop passing sympathetic resolutions.[58]

Within the state of Wisconsin feeling ran high. Soon after Johnson's proclamation and the failure of the Fenian invasion, activity within the state mirrored the national scene. While Fenianism was not the most important issue in the congressional elections in Wisconsin that fall, it provided still another weapon

---

[57] D'Arcy, *op. cit.*, p. 242, citing the *Congressional Globe*.
[58] *Ibid.*, p. 243.

to be used against Johnson by the Radical Republicans and was used for all it was worth. In Milwaukee a mass meeting was called June 12, 1866, by Centre Burke, a city councilor. Reportedly 3,000 Irishmen and others attended, presenting the political anomaly of Irishmen boisterously cheering the Republicans. The speakers, John P. Hodnett of New Jersey, McGrath of Beaver Dam, Byron C. Paine, and C. K. Martin vehemently denounced President Johnson, praised the Radicals in Congress, pledged hatred for England, and loyalty to the Irish cause. Hodnett played his role of guest speaker excitably and enthusiastically with an "eloquence that never fails to find its way to the Irish heart."[59]

> When the proclamation of President Johnson had been issued and enforced by the officers of the army in the most rigid manner, the Fenian cause looked dark indeed, and nothing but despair stared the many friends of Irish independence in the face. In that darkest moment, letters were received at headquarters, from the noble Stevens of Pennsylvania, Clark of Ohio, and others, saying, The American Congress will never desert you. We will repeal the neutrality laws, by an overwhelming vote, and if the President vetoes it, we will pass it over his head. The words sent a thrill of joy to our hearts, and I was sent here to speak to you on this occasion. . . . The Irish are out of their swaddling cloths [sic], and now are ready to throw off the political allegiance which has bound them so long. We say boldly and plainly, gentlemen, the independence of Ireland is nearest and dearest to our hearts. We will sustain the party which sustains us. We hold the balance of power in this country, and we shall exercise it, like a freeman, at the ballot box. (Tremendous cheering from the crowd.)[60]

One newspaper account of the meeting closed with this glib statement: "One could see their whole hearts were earnest in the movement, and that the tie which had so long bound the Irish to the Democratic party was broken forever."[61] Hodnett and his

---

[59] Milwaukee *Daily Wisconsin,* June 14, 1866; Milwaukee *News,* June 14, 1866.

[60] Milwaukee *Daily Wisconsin,* June 14, 1866.

[61] Milwaukee *News,* June 16, 1866.

friends addressed other Irish meetings within the state but their reception was not always one of unanimous approval. In Cedarburg, Ozaukee County, Irish Democrats objected to the denunciation of President Johnson and the new loyalty to the Republican Congress.[62]

Democratic organs, particularly those edited by Irish Americans, censured the Radicals' simulated "love for the Irish." Sam Ryan's Appleton *Crescent* was particularly vehement and passionate in its denunciation of the Irishman who would betray the cause by voting the Radical ticket as "one of those men who would sell Ireland's hopes for a British guinea and his soul to the devil for a Yankee greenback."

> By the performance, the Fenians can see how much regard a *Radical Congress* has for them. Why did not the Howe-Sawyerites repeal the damnable *Neutrality Laws* before they adjourned? Why did they not leave the way open so that every U. S. Officer, Civil and Military, should not be bound, as he now is, to prevent armed expeditions from sweeping British insolence out of Canada? Radicalism chuckles over its feat of adjourning Congress without repealing the Neutrality Laws, because it hates the Irish.[63]

A common argument among the Democrats insisted that not Johnson, or any president, but Congress had enacted the neutrality laws. The president was merely doing his "sworn duty." They insisted that the Radicals in Congress were not sincere and had conveniently referred their so-called sympathetic resolutions

---

[62] *Ibid.*

[63] Appleton *Crescent*, November 3, 1866. *Ibid.*, July 28, 1866; contains an example of Sam Ryan's (editor) fulminations against the Radicals: "'D - - N THE IRISH! They'll go with Johnson and the Democrats anyhow. It won't pay to count on them, Fenian or no Fenian, to go any other way!' Such was the sentiment recently expressed by one of the Constitution-Union hating, New England theorizing, narrow-chested radical disunionists of this country. Oh, yes, ye bond-exempted, tariff protecting puritan aristocrats. . . . They care as little for your anathemas as they do for your honied words of friendship annually bestowed upon them 'just before election.' . . . They know that they seldom err in damning you through the ballot box!"

and repeal measures to committees where they would be tabled. The Democrats also accused the Radicals of being too engrossed with Negro legislation setting the interests of the colored population above those of Irishmen and other foreign-born.[64]

While Republicans were defaming Johnson and making overtures to the Fenians another opportunity arose by which both parties attempted to ingratiate themselves with the Irish. Among the prisoners taken by the Canadians during the invasion were the Reverend John McMahon, a Catholic priest from Anderson, Indiana, and Robert Lynch, who claimed to be a reporter of the Louisville *Courier* and not a Fenian.[65] Those two were condemned to death by their captors on October 26, 1866. Reaction against this outrage was not slow on the part of Milwaukee Fenians, for Lynch had been a resident of Milwaukee and had held the office of city clerk from 1857 to 1859.[66]

Immediately plans were made for a rally to voice objections against the action of the Canadian government. The politicians of the state seized the opportunity and original announcements of the mass meeting show that among the Fenians political allegiance was divided. Those loyal to Johnson and the Democratic party were in the field first with a proposed slate of speakers including staunch Democrats: Edward McGarry, H. L. Palmer, James S. Brown, Edward Keogh, Judge Mallory, and others. The Republicans were quick to accuse the Democrats of leaving out the Fenians, C. K. Martin and Burke, because these two were not supporting Brown and Keogh for office. Brown, they claimed had approved President Johnson's proclamation against the Fenians and now was posing as pro-Fenian only to get the Irish vote.[67] According to their creed every Fenian was obliged in gratitude to

---

[64] Manitowoc *Pilot*, June 22, August 31, 1866; Milwaukee *News*, June 14, June 16, 1866; Oshkosh *Democrat*, June 15, 1866; Appleton *Crescent*, July 14, 28, October 27, November 3, 1866; Watertown *Democrat*, June 14, 1866.
[65] D'Arcy, *op. cit.*, p. 75.
[66] Milwaukee *Daily Wisconsin*, October 30, November 1, 1866; *Catholic Citizen*, December 13, 1919. At a meeting of the City Council Timothy O'Brien of the third ward introduced resolutions to be sent to the president of the United States in behalf of Robert Lynch.
[67] Milwaukee *Daily Wisconsin*, October 30, November 1 and 2, 1866.

support the Radicals and the position of a Democratic Fenian was untenable.

A belated "call" for the meeting of November 3, signed by Centre Burke who was supporting the Radicals, was issued a few days after the first announcement had appeared. By contrast it listed the Republican spokesmen first and foremost: Governor Lucius Fairchild, Matthew Carpenter, Judge Levi Hubbell, C. K. Martin, and then the Democrats, expressing the hope that Michael Scanlan of Chicago and Hodnett would be present.[68]

Since the Democratic faction had been first to announce the rally, the Republicans, put on the defensive, accused their opponents of making political capital of the situation, and after the meeting scornfully reported that Brown's and McGarry's speeches were no more than political harangues, but Fairchild's, Carpenter's, and Hubbell's remarks were sincere, lucid, and logical. Fairchild, they reported, had sent a request to the Canadian government requesting the release of Lynch. The Republicans evidently felt that their success during the preceding months in rousing the Fenians to Radical support was being challenged, hence their attempts to throw cold water on the proceedings.[69] As late as 1874 the Republicans were using the affair to corner the Irish vote in Milwaukee County:

> Carpenter is developing great strength here, and unless there is a great change before November you will not be ashamed of Milwaukee County. The Irish just now are very enthusiastic. The reason or one of them is that they know that Carpenter worked hard for the pardon of Lynch the Fenian, and I do not believe that they can be "whipped in" to vote the Reform ticket.[70]

The storm had raged intermittently since June and at the November elections the Republican party of Wisconsin maintained its representation in Congress. Five Radicals and a Democrat,

---

[68] Milwaukee *Sentinel*, November 3, 1866.
[69] *Ibid.*, November 5, 1866; Milwaukee *Daily Wisconsin*, November 5, 1866.
[70] WSHS, Keyes Papers, H. C. Payne to Keyes, Milwaukee, Wisconsin, August 10, 1874.

Charles H. Eldredge of Fond du Lac, were again sent to the House of Representatives. Eldredge considered his election a mandate to work for the release of Lynch.[71] Just how many Irish desertions from the Democratic ranks actually occurred as a result of the Republicans' efforts is a matter for conjecture. It was maintained by the Democrats after the election that as far as could be ascertained the Fenians of Wisconsin had proved faithful to their party. They circulated the story of a prominent fourth district Fenian whom eastern Radicals with money from Massachusetts had attempted to bribe into running against Eldredge. The Fenian, of course, refused to be bribed.[72]

The political furor precipitated by Wisconsin Irishmen's participation in the Fenian movement actually marks the climax in coordinated Irish action on a political level during these first thirty years. It also seems to have been an impetus to more concerted political action during the remainder of the century.

---

[71] WSHS, Charles H. Eldredge Papers, William H. Seward to Charles H. Eldredge, Washington, D. C., January 27, 1867; Hamilton Fish to Eldredge, Washington, D. C., April 15, 1871.

[72] Waukesha *Plaindealer,* November 13, 1866. Endeavors were made during the ensuing months and years to reorganize the Wisconsin Fenians, but continued defeat in Fenian activity on the national and international scene caused enthusiasm to wane. In the fall of 1867 A. L. Morrison from the Fenian headquarters held organizational meetings and again in the spring of 1868 a state organization was attempted. During 1869 William McWilliams traveled through the state organizing circles of the Brotherhood. *Cf.* Milwaukee *Sentinel,* August 31, September 2, October 4, 1867; February 17, March 5, May 26, 29, 30, 1868; January 4, 16, 1869; April 14, 1870; Milwaukee *News,* February 18, 21, 27, 28, 1869.

CHAPTER V

WISCONSIN IRISHMEN IN POLITICS, 1866-1900

During the Civil War the Republican party in Wisconsin had maintained its control and had grown in strength through Federal patronage and the Unionist movement. The Democrats, however, still controlled certain local areas and thereafter maintained sufficient representation in the legislature to remain a constant threat to the Republican supremacy, especially in concert with dissatisfied elements which found an outlet in third party movements: Granger, Greenback, Populist, Prohibition, and finally the Progressive movement at the close of the century. In the post-Civil War period the Wisconsin Republican party became a highly organized political machine under the leadership of "Boss" Elisha Keyes. As chairman of the state central committee from 1869 to 1877, "Boss" Keyes wielded a potent influence over nominations for Federal and state patronage.[1] Another indefatigable, shrewd, and unscrupulous Republican responsible for party victory and solidarity was Henry C. Payne, for many years loyal party worker and leader in Milwaukee, who became chairman of the state central committee in 1888.[2]

---

[1] Keyes was a native of Vermont who as a child migrated to the state of Wisconsin with his parents. He had studied law and had held several political offices including that of district attorney of Dane County and later that of postmaster of Madison. He resigned the chairmanship of the Republican state central committee in 1877 when President Rutherford B. Hayes ordered that no Federal office holder could direct political organizations. Richard W. Hantke, "Elisha W. Keyes, the Bismarck of Western Politics," *WMH*, XXXI (September, 1947), 29-41.

[2] Henry C. Payne became prominent as a member of the Republican National Committee during the campaigns of 1896, 1900, and 1904 and was given credit for McKinley's victory both in Wisconsin and in the nation. Payne, often consulted by President Theodore Roosevelt, also was appointed Postmaster General by him. Payne became chairman of the National Republican Committee when Mark Hanna died. Some Republicans considered Payne a

As elsewhere in the United States the Republican party in Wisconsin became the party of money and business interests. Lumbermen who had made fortunes in the industry in Wisconsin not only subsidized Republican efforts but acted as party mentors and entered the field as candidates themselves. Cadwallader C. Washburn, Philetus Sawyer, Edward Scofield, and Isaac Stephenson were all lumbermen turned politicians. Payne, Sawyer, Scofield, and Joseph W. Babcock formed the core of a political aggregation which typified the influence against which La Follette was to wage his battle during the 1890's.[3]

The only Democratic governor to be elected between 1860 and 1890, William R. Taylor, defeated Washburn in 1873 through a combination of forces. Taylor's victory crystallized the Liberal Reform in Wisconsin which had unsuccessfully backed Horace Greeley for president in 1872.[4] Washburn summarized the situation when he wrote:

> The combined powers of darkness, Whiskey, Beer, Railroads and a sprinkling of Grangers, have been on my trail and are confident of my defeat.[5]

These very forces were active in Wisconsin politics and determined to a great extent the course of political life within the state during the last forty years of the century.

As for Wisconsin Irishmen during this period, the Fenian movement had aroused in them a nationality consciousness which sought outlet in political activity. The increase in the number and activities of Irish social organizations in Wisconsin during the last

---

more capable political strategist than Hanna himself. Payne died in October, 1904. Dorothy Ganfield, "The Influence of Wisconsin on Federal Politics 1880-1907," *WMH,* XVI (Sept., 1932), 21.

[3] For Sawyer and Spooner *cf. ibid.,* pp. 12-20; also, Richard N. Current, *Pine Logs and Politics: A Life of Philetus Sawyer* (Madison: State Historical Society of Wisconsin, 1950). For La Follette's decision to lead the reform *cf.* Robert M. La Follette, *La Follette's Autobiography* (Madison, 1913), pp. 86-90. Ganfield, *loc. cit.,* p. 20, discusses Babcock's career.

[4] Deutsch, "Disintegrating Forces," *WMH,* XV (December, 1931), 168-181.

[5] WSHS, Woodman Papers, Washburn to C. Woodman, Madison, November 4, 1873, cited in Deutsch, "Disintegrating Forces," *loc. cit.,* p. 296.

thirty years of the nineteenth century also evidenced and contributed to this ethnic awareness. Politicians, realizing the potentialities, made repeated efforts to control and direct the Irish vote. Republican predominance in national and Wisconsin state politics after the Civil War had, moreover, an important moderating effect on Irish participation in the political life of the state, for Irishmen belonged to the Democratic party and could hope for little in the way of state offices or political spoils. Some reached the state legislature each term, but it was usually on a local level in areas where the foreign element was strong that Democrats could muster a majority and Irishmen achieve their political successes.

Irish communities on the whole retained their traditional Democratic party allegiance throughout the century.[6] Erin Township, Washington County, for example, was solidly Democratic. In 1860, however, there was a break in the ordinarily unanimous Democratic vote when one Republican vote was cast.[7] This allegiance to the Democratic party in Erin continued. In the 1872 presidential campaign Grant received only 8 votes, Greeley 213 and in the 1875 gubernatorial contest no votes were cast for Ludington, the Republican candidate.[8] By 1888, although the majority was still voting the Democratic ticket, the Republicans succeeded

---

[6] Herman Deutsch, "Disintegrating Forces in Wisconsin Politics of the Early Seventies," *loc cit.*, p. 168.

[7] WSHS, Wendell A. Anderson Papers, William N. Walters to Anderson, West Bend, Wisconsin, August 10, 1876. According to Walters the Republican was John Daly of Monches. Quickert, *loc. cit.*, p. 1101, tells the story that until 1860 no Republican vote had ever been cast in the town of Erin. That year one ballot was cast for Lincoln. The tellers judging an error had been made threw it out. But in each successive election the Republican vote appeared. Upon investigation the traitor was discovered but exonerated. He had become ill in New York and was nursed back to health in the home of a fellow countryman who would accept no monetary recompense for his kindness but instead exacted a promise from his indebted friend to vote the Republican ticket the rest of his life. *The Blue Book of the State of Wisconsin* (Madison: 1862), p. 150, records for Erin, 182 votes for Douglas, 1 for Lincoln.

[8] *Blue Book of the State of Wisconsin* (1876), p. 383.

in polling sixty-seven votes which dropped, however, in the Bennett Law election of 1890 to thirty-nine.[9]

The township of Erin Prairie in St. Croix County maintained an even better Democratic record. In each of the elections just cited the Republicans never polled a vote of more than ten.[10] One visitor to that locality noted their staunch Democratic faith when he wrote:

> ... indeed, I believe, did Joe Elwell, of the La Crosse *Republican,* settle on lands here, these warm hearted fellows would give him a helping hand, although he used to gnash his teeth with rage, and say hard things of Erin Prairie, when he thought of its solid Democratic vote —two hundred and forty, my masters, and not a black sheep or one infected with the radical scab among them.[11]

Much the same could have been said for the town of Holland, Brown County, which never gave more than twelve votes for a Republican candidate, and other predominantly Irish communities practically always polled a Democratic majority.[12]

There were, nevertheless, Irish defections from the Democratic party in the state after the Civil War. The Fenian episode undoubtedly had something to do with this. Republicans, moreover, employed other means to attract Irishmen to their ranks.[13] Some

---

[9] *Ibid.* (1891), p. 248. The Republican voters by 1888 were probably Norwegian.

[10] *Ibid.* (1862), p. 150; (1875), p. 380; (1891), p. 242.

[11] St. Paul *Northwestern Chronicle,* December 21, 1867, a correspondent.

[12] *Cf. Blue Book* for the years 1862, 1876, 1885, 1891.

[13] The Republicans expended more effort to obtain German allegiance to their party. Here they ran into the problem of reconciling the New England Puritan element of the party who favored temperance and Sunday laws with the German element utterly opposed to such legislation. Alexander M. Thomson, *op. cit.,* pp. 140-141: "To enlist the Germans in support of the Republican party was early seen to be a prime necessity in order to insure success, and one or more places on the State ticket must be assigned to that nationality. After Randall was nominated [1857] it was deemed to be imperative that a German be nominated for second place, but who should it be? That was the question. All the more prominent leading influential Germans had already joined the Democratic party, which had with rare wisdom and sound policy given them good places at the public crib...."

effort was expended in playing up the so-called inconsistency of the Democratic party which advocated equality for all nationalities, especially the Irish, but clamored for proscription against the Negro; whereas the Republican party of Wisconsin proclaimed to have settled the question long before to the benefit of both groups.[14] Although the Negro question was their prime political instrument on the national scene it really had little effect on the ordinary Wisconsin voter other than in the realm of theory.

A sign that Irishmen were deserting the Democratic party, and probably also a tactic for drawing Irishmen, was the publicizing of Irish converts to Republicanism. Letters appeared during the 1860's and 1870's in Republican newspapers which were designedly intended to attract the "more intelligent and independent" members of the Irish nationality. One from the pen of an "enlightened" Irishman of Milwaukee, James Tierney, claimed that a political evolution was taking place among Irish people in that city. The overthrow of slavery and triumph of the Republican party had brought many into its fold and there had been a "change of conviction in many households where Republicanism was once scorned, and where Irishmen who voted the Republican ticket could not enter with safety."[15] The Republican party invaded the sacred precincts of the Democracy in Milwaukee's third ward with the organization of a Grant and Colfax Club in 1868 consisting entirely of Irish members. At the charter meeting about fifty Irishmen signed the roll.[16]

In 1872, presumably because of Greeley's nomination by the Liberal Republicans and Democrats, Irishmen of other localities were publicly abandoning the Democratic party at least for that presidential election. Irishmen of Beaver Dam, Westford, Fox Lake, Calamus, Portland, and Elba were meeting at Juneau, Dodge County, in the interests of Republican nominations while

---

[14] Milwaukee *Sentinel*, November 3, 1865.
[15] *Ibid.*, August 9, 1867, citing the Chicago *Irish Republic;* June 29, November 3, 1863; October 31, 1876. Democrats turned Republican were considered by their fellow-countrymen almost as bad as those who lost the Catholic faith.
[16] *Ibid.*, October 26, 1868.

a large group of former Irish Democrats of Madison met to form a Grant and Wilson Club of more than one hundred members. Predictions foretold a larger Irish Republican vote than had ever before been polled in Madison.[17]

Republicans were not just passively receiving Irishmen into their ranks, but with dissatisfaction rampant against the Reform's candidate, wherever nationality could be added to their advantage as a campaign measure they were making the most of it. So while newspapers reported that Irish Republicans were becoming more numerous, party workers were using devious methods to attract the Irish vote in specific localities. In Beaver Dam, for example, where it was publicly announced that Irishmen were becoming Republicans, a party worker reported to his "Boss":

> I think we done more *hard* and *dirty* work in this City than was ever done before.... We lost a good many Irish. ... The *R.R. Irishmen* voted for Coleman.... Thank God it is ours, for a few of us boys have slept with these Irish and Polanders for the last three days and welcome sweet rest.[18]

One of the most common means employed to obtain Irish votes was to put Irishmen on the local ticket as bait to draw their fellow-countrymen with the hope that nationality would be stronger than party lines.

> We were all hands over to Columbus last Saturday and had a good meeting. We nominated our Co. ticket and put two or three Irishmen who will draw some and we think it will help in our Assembly district.[19]

---

[17] *Ibid.*, September 7, 1872; October 17, 1872.
[18] WSHS, Keyes Papers, C. E. Lewis to Keyes, Beaver Dam, Wisconsin, day after the battle, November, 1874.
[19] WSHS, Keyes Papers, C. E. Lewis to Keyes, Beaver Dam, Wisconsin, September 18, 1872. On October 1, 1872, Lewis wrote to Keyes: "Things are working all right so far as I can observe. John Malone our candidate for sheriff is stirring up the Irish. I will draw for that $50 for him tomorrow and I think it a good investment he goes the whole thing."

During the same campaign (1872) Republican politicians were working for Irish support in Neenah and Menasha, Milwaukee, Sheboygan, Janesville, and Clyman by getting locally influential Irishmen to run for office on their ticket.[20] Around Chippewa Falls the county chairman felt that despite their labors the foreign vote would be polled against them. Party workers, however, were not giving up for

> ... all the mischief they can hit upon and something new in a circular ... have very good effect among the French & Irish and the country are flooded of them.[21]

Although circulars were seemingly not distributed as freely in 1872 as in later campaigns, they were placed where it was felt they would accomplish the all-important purpose of influencing Irishmen to vote the Republican ticket.

Persons with some "influential connection" were frequently used to represent Republicanism to the Irish. Thus Matt Carpenter's favorable Fenian attitude during their crucial days made him of value in Milwaukee and elsewhere[22] and Sam Birdsal's former positions as captain of the Irish military company, the Montgomery Guards, and as former Democratic office-holder turned Republican were considered assets to the party when he became a stump speaker in Milwaukee.[23] For the sake of balance in state offices, James S. White of Milwaukee, "a Democrat of mild, harmless type," was urged upon Keyes for appointment by the

---

[20] WSHS, Keyes Papers, A. Keyes to Elisha Keyes, Menasha, October 29, 1872; N. Thatcher to Keyes, October 29, 1872; J. B. Shaw to Keyes, Milwaukee, October 28, 1873; Nathan Cole to Keyes, Sheboygan, Wisconsin, October 19, 1874; J. T. Moak to Keyes, Watertown, Wisconsin, January 4, 1875; S. J. Conklin to Keyes, Watertown, Wisconsin, November 19, 1874; James Bintliff to Keyes, Janesville, Wisconsin, November 19, 1874; December 31, 1874. Much depended upon the local party henchmen; how active, astute, honest, or unscrupulous they were.

[21] WSHS, Keyes Papers, O. R. Deeke to Keyes, Chippewa Falls, Wisconsin, September 9, 1872; July 20, 1872.

[22] WSHS, Keyes Papers, H. C. Payne to Keyes, Milwaukee, Wisconsin, August 10, 1874; Milwaukee *Sentinel,* November 6, 1874.

[23] WSHS, Keyes Papers, Sam Birdsal to Keyes, Washington, D. C., September 12, 1872.

governor to a position on the Board of State Prison directors. The wisdom displayed in choosing a man of his character lay in the fact that even though he had often helped the Republicans in Milwaukee he was "so prominently identified with the Democratic party that his appointment would be extremely popular with the best element in that party, besides being acceptable to the Republicans."[24]

Democratic tactics did not differ perceptibly from those of the Republicans.[25] There was an essential difference, however, in that the Democrats were seeking to retain the Irish vote while Republicans were working to get what they had never previously possessed. Therefore the latter were probably expending more effort than the former. The importance of local issues, personalities, and animosities was not lost sight of by either party and these were often used to cloud the national issues.

> In this town the saloons spawned forth upon me like an avalanche—and although I received 107 straight Republican votes, yet by the St. Paul road importing votes and digging up all the Irish that had not been dead over 20 years, they swore in enough so that Chase got 112 in the town. The presidential election is as entirely lost sight of by them as they know there was no chance for Greeley and the entire concentrated power of copperheads and soreheads was hurled upon me. They paid no attention to our sheriff matter—no attention to Greeley but simply anything to beat "Frank" [Leland].[26]

Money was used to convince some Irishmen for which party to vote. It seems to have flowed more freely from Republican than Democratic pockets. One Republican confessed to "Boss Keyes":

> I want to work ... all day among the Irish of this town.

---

[24] WSHS, Keyes Papers, H. Howell to Keyes, Office of the Board of Public Works, Milwaukee, October 25, 1873. He also stated: "White's father was an Irishman, and he is a good, sincere Catholic."

[25] WSHS, Keyes Papers, H. C. Payne to Keyes, Milwaukee, October 29, 1872; Nathan Cole to Keyes, Sheboygan, Wisconsin, October 26, 1874.

[26] WSHS, Keyes Papers, Frank Leland to Keyes, Elkhorn, Wisconsin, November 6, 1872.

I gave them money last fall and I cannot do anything with them without money this fall.[27]

It must be noted here that there was reason for the interest of both Republicans and Democrats in the Irish vote during these years of the early 1870's. Republican prestige was suffering a setback occasioned by the temperance and Liberal Reform movements while Democrats who had coalesced with the Reform were painfully aware of the desertion of some of their party to the regular Republican ranks. The attempts of the parties to draw the Irish was merely part of the larger efforts to hold their parties together, on the one hand, and to facilitate the division within the opposing party, on the other. The defeat of Greeley and the temporary triumph of anti-temperance and reform demonstrates in the first instance the weakness of the reform forces in choosing a candidate unsatisfactory to both Germans and Irish and in the second, the strength of the party when Germans and Irish were united. The victory of the Liberal Reform in Wisconsin was achieved partly because practically all of the Germans—forty-eighters of the Reform, Protestants and Catholics of the Democratic party—found common ground in opposition to the temperance movement.

Since German Catholics and Lutherans generally belonged to the Democratic party, they were united in their political allegiance, but on the basis of religion little love was expended by either group for the other. Within the Catholic Church the German and Irish nationalities were frequently at odds, and when their religion was attacked from the outside they did not always unite in a common defense. Politicians, alert to the religious situation, and reasoning too glibly from the premise that priests and ministers influenced not only the religious but also the political beliefs of their congregations often acted accordingly. It is not surprising, therefore, to find both parties in courting the Irish

---

[27] WSHS, Keyes Papers, O. R. Jones to Keyes, Beaver Dam, Wisconsin October 28, 1875; A. J. Turner to Keyes, Portage, Wisconsin, August 24, 1875; P. R. Tierney to Keyes, Madison, Wisconsin, December 11, 1875; **Milwaukee** *Sentinel*, November 6, 1874.

vote, also attempting to influence Catholic priests who, they felt, could help the party's cause among voters and candidates.[28]

Nor was it unusual for the Republicans, since they held the allegiance of nativists and the German anti-clericals, to stir up anti-Democratic and anti-Catholic prejudice, reaping the reward in Republican and Democratic anti-Catholic votes. This could be done in two ways: they might demonstrate that Democrats or a particular Democratic candidate was anti-clerical or anti-Catholic; or they might sound the alarm among Protestant Republicans and Democrats of a Democratic-Catholic alliance. An instance of the former tactic was the contemplated circulation of a letter among Catholics of southwestern Wisconsin, most of whom were Irish. The letter, containing an attack on a local Irish Catholic priest and making charges against the Catholic clergy, had been written by the opposition Democratic candidate and had appeared a year previously in a local newspaper.[29] The second method had been employed many times, but the issues were usually not so specifically delineated as in the campaign of 1875. With a kind of prophetic significance for future struggles, charges of a Democratic-Catholic alliance grew out of statements concerning public school support written into the platforms of both parties. To win the support of German Protestants, the Republicans inserted into their platform a clause supporting free education and the public school system and calling not only for the taxation of all for its support, but also for no division of the school fund for any sectarian purpose.[30] The Democrats also pledged their support of the public school system but omitted to stipulate specifically for "taxation of all for its support." This loop-hole pro-

---

[28] WSHS, Keyes Papers, J. B. Shaw to Keyes, Milwaukee, October 28, 1873; J. T. Moak to Keyes, Watertown, Wisconsin, January 8, 1875.

[29] WSHS, Keyes Papers, B. J. Carter to Keyes, Prairie du Chien, Wisconsin, October 3, 1876.

[30] Deutsch, "Yankee-Teuton Rivalry in Wisconsin Politics of the Seventies," *loc. cit.*, p. 409. One of the most bitter battles and subsequent Republican defeat was to take place in 1890 over the Bennett Law, a compulsory school law which the Democrats and Catholics in general opposed. *Cf. infra*, pp. 168 ff.

vided the Republicans with their ammunition. The plan of attack was being considered early in the campaign:

> What do you think about the policy of opening the fight on the Democratic Catholic Alliance against the schools? I have some good material that might be used with effect. It might kick back a little here, but it would be a good point in the interior. And after all, how many Catholic votes will we get in any event? Perhaps it will be better to wait till after the Democrats have spoken. And then perhaps the matter might be presented better in a tract, and sent only where it would do the most good.[31]

The Republicans did include a charge in their German campaign circular that the Democrats had consulted with John Martin Henni, Archbishop of Milwaukee, prior to the insertion of the school clause into their platform. This accusation was followed by a "subtle but irrelevant" comparison between the taxation question and the struggles of Luther and Bismarck with the Papacy. Then came the outright charge that Democracy was in alliance with Rome and had left open a way for a future proposal to tax only those whose children were attending the public schools.[32]

It should be noted that the circular was printed in German, was to be used in Protestant German localities, and that the attack was not launched publicly in the newspapers. Democrats retaliated so as to show they recognized the strategy. The Milwaukee *News* and *Seebote,* English and German Democratic organs, determined to give the matter publicity, printed the Republican circular in English and German forwarding it to Catholic priests and societies throughout the state. Other Democratic newspaper editors and local leaders did likewise, some distributing the Republican circular with the title, "Democratic Supplement."[33] They

---

[31] WSHS, Keyes Papers, A. C. Botkin to Keyes, Milwaukee, Wisconsin, August 21, 1875.

[32] Deutsch, "Yankee-Teuton Rivalry in Wisconsin Politics of the Seventies," *loc. cit.,* p. 409.

[33] WSHS, Keyes Papers, H. C. Payne to Keyes, Milwaukee, October 24, 1875; Anderson Papers, N. H. Emmon to J. G. Knight, Stevens Point, Wisconsin, October 28, 1875; William Walters to Anderson, West Bend, Wisconsin, October 28, 1875.

brought the issue into the open through their newspaper columns and thus strengthened their opposition by making known to all Democrats, including the Irish Catholics, the trick which was being used against them. Republicans had anticipated that a use of the circular would bring more Protestant Germans to the polls, thus increasing their total vote. The ruse was successful as planned in localities where German Protestants were numerous.[34] Where Irish and German Catholics were numerically strong, however, some of the local Republican politicians lost their patience when the party lost votes; while Catholic voters, Irishmen among them, flocked to the polls to defend their faith by voting the Democratic ticket.[35] In Milwaukee itself where the third ward Irish were lining up in opposition, the Republicans resorted to threats of retaliation. H. C. Payne wrote of his tactics to Keyes:

> I have had an interview with the leaders of the irish [sic] Catholics in the 3rd ward, and notified them that if that ward gave over 500 against Ludington, they should never have another cent from the state for their institutions in this city. And told them that we meant business when we said it. We are encouraged by the situation in the city. But we are dealing with a damned treacherous crowd.[36]

The circular caused so much trouble that Ludington himself

---

[34] WSHS, Keyes Papers, J. T. Moak to Keyes, Watertown, Wisconsin, October 28, 1875; W. S. Greene to Keyes, Milford, Wisconsin, November 1, 1875; Ed Coe to Keyes, Whitewater, Wisconsin, November 3, 1875.

[35] WSHS, Keyes Papers, John Brackett to Keyes, Eau Claire, Wisconsin, September 23, 1875; H. S. Sackett to Keyes, Berlin, Wisconsin, October 25, 1875: "That d--d Catholic slur is raising hell here." Frank Leland to Keyes, Delavan, Wisconsin, November 3, 1875: "The Irish nearly all went against us on the Henni pamphlet." Ed Coe to Keyes, Chippewa Falls, Wisconsin, November 3, 1875; William Richardson to Keyes, Chippewa Falls, Wisconsin, November 3, 1875: "That Document you sent me raised *Hell* and set the Priests all to work here 3 in No. and We could not do anything with the Catholics for love or money which we used to some extent." Catholics in Chippewa Falls were chiefly Irish and French.

[36] WSHS, Keyes Papers, Payne to Keyes, Milwaukee, October 30, 1875. The third ward actually gave Taylor a majority of 330. *Cf. Blue Book* (1876), p. 375.

had to do some suave campaigning to soothe the troubled waters: "He is getting up a 'gag' on the Catholics that will work."[37] Since the campaign was not fought chiefly on the school and religious issues but upon other questions which were of greater import, the results of this Republican strategy cannot be measured, at least not in the terms of votes.[38] The Republican governor was elected and the party was to remain in control until the school issue reëntered state politics in 1890. This attempt to insert religion into the political campaign was not particularly consequential nor unique, but is of value to this study in so far as it demonstrates the complications involved in the Irish-German relationship. The anti-Catholic circular was not directed at the Irish, but in this instance they considered an attack on their religion and the Democratic party as an attack on themselves. This was neither the first time nor the last that the religious issue was injected into a campaign; neither did this particular incident mark an end to attempts on the part of Republicans to draw the Irish vote to their side.

In a different form the religious issue was carried into the presidential campaign of 1876 particularly by means of circulars secretly sent through the mail to German Protestants by a Milwaukee German Republican newspaper, the *Germania*. The accusation this time joined Tilden and the Catholics, narrowing the election issues to "Hayes *versus* Catholicism."[39] Irishmen did support Tilden.

The usual report during the campaign amounted to: "The Irish population supports T & H [Tilden and Hendricks] to a man, are making big efforts." Democrats, nevertheless, were becoming

---

[37] WSHS, Keyes Papers, Payne to Keyes, Milwaukee, October 28, 1875.

[38] In some of the Irish towns as Erin, St. Croix County; Shields and Emmet, Dodge County; Westport, Dane County; and Osceola, Fond du Lac County, the vote was heavier than usual and fewer Republican votes were cast than in the presidential election of 1872. In some others this was not the case.

[39] WSHS, Anderson Papers, S. D. Hubbard to Anderson, Union River, Wisconsin, October 24, 1876; William Walters to Anderson, West Bend, Wisconsin, November 15, 1876; Edward Bragg to Anderson, Fond du Lac, Wisconsin, November 25, 1876.

alarmed at the "Cooper sentiment" for Greenback inflation,[40] which became apparent among Irishmen, many of whom subscribed to the New York *Irish World* which was campaigning for the Greenback Party. In some localities Irishmen were organizing themselves into Cooper clubs.[41] Since Democrats knew that Irish votes for the Greenback candidate meant a loss for them, they attempted to stop the leakage by means of speakers and documents. Republicans, on the other hand, welcomed anything that augured a split in the opposition's vote and in at least one section of the state felt that it would be clever and profitable strategy to circulate the *Irish World* among Irish Catholics for "there is nothing like giving our 'coffee out of their own pot.' "[42]

The Republicans continued to use the *Irish World* as campaign literature among the Irish in subsequent elections, particularly in 1884 and 1888.[43] During the Cleveland-Blaine campaign this Irish-American publication supported Blaine and close to election time ran a series of articles on protection *versus* free trade. Irish-Americans were urged to procure the last pre-election number for convincing proof that England would view the election of Cleveland as a victory for free trade.[44] Moreover, the Wisconsin Republicans who had formerly tried the strategy of rousing anti-Catholic feeling to draw out the German Protestant vote made a bid for Irish support of their presidential candidate in 1884 on the grounds that because Blaine had relatives who be-

---

[40] WSHS, Anderson Papers, E. Bragg to Anderson, Sheboygan, Wisconsin, October 1, 1876; August Meyer to Anderson, Port Washington, Wisconsin, October 2, 1876; George A. Halsey of National Democratic Committee to Anderson, New York, October 27, 1876. The national committee was sending out circulars to counteract the Greenback *Irish World*. Keyes Papers, J. W. Johan to Keyes, Cedarburg, Wisconsin, August 28, 1876; O. W. Block to Keyes, Oconto, Wisconsin, September 29, 1876.

[41] WSHS, Anderson Papers, August Meyer to Anderson, Port Washington, Wisconsin, October 2, 1876.

[42] WSHS, Keyes Papers, H. W. Reeve to Keyes, Sandusky, Wisconsin, October 5, 1876. Sandusky is located in Sauk County.

[43] Janesville *Gazette*, November 1, 1884; WSHS, Ellis B. Usher Papers, D. E. Sherman to Usher, Lake Geneva, Wisconsin, October 6, 1888; S. F. Frawley to Usher (telegram), Eau Claire, Wisconsin, October, 1888.

[44] Janesville *Gazette*, November 1, 1884.

longed to the Catholic faith he was sympathetic toward adherents of that religion.[45]

There is practically no way of evaluating the extent of the effects of these Republican efforts during the 1884 campaign. Democrats indeed admitted the desertion of more Irishmen than ever before from their ranks.[46] Despite this secession of some Irishmen the Republican "Irish vote" was considered insignificant in comparison with the Democratic "Irish vote," proof that the effort to divide the vote of Irish Democrats had not been altogether successful.[47]

Four years later in the campaign between Harrison and Cleveland the tariff again emerged as the most important issue on the national level but not the decisive one.[48] In Wisconsin, however, the tariff seems to have been considered by both parties the key to the Irish vote.[49] Besides distributing the *Irish World* and

---

[45] WSHS, William F. Vilas Papers, F. W. Jewett to Vilas, Jewett Mills, Wisconsin, July 18, 1884. Blaine's Irish mother had been a Catholic and his sister was superior in a Catholic convent. Blaine had sympathized with the Irish cause and had shown animosity toward England when he was Secretary of State.

[46] WSHS, Usher Papers, A. F. Warden to Usher, Plymouth, Wisconsin, February 6, 1888; M. C. Mead to John E. Wright, Plymouth, Wisconsin, August 27, 1888; J. D. Putnam to Usher, River Falls, Wisconsin, June 27, 1888; August 28, 1888; F. L. Colgrove, River Falls, Wisconsin, August 30, 1888; Robert M. Crawford to Wright, Mineral Point, September 2, 1888; H. H. Cohn to Usher, Monroe, Wisconsin, September 30, 1888; J. G. Wickham to Usher, Beloit, Wisconsin, September 19, 1888; J. W. Murphy to Usher, Chicago, September 3, 1888.

[47] *Catholic Citizen*, November 29, 1884.

[48] The decisive factors in Cleveland's 1888 defeat are usually regarded as the defection of Tammany Hall in New York State, G.A.R. support of the Republicans, and the large campaign fund at the disposal of the Republican party. *Cf.* Allan Nevins, *Grover Cleveland; a Study in Courage* (New York: Dodd, Mead and Company, 1932), pp. 414-442.

[49] There is no conclusive evidence that Sir Lionel Sackville-West's letter had a decisive influence on the vote in Wisconsin. The campaign had aroused a great deal of Anglophobia because of Cleveland's stand on tariff reduction. His opponents charged that England, strong for free trade, had bribed him into his position on the tariff. The Sackville-West affair grew out of the Republican controlled Senate's refusal to ratify the Bayard-Chamberlain pact, a negotiated settlement of the United States-Canadian fishery disputes.

Michael Scanlan's *Why Ireland Is Poor*,[50] the Republicans sent John F. Finerty of Chicago, editor of the *Citizen* and member of Congress from Illinois, throughout the state of Wisconsin to speak at rallies and political gatherings, especially in localities where Irishmen were numerous.[51] Wisconsin Irish Republicans including Bryan J. Castle, John T. Kelley, and J. Touhey were also engaged

---

Cleveland retaliated with a strong message to the Senate recommending that Congress give the President power to suspend the operation of laws and regulations which permitted the transportation of bonded goods across the Canadian border. The House passed such a measure but the Senate refused to cooperate. This action on the part of Cleveland was loudly acclaimed by anti-British Americans particularly the Irish. Republicans accused Cleveland of merely courting Irish support for the coming election. It was at this point that Sir Lionel Sackville-West, the British minister in Washington, received a letter from a Californian, George Osgoodby, posing as a naturalized citizen of English birth, in which the minister was asked to explain Cleveland's position regarding England. Undiplomatically Sackville-West answered that Cleveland despite his retaliatory message, would undoubtedly, if elected, adopt a conciliatory attitude toward England. The letter, turned over to the Republican leaders by Osgoodby, was published just before the election and the cry raised that to vote for Cleveland was to vote for the interests of England. Cleveland peremptorily dismissed the British minister, but the incident is generally considered to have lost Cleveland the election. *Cf. ibid.*, pp. 428-442.

[50] WSHS, Usher Papers, D. E. Sherman to Usher, Lake Geneva, October 6, 1888. Michael Scanlan was editor of the Chicago *Irish Republic* which he and two others founded as a Fenian organ in 1867. By the end of the same year the paper had become primarily an organ of the Republican party. W. H. Putnam to Usher, River Falls, Wisconsin, June 11, 1888, wrote: "The Irish have been flooded with enflamitory [sic] documents calculated to arrouse [sic] their hatered [sic] of England and consequently change them to Republicans on the tariff question."

[51] WSHS, Usher Papers, John Morrissey to Wright, Elkhorn, Wisconsin, August 25, 1888; Wm. Kennedy to Usher, Appleton, Wisconsin, August 27, 1888; John Harrington to Usher, Oshkosh, Wisconsin, August 30, 1888; J. W. Murphy to Usher, Chicago, September 3, 1888; Andrew Een to Usher, Stevens Point, Wisconsin, September 3, 1888, September 13, 1888; Robert M. Crawford to Usher, Mineral Point, Wisconsin, October 2, 1888; D. E. Sherman to Usher, Lake Geneva, October 6, 1888; John Meehan to Usher, Darlington, Wisconsin, October 8, 1888; Dennis J. Murphy to Usher, Highland, Wisconsin, October 15, October 18, 1888; W. Brawley to Usher, Mauston, Wisconsin, October 5, 1888.

as speakers to persuade Irish-Americans to follow their political example.[52] It was hoped that these speakers would hold the allegiance of the "Blaine Irish" and convert more Irishmen to the Republican cause. Among the Irish audiences they never lost the opportunity of condemning free trade chiefly on the basis that it ruined Ireland and that the United States' abandonment of protection was playing into England's hands.

Local Democratic leaders respected Finerty's ability and urged the state committee to send effective speakers to offset the Chicago Republican's arguments concerning the tariff.

> Now what we want is a set of speakers who will handle this question [tariff reform] in a way that will and can be understood and appreciated by the farmers, men who will bring it home to them and make it savor of the corn field and kitchen.[53]

The Democrats relied almost wholly on home talent; that is, on party members living within the state. J. L. O'Connor, district attorney of Dane County; William Kennedy, state senator from Appleton; and Thomas Cleary, an attorney of Platteville and brother of James Matthew Cleary, Catholic priest and lecturer of Catholic Total Abstinence fame, were among the more popular Irish-American speakers.[54]

---

[52] WSHS, Usher Papers, T. F. Scanlon to Usher, Lyndon Station, Wisconsin, September 24, 1888; John E. Dennis to Usher, Glen Beulah, Wisconsin, October, 1888; Lynn Pease to Usher, Montello, Wisconsin, September 11, 1888; Wm. Murphy to Usher, Briggsville, September 15, 1888; Ralph Hume to Usher, Chilton, Wisconsin, October 10, 1888.

[53] WSHS, Usher Papers, A. J. Kinney to Usher, Hudson, Wisconsin, October 6, 1888; Dennis J. Murphy to Usher, Highland, Wisconsin, October 15, 1888: "We with our home talent cannot withstand this assault and we would kindly ask you to send us some one who can offset and refute Finnerty's speech in grand style. If you have any heavy Irish timber this is the place for him to do efficient work. A man of ordinary calibre would have no business here after Finnerty. We want a heavy man that knows Finnerty's record and can talk to it."

[54] WSHS, Usher Papers, W. Brawley to Usher, Mauston, Wisconsin, September 20, 1888; H. H. Cohn to Usher, Monroe, Wisconsin, September 30, 1888; Brawley to Usher, Mauston, October 5, 1888; D. C. Fulton to

Again in this election accurate estimates of the results of the two parties' efforts to control the Irish and Irish-American vote are difficult to obtain. The information on the election is one-sided since only the Democratic chairman's correspondence is available. It reveals, however, that the Irish furnished a good target for the Republican strategy and that the Democrats were forced to the limit in their efforts to retain Irish loyalty and to win back into the fold those who had left it four years earlier. The sons of Erin, Irish-born and second generation, were being torn between their traditional and yet more recent loyalty to the Democratic party and their ancient hatred of England. The tariff was a touchy question among them as one Irish Democratic chairman warned:

> I am creditably [sic] informed that your Hon. body proposes heading our Ticket Tariff reform It is my opinion If you use any heading of that kind It will loose [sic] us many hundred votes especially among the Irish voters as they are very timid on that point.[55]

Wherever the Irish vote was concerned, moreover, the battle in 1884 and 1888 was concentrated chiefly on the national election. Local issues were at least not the subjects of correspondence. It would seem that the Republican strategy was just this —to obtain the Irish vote through the national issue and to play upon local issues for the German and American vote. As the *Catholic Citizen* pertinently queried:

> In this connection, the fact that the Republican managers are making strenuous appeals to the "Irish vote," suggests the inquiry: How have they met the Democrats

---

Usher, Madison, Wisconsin, October 5, 1888; A. J. Kinney to Usher, Hudson, Wisconsin, October 6, 1888; John Morrissey to Usher, Elkhorn, September 19, 1888; A. M. Valentine to Usher, Janesville, Wisconsin, September 27, 1888; Dennis J. Murphy to Usher, Highland, October 18, 1888; Wm. Kennedy to Usher, Appleton, Wisconsin, August 27, 1888; T. L. Cleary to Usher, Oshkosh, Wisconsin, October 1, 1888; Ralph Hume to Usher, Chilton, Wisconsin, October 10, 1888.

[55] WSHS, Usher Papers, Henry Carr to Usher, Collins, Wisconsin, November 2, 1888.

in Irish-American nominations? It is an established rule with politicians to recognize on their tickets the "elements" for whose support they are under obligations. The Republican State ticket recognizes the "German" and "Norwegian" but fails, and has quite systematically failed to recognize the "Irish," giving some color to the common complaint that an "Irishman has no place in the Republican party."

But there are our Republican managers talking about the "Irish vote" as a distinct political element, and claiming to expect a large accession from it.[56]

The Republicans, after all, did not need the Irish vote under ordinary circumstances to keep themselves in power on a state level. Within certain local areas, towns and counties, where Irish were numerous, however, the Republican party could have profited by converting the Irishmen to their side; hence their efforts in that direction.[57]

In the off-year election of 1890 a political upheaval occurred which placed the Democrats in control of the state government. The Democrats, who were organized under a state central committee as were the Republicans, had worked throughout the second half of the century against such odds as scant financial support and continued defeat; therefore, they had no spoils for distribution to the loyal party workers. However, national issues, particularly the tariff, and local conditions combined in 1890 to bring about a total defeat of the Republican party in the state. This was the year of the Bennett Law campaign.

The controversy centered about a compulsory school bill which had been passed by the state legislature and had become law in

---

[56] September 27, 1884.

[57] There is also probably truth to the supposition that the Republicans, expecting to lose some rural support because of their endorsement of a protective tariff, courted the Irish on that very question. WSHS, Usher Papers, John Rose to Usher, Galesville, Wisconsin, November 4, 1892, reveals rural Irish opposition to one phase of protection: "I was just informed that some of the Irish Democrats of Ettrick were a going to vote against Cobourn [sic], on a/c of him not voting for free Lumber and binding twine . . . it would be undoubtedly good if you would write and fully explain how and why it was done."

April, 1889. The measure required every child between the ages of seven and fourteen to attend school "in the city, town or district" in which he resided for a period of at least twelve weeks in each year. No school was to be regarded as a school unless there was taught therein "reading, writing and arithmetic and United States history in the English language."[58]

The large German population of Wisconsin was involved particularly because Lutherans and Catholics of that nationality maintained parochial schools in which the German language was used if not exclusively, at least extensively. The German Lutherans were the first to take up the cudgels at their synods in June, 1889, and by the spring of 1890 Lutherans and Catholics were demanding that the repeal of the law be made an issue in the 1890 campaign.[59] Popular debate, when not attacking the churches, cen-

---

[58] *Laws of Wisconsin* (1889), Chap. 519. William D. Hoard, who had been elected governor in 1888, took the stand in his inaugural address to the state legislature in favor of a compulsory school law and "advocated giving city and county superintendents authority to inspect all schools and require that reading and writing in English should be daily taught therein. As if acting in concert, the *Sentinel* [Milwaukee] and Mr. Thayer [State Superintendent of Public Instruction] endorsed the stand taken by Hoard, who afterwards admitted that his message was aimed at sectarian schools." William F. Whyte, "The Bennett Law Campaign in Wisconsin," *WMH*, X (June, 1927), 376. *Cf.* also, Louise P. Kellogg, "The Bennett Law in Wisconsin," *WMH*, II (September, 1918), 3-25.

That same year on February 13, in the Senate, Levi E. Pond of the twenty-seventh district (Adams, Columbia, and Marquette Counties) introduced "A bill to provide for statistical reports from principals or teachers of commercial, parochial, and other private schools in the state of Wisconsin and for the publication of summaries of such reports in the biennial report of the state superintendent." From the statistics so supplied the state would judge whether sufficient instruction was being given in the English language and on that basis whether the institution qualified as a school according to state law. Petitions against the bill, particularly from German Lutherans and Catholics, flooded the Senate and the measure was not passed by that body. About twenty-five of the protests against the Pond Bill originated among groups of Irishmen and at least five of these had been instigated by Irish Catholic clergymen. What connection, if any, there was between the failure of the Pond Bill and the introduction of the Bennett Law into the Assembly has not been established.

[59] Kellogg, "The Bennett Law in Wisconsin," *loc. cit.*, pp. 10, 14.

tered chiefly around the language question while the Democratic platform, the Lutheran manifesto, and the Catholic Bishops' statement based objections upon interference with parental rights and the threat to the existence of parochial and private schools. In many cities of Wisconsin, including Milwaukee, the spring mayoralty elections resulted in Democratic victories as the climax of campaigns influenced to a greater or less degree by this issue.[60] During the summer the Democrats not only watched the Republicans line up in support of the issue but planned how they could best use it to put their opponents on the defensive.

Events played into the Democrats' hands so well that when the Republicans devised their campaign platform they had only slightly moderated their proposals by promising to revise the statute so as to recognize more explicitly the right of the parent or guardian to select the time of year and place, "whether public or private or wherever located" in which his child or ward should be educated.[61] The Democrats, on the other hand, pledged themselves unequivocally to repeal the obnoxious law. In their plank on the school issue they maintained that existing compulsory education and child labor legislation were sufficient if enforced; they opposed "needless and unjust interference" with rights of parents and liberty of conscience; upheld the public school system which they had founded, denounced the Bennett Law "as unnecessary, unwise, unconstitutional, un-American and un-Democratic," and demanded its repeal.[62] As a result of the campaign the Democratic victory in 1890 was complete with the executive and legislative branches brought under their control. Of the Congressmen elected only one was Republican. The legislature repealed the Bennett Law when it met in 1891.[63]

The 1890 campaign is an example of the interplay of state and

---

[60] Appleton *Crescent*, April 5, 1890; *Catholic Citizen*, April 5, 1890.

[61] *Blue Book* (1891), p. 390.

[62] *Ibid.*, p. 394.

[63] Substitute measures for the repealed Bennett Law were presented in the assembly by Humphrey Desmond, an Irish-American of Milwaukee, the first assembly district. These became the child labor law and compulsory school attendance law which governed the matter for some time. Cf. *Laws of Wisconsin* (1891), chaps. 109, 187.

national issues in a state election, and also of the difficulty of evaluating the effect of the various forces at work. Events comparable in result to what happened in Wisconsin were taking place in other Republican states with the consequence that the United States Congress came under Democratic control. Certainly if the Bennett Law was not the deciding factor in the Badger state, it was the most publicized issue in the campaign. Although the McKinley tariff and the state treasury issues were actually of greater political significance to both parties, the average voter was probably more aware of the Bennett Law as a phase of the campaign and his voting motivated more by this issue than the other two. This is especially true of the Lutherans and Catholics who felt that the existence of their schools was at stake. It seems hardly possible that the tariff could have effected the party realignment which resulted when the Bennett Law became an issue.[64] The Democrats might have won in any case, but certainly not with the large majority actually attained.[65]

---

[64] Comparisons of vote totals in Wisconsin for 1884, 1886, 1888, and 1890 indicate this party realignment. The votes cast for governor in 1886, an off year, total approximately 34,000 fewer than in 1884; in 1890 the votes cast numbered about 46,000 less than in 1888. The loss in the Republican vote between 1884 and 1886 was about 28,000 and in the Democratic vote about 32,000. On the other hand, the loss in the Republican vote between 1888 and 1890 was about 44,000, while the Democratic votes increased by about 5,000. Thus where the normal trend in an off year election was downward for both parties, in 1890 the opposite occurred in the Democratic vote. Allowing for a lighter vote in both parties, the increased Democratic vote would seem to indicate two things: first, a goodly number of Republicans deserted their party in this election. That Republicans just stayed home is hardly the explanation; and secondly, Catholics and Lutherans turned out in large numbers to vote the Democratic ticket.

[65] Plumb, *op. cit.*, p. 91. Thomson, *op. cit.*, p. 239, states: "The Bennett law issue proved disastrous to the Republican party." The Waukesha *Democrat*, November 8, 1890, observed that the McKinley tariff had as much if not more to do with the outcome than the Bennett Law. Joseph Schafer, "Editorial Comment," *WMH*, X (June, 1927), 458-460, insists on the importance of the other issues, especially the McKinley tariff in congressional elections, for this was the cause for Republican defeats in other mid-Western states. WSHS, N. P. Haugen Papers, W. F. Street to Haugen, Madison, Wisconsin, Nov. 9, 1890, admitted that the Catholics (Irish and German) and Lutherans had voted to a man while Republicans "stayed at home."

During the 1890 campaign Irishmen were in the fight as usual but they were not presenting a united front. The Republicans were trying to get the "'Dutch' Catholics and the Irish Catholics at loggerheads" while the Democrats, since the Lutherans and Catholics had united, were interested in holding the Irish Catholics in line.[66] A number of factors tended to modify the Irishman's position. Two loyalties drew him to the side of opposition to the law: allegiance to the Catholic Church and to the Democratic party. On the other hand, however, Irish Catholics had been contending against what they called the German dominance of the Church in Wisconsin and the rise of German influence within the Democratic party.[67]

In closer connection with the school issue, moreover, was the fact that the German parishes, not the Irish, had more generally built parochial schools. So the school question did not interest the Irish to the extent nor in the same way that it aroused the Germans. Many of the Irish had not only been educated in the public school system, but also had become teachers in the public schools, and quite a number had risen to the position of local superintendent. It was natural, then, that they should feel the need of being loyal to that institution. It was precisely on this point, however, that the issue became confused. These Irishmen along with other proponents of the Bennett Law took the stand that attacks on the law were attacks on the public school system. Typical of the sentiment of Catholic Bennett-Law Irishmen is the letter of S. N. Hawkins, a native Irishman of New Richmond, St. Croix County, to John Nagle of Manitowoc.

> I learn from the clippings from papers that you are in favor of the principles of the so-called Bennett Law and opposed to the Democratic platform of that issue. I hear that you are an Irishman and a Catholic, also the editor of a democratic paper. If reports are true then I believe that you have taken a stand that in the near future will redound to your credit. I should be pleased to get a couple of the issues of your paper containing your views on this

---

[66] WSHS, Usher Papers, Brawley to Usher, Tomah, Wis., Apr. 7, 1890.
[67] Whyte, "The Bennett Law Campaign," *loc. cit.*, p. 384.

important matter. We have a large settlement of Irish Catholics in this county many of whom argue that it is a stab at their religion and who may be befogged into voting on that theory. But I am happy to be able to say that quite a few are getting their eyes open to the real situation and will act accordingly. I am of Irish birth and belong to the Catholic church, but I have been reared from infancy in America and educated in the public schools and I do not now see any reason why I should slap my Alma Mater, but on the contrary I believe that it is manifestly my duty to do what I can to expose that fallacious doctrine enunciated by the democracy in their platform.[68]

As a matter of record, however, the Lutherans and Catholics were not attacking the public school system, but were maintaining their independence of it.[69] As the *Catholic Citizen* clearly stated:

We do not attack the public school system. Our contemporary [Milwaukee *Sentinel*] cannot quote a single editorial expression from this journal attacking the public school system. We are willing to criticize, although we have not done even that to our knowledge. Neither does the opposition to the Bennett Law, Lutheran, Democratic or Catholic, attack the public schools. Does the Lutheran manifesto do so? Does the Democratic platform do so? Does the Bishops' protest do so? The only people who are putting the public schools into controversy are the Bennett Law people.[70]

Mixed with the charges that the public school system was being attacked there was serious and sincere advocacy of the Bennett Law not only as a compulsory but also as a necessary Americanizing school measure. Nagle, an Irish-American Democrat, former public school superintendent in Manitowoc, and editor of the Manitowoc *Pilot,* took a definite stand in favor of the Bennett Law. He became one of its staunchest defenders through the

---

[68] Manitowoc *Pilot,* October 16, 1890.
[69] Whyte, "Bennett Law Campaign in Wisconsin," *loc. cit.,* p. 385.
[70] *Catholic Citizen,* October 4, 1890.

editorial columns of his newspaper and first among promoters of the Democratic Bennett Law League.[71] On the other hand, Edward McLaughlin, superintendent of the public schools of Fond du Lac, put himself on record with the opposition as thoroughly convinced that the law was unjust, unnecessary, deceitful, and dangerous.[72] In Milwaukee, P. J. Somers, an Irish-American and Catholic, president of the Milwaukee city council, former superintendent of the public schools there, also upheld the Democratic party's platform of opposition.[73] An Irish-American lawyer and city attorney of Stevens Point, John Brennan, wrote vigorously during the campaign in behalf of the Bennett Law and addressed an open letter to the bishops of Wisconsin which caused a great deal of comment and discussion.[74] Two other representative Irishmen were to be found in Peter Doyle, Wisconsin Secretary of State, 1874-1878, and loyal Democratic politician from Prairie du Chien, and Jeremiah Quinn of Milwaukee, a former Fenian leader and tax commissioner.[75] The former took a stand with his party and Archbishop Heiss, while the latter supported the Bennett law.

Charges against the German Lutherans and Catholics became so bitter that some Irish Republicans, although loyal to their party and the school law, repudiated such tactics.[76] D. E. Murphy

---

[71] Plumb, *op. cit.*, p. 91.

[72] Manitowoc *Pilot,* July 3, 1890.

[73] *Ibid.,* May 22, 1890. Somers became mayor when in this 1890 election, George W. Peck, elected mayor of Milwaukee in the spring of 1890, became the Democratic governor of Wisconsin.

[74] Andrew J. Aikens and Louis A. Proctor, *Men of Progress for Wisconsin* (Milwaukee, 1896), p. 254.

[75] *Catholic Citizen,* February 15, 1890, citing the Milwaukee *Journal;* October 25, 1890; Milwaukee *Sentinel,* October 21, 1890. Quinn was answering a man named Donnelly who had placed himself in opposition to the Bennett Law as an Irish-American.

[76] The Forty-eighter liberal Turners in the Republican party along with the nativist element hurled the traditional anti-clerical and anti-Catholic charges. The German Turners were aligned in opposition to practically all other Germans in the state along with the Irish and Polish Catholics. Norwegians quite generally remained loyal to the Republican cause.

in a published letter to the Young Men's Republican Club of Milwaukee observed that,

> many very unwise people (among whom are some fanatics) would have your minds poisoned against a very worthy class of our fellow citizens, *viz.*, Catholics and Lutherans. . . . Let me say in conclusion to my young Republican friends, that he who would pour the poison of prejudice into your minds against any nationality or religious body is not only unwise and unpatriotic, but above all un-American.[77]

That Irishmen were divided on the issue and not in complete consonance with the German bishops should not be surprising when it is known that their neighbor to the West, Archbishop Ireland of St. Paul, wrote to Governor Hoard his approval of the law despite the Milwaukee Archbishop's stand against it.[78] Moreover, the death of Archbishop Heiss occasioned further complications. The question of a successor to the Milwaukee Archbishopric caused some agitation for the appointment of a non-German as had been the case in 1878 when the matter of a coadjutor to Archbishop Henni had resulted in a controversy between the English-speaking (predominantly Irish and Irish-American) and the German Catholics. In its efforts to make an issue of nationality for the purpose of dividing the Catholic vote, the leading Republican paper reported a Catholic priest as saying that "if the Ger-

---

[77] *Catholic Citizen,* October 18, 1890, citing the Milwaukee *Sentinel.* John T. Kelley also spoke out against the trend the campaign was taking in some Republican quarters.

[78] Whyte, "The Bennett Law Campaign in Wisconsin," *loc. cit.,* p. 385. Whyte also states that Archbishop Ireland in a personal interview with Hoard was reported as saying: "Governor, you must stand up, I must stand up, all who believe in America must stand up and fight this poisonous spirit of foreignism." In taking this position Ireland was acting in character. For his stand on public and parochial school relations and his Faribault-Stillwater Plan *cf.* Daniel F. Reilly, *The School Controversy (1891-1893)* (Washington: Catholic University of America Press, 1943). For Ireland's part in working against excessive Germanism in the Church *cf.* James H. Moynihan, *The Life of Archbishop John Ireland* (New York: Harper and Brothers, 1953), pp. 63-78.

man Catholics should be victorious in the elections this year, that would be the end of all hopes of ever having an English-speaking bishop in the State."[79] The *Catholic Citizen* let it be known that the salvation of the souls of the Irish Catholics did not depend upon their having an English-speaking hierarchy in the state. "The present object is not to win a victory for the 'German Catholics,' but to inflict a defeat on Know-Nothingism, demagogy and falsehood."[80]

As has been seen there were Irish Catholics who stood on the side of the Bennett Law. But among the Irish and Irish-American clergy there seems to have been the conviction that the Bennett Law, because of the possibility of its being interpreted and used adversely to parochial schools, should be repealed. The Catholic position was upheld by the Reverend Michael O'Brien of Oshkosh in answer to charges made by a Lutheran parochial teacher of the same city. O'Brien held that both school systems, public and private, served a definite purpose and that Catholics, far from seeking a division of funds, were willing to bear the burden of supporting their own schools while at the same time they were saving the state and local governments large sums.[81] The Reverend J. W. Vahey was using his pen against the Bennett Law in the columns of the Dodgeville *Sun*.[82] When the Milwaukee *Sentinel* charged that English-speaking Catholic clergy were opposed to the stand taken by the Germans, the *Catholic Citizen* took a canvass of the priests in the city of Milwaukee and came up with a firm denial of the charge and a positive affirmation that "all the pastors of the English-speaking congregations are against the Bennett Law, and strong endorsers of the bishops' protest."[83]

---

[79] Milwaukee *Sentinel*, September 22, 1890.

[80] *Catholic Citizen*, September 27, 1890.

[81] Appleton *Crescent*, April 5, 1890.

[82] *Catholic Citizen*, September 27, 1890.

[83] *Ibid.*, March 22, June 21, 1890. The issues of July 26 and November 1, 1890, contain letters from English-speaking clergymen opposing the Bennett Law and claiming that the Irish were loyal to the Church's position. The September 30, 1890 issue, contains a letter from the Reverend Mathias Hannon, an Irish-born pastor stationed at Darlington, Wisconsin, in which he pledges loyalty to Hoard and the Republicans but repudiates the Bennett

As the controversy continued and election day approached, Irishmen were warned that they should not allow themselves to be diverted by false issues when they cast their ballots.

> The English language is not an issue. The appointment of an English-speaking Archbishop is in no way involved in the issue of this State election. If either of these issues were before the people, we should take altogether a different side. It is a principle which affects both our religion and our rights as citizens that is at stake in this election.[84]

These lines reveal the position of the average Catholic Irish-American, clerical and lay. It is difficult to see any logical connection between the outcome of the Bennett Law issue and the nationality of the future archbishop. The attempt to combine the two must be interpreted as just another means employed by the opposition to defeat the Bennett Law opponents. A division of the votes of Catholics along national lines would increase the pro-Bennett Law vote only slightly, but would split the Democratic vote to the benefit of the Republicans.

Democrats who opposed the stand their party had taken, formed the Democratic Bennett Law League and many of the members were of Irish descent.[85] The Louisville Catholic *Record* charged that the League was composed chiefly of "Irishmen who are dis-

---

Law in some of its provisions: "On the Bennett Law I think I am sound. I believe it to be a usurpation of parental rights, unwise and unnecessary. I believe that the father is head of the family, and on him devolves the right to educate the child. Now comes the right of the State. I believe the State has the right to compel parents by fines and imprisonment, to send their children to schools where they can acquire a knowledge of the legal language of the State. That the Republican party is inimical to the parochial schools is all bosh, and has no foundation."

[84] *Ibid.*, November 1, 1890, letter to the editor from an English-speaking priest.

[85] Whyte, "The Bennett Law Campaign in Wisconsin," *loc. cit.*, p. 388; Plumb, *op. cit.*, p. 93. The Milwaukee *Sentinel* published names of prominent Bennett Law Democrats in heavy black type as a role of honor.

pleased with the Germans for resolving to defend their race schools." It further charged:

> If the Catholic bishops of Wisconsin were named Ryan or O'Brien, no Irishman would openly come forward in favor of a law which the church wishes to have repealed. But as the bishops' names are Flasch and Katzer, the "haughty" sons of the Emerald Isle probably do not regard them as genuine bishops.[86]

Just what the balance of nationalities was in the Bennett Law League would be difficult to say, but some of its principal proponents were Irish-Americans: John Nagle of the Manitowoc *Pilot*, Hugh Ryan, and W. H. Timlin of Milwaukee were among its officers.[87] Some time before the election the League sent to thousands of Wisconsin voters a bitter and bigoted attack on the Lutherans and Catholics which charged that the two church groups had united against "our republican commonwealth . . . to disrupt our free government and snatch away from it one of the fundamental rights which every civilized and, before all, every republican state claims, holds dear and freely exercises." The circular was filled with unsubstantiated generalities. The League had adopted the Turner and nativist tactics.

> Misled church communities have held meetings and passed resolutions; fanatical bishops have issued bitter proclamations, and the Democratic party has crawled to the Cross. . . .
> Let such an unnatural and contemptible coalition gain the ascendancy and there will be no end or measure to its greed for power. The *Church*, it is well known, has a BIG STOMACH; its craving for power and influence is insatiable, especially when, as in this case, it turns unfaithful to its mission, making politics its business instead of serving God.[88]

---

[86] Manitowoc *Pilot*, October 2, 1890, citing the Louisville *Record*.
[87] *Catholic Citizen*, October 4, 1890. Plumb, *op. cit.*, p. 92, mentions that a large number of prominent leaders became Bennett Law Democrats, many of them of Irish descent.
[88] Cited in the *Catholic Citizen*, October 4, 1890.

In 1890 the non-German Catholic Press of Wisconsin, which consisted of the *Catholic Citizen* published in Milwaukee and the Catholic *Sentinel* of Chippewa Falls, opposed the Bennett Law. The Catholic *Sentinel* was reported to be "heart and soul opposed to any plan which would take our parish schools out of the hands of the Church."[89] The *Catholic Citizen,* beyond doubt the chief Irish Catholic organ in Wisconsin, was not immediate in its all-out condemnation of the Bennett Law, but once the protest of the Catholic bishops had been published its loyalty to them remained unquestioned. The editors were relentless in answering the charges of the opposition, in defending the Catholic position, and in pointing out the resemblance between Know-Nothingism and the attacks of many of the Bennett Law protagonists. Its editor at the time, E. A. Bray, had been accurately described as "a very

---

[89] *Ibid.,* August 8, 1890. Publication of the *Catholic Sentinel* had been inaugurated by the Reverend C. F. X. Goldsmith in 1889 and was edited by him until his death, November 24, 1890, when it was taken over by Arthur Gough. Gough was a native of Ireland with an interesting and exciting background which probably constitutes much of the reason for his independent and liberal views. Issues of the paper from 1889 to 1892 cannot be located. November 1, 1894, however, the editor stated: "Every Catholic should vote for the present state officers. It is a debt due for their action on the Bennett Law." Gough was born in Londonderry on February 11, 1826. After his education at Queen's University he engaged in civil engineering. In 1850 he was appointed inspector of the national schools which position he held for sixteen years. During this time he studied law and wrote numerous articles for Irish newspapers chiefly on mathematical subjects. Gough was admitted to the bar and practiced before the Queen's Bench in Ireland. Also during these years Gough, personally acquainted with James Stephens, Fenian leader, was sympathetic with the Fenian cause. In 1866 he was imprisoned for writing a poem which ridiculed the Lord Lieutenant of Ireland. Shortly after, when given a choice of remaining in prison or quitting the country, Gough chose the latter and sailed for America with his four children. His father, brother, and a sister had preceded him to Chippewa Falls, Wisconsin. When Gough arrived in Wisconsin, he worked first in the woods as a lumberjack, studying Wisconsin law in his spare time. In December, 1867, he was admitted to the bar and in 1869 became judge of Chippewa County. Gough was highly esteemed as a lawyer and judge. He died September 21, 1918. *Cf.* Chippewa Falls *Herald,* September 21, 1918; Chippewa Falls *Daily Independent,* September 13, 1908; February 11, 1912; February 11, 1916; *Diamond Jubilee of Notre Dame Parish,* pp. 135-136.

independent fellow" and the paper had a wide circulation among English-speaking, therefore Irish and Irish-American Wisconsin Catholics.[90] Immediately after the 1890 Democratic victory the editor summarized its attitude towards the Republican party:

> The *Citizen* believes that the masses of the Republican party in Wisconsin are liberal minded men who intended no harm to the church schools and preferred no interference with them. But the Bennett law drew all the sectarian, bigoted, fanatical and crazy impurities in the Republican body (and some in the Democratic also) to a head and the consequent boil governed the Republican party rather than its brains. The party that has given the nation a Mat. Carpenter, a Howe and a Fairchild was run this time by men of the county fair and school "deestrict" range of intellect, with the assistant inspiration of the Presbyterian conference and the light weight "educator."
>
> The result is a defeat as crushing as it is deserved. It is the sure consequence of a great party adopting a narrow and meddlesome course and endeavoring to defend a weak and unstatesmanlike measure by a campaign of misrepresentation and ignominy.[91]

Two other papers edited by Irish-Americans were the Appleton *Crescent* and the Manitowoc *Pilot*. The *Crescent's* editor staunchly vindicated the Democratic position, not so much as an Irishman but rather as a Democrat. And as has been seen, John Nagle of the Manitowoc *Pilot,* rather than give up his allegiance to the Democratic party, joined the group of disaffected members in the Democratic Bennett Law League and used his power to uphold the League's stand.

With their success in 1890 the Democrats faced the task of retaining the coordination and harmony achieved during the campaign and of satisfying the heterogeneous elements within the party, especially in distribution of the spoils. One important con-

---

[90] WSHS, Usher Papers, Brawley to Usher, Mauston, Wisconsin, April 14, 1887.
[91] *Catholic Citizen*, November 8, 1890.

sideration was necessarily that of nationality. The party's adherents were a mixture of "hyphenated Americans" chiefly of German, Irish and Polish extraction.[92] The Germans, furthermore, were divided in their religious allegiance between Lutherans and Catholics. To achieve harmony required consummate patience, tact, and skillful diplomacy on the part of party leaders who found aggressive Irishmen one of their chief problems.

> The difficulty that we have to contend with is shown in this case. Our leaders, like Colonel Knight, not speaking German, don't pay attention to the German element that they should; the Irishman on the other hand can make himself understood in the English language, which he does most vehemently, hence he receives attention; the German notices it, and, in his slow quiet way, waits for the time to take his revenge.[93]

One of the initial problems confronting the Democrats after the 1890 victory concerned the speakership in the assembly. Irishmen were contending against one another for the position: Edward Keogh of Milwaukee and James J. Hogan of La Crosse, each claiming the honor for service rendered or being pushed by some interest.[94] Hogan held the position until 1893 and Keogh succeeded him. Edward C. Wall, Democratic party leader in the state, was in a delicate position because openly to oppose Irishmen who were clamoring for some major appointment would create ill-will, especially since he knew he would be compelled to refuse some appointments demanded by the Irish.[95] And since the Democrats had relied so heavily on the German support dur-

---

[92] Large numbers of Polish immigrants located in Milwaukee during the 1880's and 1890's. By 1891 a contemporary described the southwestern section of the city of Milwaukee as another Poland. They joined the Democratic party and became aggressive in political affairs. *Cf.* Still, *op. cit.*, pp. 268-269.
[93] WSHS, Vilas Papers, E. C. Wall to Vilas, Milwaukee, August 26, 1891.
[94] WSHS, Usher Papers, Brawley to Usher, Mauston, Wisconsin, December 6, 1890; Wall to Usher, Milwaukee, December 6, 1890; J. E. Dodge to Usher, Racine, Wisconsin, November 10, 1890.
[95] WSHS, Usher Papers, Wall to Usher, Milwaukee, December 6, 1890.

ing the campaign it was considered necessary to keep them satisfied. As one local politician put it:

> ... one serious danger we labor under is that appointments will be too numerously secured by the Irish to the exclusion of the much more deserving Germans.[96]

Wall's patience finally gave way:

> Clarence gave me as one of the reasons why he would have to support Regan, that Regan's friends helped prevent the division of Ashland County. Great God, have all little things like that got to be brought into our state politics?
>
> This morning the Governor tells me that Clarence is in favor of the appointment of an Irishman at Hurley as Deputy Warden at the State Prison.
>
> At that rate we might just as well hang up our hopes of success. Nothing but Irish appointed to office. . . . I told all of them [State Board of Control] that I had no one to recommend for office; I have declined to recommend people, but I did make suggestions as to policy and one of those was that particular attention should be paid to the Germans and the Norwegians. I find now that an Irishman is pushed for pretty near every prominent place.[97]

The nationality problem did continue to plague him and Wall's ingenuity was taxed to the utmost. He had found it useful to cultivate the friendship of and to work closely with the Lutheran and Catholic clergy. During the 1892 mayoralty campaign in Milwaukee where the Democratic candidate, P. J. Somers, was a Catholic Irish-American, and where in nominations for aldermen the "Catholics and Irish, as usual, walked away with everything," Wall maneuvered the Lutheran vote through the help of his "Ministerial friends."[98] As a result the party voted solidly and Somers was elected.

---

[96] WSHS, Usher Papers, Dodge to Usher, Racine, November 1, 1890.

[97] WSHS, Vilas Papers, Wall to Vilas, Milwaukee, July 9, 1890.

[98] WSHS, Vilas Papers, Wall to Vilas, Milwaukee, March 18, March 26, March 29, April 6, 1892. Two prominent Lutheran ministers supported Wall and helped him prepare and send out circulars to the Lutheran voters shortly before the elections.

The German Lutherans continued to complain to Wall that they were out of place in the Democratic party, "only good enough to elect Irish and Polish Catholics to the offices" and that "their ambition must not aspire to more than a $1,200 position at Madison." The Republicans, consequently, were courting their vote.[99] The German Catholics were not satisfied either and at one time threatened to adopt a resolution at one of their meetings condemning Wall. The *Columbia* editorialized their position complaining of the treatment German Catholics were receiving "at the hands of Boss Wall and his consorts."

> Any Irish office seeker or boodle politician has under the present party management a hundred times more chance of securing office and honors than the old-time, capable, and worthy German Democrats, honorable and prominent men who do not seek after office and honors and do not seek after emoluments.[100]

Evidently one reason for some of the Catholic dissatisfaction, German and Irish, concerned the Marquette statue which the Wisconsin legislature intended to present to Congress for Statuary Hall in the national capitol. Senator Vilas had placed himself in opposition to the statue. The *Columbia* immediately raised the cry that he was trying to please the Lutherans. Wall's quick action, however, stopped them from making it an issue.[101] He feared

---

[99] WSHS, Vilas Papers, Carl F. Huth to Vilas, Milwaukee, February 6, 1893.

[100] *Columbia*, May, 1892. The *Columbia* was a Milwaukee German Catholic paper. WSHS, Vilas Papers, Wall to Vilas, Milwaukee, May 13, 1892, claimed that the meeting was called for the purpose of electing delegates to the Green Bay Catholic convention of German societies. Wall told Vilas that he did not know why they were condemning him; that Archbishop Katzer and Monsignor August Zeininger, Chancellor of the Archdiocese of Milwaukee, were his friends.

[101] WSHS, Vilas Papers, Wall to Vilas, Milwaukee, May 18, 1892. As soon as Wall saw the *Columbia* attack on Vilas because of his position regarding the Marquette statue, he wrote to Monsignor Zeininger who stopped the *Columbia* from further attacks on Vilas. He informed Vilas of his action and cautioned him against his position of opposition, for Wall

that Republican Germans would enter the fight and the outcome prove fatal. Moreover, the *Catholic Citizen* was ready to take up the issue thus pushing the Irish Catholics into the affair. And, as Wall concluded, "over such a trivial matter as a statue in Statuary Hall, that had been asked for by the Legislature of Wisconsin, our whole great work might be upset."[102]

Despite his efforts to unite the national and religious elements of the party, Wall realized there were limits to such a policy, and when J. L. O'Connor, a Catholic Irishman and attorney general from 1891-1895, was suggested as a possible candidate for governor in 1894 on the Democratic ticket, Wall worked against the nomination. He expressed the opinion that, among other things, O'Connor's nationality and religion would militate too strongly against his election.[103]

The problem of nationality and religion within the Democratic party was already a touchy one when the entrance of the American Protective Association into politics during the early 1890's tended to sharpen the differences. In Wisconsin the association never flourished as well as in some of the neighboring states but it did function with some success in the municipal and state elections of 1894. Since the association was generally identified with the Republican party, the Democrats were again faced with the necessity of effecting a cohesion of their forces in the face of an attack on religion. This time, however, the assault was launched against all Catholics, thus involving the Irish and Polish, but only a portion of the Germans. Wall conceived a plan whereby he

---

believed that one-half of the Democratic party in Wisconsin were Catholics, a large proportion German Catholics. Hence his feeling that dissension within the party on the part of Catholics would prove fatal.

[102] *Ibid.*, WSHS, Vilas Papers, Wall to Vilas, Milwaukee, June 20, 1893, points out that the Polish Catholics were also an element to be placated. Wall was contemplating the possibility and practicality of a Polish United States Marshal: "I do not know whether this will be at all practicable. If it were, it would be a splendid solution of the problem, for we would have then recognized the Irish, the German Lutherans and the Polanders, which are the sources from which we get our votes for victory. At any rate, we must do something now to satisfy them and keep everything in line.

[103] WSHS, Vilas Papers, Wall to Vilas, Milwaukee, March 27, 1893.

hoped the Lutherans could be persuaded to condemn the A.P.A. on the grounds that it was a secret society. In this way the fight would have been instigated independently of the Catholics and, after the Lutherans were in line, Wall proposed having the Catholics step in. He felt that fighting the A.P.A. had definite advantages: it would solidify the entire Catholic vote, German and Irish; and through it more obnoxious and annoying political issues could be kept in the background.[104]

The A.P.A. was neither the most important nor the deciding factor in the elections and although Wall's strategy failed to bring victory to the Democrats it did moderate the opposition's success. The Republicans admitted that had the Democrats not raised the "A.P.A. scare" the Republican majority, at least in the Milwaukee municipal elections, would have been much greater.[105] Only the Polish and Irish vote seemed to have remained staunchly Democratic. Irishmen fought the association in their press and on the lecture platform.[106] The *Catholic Citizen* warred incessantly against A.P.A. intolerance and bigotry while the *Catholic Sentinel* also joined the fight but with somewhat less vigor and consistency. Irish rebuttal was frequently directed at the Orange tint of the A.P.A. membership.[107] For some reason German Catholic opposition was not so strong as the Irish or at least not as vehement. Archbishop Frederick X. Katzer had cautioned against mere denunciation and urged instead a positive attitude. When the German Catholic societies met in convention in Sheboygan, May, 1894, Katzer called for a resolution which would assert and explain the loyalty of Catholics as citizens of the United States instead of denouncing the A.P.A.[108]

---

[104] WSHS, Vilas Papers, Wall to Vilas, Milwaukee, May 12, 1893.
[105] *Catholic Citizen*, April 7, 1894.
[106] *Ibid.*, March 17, 1894.
[107] Humphrey Desmond, *The A.P.A. Movement* (Washington, D. C.: The New Century Press, 1912), pp. 9, 45, describes the membership as consisting of the more vigorous Protestants and reinforced by certain elements of immigration, more especially the Scandinavian and so-called Anglo-Canadian. In Milwaukee in 1894 the Germans and Norwegians made up a clear majority in the A.P.A. councils.
[108] *Catholic Sentinel*, May 24, 1894.

Irish Catholics felt that such a position was too much like giving up a good fight. They preferred having the reputation of being the A.P.A. target. As the editor of the *Catholic Sentinel* put it:

> The Archbishop well knows that there is but feeble opposition against the German Catholics from the Orange and Tory bigots. The Irish Catholics are the ones they are after, and it is not because of their faith but because of their activity as politicians that they are slandered and misrepresented.[109]

The A.P.A. issue, scandals under the Democratic administration within the state, the tariff question, and the economic depression, which had begun to make itself felt, militated against the popularity of the Democrats and the elections of 1894 and 1896 returned the Republicans to power. A writer of the time summed up the situation within the Democratic party itself:

> The Democratic party of this state and nation being unused to power lacks homogeneity and constructive capacity.... Every thing new is examined with a critical eye and its defect [sic] are noted. There are Germans, Irish, Polish, Bohemians and Yankees in the Democratic party. It is a federation and a discordant one when in power. Each nationality or religious sect watches the other with a jealous eye and often refers to it with ungracious comment.[110]

In 1896 the Democrats in state convention declared for gold but at the national convention Bryan made his "cross of gold" speech and a split occurred. The majority of the Wisconsin Democratic party followed the silverites under Wall, while Usher headed the gold Democrats among whom were Vilas and Nagle. The Irish of Wisconsin seem to have followed the majority into the Bryan camp despite the attempts of the sound money Democrats to draw their allegiance.[111] The gold Democrats circulated

---

[109] *Ibid.*
[110] Plumb, *op. cit.*, p. 107, citing "a writer of the time."
[111] WSHS, Usher Papers, William M. Knauf to Usher, Chilton, Wisconsin, September 21, 1896; Stuart MacKibbin to Usher, South Bend, Indiana,

Archbishop Ireland's statement to persuade the Irish of the soundness of the gold position.[112] The Democratic press was divided between the two groups, Nagle among the Irish-Americans staunchly supporting the gold faction in the columns of the *Pilot.* The editor of the *Catholic Sentinel* was on the side of Bryan and silver.

To determine the position of Irishmen on political issues toward the end of the nineteenth century when the La Follette reform was coming to the fore, becomes increasingly difficult because, for all practical purposes, the Irishman had merged with the rest of Wisconsin's heterogeneous population. Some rural Irishmen were leaving their father's farms and locating in the cities, while distinctively Irish wards were losing their "nationality" through the immigration of other foreign groups and the rise of their own to better financial status. In Milwaukee, for example, the newly arrived Italians began to crowd into the third ward and in 1892 a disastrous fire concluded the process of scattering the Irish into other parts of the city.[113]

Where it is possible to isolate the Irish vote in the 1900 election—in Erin Prairie, St. Croix County and Erin, Washington County—there was no evidence of a significant defection to the La Follette branch of the Republican party. Where Irishmen had

---

October 8, 1896; W. C. Leitsch, Columbus, Wisconsin, October 16, 1896; George Krouskop to Usher, Richland Center, October 21, 1896. W. A. Wyse to Usher, Reedsburg, Wisconsin, October 26, 1896: "We have quite a large Bryan following in this county [Sauk], especially amongst the Irish. They are too strongly wedded to the PARTY to vote otherwise. . . . In Richland County there is a strong Bryan sentiment in the northern part amongst the Irish."

[112] WSHS, Usher Papers, George Krouskop to Usher, Richland Center, October 21, 1896; W. A. Wyse to Usher, Reedsburg, Wisconsin, October 26, 1896. During the campaign of 1896 Archbishop Ireland, after William Jennings Bryan left St. Paul, declared his adherence to the Republican platform as enunciated at St. Louis. Among other things he "discoursed on the free-silver theory like a professor of economics, prophesying that it would bring on a financial depression beyond anything hitherto experienced." *Cf.* Moynihan, *op. cit.,* p. 261.

[113] The third ward fire destroyed property worth $5,000,000 and 1,893 people were left homeless. *Cf.* Still, *op. cit.,* p. 359.

become scattered, however, the psychology of group voting was lacking, and Irishmen were more likely to break with their traditional allegiance to the Democratic party and to become independent in their voting habits. To the end of the century, therefore, Irishmen had generally remained with the Democratic party.

Possibly Milwaukee was the most fertile ground in Wisconsin for the development of Irish political acumen. For that city had been a Democratic stronghold until after 1870 even though the state had long before succumbed to Republican domination.[114] In the early years the Irish of Milwaukee had developed some strong leaders: John White, Garrett M. Fitzgerald, Timothy O'Brien, Doctor James Johnson, Edward McGarry, Hans Crocker, Richard Murphy, Andrew McCormick, and Edward O'Neill. These men are credited with having mobilized the Milwaukee Irish into a politically staunch faction of the regular Democratic machine.[115] John White as organizer and captain of the Emmett Guards became political leader of the Irish element in Milwaukee from 1844-1856 along with Timothy O'Brien, who is considered one of the shrewdest Democratic politicians Milwaukee has known.[116]

---

[114] *Ibid.*, p. 133.

[115] *Ibid.*

[116] John White ran for office of sheriff in 1844 on the Democratic ticket, but the nativists "double crossed" him and the entire ticket was elected with the exception of White. James S. Buck, *Pioneer History of Milwaukee from the First American Settlement in 1833* (Milwaukee: Swain and Tate, 1881-90), II, 223, says: "Such was the wrath of the Irish thereat, that for the next four years every candidate for Democratic honors stood a better chance to be struck with lightening than he did for a place on the slate, unless he would swear unequivocally that he voted for John White for sheriff in 1844." White was elected sheriff in 1851 and was collector of the port before that time and again under President Pierce.

Timothy O'Brien, familiarly called "Father Tim," had come directly to Milwaukee from Limerick in 1842 and besides providing aggressive political leadership served in some official capacity from the time he was elected city marshal in 1848 until close to the time of his death in 1888. In contrast to the usual brevity of aldermanic terms by annual turnover, O'Brien served in that capacity for fifteen years as representative of the third ward. Other positions in which he served are: city marshal, captain of police, deputy sheriff, coroner, county supervisor, crier of the court, superintendent of the

Control of Milwaukee city politics in the 1850's had been concentrated largely in the hands of a railroad group who controlled the votes of contractors and laborers.[117] Also in these early days of Milwaukee history there was frequently more contention among the various elements of a given nationality than between one nationality and another. An example of this occurred in August, 1855, when the Irish Democrats from four country towns of Milwaukee County, resenting the third ward control of the sixth state senatorial district, bolted and attempted to force through their own candidate for state senator against O'Neill. They were no more successful against the third ward bosses than an isolated group of Irishmen could have been in defying Tammany Hall in New York.[118]

After 1856 the political leadership of the Irish passed to O'Neill and Edward Keogh.[119] The Irish succeeded in advancing O'Neill

---

poor, and ward foreman. *Cf. ibid.*, III, 300; Milwaukee *Sentinel*, August 25, 1888; *History of Milwaukee, Wisconsin, from Pre-historic Times to the Present Date* (Chicago: The Western Historical Company, 1881), p. 1593.

[117] Still, *op. cit.*, pp. 143-147.

[118] Milwaukee *Sentinel*, August 27, October 16, 17, 1855. The sixth district was composed of the third ward of the city of Milwaukee and the towns of Franklin, Oak Creek, Greenfield, and Lake.

[119] O'Neill, a native Irishman, had entered the city in 1850 and already in 1853 had been elected to represent the third ward in the state assembly. He subsequently served another term in the assembly and two terms in the state senate. O'Neill served in other offices besides that of mayor and became a prominent banker in Milwaukee.

Edward Keogh, who came to Milwaukee from County Cavan, Ireland, when seven years of age, grew up in the third ward and at the age of twenty-five became a member of the state assembly. Keogh's political acumen is demonstrated in the fact that he was returned to the legislature as senator in 1862 and 1863, and as assemblyman each year from 1876 to 1881, again in 1883, and for four terms from 1887 to 1893. During the last term he held the position of speaker in the assembly. Keogh, a printer by trade, sustained intimate relations with the Milwaukee municipal government chiefly through his printing contracts—so much so that he was considered to be one of the best posted men in Milwaukee on municipal affairs. In the state legislature Keogh is best known for promoting legislation on elections, caucuses, and the Australian ballot. At the time of his death the *Catholic Sentinel* reported that he wielded perhaps as much influence as any other man in state politics and was leader of the Democratic party in the legislature. *Cf. Catholic Sentinel*, December 1, 1898.

to the mayoralty for four one-year terms (1863, 1867, 1868, 1869). Frequent "deals" with the Germans, who were constantly increasing in number and political aggressiveness, became necessary. In 1867 the municipal elections terminated in a compromise made between the Irish and Germans whereby O'Neill became mayor, G. C. Trumpf, treasurer, and Fred Williams, comptroller. As long as cooperation on the part of the two nationalities could be manipulated by the politicians in control, the Democratic party gathered strength. In 1868 they achieved a sweeping victory and by 1869 the Republican opposition had folded up. Despite the Democrats' success in 1870, that year marked the end of their undisputed control of Milwaukee politics. Significantly it was during this election that the German and Irish Democrats contended for the position of comptroller, the Irish obtaining it for Jeremiah Quinn.[120] Outside the party, German opposition to the Irish Democrats was notable among the forty-eighters who were particularly strong in Milwaukee.

The Irish passed from a predominant position in the early days to that of holding the balance in the city's politics, but in the 1890's the Polish replaced the Irish in this latter capacity. The political power of the Irish had begun to wane. In 1891 the *Sentinel* summarized the situation:

> At present, the Polish voters hold a balance of power, even without the Irish voters.... The most of the Irish-Americans are Democrats, and they vote with a good deal of solidarity, but the exceptions are increasing, and anyhow the number of Irish is so small now that they are hardly to be considered. The Germans, with the exception of the German Catholics, do not vote solidly as a group in ordinary times.[121]

In order to evaluate properly the activity of Irishmen in Wisconsin politics it should be noted that they were at a disadvantage politically because of their fewness in number compared with the Germans, Norwegians, and other nationalities including native

---

[120] Still, *op. cit.*, pp. 162-163.
[121] Milwaukee *Sentinel*, April 6, 1892.

Americans, and because of their adherence to a minority party. On account of their political adroitness, however, they could not be disregarded. Politically they were not always docile nor were they masters of their own destiny, but rather they constituted a faction whose vote was sought by various means, whose interests were exploited for the benefit of the party, and who were placated or kept in line by means of small shares in the spoils. They were controlled by the Democratic machine in which some of them became mentors as did Edward Keogh, Peter Doyle, J. L. O'Connor, Edward Ryan, and John Nagle. If the Democratic party had been in the position of dominance within the state instead of the Republicans, it is highly probable that the Irish politicians among them would have risen to greater political heights. The short period of Democratic dominance between 1890 and 1894 demonstrates their political alertness.

Irishmen were particularly active as local Democratic chairmen and officeholders not only in Irish communities but also frequently in localities where Germans or Norwegians outnumbered them.[122] Each legislature from territorial days until the end of the century contained some Irish-born members and a larger number of Irish Americans. They were usually represented beyond their numerical proportion in the state compared with the other national groups. Political correspondence shows that no matter how disparagingly Irishmen were spoken of they were never completely ignored by either party.

Factors that motivated Irishmen in their political activity were chiefly their propensity for participation in politics, which they seemingly brought with them from their own country, their love for their native land and corresponding hatred of England, their religion, and their ambition for office. Characteristically the Irishman seems to have possessed the aptitudes for political activity

---

[122] Whyte, "Chronicle of Early Watertown," *loc. cit.*, 311, asserts that the Irish controlled the politics of the towns of Emmet and Shields, Dodge County, for fifty years. Finally in Emmet, the Germans, having become a majority, insisted on their share of town offices and forced a division. Eventually the Irish were compelled to be satisfied with the office of town clerk and by the 1920's they had not even that.

and many, before coming to Wisconsin, had learned by experience the devious methods employed by politicians. The Irishman's love for his native country or that of his forefathers, as the case might be, and his hatred for England, at times furnished politicians with specious pretexts with which to win his patronage. Politicians' support of Irish causes, as in 1852 and at the time of the Fenian movement in the 1860's, actually motivated the Irishman's voting in many cases. This is also true of the Republican use of anti-British arguments in tariff debate. Religion often motivated the Irishman's voting, for by far the majority of Irishmen in Wisconsin were Roman Catholics and bore the twofold stigma of foreigner and Catholic. As such they were frequently attacked, or their religion was attacked by the nativists and anti-clericals within the Republican party. The municipal election of Milwaukee in 1874, the gubernatorial elections of 1875 and 1890, and the presidential campaign of 1876 are instances in which evidence substantiates the fact that Irish Catholics voted in defense of their religion. Regarding his ambition it should be noted that the Irish politician has been characterized as restless and unsatisfied unless he is boss within a given realm. Lesser state offices did not tempt the Irishman as much as a local position in which he could dominate. As aldermen and ward bosses in a city like Milwaukee this innate desire to dominate could be fulfilled. In these positions an Irishman's word was law, the duty of holding the vote in line was a challenge to his ability; he was generally feared and his power respected, while recipients of his favors were ready to demonstrate their gratitude. Not only these circumstances, but also the fact that the Democratic party had few spoils to share since it was so seldom in power, can also account for the Irishman's eagerness and determination to hold local offices and positions within the party organization. For as soon as the Democrats achieved victory between 1890 and 1894, Irishmen were the bane of Democratic politicians with their importunate demands for a share in the spoils.

The reasons why Irishmen remained Democrats so consistently throughout the nineteenth century are several. Many had been Democrats before coming to the state. In the East and in Wisconsin the Democrats had solicited the foreign vote and had proved their political affection for the immigrant by obtaining liberal suffrage legislation and by working for liberal land laws. The very name, "Democrat," contained a sufficient attraction for the Irish while that of Whig repelled them. To the Irish, the Whigs and later the Republicans represented aristocracy, anti-foreignism and anti-Catholicism, while the Democrats were the party of the poor and oppressed, the refuge of foreigners. Probably the strongest factor in keeping Irishmen within the Democratic fold was the Wisconsin Know-Nothing inheritance of the Republican party, embodied in the attitude of native Americans and German forty-eighters. Irish allegiance to the Democratic party became a tradition among them, so much so that an Irish Democrat turned Republican was considered almost as much a social outcast as an Irish Catholic who gave up his Faith.

CHAPTER VI

THE RELIGIOUS AND SOCIAL LIFE OF WISCONSIN IRISHMEN

By far the majority of Irishmen who emigrated to Wisconsin professed the Catholic faith. Their entrance into the state was not Wisconsin's first contact with the Catholic Church, for French Jesuit missionaries had entered the northern regions bringing Christianity to the Indians during the latter half of the seventeenth century. From the date of the first Mass on Wisconsin soil in 1661 until 1728 these missionaries were active within the bounds of the present state. After 1728 and until 1823, Catholic missionary activity was entirely dependent upon itinerant missionaries who passed through from Detroit and St. Louis. Green Bay and Prairie du Chien were the chief centers of Catholic activity until the southwestern and the lake regions began to feel the impact of immigration from the South and East. As the pioneers pushed the frontier westward, diocesan organizations reflected the movement and Wisconsin, a part of the diocese of Quebec in 1674, passed under the jurisdiction of each of the following dioceses in turn: Baltimore (1789), Bardstown (1808), Cincinnati (1821), and Detroit (1833).[1] When Irish Catholics entered southwestern Wisconsin, most of them leadminers, they did not bring Irish priests with them. The Reverend Samuel Charles Mazzuchelli, an Italian Dominican, who had labored in Mackinac and around Green Bay in the early 1830's, came as a missionary to northern Iowa, Illinois, and southern Wisconsin in 1835. Until his death in 1864 he worked zealously visiting the mining centers, building churches in Prairie du Chien, Benton, New Diggings, and Shullsburg; visiting Mineral Point, Gratiot Grove, and other

---

[1] The Bishop of Detroit delegated jurisdiction over southern Wisconsin to the Bishop of Dubuque after that see was erected in 1837, but Wisconsin was never a part of the Dubuque Diocese.

locations where the number of Irish Catholics warranted the services of a priest.[2]

While Mazzuchelli was ministering to the needs of Catholic Irishmen in the southwest, the Reverend Patrick O'Kelley arrived in Milwaukee, May, 1839, the first resident pastor of the southeast. Besides the establishment of St. Peter's Church in Milwaukee to accommodate his heterogeneous flock of Irishmen, Germans, and Frenchmen, O'Kelley visited Racine, Mt. Pleasant, Rochester, Burlington, Southport (Kenosha), Pleasant Prairie, Salem, Oak Creek, and Greenfield. His labors in these missions kept him away from St. Peter's in Milwaukee for long periods at a time and the strenuous activity impaired his health. As a consequence trouble ensued at St. Peter's and factions between the German and Irish disturbed the administration of the parish. Moreover, the Germans desired a priest of their own nationality.[3] Bishop Peter P. Lefevere of Detroit recalled O'Kelley in 1842 and sent in his place the Reverend Martin Kundig who was well equipped to handle the situation.

Kundig came to be loved by all Catholics regardless of nationality. He solved the difficulty at St. Peter's temporarily by providing separate services for the Irish and German portions of his flock and by organizing separate societies for the Irish and Germans. Kundig counted approximately 750 Catholic families in Milwaukee and the outlying settlements. He had help in the persons of the Reverend Thomas Morrissey, an Irish-born priest who had been laboring in Ann Arbor (then called Northfield), Michigan, and the Reverend Peter McLaughlin. Morrissey's arrival in the early fall of 1842 made it possible for Kundig to tend to the missions outside of Milwaukee.[4]

---

[2] Mary E. Evans, *The Seed and the Glory* (New York: McMullen Books, Inc., 1950). The Irish Catholics came to love this holy and zealous priest. Many of them, it is said, called him Father Matthew Kelly.

[3] Peter Leo Johnson, "Reverend Patrick O'Kelly, First Resident Catholic Pastor of Milwaukee," *Salesianum*, XLV (July, 1950), 108-113.

[4] Heming, *op. cit.*, p. 555, gives the following concerning Morrissey which he obtained in an interview with Dr. Edward Johnson, pioneer of Watertown, Wisconsin: "Father Morissey was man of medium height, stout built [sic] and florid complexion, and spoke Irish as well as he did the English language.

Prior to 1842 Catholics, chiefly Irish, had located within the present counties of Milwaukee, Waukesha, Racine, Kenosha, Washington, and Ozaukee. Kundig, and sometimes Morrissey, made the rounds and extended their visits into Walworth, Rock, and Jefferson Counties. By March 28, 1843, after a period of ten months' labor, Kundig had organized twenty-five Catholic groups.[5]

Kundig's successful efforts in and around Milwaukee convinced him that Wisconsin would be the haven for many immigrants. Since the bishops of the United States were to meet in provincial council in Baltimore in May, 1843, and were expected to suggest to Rome the erection of several new dioceses, Kundig felt that Wisconsin Territory should be so designated and that Milwaukee would provide the best location for an episcopal see. To this end he bent his efforts, writing letters on the advantage of settling in Wisconsin and the bright prospects of the Catholic Church there, and sending these to the *Wahrheitsfreund* edited by his friend, the Reverend John Martin Henni of Cincinnati. More practically, with the intention of attracting the notice of the bishops of the United States to Milwaukee and to the large number of Catholics in the vicinity, Kundig organized a St. Patrick's Day celebration in 1843 in which approximately 3,000 Catholics took part with the Irish congregations playing the predominant role.[6] Henni had

---

He had no regard for personal comfort, traveling incessantly, and taking but little rest. He was regarded as a man of great endurance, capable of withstanding as many hardships and as much cold as the Indians. There is but little additional to say regarding the missionary labors of Fathers Morrissey and Kundig, more than to record their heroic courage, zeal, and piety. The field of their labors reached over a vast extent of woodland, and their unguarded and almost helpless condition while journeying from one settlement to another, was always one of danger. Their every act and effort, in fact, carries us back to the apostolic age, their one great object seeming to be a desire to keep alive the faith in all those who had left the great centers of population to make a home for themselves in this tractless wilderness. The missions of these two Fathers ended in 1846, when they were succeeded at short intervals by Fathers McKernan and John Healey."

[5] P. L. Johnson, *Stuffed Saddlebags: The Life of Martin Kundig, Priest, 1805-1879* (Milwaukee: Bruce Publishing Company, 1942), p. 198.

[6] Johnson, "Unofficial Beginnings of the Milwaukee Catholic Diocese," *WMH*, XXIIII (September, 1939), 3-16. *Cf.* also, *Stuffed Saddlebags*, pp. 186-192, 232-237. The following congregations took part, practically all of

requested of Kundig a report of the number of German Catholics in Wisconsin which, with similar reports from other localities, he hoped to publish in his paper in order to draw the hierarchy's attention to the need for German bishops. Instead, Kundig saw to it that each bishop, vicar general, and religious superior in the United States was supplied with copies of newspapers reporting his St. Patrick's Day celebration. He was thus achieving two aims in one stroke: demonstrating the need of a diocese in Wisconsin Territory and emphasizing that Milwaukee, not Prairie du Chien or Green Bay, should be the episcopal see. In his accounts of the celebration in the *Wahrheitsfreund* and the *Detroit Western Register* written within two days of each other, Kundig stressed the participation of the few German groups in the former paper, and of the English-speaking in the latter.

Owing in large part to Kundig's exertions the bishops in council suggested Milwaukee as an episcopal see and Rome appointed Henni its first bishop.[7] He was consecrated in Cincinnati on

---

them predominantly Irish: St. Peter's, Milwaukee; St. Mary's, Greenfield; St. Mary's, Kenosha; St. Stephen's, Mineral Point; Trinity, Madison; St. Ignatius', Racine; St. Bernard's, Watertown; St. Michael's, Granville; St. Patrick's, Yorkville; St. Patrick's, Brighton; St. Francis', Cedarburg; St. Louis', Franklin; St. Martin's, Geneva; St. Dominic's, Brookfield; St. Matthias', Oak Creek; St. Bridget's, Muskego; St. John's, Monches; St. Joseph's, Waukesha. Nearly all of the names of the officers of the day were Irish. The order of the day included an outdoor Mass by Father Morrissey, administration of the temperance pledge to more than one hundred persons, and then a procession of the twenty congregations and several temperance societies carrying banners which lauded the Church, America, the temperance cause, and the Irish nationality. After the parade refreshments were served and speeches given. The delegates met again in the evening to elect officers to the Wisconsin Catholic Total Abstinence Society. More speeches were delivered and with adjournment of the meeting the celebration was concluded.

[7] John Martin Henni was born June 15, 1805, in the canton of Grison, Switzerland. He was educated principally at Lucerne and took a course at the Sapienza University in Rome. As the request of Frederic Rese, vicar general of the diocese of Cincinnati, Henni came to the United States in 1828. He was ordained priest on February 2, 1829. In 1834 he was appointed vicar general of Cincinnati and pastor of the Germans there. He founded, in 1837, and edited for six years the *Wahrheitsfreund,* first German Catholic newspaper in the United States. Henni was always deeply interested in the welfare

March 19, 1844, and arrived in Milwaukee two months later accompanied by his friend, the Reverend Michael Heiss, future bishop of La Crosse and Archbishop of Milwaukee. Henni found six resident priests in his diocese: Frederick Baraga at La Pointe, Fleurimont Bonduel at Green Bay, Theodore J. Van den Broek at Little Chute, McLaughlin, Morrissey and Kundig.[8]

The total Catholic population of Wisconsin in 1842 was estimated to be about 7,000.[9] By 1845 immigration had increased the total to a reported 25,090. Of these 14,538 were Irish, English, Scotch, and American; 5,628 French; 2,776 German, and 2,148 were Indians.[10] Thus Irish Catholics, located chiefly in the lead region and southeastern Wisconsin, were the more numerous portion of Henni's flock.

After Bishop Henni became established in Milwaukee in 1844, Kundig labored outside the city from 1845 to 1859, with the ex-

---

of the German Catholic population. As Bishop of Milwaukee he established St. Francis Seminary, introduced into the diocese various religious orders of men and women. In 1875 he became archbishop when the diocese was raised to an archbishopric. Henni died six years later on September 7, 1881.

[8] Heming, *op. cit.*, p. 310, asserts that Morrissey and McLaughlin were assisting Father O'Kelley. This hardly seems possible. Morrissey more likely came in 1842. McLaughlin is mentioned by Johnson, *Stuffed Saddlebags*, p. 243, as teaching catechism at St. Peter's. Father McLaughlin, assistant at the Cathedral parish in Milwaukee, preached the English sermon at the laying of the cornerstone of the Cathedral, December 5, 1847, and of Holy Trinity Church, July 15, 1849, in the same city. *Cf.* Heming, *op. cit.*, p. 271.

[9] During the early 1830's the Catholic population was liberally estimated at 1,500 whites and 1,000 Indians with approximately an additional 100 persons located near La Pointe. By 1840, Wisconsin Territory, including eastern Minnesota, was estimated to have approximately 3,600 Catholics, 10,000 Protestants, 16,000 infidel Indians, and 11,000 Catholic Indians. Johnson, *Stuffed Saddlebags*, p. 168.

[10] *Ibid.*, p. 168, citing the *U. S. Catholic Magazine* (February, 1845), p. 132. This same periodical in its October, 1845 issue, pp. 673-674, gave the following figures showing an increase: total number of Catholics in Wisconsin, 27,000; Irish 16,000; German 8,000. More than two-thirds of the Catholics, 19,000 were reported as residing in the counties of Milwaukee including present day Waukesha; Washington including present day Ozaukee; Racine including the present Kenosha; Walworth, Rock, Green, Dane, Dodge, Jefferson, and Portage.

ception of a year at St. John's Cathedral, 1854-1855. His work took him among the Irish and Germans, but "Tactful . . . energetic, and bilingual, Kundig was acceptable to all."[11] He served as pastor in Kenosha from 1845-1849, at St. Martin's, Franklin Township, Milwaukee County, from 1848-1849, and approximately a year each in Waukesha, Racine, and Beaver Dam. From each of these locations he reached out to neighboring stations and hence by 1859 had worked among Catholics in counties as far west as Dodge, Dane, Columbia, and Green Lake (then a part of Marquette County). He even paid a visit to Mineral Point and Dodgeville in Iowa County.[12]

The establishment of the diocese of Milwaukee and the publicity given Catholicity in Wisconsin by O'Kelley, Kundig, and others, attracted Irish priests and seminarians who were willing to undertake the arduous duties of a missionary for the purpose of preserving the faith among their fellow countrymen.[13] The

---

[11] *Ibid.*, p. 207.

[12] *Ibid.*, pp. 204-226. Since most of Kundig's efforts in these locations were among Irish Catholics, Johnson entitles the chapter dealing with them, "Soggarth Aroon," a title truly indicative of Kundig's relationship with the Irish. Among the churches which Kundig built were several St. Patrick's, two St. Malachy's, and a St. Columbkill (originally St. Aidan). Some Irish churches were named for the Blessed Virgin and St. Joseph; some for the donor or an active layman, such as St. Bernard's in Watertown named after Bernard Crangle. *Cf.* George T. Meagher, *A Century at St. Bernard's* (Milwaukee: Sentinel Bindery and Printing Company, 1946), p. 7.

[13] Some Irish-born priests who reached Wisconsin had been invited to the United States by bishops of other dioceses; some came as students from seminaries in Ireland at the request of bishops in eastern dioceses. Then either before or after ordination they entered the Milwaukee diocese. The Reverend Joseph Smith emigrated to the United States at the invitation of Archbishop John B. Purcell of Cincinnati. Having made the acquaintance of Bishop Henni he joined the diocese of Milwaukee and was ordained by that prelate on June 14, 1850, at Notre Dame, Indiana. *Cf.* Meagher, *op. cit.*, p. 15. The Reverend Hugh McMahon was ordained for the Philadelphia diocese in 1848 where he labored until 1855. That year he volunteered for the Milwaukee diocese in which he labored until his death in 1898. *Cf.* Heming, *op. cit.*, pp. 494-495; *Catholic Sentinel*, October 6, 1898. Patrick Donohoe, at St. John's Cathedral, Milwaukee, 1853-1890, was another Irish-born priest ordained by Bishop Kenrick who labored first in Philadelphia and then

Reverend William Quinn who arrived in the fall of 1844, the Reverend Michael McFaul, and Father Morrissey followed Kundig into the Irish parishes around Milwaukee thus relieving him of a portion of his burden. In Walworth and Rock Counties a pioneer Irish-American priest, Patrick McKernan, made it less necessary for Kundig to spend time there. McKernan resided at Racine in 1845 and at Lake Geneva in 1846 extending his missionary tours into the region surrounding these localities. In 1850, besides the Irish-American missionaries, there were at least eight Irish-born priests working among the Irish Catholics in the diocese.[14] By 1860 the number of Irish-born priests had increased to thirty-four.[15]

---

entered the Milwaukee diocese. *Cf.* Heming, *op. cit.*, pp. 313, 1022. Another, Edward O'Connor, had been the first priest ordained by Bishop John Timon for the Buffalo Diocese in 1848. He also later entered the Milwaukee diocese where he practiced the ministry until his death in 1873 at Waukesha. *Cf.* Milwaukee *Sentinel*, February 7, 1873.

[14] The following priests were found listed in the 1850 manuscript census: John Bradley, Milwaukee, first ward; James Colton, town of Menomonee, Waukesha County; John Conway, town of Franklin, Milwaukee County (Conway is mentioned in Heming, *op. cit.*, pp. 414, 415. spelled Conway and Conroy; also with the name James instead of John. The 1860 census lists a John Conroy, mentioned also in Heming, *op. cit.*, p. 430); James V. Daly, Hazel Green, Grant County (probably a Dominican); John Healy, village of Watertown, Jefferson County; Patrick Kain, town of Cottage Grove, Dane County; Francis Prendergast, Cedarburg, Ozaukee County. Michael McFaul, a native Irishman ordained by Bishop Henni, September 29, 1847, was not found in the census. P. L. Johnson, "The American Odyssey of the Irish Brigidines," *Salesianum*, XXXIX (April, 1944), 62-63, mentions that McFaul held various pastorates in the Milwaukee diocese until 1858 when he went to Missouri.

[15] The Irish-born Catholic priests in Wisconsin in the year 1860 were: Patrick Bradley, Saukville, Ozaukee County; George Brennan, Racine, second ward; James Colton, Shullsburg; John Conroy, Janesville; William Dougherty, Cedarburg; Patrick Donohoe, Milwaukee; Michael Downey, Porter, Rock County; James M. Doyle, Portage; Richard Dumphy, Whitewater; P. O. Farrell, Franklin; Moses B. Fortune, O.P., Hazel Green; E. Gray, Ripon; Joseph Harriman, Watertown; Martin Hobbes, Oconomowoc; Thomas Keenan, Oshkosh; Lawrence N. Kenney, East Troy; J. J. Kinsella, Oak Creek, Milwaukee County; F. P. McCormack, O.P., Hazel Green; Francis McGann, Mineral Point; J. M. McGowan, Water-

In contemporary reports the term Irish is used to include the Irish-born and Irish-American priests. Hence when the Reverend Michael Heiss summarized the growth of the Catholic Church in Wisconsin, he could state in 1847:

> Our diocese, which is now three years old, counts twenty-nine priests and over thirty-thousand Catholics. Of the twenty-nine priests fourteen are Germans; the other Irish, French and Italian.[16]

Again in 1861 he wrote:

> The diocese . . . comprises the entire state of Wisconsin, nearly as much territory as its erection in the year 1844. At that time the bishop of Milwaukee had only six priests of his own, and in the vast territory hardly more than 9 to 10,000 Catholics, who possessed only four inexpensive and unfinished churches and chapels, and besides, 23 others under construction, with a total of 117 priests and a Catholic population of approximately 190,000 souls. The largest part of the population consists of Germans and Irish who are about equal in number. Besides these we have some Canadian, Dutch, Belgian, and also a few Polish and Bohemian parishes, and two missions among the Indians. It is not difficult to understand what incessant zeal, untiring solicitude, and keen prudence are required to govern a new, quickly developing and extensive diocese in order to preserve peace and harmony among the different elements and to foster and promote Catholic life.[17]

---

town; John McGuirk, Elba; Hugh McMahon, Chilton; Peter Montague, Kildare; James Morris, Fox Lake; Patrick Murphy, Fitchburg; Patrick O'Farrell, Waukesha; Patrick Pettit, Lyndon, Sheboygan County; Thomas L. Powers, O.P., Hazel Green (Vice President of St. Thomas College, Sinsinawa Mound); George T. Riordan, Kenosha, first ward; Henry Roche, Delavan; Richard Roche, Mauston; Joseph Smith, Watertown, third ward; Francis Stroker, Willow Springs; Richard Sullivan, Monroe; John W. Tiernan, Merton.

[16] *Salesianum*, X (October, 1914), 16-23, Reverend Michael Heiss to Reverend Kilian Kleiner, Milwaukee, May 4, 1847.

[17] *Ibid.*, XL (October, 1945), 169-170, Heiss to Board of Directors, Ludwig-missionsverein, Milwaukee, August 30, 1861.

The organization of Irish congregations in Wisconsin generally followed a similar pattern. When a group of Irish Catholics had settled within the same vicinity they usually requested the nearest missionary to attend to their spiritual needs, or a missionary on his travels would find several families to whom he would minister and possibly make provision for their organization into a congregation.[18] Celebration of the first Mass in a locality was considered an event worthy of note. Masses were commonly said in a private home chosen for its location, size, or even the prominence of the family within it. Such visitations of a missionary were continued at intervals—weekly, monthly, or less frequently—depending upon circumstances. Sometimes several years passed before the settlers succeeded in building a church, their efforts then producing a frame building or merely a crude log structure erected on property donated by one of the settlers; for it was a matter of using the materials at hand.[19] Where expenses were incurred Catholics

---

[18] Sometimes an accident or illness was the immediate occasion for seeking the services of a priest. For example, in Bear Creek Township, Sauk County, in the fall of 1855. James Donohoe, son of Patrick Donohoe, was injured fatally when he was attempting to fell a tree. Some of the settlers who had come from Madison knew that a priest was stationed at Sauk City. The priest, Maximilian Gaertner, was sent for. His arrival marks the coming of the first priest among the Irish settlers in that area who ultimately formed the parish of St. Patrick, Loreto. James Donohoe died before the priest arrived and his funeral Mass, said in the home of Patrick Donohoe, was the first Mass offered in Bear Creek Township. Father Gaertner, now aware of the presence of these Irish Catholics, continued to visit this Irish settlement about once a month, saying Mass in the home of Patrick Donohoe. A church was not built until 1860. *Cf.* Duren, *op. cit.*, pp. 5-8.

[19] Also typical of this procedure was the church building in Loreto. There John Rice donated three acres of his land. Duren, *op. cit.*, p. 10, describes the situation: "The location for a church having been determined, the ground obtained, and building timber to the amount of $14.00 bargained for with one Spelle, the zealous little band of Irishmen resolutely went to work to fell trees and hew logs on the same day after the meeting, for the decision was in favor of a log structure, since this gave the only possible prospect of success, because the people were all poor and needy, having settled in this town with empty pockets and bare hands and could raise but little cash money for building a church. But they brought with them from their dear old native land Irish grit, sinew, bone, and muscle with which they could erect a log church building in this locality, where splendid building timber

were often assisted by the donations of their non-Catholic friends.

In the counties surrounding Milwaukee, Kundig was the first to say Mass in many of these settlements, but as Irish priests and other missionaries became more numerous the primitive status of Catholicity gave way to more efficient parish organization. Likewise, Catholic congregations became more numerous as the foreign immigrants particularly aided in pushing the frontier to the western and northern bounds of the state. Bishop Henni, with Heiss and other German priests interested in the growth of the diocese and the state, labored zealously to promote German Catholic immigration into Wisconsin and at the same time to provide German Catholic priests. Their spirit is revealed in a letter of Adelbert Inama written in 1846:

> The Bishop must give due consideration to this [Irish] part of the Catholic population, as they are still in the majority; however, the German tongue will soon achieve a parity and become the first jewel in the Bishop's mitre.[20]

The settlement of German Catholics among the Irish aggravated the nationality problem within the Church. The basic cause of the friction probably lay in the language problem, although other factors such as differences in customs and personalities contributed to the difficulties. The bishop aimed to provide each parish with a priest of the same nationality as the predominant portion of his flock, but this was not always possible.[21] And even where

---

was plentiful at the time; but above all they brought with them to this wilderness deep down in their Irish hearts the dear old Catholic faith of Ireland. This impelled them onward; this united their efforts; this made them surmount every difficulty, and forgetting every hardship in erecting an edifice for the service of the Most High." Although the church was begun in 1860, it was not completed until 1865 because of the Civil War.

[20] Inama, *loc. cit.*, p. 85.

[21] A remark in a letter of Father Inama demonstrates this attitude toward national parishes: "The fifth district lies about thirty miles north of the Baraboo, a tributary of the Wisconsin. The Catholic population is almost entirely of Irish descent and counts already eighty families. . . . Father Gaertner is visiting the community regularly, until they shall receive a priest of their own nationality." Inama to Archbishop of Vienna, Prairie du Sac, Wisconsin Territory, February 14, 1853, in *WMH*, XII (September, 1928), 95.

this was done the minority nationality within the parish was usually dissatisfied and trouble frequently ensued.

It can be readily understood that the newly arrived Germans, because of their inability to speak and understand English, were in definite need of a German-speaking priest. Instructions could not be given nor could the Sacrament of Penance be administered unless the priest could speak German. The Germans, moreover, clung to their language, particularly where their religion was concerned. Priests and people firmly believed that: "Mit der Sprache geht der Glaube"; hence, the establishment of German parishes and parochial schools. The Reverend Anthony Urbanek, a German missionary, in reporting the need for German Catholic schools in the Milwaukee diocese used this very argument: the Germans, if Anglicized, lose their Faith. Regarding the Irish, however, he wrote: "On the other hand, Irish children, if well instructed by their priest in any English Catechism, generally are saved to the Catholic faith."[22]

This problem involving nationality conflict within parishes continued to be troublesome throughout most of the nineteenth century. Various solutions were tried. In some parishes the instructions were always given in English, but a German priest from a neighboring mission would perodically visit the parish in order to preach and take care of the needs of the German portion of the flock. A few Irish priests were bilingual; others of Irish descent, especially those who had received their training at St. Francis Seminary in Milwaukee, learned to speak German. They would then arrange to have two Masses on Sunday with instructions in German at one and in English at the other.[23] Where the pastor of a congregation was unable to preach in German,

---

[22] Anthony Urbanek to the Most Reverend Vincent E. Milde, Archbishop of Vienna, Wisconsin, 1853, *WMH*, X (September, 1926), 87.

[23] The Reverend Thomas Keenan, born in County Tyrone, Ireland, could speak German. Heiss wrote of him: "Here [Oshkosh] there are two Catholic churches, one for the Irish and the other for the Germans, but both are under the administration of one priest, who, though Irish, speaks German pretty well. Here too, the Germans have a Catholic school." Heiss to Board of Directors of Ludwig-Missionsverein, Milwaukee, August 30, 1861, in *Salesianum*, XL (October, 1945), 175.

the portion of his flock of that nationality was neglected in so far as instruction was concerned. According to a contemporary report, such a situation obtained in Racine in 1852 before the Germans built their own church. There the Reverend John W. Norris celebrated two High Masses each Sunday, one at nine o'clock for the Germans and one at eleven o'clock for the Irish congregation. According to the report, only the Irish were treated to a sermon. At afternoon Vespers the lecture on the truths of the Catholic Church was also given in English.[24]

These solutions were at best merely temporary. Wherever circumstances allowed, two separate congregations were formed, each with its own church and pastor.[25] Ironically, in some instances, because of the scarcity of clergy, one priest was forced to serve both parishes. Nationality became the usual basis for parish division throughout Wisconsin, particularly where both Irish and Germans lived in close proximity. In 1859 a correspondent wrote to the Boston *Pilot:*

> It is nothing at all unusual to see an Irish Congregation, comprised of from fifty to two hundred farmers and their families living in a circuit of about a mile around their neat little church to which is attached a few acres of

---

[24] Boston *Pilot*, March 13, 1852, letter from Edward Gillin, Racine, Wisconsin. When Catholics held a celebration, such as a church dedication, sermons were usually delivered in both languages. In some of the mixed congregations the Germans built a parochial school and the student body was drawn chiefly from German homes. This was the situation in Fond du Lac in 1861. Heiss to Ludwig-missionsverein, Milwaukee, August 30, 1861, *loc. cit.,* p. 174.

[25] The following are examples of German congregations which separated from Irish parishes: Appleton, St. Joseph's from St. Mary's in 1868; Highland, Iowa County, St. John's from St. Phillip's in 1860; Kenosha, St. George's from St. Mark's in 1849; Madison, Holy Redeemer from St. Raphael's in 1859; Milwaukee, St. Mary's from St. Peter's in 1847; Mineral Point, St. Mary's from St. Paul's in 1870; Racine, St. Mary's from St. Luke's in 1845. In Clyman, Dodge County, the Irish-German conflict became so heated that the Bishop had to settle the affair. For two such cases, *cf.* Theodore Roemer, *Saint Joseph in Appleton; the History of a Parish* (Menasha, Wisconsin: George Banta Publishing Company, 1943), pp. 16–27, and Heming, *op. cit.,* pp. 454–455, which describes Bishop Henni's intervention in Madison.

land and the residence of their zealous pastor, and on the next eminence, beyond the stream, or grassy marsh, a German church in the midst of a numerous and faithful congregation of industrious farmers, who care very little about becoming Yankeeized, either in language or manners. . . . In no other state have the Irish and German emigrants flocked together, and built up settlements exclusively Irish or German like in it.[26]

Through the efforts of Bishop Henni and his priests the Milwaukee diocese, by 1856, had its own seminary for the education of priests. Here nationality again caused friction. When funds were being collected appeals were made especially to the German Catholics. Heiss and the Reverend Joseph Salzmann had reasoned that aid might be forthcoming from the Irish and other nationalities after it had been demonstrated that the enterprise was not impossible.[27]

Heiss after writing about the laying of the cornerstone for the seminary wrote:

So some thought that the seminary would become an institution solely for the Germans. When, however, we also accepted Irish youths, certain parties spread the suspicion that it was planned to displace the Germans gradually and to make the seminary Irish. Both these suspicions were unfounded. We desire to establish a diocesan seminary, that is to say, one which is adequate for the needs of the diocese the faithful of which are chiefly German and Irish. The preacher explained this clearly and I am informed that everybody was satisfied with the pronouncement that in the future seminary the German element would be always amply considered, but indeed without neglecting other nationalities.[28]

---

[26] Boston *Pilot*, August 20, 1859, letter from a resident of Washington County, Wisconsin, July 29, 1859.

[27] Heiss was the rector of the seminary from 1856 to 1868 and Salzmann the procurator, 1856 to 1874. Both men were untiring in their efforts to put the seminary on a sound footing.

[28] *Salesianum*, XXXIX (July, 1944), 117-118, letter of Heiss to the Ludwigmissionsverein, Nojoshing near Milwaukee, July 21, 1855.

Both Irish and German students studied and were ordained at the seminary throughout the century. This institution served somewhat as a tempering influence within the diocese. The close intermingling of students of various nationalities helped to break down prejudice and many of the non-German students learned to speak the German language.[29] On the other hand, however, the Irish frequently accused the seminary officials of partiality towards students of German descent. In 1896 the *Catholic Citizen,* in an editorial, noted that Wisconsin state institutions of higher learning had graduated that year a rather large number of Irish-American students; also, that the majority of graduates from the colleges of Marquette in Milwaukee and Sacred Heart in Watertown bore Celtic names. On the other hand, the graduation class of Pio Nono College and the ordination class at the Seminary were composed entirely of German and Polish-Americans. The editor queried:

> What is the explanation of the situation? Is there a dearth of vocations for the priesthood among the Irish-Americans of Wisconsin? Or is there something inhospitable about the atmosphere of St. Francis? We pause for meditation.[30]

Again in 1899 the *Catholic Citizen* pointed out that more than half of the St. Patrick's churches in Wisconsin were provided with German-American pastors. In a list selected at random, the editor gave the location of seven parish churches and six mission churches dedicated to St. Patrick with the names of their German-American pastors.[31] This editorial provoked a discussion among Irish priests which was carried on in the *Citizen's* columns from

---

[29] *Salesianum,* XLII (January, 1947), 22, letter to Salzmann to the Ludwig-Missionsverein, Nojoshing, Wisconsin, October 3, 1864. Salzmann wrote regarding the class of 1863: "In the past scholastic year twelve were ordained to the holy priesthood here. Nine of the foregoing were ordained priests for our diocese, of whom four are of German, three of Irish, and two of Dutch descent. All are able to speak German."

[30] *Catholic Citizen,* June 26, 1896.

[31] *Ibid.,* August 19, 1899. Trouble in East St. Louis where an Irish congregation was resisting a German pastor provoked the article.

September to December, 1899. Some maintained that the reason for the "passing" of the Irish priesthood in Wisconsin was a lack of vocations among Irish-Americans. Others contended that there was no lack of vocations but rather that Irish vocations were not fostered by the Wisconsin hierarchy and seminary officials. One of the chief accusations against the seminary was that it had maintained a policy of discrimination against Irish students particularly in regard to fees charged for their education.[32]

This contention that German dominance of the Church in Wisconsin was injurious to Catholic growth especially among the non-German, or English-speaking Catholics, was merely a reiteration of charges which had been made frequently by the Irish clergy and which in the late 1870's and again in 1890 led to concerted action on both sides. In these two instances a successor to the Archbishopric of Milwaukee was at stake. As soon as it became known in the spring of 1878 that Henni, aged and infirm, was seeking the appointment of a coadjutor with the right of succession, and that he proposed his German friend, Heiss, Bishop of La Crosse, for the position, the Irish and American clergy of the Milwaukee Archdiocese took steps to prevent such an appointment. They lined up their arguments in letters and memorials to James Gibbons, Archbishop of Baltimore, counting on his influence with Rome to prevent the appointment of a German.[33]

---

[32] *Cf. Catholic Citizen*, September 9, 16, 23, 1899; October 7, 14, 21, 28, 1899; November 4 and 11, 1899; *Catholic Sentinel*, November 16 and December 7, 1899; Milwaukee *Sentinel*, November 25, 1899. The principal participants were J. J. Loughran, Minden, Nebraska; R. J. Smith of the Seminary faculty; a priest who signed himself "Old Soggarth," and one who simply signed "A Priest." Smith had refuted the accusations regarding the increased fee for Irishmen with an example from an old seminary ledger. The participant who signed himself "A Priest" demonstrated how he, the poor Irish student used as Smith's example, paid not only the full sum but interest besides. One phase of the discussion was centered upon a plan for financing the education of young Irish seminarians.

[33] AAB, 73-S-1, George L. Willard to Gibbons, Fond du Lac, Wisconsin, May 7, 1878; 73-S-2, Committee of Priests of Archdiocese of Milwaukee to Gibbons, Milwaukee, May 8, 1878; 73-S-13, H. F. Fairbanks to Gibbons, Whitewater, Wisconsin, May 23, 1878; 73-W-2, Willard to Gibbons, Pio Nono College, St. Francis, Wisconsin, September 7, 1878; 73-W-10,

One memorial to the Baltimore prelate stated that the United States census of 1870 revealed a native-born population in Wisconsin of approximately 690,000 and a foreign population of about 360,000. The memorial estimated the Catholic population at 290,000 of which 120,000 were Irish or of Irish descent, about 117,000 German or of German descent, and the remainder of other nationalities.

The memorial pointed out that the Archbishop and two bishops in Wisconsin were German, that all ecclesiastical officials were German but one, a Belgian, and that there never had been an English-speaking priest in any of these positions. Moreover, not only was the seminary under German domination, but a number of purely English-speaking parishes in the Milwaukee Archdiocese was under the charge of German priests. According to the Irish faction, the La Crosse diocese had five English-speaking priests and Green Bay only four, the proportion of priests to Catholics in these two dioceses was about one to 1,000 and 40,000 English-speaking Catholics were under the ministration of German priests. All sermons and instructions in these parishes were in German or broken English.

The memorial concluded with the following contention:

> These facts prove a thorough and complete rule of one nationality, which chance has placed in its possession, and a seeming determination on the part of that nationality to keep all the influence and authority in its own hands, and within the province of Milwaukee to build up a new Germany in the Church. The injury to Catholicity by such a course is evident. What could more hinder its true and permanent progress and development? Our only hope is that the successor or coadjutor with the right of succession of our highly esteemed Archbishop, will not be a German, but English speaking.[34]

Martin Kundig, Vicar General, Patrick Donahoe, pastor of St. John's Cathedral, James J. Keogh and Edward P. Lorigan, assistant pastors at Cathedral, to Gibbons, Milwaukee, September 23, 1878; 73-W-11, Thomas Fagan to Gibbons, St. Francis Seminary, Milwaukee, September 25, 1878; 74-F-5, E. J. Fitzpatrick to Gibbons, St. Francis Seminary, December 23, 1878.

[34] AAB 73-S-2, Committee of Priests of the Archdiocese of Milwaukee to Gibbons, Milwaukee, May 8, 1878. The group consisted of P. F. Pettit,

In the archdiocese, discussion of the question at first seems to have been carried on among the clergy quietly. Neither group of priests, Irish or German, wanted to arouse the suspicions of the other, but when about fifty German priests gathered at Saukville for a celebration in September, the news leaked out that they had discussed the plausibility of sending a petition to Rome urging the necessity of a German successor to Henni and also that such a petition had been signed later by some of the German clergy and was sent to Rome.[35] When this latter fact became known the storm broke loose. Milwaukee newspapers gave the matter publicity.[36] Thomas Fagan of the seminary faculty, an extremist on the issue of German dominance, spearheaded an assault on the German clergy and their un-American designs. He injudiciously launched an attack against Heiss, a fact which was not only embarrassing to the Irish and American priests, but which was also detrimental to their efforts.[37] The *Catholic Citizen*, edited

---

pastor, Madison, Wisconsin; George L. Willard, pastor, Fond du Lac, Wisconsin; H. F. Fairbanks, pastor, Whitewater, Wisconsin; Thomas Fagan, professor at Seminary of St. Francis, St. Francis, Wisconsin; Joseph J. Keenan, professor at Pio Nono College, St. Francis, Wisconsin; James J. Keogh, assistant pastor, St. John's Cathedral, Milwaukee. Three of these, Pettit, Keenan, and Keogh, were Irish-born.

[35] *Catholic Citizen*, December 21, 1878; January 4 and 18, 1879.

[36] Articles appeared in the Milwaukee *News*, December 15, 17, 18, 22, 24, 25, 29, 1878; January 1, 19, 29, 1879; February 1, 1879; Milwaukee *Sentinel*, December 16, 21, 23, 1878.

[37] In some issues of the Milwaukee *News* in a column under the heading "St. Francis Jottings" or a similar title, news items from St. Francis Seminary were printed. Derogatory and sarcastic references to the German side of the coadjutor controversy were frequently inserted in the column. The Dec. 25 and January 1 issues of the *News* contained letters signed "Clio," which attacked the German clergy and also Bishop Heiss. The first of these was an answer to Kilian Flasch of the seminary who had in the December 22 issue refuted the charges against the German clergy. Flasch also sent out a circular in defense of Bishop Heiss, who had been charged falsely with consenting to the petition which asked that he be made coadjutor. The newspaper articles from the seminary and the letters signed "Clio" were attributed to Fagan. His charges against Heiss made in a letter to Gibbons coincide with those of the newspaper. E. J. Fitzpatrick of St. Francis Seminary wrote to Gibbons that Fagan, who "some think is of unsound

by George L. Willard, an American priest, and E. A. Bray, a Catholic layman, at first procured a denial that a petition had issued from the German clergy at the seminary, but during the month of January, 1879, after an investigation, undertook to present the facts, not, however, without commending the Irish faction:

> It is due to the Irish priests to say that no effort has been made to get an Irishman for Coadjutor. Had this petition which was sent to Rome been for an American, who is able to speak the different languages used by Catholics in this diocese—An American in his tastes, inclinations, dispositions and patriotism, it would not have been sectarian, national or anti-Catholic. We would sign such a petition and every priest in the whole province could sign it with a good conscience.[38]

mind" sent articles to the local papers calumniating Heiss and giving scandal. AAB, 74-F-5, Fitzpatrick to Gibbons, St. Francis, Wisconsin, December 23, 1878; 73-W-11, Fagan to Gibbons, St. Francis, Wisconsin, September 25, 1878. However, in a letter to James A. McMaster, editor of the New York *Freeman's Journal*, George L. Willard, editor of the Milwaukee *Catholic Citizen*, mentions that Father Fagan was turned out of the seminary by the Germans because they imagined that he had written some of the articles appearing in several newspapers. Willard relates that Fagan knew the authors, had a better education than the German rector of the seminary, and was too high-minded to engage in such actions. It was Father Fagan, Willard maintained, who kept him from coming out too strongly in the *Catholic Citizen* against Peter J. Baltes, Bishop of Alton, Illinois, in his controversy with McMaster. George L. Willard, St. Francis, Wisconsin, to McMaster, March 26, 1879. The original of this letter is in the Archives of the University of Notre Dame.

[38] *Catholic Citizen*, January 4, 1879. *Cf.* also, the issues of January 18, 25, and February 1, 1879. Willard was pastor at Fond du Lac, Wisconsin, but became editor of the *Catholic Citizen* in November, 1878, at which time he also became a professor at St. Francis Seminary. Willard was a convert to Catholicism. In a letter to Gibbons on the coadjutor question he had written: "We have a powerful organization of German priests in our diocese. Our good Archbishop being a German with German proclivities, induced them to come here. We have had frequent importations of priests and students from Germany, while our own young men of splendid talents and intellect, Americans or Irishmen, have been allowed to attach themselves to other dioceses when they entered theology. Wherever one or two German

Gibbons took cognizance of the Irish priests' communications and sought the opinion of other members of the American hierarchy. Joseph Dwenger, Bishop of Fort Wayne, and John Lancaster Spalding, Bishop of Peoria, were suggested for the post. When the six bishops of the province of Milwaukee met for the purpose of choosing names for the terna to be sent to Rome, Thomas L. Grace, Bishop of St. Paul, succeeded only with some difficulty in getting Spalding's name on the list. He had been encouraged by Kundig to push Spalding's nomination. Kundig had assured Grace that Spalding would be acceptable and that there was, "among the intelligent and influential German Catholics of Milwaukee, a leaning toward Bishop Spalding." Bishop Grace informed Gibbons of Spalding's acceptability and added:

> I share the opinion of the Vicar General Kundig, the oldest and most respected among the German priests of the Archdiocese, that the appointment of a coadjutor who will be likely to change the existing policy and give a different tone to the Church in Wisconsin, is of vital importance to the interests of religion and the advancement of the Church.[39]

What was the position of the Irish Catholic laity on this question of a German hierarchy in Wisconsin? It seems evident that

---

families settle, it makes, in the opinion of these, a *mixed* congregation, to be presided over by a German priest, no matter if there be 100 or more Irish families in the same place. This forms the foundation for our good Archbishop's oft repeated remark that he must have all German priests for his diocese. These German priests have frequent meetings, the principal and ulterior object of which is to perpetuate a young Germany here. The fact of my being an *American not an Irishman*, as also speaking the German language, has led them to repose more than usual confidence in me, hence I have been made cognizant of many of their plans. . . . They have concluded that Rt. Rev. M. Heiss, the present Bishop of La Crosse, must be transferred to Milwaukee and Rev. Father Flasch be made Bishop of La Crosse. We, the American and Irish priests, have remained quiet, thinking there could scarcely be a possibility of another German Bishop here, but now we feel that we must act. . . ." AAB, 73-S-1, Willard to Gibbons, Fond du Lac, Wisconsin, May 7, 1878.

[39] AAB, 73-W-3, Thomas L. Grace to Gibbons, St. Paul, September 8, 1878.

they stood on the side of the Irish and American clergy, although they seem not to have published their views to any great extent.[40] If their attitude toward German pastors carried over to the bishops, who not only brought many German priests into the three dioceses, but also appointed them pastors, there is no question about the people's preference for an American coadjutor. Communications of the Irish and American clergy to Gibbons claimed to speak for both the English-speaking clergy and laity.

> We are convinced that an English-speaking Bishop is very much needed in Milwaukee, and we are expressing the desire of priests and people, when we pray for the appointment of Bishop Spalding.[41]

The editors of the *Catholic Citizen* admitted that they had received many letters expressing opinions on both sides of the question.[42] Some of these were probably from Irish laymen, but the Catholic laity evidently realized that their reaction would have little influence on the Holy See's decision.[43]

Open controversy subsided after January 19, 1879, chiefly because of a circular which Archbishop Henni issued to his priests containing a condemnation of the attacks on Heiss and forbidding

---

[40] The Milwaukee *Wisconsin* contained a letter from a "Catholic" who objected to the controversy, but who was anti-German as far as the coadjutor was concerned. He wrote: ". . . there are a large number of priests and Catholics who are conscientiously and justly opposed to the idea of a German coadjutor." Cited by the *Catholic Citizen*, January 4, 1879. Whether the "Catholic" who wrote the letter was a priest or a layman is open to question.

[41] AAB, 73-W-10, Group of Milwaukee Priests to Gibbons, Milwaukee, September 23, 1878.

[42] *Catholic Citizen*, January 18, 1879. The editors stated: "Were we to publish all of these letters we should fill our entire space, to the exclusion of other matter, and be obliged to issue a supplement besides."

[43] The problem was not purely local. Other dioceses where the German element was strong were having similar troubles. The Milwaukee *News*, January 17, 1879, published a sarcastic letter which referred to the resignation of Archbishop Purcell and the efforts of German priests there to obtain a German successor. The writer suggested that if they were looking for a *modus operandi* the dioceses of Wisconsin could furnish it: circulate a petition and then deny having done it.

the clergy to write or incite the publication of articles about the coadjutorship in the secular press.[44] The attacks on Heiss elicited expressions of regret and loyalty from his clergy of the La Crosse Diocese both Irish and German.[45]

Another moderating factor occurred after the death of Father Kundig, March 9, 1879, in the appointment of Patrick J. Donahoe, pastor of the Cathedral, a predominantly Irish parish, to the position of vicar general to succeed Kundig.[46] The Archbishop realized that such a move would lessen the effect of the charge that there had never been an ecclesiastical officer in the archdiocese of other than German birth or descent. About a month after Donahoe's appointment, however, Henni found it necessary to appoint a vicar general for the Germans also.[47] Whereas Kundig had been acceptable to the Irish because of his broadmindedness on the nationality question, Donahoe was not completely satisfactory to German element, the language problem alone causing great difficulty. Merely placing Irishmen or Americans in positions of authority was not an effective solution; neither did it demonstrate a realistic attitude toward this complex problem. Proverbially Rome is slow to act and this case of appointing a coadjutor was no exception; but Heiss was appointed, March 14, 1880.

Irish-German antipathy within the Church in Wisconsin was part of a nationwide antagonism that reached a crisis in the 1880's, and in the 1890's evolved into what became known as "Cahenslyism."[48] As had been the case in Wisconsin this antipathy origi-

---

[44] ADL, Circular sent by Henni to his priests, Milwaukee, January 19, 1879.

[45] ADL, Priests of La Crosse Diocese to Heiss, January 25, 1879. This letter was also published in the *Catholic Citizen*, February 1, 1879, and in the Milwaukee *News*, January 30, 1879. Bishop Grace also wrote to Heiss protesting the attacks on Heiss and expressing the loyalty of the clergy and laity of the St. Paul Diocese.

[46] *Catholic Citizen*, March 15, 1879.

[47] *Ibid.*, April 12, 1879.

[48] The Germans' insistence on a more realistic attitude toward their needs reached a crisis in 1886 when P. M. Abbelen, Vicar General of the Milwaukee Archdiocese, took to Rome a memorial presenting the demands of the German Catholics in the United States. Their requests were chiefly the following: the same rights should be given German, French, and Slavic

nated with the clergy and hierarchy rather than among the laity. Milwaukee's Archbishops Heiss (1880-1890), and Frederick X. Katzer (1890-1903), were considered leaders of the German faction, but since most of the controversy was carried on among the hierarchy and by them with Rome, there is little recorded evidence of local factions among the clergy and laity in Wisconsin. That the question was alive among the clergy, however, is shown

parishes as were given parishes in which the English language was used; immigrants of the first generation should be obliged to attend their national parishes; the German language should be taught in the German parochial schools; mixed parishes should be provided with a priest who understood German; and finally, the ordinary of each diocese should be obliged to provide a German vicar general for the German element in those dioceses where there was an Irish vicar general. This memorial claimed that the German minority within the Catholic Church in the United States was being unjustly restricted by the Irish majority. This presentation of the affair as a German-Irish conflict aroused the wrath of a number of the American Hierarchy, particularly Bishops Ireland of St. Paul and John Keane of Richmond, who were on their way to Rome when the memorial was presented. When it seemed that the question had been settled, in 1891, Peter Paul Cahensly, secretary of the St. Raphael Society for the protection of German Catholic emigrants, presented to Rome a memorial which had been adopted by the Society at a meeting held in Lucerne, Switzerland, December 9-10, 1890. The memorandum, suggesting means of safeguarding the Catholic faith of emigrants to the United States, contained alarming statistics on immigrant losses to the Faith in the United States. The report was presented to the Holy See with the recommendation that national groups in the United States be represented in the episcopacy in proportion to their numerical strength. Reports of the memorial to the United States emphasized the German aspect and were interpreted as though there were collusion between German Catholics and the German hierarchy in the United States with those in Europe with intent to Germanize the Church in America. Immediately controversy raged. Members of the hierarchy in the United States led by James Cardinal Gibbons and Archbishop Ireland remonstrated with Rome and the memorial was ultimately rejected. With the hierarchy likewise lined up in two camps, the so-called liberal *vs.* conservative, on Archbishop Ireland's school plans, the nationality question continued to be a matter for heated discussion. Controversy gradually died out in the early years of the twentieth century. *Cf.* Colman J. Barry, *The Catholic Church and German Americans* (Milwaukee: The Bruce Publishing Company, 1953), pp. 44-85, 131-236; John Tracy Ellis, *The Life of James Cardinal Gibbons* (Milwaukee: Bruce Publishing Company, 1952), I, 331-388.

by the organization of the American Catholic Clerical Union in Milwaukee in 1891 by priests largely of Irish ancestry who were opposed to what they believed were the aims of the German American Priests' Society.[49] The *Catholic Citizen* treated "Cahenslyism" extensively throughout this period but dealt with it as something which existed beyond the confines of Wisconsin.

In 1890 attempts were made by the American hierarchy, particularly by Archbishop Ireland, to prevent Katzer's appointment to the Archbishopric of Milwaukee to succeed Heiss, but they were not successful. Very little concerning the nationality of Heiss's successor appeared in the secular press, except in connection with the Bennett Law.[50] The *Catholic Citizen* discouraged discussion of the subject. Its forward-looking attitude on the question of national differences within the Church was expressed in an editorial as follows:

> One true attribute of our Catholicity would be a disposition to give each other's national proclivities a wide scope. Non-interference is pretty good policy in the polyglot stage of the Church. Breadth, tolerance and consideration are the dictates of Christian charity. We will all be Americans in a hundred years.[51]

In addition to Cahenslyism, the so-called school question formed

---

[49] Barry, *op. cit.*, p. 126, cites Archbishop Ireland's approval of the American Catholic Clerical Union in a letter to Monsignor Denis J. O'Connell: "The 'American Clerical Union' in Wisconsin is doing a splendid work. It has frightened the Germans, & driven them to their lairs. The 'Union' is managed with great prudence. It professes a great admiration for the zeal & success of the German 'Verein,' and professes to walk in the footsteps of the latter."

In 1883 Heiss wrote to a friend that he had been called to Rome to discuss questions concerning American Church affairs. Evidence that the nationality problem was still acute in the Archdiocese is contained in the following statement: "I have to appoint an administrator for the time of my absence, which is no easy thing on account of the different nationalities." Heiss to Kilian Kleiner, Milwaukee, June 11, 1883, *Salesianum*, XIII (July, 1918), 32-34.

[50] For injection of this question into the Bennett Law campaign *cf. supra.*, pp. 175 f.

[51] *Catholic Citizen*, January 11, 1890.

an integral part of the controversy over the "Americanization" of the Church in the United States. With political fights breaking out in a number of states comparable to that over the Bennett Law in Wisconsin, the so-called liberal members of the hierarchy led by Ireland and Gibbons took it upon themselves to present the Church in America as an institution not only devoted to the religious needs of its people, but one which was adaptable to American democratic principles. Regarding education, Gibbons and Ireland defended the parochial schools but took advantage of occasions to commend the public school system.[52] They considered Catholic parochial schools as supplementary to the public school system, not in opposition to it. Ireland called for state support of Catholic schools or the teaching of religion in state schools. In August, 1891, the St. Paul prelate put his theory into practice with an arrangement whereby the school boards of Faribault and Stillwater, Minnesota, took over the two parochial schools within their localities.[53]

Katzer and the German hierarchy in general were bitterly opposed to Ireland's action on the grounds that it was compromising the Catholic position. Moreover, they feared for their German parochial schools, but reasons for their opposition also involved the struggle over Cahenslyism. On the other hand, some of the Irish and Irish-American clergy and laity of the Milwaukee Archdiocese expressed themselves as favorable toward Ireland's stand on the school question. James M. Cleary, a priest of Irish descent and pastor of the Irish parish in Kenosha, was definitely on Ireland's side when he wrote that the system inaugurated by Ireland in Minnesota had been in vogue for some time in several

[52] Gibbons presented the case for the Catholic parochial school in an address delivered to the National Education Association, which met in Nashville in July, 1889. When the same organization met in St. Paul, 1890, Ireland addressed the convention on "State Schools and Parish Schools." He praised the public school system and regretted the necessity of maintaining a parochial school system. Daniel Reilly, *op. cit.,* pp. 39-50.
[53] *Ibid.,* pp. 67-105. According to the arrangement the school boards would hire the religious teachers and pay them their salary. No religion would be taught during school hours.

of the German settlements in Wisconsin.[54] Another Irish-American priest who became vocal on the question was Michael J. O'Brien, pastor at Fort Howard. He had been a teacher in the public schools for three years before beginning his studies for the priesthood. Speaking at the ceremonies accompanying the laying of the cornerstone of the normal school at Stevens Point, April 26, 1894, O'Brien said:

> The Catholic Church is not an enemy of public schools, and if her people desire to teach their children the primary branches in their own schools, they should have that privilege. . . . With Bishop Ireland, whom we all know so well and admire so much, I would say, "God bless the public schools; may they dot the valleys and the hillsides." There may be some of our people who are not in favor of public schools; there may be some people who are opposed to us, but in neither case should be drawn general conclusions that these are the sentiments of the whole.[55]

Representative of a large portion of the Irishmen resident in the state of Wisconsin, 150 delegates to the state convention of the Ancient Order of Hibernians held in Fond du Lac, July, 1894, adopted a resolution which stated they were not hostile to the public schools and further declared:

> We believe it [education] to be one of the fundamental parts of our government; and we oppose as both illegal

[54] Humphrey Moynihan, "Archbishop Ireland," *Acta et Dicta*, VI (October, 1933), 23. Cleary and Ireland also worked together closely in the Catholic Total Abstinence movement. Cleary later joined Ireland's Archdiocese. An interesting accommodation in regard to public schools was that instituted by the Reverend Caspar Rehrl, founder of the Sisters of St. Agnes at Barton, Wisconsin. In the rule which he drew up for their guidance, Rehrl stated that the Sisters would be occupied chiefly in rural schools and that they could not achieve their aim unless they were to take charge of public schools. He insisted that they keep state regulations regarding textbooks, that they admit non-Catholics to religious instruction by written permission only, and that they observe the arrangements whereby religious exercises and instruction would be entirely separate from the functioning of the public school. Johnson, *Stuffed Saddlebags*, p. 243.

[55] *Catholic Sentinel*, May 10, 1894. O'Brien had made a similar statement during the Bennett Law Campaign, *supra*, p. 176.

and unwise any steps taken towards a division of the public school fund. We recognize the right of each religious denomination to maintain at its own cost proper schools for the Christian education of its youth, but we deprecate the bitter controversies and confusion that would inevitably follow an attempt to divide and parcel out the public funds for their support.[56]

There is reason for the Irish attitude toward Ireland's plan. As a matter of record, when a free public school system was being installed in Kenosha, 1844-1845, one of its strongest proponents and supporters was Father Kundig. At that time Irish Catholics constituted the largest foreign group in Kenosha and because of their economic status a free school system was to their advantage.[57] Religious instruction could be provided outside of school hours. This was somewhat in the tradition of the Irish who did not have parochial schools taught by religious in their native country, where the teachers, however, were Catholic. Similarly, in the late 1890's, the seven public schools in the area around Erin Prairie in St. Croix County were all conducted by Irish Catholic teachers.[58]

Frequently in Irish rural communities the church and public school were the center of practically all activity. Two specific examples are the communities of Meeme and Monches. One writer has made the claim that in the former locality the public school was so inseparably associated with the Catholic church that peo-

---

[56] *Catholic Sentinel*, July 26, 1894.

[57] Schafer, "Origin of Wisconsin's Free School System," *WMH*, IX (1925), 35. When the voters of Kenosha gave their consent to the establishment of a tax-supported school, the question of a building arose. Kundig offered the basement of the Catholic church as a temporary expedient. On June 16, 1845, the first free public school in Wisconsin was opened in the basement of a Catholic church. In June, 1846, the first ward public school in Milwaukee was likewise opened in the basement of St. Peter's Catholic Church. No religious instruction was given during school hours. In 1849, an arrangement similar to Ireland's plan obtained at Hazel Green. The Dominican Sisters of Sinsinawa opened a school there which both Catholics and Protestants attended. The daily religion class for Catholics was taught after the regular school hours. The situation was reversed when a Catholic school was substituted for the public one. Johnson, *Stuffed Saddlebags*, pp. 246, 243.

[58] Heming, *op. cit.*, p. 811.

ple spoke of both as though they were one.[59] The same writer pointed out that scarcely an Irish family existed in which one or more members were not teachers and that there were numerous instances where every child in a large Irish family had taken up public school teaching.[60]

All of these circumstances contributed to the Irishman's acceptance of the public school. Typical of their attitude is the wording of an article which appeared in the *Catholic Sentinel*. The editor noted that when the "rage for parochial schools was at its height" the Catholics of New Richmond, St. Croix County, had built a parochial school, but that, since the Reverend Dr. William E. Degnan took charge of the mission, the school was closed and the children attended the public school "with very good results."[61]

Education in Wisconsin during the 1840's and 1850's depended almost wholly upon local efforts. In some instances teachers who conducted schools financed their work by charging a fixed sum per pupil. In Milwaukee and other populated areas which were developing into cities, some of the wards rented a building and hired a teacher, meeting the expenses through a local tax levy. Since there was no general school tax, educational opportunities varied greatly and generally there were no provisions for the poor. In some instances private or parish groups organized free schools which the poorer children could attend.

The early schools set up by Kundig in Milwaukee were of the latter type. In 1842 Kundig opened a school for girls conducted by Catherine Shea and one Miss Murray, also one for boys conducted in a room in the basement of St. Peter's Church under the tutelage of Joseph Murray.[62] Early schools were also established in the Irish parishes of the lead region, also in Watertown and

---

[59] Holmes, *Old World Wisconsin*, p. 183.
[60] *Ibid.*, p. 182.
[61] *Catholic Sentinel*, January 3, 1895. The editor did not know the reason for this action on the part of Degnan. It may have been chiefly economic.
[62] Johnson, *Stuffed Saddlebags*, pp. 179-180. The first name of Catherine Shea's companion teacher is not given. In another room in the basement of St. Peter's, boys from German families attended classes conducted by a German teacher.

Janesville.[63] The pastors of the parishes in which these schools were located had usually instigated their foundation, but they were not parochial schools in the same sense that that term is used today. Some of them eventually became public schools and others gradually evolved into strictly parochial or parish schools under the immediate direction of the pastor with a religious community of sisters providing the teachers.

One of these earliest teaching sisterhoods with its origins in Wisconsin is the Order of St. Dominic established by Mazzuchelli at Sinsinawa Mound, Grant County, in 1847.[64] As distinguished from other religious communities of women the Sinsinawa group has been referred to as the "oldest English-speaking religious

---

[63] In 1847, St. Paul's School was organized in Mineral Point, Rose Dunbar, *History of St. Paul's Church* (Mineral Point, 1942). The school at Shullsburg was taught by William Ahern, a graduate of Maynooth, and Bridget Cummings. Cf. W. Raymond Jamieson, *A Brief History of St. Mathew's Church at Shullsburg* (Shullsburg, 1925), p. 9. Father Mazzuchelli also established schools at Benton and New Diggings in the lead region. Prior to 1857 a school was conducted in St. Bernard's Parish, Watertown, by Daniel Collins with the assistance of Annie Hoye. Cf. Meagher, *op. cit.*, p. 19. The school in St. Patrick's Parish, Janesville, was taught by Thomas Tracey. Cf. *History of St. Patrick's Church, Janesville, Wisconsin* (Janesville, 1925). Mazzuchelli also founded a college, St. Thomas, at Sinsinawa Mound for the higher education of young men. The college was staffed by members of the Dominican Order under the presidency of Mazzuchelli. Some of the professors were Irish as were also some of the students. In 1849 he placed the college under the direction of the Dominican Fathers whose provincial headquarters were in Somerset, Ohio. Because of an insufficient number of priests to staff the institution it was closed in 1866. Samuel S. Mazzuchelli, *Memoirs Historical and Edifying of a Missionary Apostolic*, tran. Sister M. Benedicta Kennedy (Chicago: W. F. Hall Printing Company, 1915), pp. x, xi.

Of later origin was Sacred Heart College, Watertown, established in 1872 by the Holy Cross Fathers from South Bend, Indiana, who were in charge of St. Bernard's, the Irish parish there. Lists of graduates, officers and members of societies of the school reveal that students of Irish descent were in the majority. The college eventually became a novitiate for training brothers of the Holy Cross Congregation. Meagher, *op. cit.*, pp. 50, 60, 115-117.

[64] Heming, *op. cit.*, p. 964, Mazzuchelli, *op. cit.*, p. xi. For a few years the young community had its motherhouse at Benton, but in 1867 moved again to Sinsinawa.

community of women in Wisconsin, or more properly, Irish-American Order of the State."[65] Most of the other foundations of religious women established in Wisconsin were either branches of older German communities or were new American foundations established by German women.

Mazzuchelli had set out to establish a community which would draw the daughters of the pioneer settlers. Not motivated by the nationalistic spirit of so many of the other European founders, he seems to have placed his confidence in the new country and the Catholic emigrants who had come to settle in it. His intention was not to found an "Irish-American" community as such. Nevertheless, the surnames of the first four members of the community were definitely Irish: Fitzpatrick, two Conways, and Cahill. Mazzuchelli referred to these women as his "four cornerstones." Mother Emily Power, long the guiding spirit of the Community and her three sisters were Irish-born.[66] Since the Community was established in southern Wisconsin, where most of the Catholics were Irish-born or of Irish descent, many of its recruits were drawn from that area. This also helps to account for the Irish family names of many of the Sisters. The three Sisters of this order teaching in Prairie du Chien, 1860, were of Irish birth.[67]

Of more immediate Irish origin, but not permanent, was the foundation of the Brigidines in Kenosha in 1851. With the aid of the Reverend Michael McFaul, pastor of St. Mark's parish, two members of the Brigidine Sisterhood emigrated to Kenosha from Mountrath, County Carlow, Ireland. Soon after their arrival they opened St. Mark's Female School. According to an 1852 report the number of sisters had increased within a year to three professed sisters and several novices.[68]

---

[65] *Catholic Citizen,* November 15, 1878, communication from a reader.

[66] Sister M. Eva, O.P., to the writer, Sinsinawa, Wisconsin, September 6, 1951. A list of the members of the Sisterhood who were admitted to profession between the years 1849-1878 discloses a majority of Irish surnames.

[67] In the 1860 census they were listed as Sisters of the Church: Mary Agnes Barry, Mary C. Williams, and Mary A. Burns (probably Byrne).

[68] P. L. Johnson, "The American Odyssey of the Irish Brigidines," *Salesianum,* XXXIX (April, 1944), 64; Boston *Pilot,* March 13, 1852, Edward Gillin to editor, Racine, Wisconsin, Feb. 2, 1852.

In attempting to establish the Community on a firm financial foundation, Bishop Henni appealed to the Society for the Propagation of the Faith.[69] The Community, however, did not prosper. It seems that the two founders had left Ireland without the approval of their superiors, including that of their local ordinary. Since their work did not expand beyond the one school for girls in Kenosha, their income must have been very meager. Moreover, there were not only frequent transfers of the pastors at St. Mark's to other parishes during these years, but the pastor was also often absent visiting the surrounding missions. These conditions undoubtedly contributed to the insecurity of the institution. The Sisters left Kenosha sometime in 1855 and after attempts to locate in other parts of the United States, these Irish Brigidines disbanded in 1869 and the members entered other religious communities in the United States and Canada and some returned to Ireland.[70]

Another religious community of women with an Irish background which founded a motherhouse in Wisconsin was the Sisters of Mercy. Mother M. Francis Jackson with five other sisters and three postulants at the invitation of the Reverend James Doyle arrived in Janesville during November, 1870, from Sterling, Illinois. In April, 1871, the first reception ceremony took place. In the meantime the sisters had opened St. Joseph Academy for girls. Financial difficulties in 1876 forced Father Doyle to close St. Patrick's church and school at Janesville. The sisters, therefore, moved to Fond du Lac where they cared for the orphans and taught in the basement of St. Joseph Church. When in 1885 the church and school reopened in Janesville, the sisters returned, purchased property for a convent, and reopened their academy.[71]

---

[69] *Ibid.*, p. 64. The letter of Henni is cited: "The Sisters of St. Bridget; as I declared in my last year's report, arrived here from Ireland extremely needy, but now are doing very well in teaching a large school of poor children. At present they have hardly a home of their own, because means are lacking for which I awaited in vain from Europe. Nevertheless, in order to settle them permanently I was obliged again to contract a debt of $600."

[70] *Ibid.*, pp. 61-67.

[71] Sister Mary Josephine Gately, *The Sisters of Mercy, Historical Sketches, 1831-1931* (New York: The Macmillan Company, 1931), pp. 366-368. Sister M. Ernetta to the writer, Janesville, Wisconsin, August 25, 1951.

The Daughters of Charity of St. Vincent de Paul, whose motherhouse was in Emmitsburg, Maryland, and who entered Milwaukee in 1846, numbered some Irish members and conducted a school for the girls of the Irish parishes in Milwaukee.[72] Quite naturally the English-speaking communities of religious women were, where possible, given charge of parochial schools in Irish parishes, while the German communities were called on to staff the German schools. There were exceptions, however, to both of these arrangements.[73]

Not all of the Irishmen in Wisconsin were Catholics, but Irish Protestants, scattered in localities in various parts of the state, were few by comparison. Something has already been told of the groups in Lima Township, Rock County; Koshkonong Township, Jefferson County; in Exeter, Green County; and in the townships of Medina, Cottage Grove, Sun Prairie, and Fitchburg, Dane County.[74] Moreover, the number, location, and religious affiliations of Irish-born Protestant clergymen, although not an infallible, are at least a possible indication of the existence of Irish Protestant congregations. In 1850 there were approximately eleven Irish-born Protestant ministers in Wisconsin. Of these, three were recorded in the 1850 census as Baptists, one as an Epis-

---

[72] Michael Heiss to Board of Directors of the Ludwig-missionsverein, Milwaukee, August 30, 1861, *Salesianum*, XL (October, 1945), 170. P. L. Johnson, *Daughters of Charity in Wisconsin* (Milwaukee, 1946), p. 8.

[73] The School Sisters of Notre Dame, of German origin, took over St. Mark's in Kenosha when the Brigidines left. Johnson, "American Odyssey of the Irish Brigidines," *loc. cit.*, p. 64. The Franciscan Sisters of Perpetual Adoration, La Crosse, Wisconsin, founded by a number of German Tertiaries at St. Francis, Wisconsin, in 1849, taught in Janesville from 1865 until 1870, when the Sisters of Mercy took their place. At that time the Motherhouse of the Franciscan Sisters was at Jefferson, Wisconsin. ASRC, Sister M. Bonaventure Schoeberle, "Our Missions" (Unpublished manuscript), pp. 13-14. Concerning the Franciscan Sisters at Janesville, Heiss, director of the Community, wrote: "The last named (the school at Janesville) is the most important because it is the largest and it is an entirely Irish parish. The priest at Janesville takes great interest in the good cause and I hope that our sisters will find a very fertile field of labor. . . ." Sister M. Mileta Ludwig, *A Chapter of Franciscan History* (New York: Bookman Associates, 1949), p. 127.

[74] *Supra*, pp. 67, 71, 73-74.

copalian, two as Methodists, two Presbyterians, and three were listed without any designation of sect. By 1860 the number of Irish-born Protestant ministers had increased to fifteen. Of these, Irish Baptist ministers had decreased to two, Methodist, Episcopalian, and Presbyterian clergymen had each increased to four, and one minister was listed without the sect designated. It is interesting to note that none of the ministers recorded in the 1850 census was again listed in the 1860, nor were any of the locations repeated.[75] Most of these were probably itinerant missionaries, particularly the Baptists and Methodists. One reason for the increase in Episcopalian clergymen was the founding of the Episcopal Seminary at Nashotah, Waukesha County. One of the Irish Episcopalian clergymen was stationed in 1860 at Nashotah and one of the students there was Irish-born.

Much of the social life of Wisconsin Irishmen was carried on within the parish organization. This is particularly true of their participation in the Catholic Total Abstinence movement, the Ancient Order of Hibernians, and in certain literary and dramatic societies. Frequently and quite necessarily the pastor of the congregation was the organizer and leader in these movements, especially of the Catholic Total Abstinence Societies.

The need for promoting temperance among Irish Catholics in

[75] In 1850, the Baptist ministers were located in Berlin, Marquette County; Appleton, Outagamie County; Port Washington, Ozaukee County. In 1860, the two Baptists were in Hubbard, Dodge County and in Wheatland, Vernon County. The Episcopalian clergyman in 1850 was stationed in Nekimi, Winnebago County; in 1860, the four Episcopalians were in Green Bay, in Kenosha, in Prescott, Pierce County, and in Summit, Waukesha County. The two Methodists were located in Greenfield (later Fitchburg), Dane County and in Nepeuskun, Winnebago County in 1850. The four Methodist Ministers listed in 1860 were in Sun Prairie, Dane County; Mineral Point, Iowa County; Pepin, Pepin County, and La Grange, Walworth County. The 1850 census listed a New Style Presbyterian clergyman in Two Rivers, Manitowoc County, and a Reformed Presbyterian in Harmony, Rock County. The 1860 census recorded two Old Style Presbyterians, one in Dekorra, Columbia County, and one in Fitchburg, Waukesha County. The three Protestant clergymen listed without their sect in 1850 were located in Racine, Delavan, Walworth County, and in Hartford, Washington County; in 1860 a Protestant minister was located in Milton, Rock County.

Wisconsin was not peculiar to Irishmen within this state, for the Reverend Theobald Mathew had sought to remedy intemperance by organizing Catholic Total Abstinence Societies in Ireland and the movement had spread to the United States with the large influx of Irish immigrants.[76] In Wisconsin, Mazzuchelli was active in promoting temperance because, as he pointed out in his memoirs, Americans, lacking the means of producing wines common to Europe, made extensive use of "strong spirits extracted from Indian corn." Many of the immigrants from Ireland, "notwithstanding the Faith, the generosity, the honesty, the industry and all the other virtues that so eminently distinguish the race, were often too weak upon this one point, giving themselves up in bondage to the vice of intemperance."[77] Recognizing the evil within the lead region, Mazzuchelli organized total abstinence societies in the congregations he set up.

> From the year 1839 when the Societies had become established in the various Missions recorded in these Memoirs, piety actually made visible progress from day to day, in proportion as the virtue of Temperance won its blessed victories among the people; peace and plenty reigned in the families, Catholicity won the respect and reverence of its very enemies, and the Faith spread among the more sincere of those outside the Church. Many of the Catholic Irish abandoned entirely the dangerous traffic in intoxicating drink and sought more honorable means of subsistence.[78]

These societies were probably the first Catholic temperance societies organized within Wisconsin. Mazzuchelli opened their membership to Protestants who, he said, were impressed by the re-

---

[76] Sister Joan Bland, *Hibernian Crusade: The Story of the Catholic Total Abstinence Union of America* (Washington: The Catholic University of America Press, 1951), pp. 7-20.

[77] Mazzuchelli, *op. cit.*, p. 282.

[78] *Ibid.*, p. 283. Mazzuchelli included in his Memoirs a facsimile of the certificate given to those who took the pledge. The formula, printed within the outline of a cross, was as follows: "I, N. N., promise to abstain from any intoxicating drink, unless used medicinally and by order of a physician." The certificate indicated the duration of the pledge, when it was taken, and contained the signature of the priest who administered it. According to the wording of the certificate the priest was the president of the society.

sults that temperance produced among the Irish Catholic citizens.[79] As has been noted previously, Father O'Kelley, the first resident priest in Milwaukee, organized a total abstinence society within St. Peter's parish as early as 1841.[80] His work in promoting temperance was eulogized by the secular press which reported that 250 Catholics had taken the pledge from O'Kelley.[81] That other societies had also been founded within the vicinity of Milwaukee is evident from the demonstration maneuvered by Kundig in 1843.[82] The Fourth Provincial Council of Baltimore, held in 1840, recommended the establishment of temperance societies in all Catholic parishes. Kundig was encouraged also by the exhortations of his ordinary, Bishop Lefevere of Detroit, who had written to the Cincinnati *Catholic Telegraph* that he hoped to see total abstinence societies established in every parish in his diocese.[83] Kenosha, probably as a result of Kundig's efforts, had a Catholic Total Abstinence Society already in 1845; the Irish in Dublin, Grant County, had established a Catholic Temperance Association before 1846, and the Reverend Michael McFaul had organized a society in Janesville in 1852 or 1853.[84]

Evidence of temperance societies and their activities between the years 1845 and 1872, however, is very meager. Moreover, the secretarial records of the state Catholic Total Abstinence Union, founded in 1871, were destroyed by fire. Proceedings of some of the annual state conventions are extant in the *Catholic Citizen,* and participation of Wisconsin societies in the Catholic Total Abstinence Union of America is recorded in the published proceedings of the Union's conventions.[85]

---

[79] *Ibid.,* p. 284.
[80] *Supra,* p. 137.
[81] Milwaukee *Sentinel,* May 18, June 8, 1841.
[82] *Supra,* p. 196, n. 6.
[83] Johnson, *op. cit.,* p. 231.
[84] Boston *Pilot,* September 20, 1845; McLeod, *op. cit.,* p. 233; Boston *Pilot,* June 25, 1853, letter from a correspondent, "T. J." Janesville, Wisconsin, June 2, 1853.
[85] Proceedings of all the state conventions are not available because extant issues of the *Catholic Citizen* for the nineteenth century date from December, 1878, to April, 1880, and from 1882 to 1900. Further research in Wisconsin newspapers may uncover the proceedings of state conventions from 1872 to 1878 and for 1880 and 1881.

Although the first meeting to organize Catholic Total Abstinence on a statewide scale was held in 1871, the first actual state convention met June 18 and 19, 1872, at Watertown.[86] The meeting in 1871, attended by several leading Catholics and priests, reportedly convened for the purpose of organizing a society which would promote total abstinence from "all intoxicating drinks and liquors."[87] At the first State Convention in Wisconsin the Reverend George L. Willard of Fond du Lac was elected president, Dr. D. W. Nolan of Milwaukee, recording secretary, William D. Stacy of Watertown, corresponding secretary, the Reverend James O'Malley of Montello, treasurer, and John Clark of Beaver Dam, sergeant-at-arms.[88]

At the second National Convention of the Catholic Total Abstinence Union of America, held in October, 1872, Willard, as a delegate from Wisconsin, described the state convention of 1872 as a meeting of four or five societies in a small village of about 3,000 inhabitants. He estimated the attendance at 7,000, which seems to have been a considerable exaggeration.[89] Although there were about twenty Catholic Total Abstinence societies in Wis-

---

[86] *Catholic Citizen,* July 11, 1896. The state conventions were numbered from the year 1871, hence 1896 was the twenty-fifth anniversary of the founding of the state total abstinence movement. *Cf.* also, Heming, *op. cit.,* p. 1078; Meagher, *op. cit.,* p. 42. The evolution of the Watertown St. Bernard's Temperance and Benevolent Society is interesting. Father Kundig had organized a temperance society in Watertown which took part in the Milwaukee St. Patrick's day celebration in 1843. In March, 1867, a Hibernian Benevolent Society was founded which seems merely to have been the Tara Hall Circle of the Fenian Brotherhood reorganized for a different purpose. Shortly after his arrival as assistant pastor at St. Bernard's the Reverend Thomas Pope Hodnett added temperance to the aims of the organization and had it incorporated under state laws as the St. Bernard Temperance and Benevolent Society of the city of Watertown, Wisconsin. The society was very active, establishing a library and reading room. After Father Hodnett was transferred from the parish the society continued to prosper and seems to have been the center of parish activity for some time. *Ibid.,* pp. 29-30, 33-35.
[87] *Catholic Citizen,* July 11, 1896.
[88] Heming, *op. cit.,* p. 1078.
[89] *Proceedings of the Second General Convention of the Catholic Total Abstinence Union of America* (1872), p. 9.

consin, only six of them were reported as belonging to the state and national unions.[90]

The number of Wisconsin societies belonging to the national and state unions varied from year to year. Some total abstinence societies in the state did not belong to either union and some were affiliated with the state, but not the national union. In 1878 the state union counting forty societies reached the high point in its history.[91] In 1891, twenty-three men's societies and six ladies' societies marked the peak of Wisconsin's membership in the national union.[92]

Practically the entire membership in Wisconsin was Irish or of Irish descent and was confined to Irish parishes, although there was an active society among the Indians of the Keshena Reservation, some members and promoters were of early American ancestry, and a very few were German, Dutch, and French. The Germans quite generally regarded the total abstinence movement with the same scorn expressed by the Reverend Francis X. Paulhuber who wrote that the temperance law was "satisfactory for the English and Irish because as everybody knows they drink solely to get drunk," while the Germans knew how to drink in moderation.[93]

In their letters to the national and state conventions the German hierarchy of Wisconsin expressed appreciation for the good which the organization was accomplishing. When the state convention met in Green Bay in 1884, Bishop F. X. Krautbauer was present in the sanctuary during the Mass and opened the convention with prayer.[94] These men were never the strong supporters and promoters of the movement, however, as were, for example, Archbishop Ireland, Bishop Joseph Cotter of Winona, and Bishop John J. Keane of Richmond, later Archbishop of Dubuque. The German bishops of Wisconsin could recognize virtue in tem-

---

[90] *Ibid.*, p. 18.
[91] *Proceedings of the CTAU of A,* VIII (1878), 29.
[92] *Ibid.,* XXI (1891), 5.
[93] Francis X. Paulhuber to the Ludwig-missionsverein, Milwaukee, Wisconsin, July 22, 1855, in *Salesianum,* XXXIX (October, 1944), 176.
[94] *Catholic Citizen,* June 23, 1883.

perance, but not in total abstinence. The difference in viewpoint between the Irish clergy and the bishops was stated by the Reverend James O'Malley, one of the founders and presidents of the Wisconsin Union, when he expressed himself in opposition to Bishop Sebastian G. Messmer of Green Bay:

> I must differ from the bishop, on this point, for I earnestly believe that total abstinence is the one and only cure for intemperance. The bishop may have his opinion, but I think I am right in my position. I have worked to that end and shall continue to do so. Some of the ablest men in the Catholic Church are total abstinence men.[95]

The Reverend J. M. Cleary, probably the most active total abstinence agitator in Wisconsin, president of the Wisconsin Union a number of times, and also of the National Union, ultimately left the Milwaukee Archdiocese in November, 1892, to join the Archdiocese of St. Paul.[96] There were rumors in the press, which were denied, that Cleary took this step because his activity and views on total abstinence were in opposition to Archbishop Katzer's, but his close association with Ireland in total abstinence work and the more or less constant friction between the two archbishops probably formed part of the reason for Cleary's step into Ireland's Archdiocese.[97]

Most of the priests active in the state union were also Irish or of Irish descent. The following clergymen held the office of pres-

---

[95] *Ibid.*, September 1, 1894. For Messmer's proposed national Catholic Temperance League, *cf.* Bland, *op. cit.*, p. 191. Messmer felt that the total abstinence movement was too limited in its appeal, that a program of temperance could include nationalities among whom alcoholic beverages were considered a necessity of life.

[96] Record in Chancery Office, Archdiocese of St. Paul. Father Cleary had become lecturer for the national union in 1887 and had been released from his parochial duties by Archbishop Heiss at the request of Bishop Ireland. That year most of his time was devoted to lecturing throughout the United States, although he maintained his residence in Kenosha. Evidently he had again resumed his pastoral duties in Kenosha, however, when Archbishop Katzer released him.

[97] *Catholic Citizen,* September 24, 1892, citing the Milwaukee *Evening Wisconsin;* October 1, 1892; *Catholic Sentinel,* September 29, 1892.

ident at some time during the union's history prior to 1900: G. L. Willard, James O'Malley, J. M. Cleary, E. M. McGinnity, M. J. Ward, W. J. Fitzmaurice, J. S. Campbell, L. P. O'Reilly, and F. J. Fiss. These men, with other pastors of Irish parishes, believed firmly in total abstinence and worked faithfully for the cause. Although officers in local societies frequently were laymen and the pastor was spiritual director, the presidents and vice-presidents of the state union were priests and the offices of secretary and treasurer were held by laymen. During the 1890's when ladies' societies were admitted into the state union, women were elected annually to the office of secretary and one or two of them to an honorary vice-presidency.[98]

The history of the Catholic Total Abstinence Union of Wisconsin quite generally parallels that of the Catholic Total Abstinence Union of America. The proceedings of both groups reveal discussion of insurance, the position of the union on administration of the pledge, its relations with non-Catholic temperance efforts, its stand on high license, observance of the Sunday, temperance legislation, and the ever-present question of dues and fund-raising projects, such as assistance to the Irish Land League and the establishment of a Father Mathew Chair at the Catholic University of America.

Although the Wisconsin Union did set up the Catholic Total Abstinence Aid Association in 1879 to provide insurance benefits for its members, the project failed.[99] The Wisconsin union also advocated administration of the pledge to first communicants and confirmation classes as early as 1887.[100] Throughout the history of the state union, newspaper reports were filled with platitudes about good will among Protestant and Catholic abstainers. In some localities Protestants reportedly attended lectures by Catholics, sometimes in large numbers, and took the pledge from a priest along with Catholics, but they were not admitted to the

---

[98] Nellie Kane of Ashland and Agnes Brooks of Watertown were especially active in the state union.
[99] *Catholic Citizen*, June 28, August 30, October 25, 1879.
[100] *Ibid.*, July 2, 1887. This custom was first mentioned in the resolutions of the National Union at the 1890 Convention. *Cf.* Bland, *op. cit.*, p. 162.

state union. By 1890, under the leadership of Father O'Malley, there was a definite trend toward the admission of women and Protestants into the societies affiliated with the state and national unions. In 1888 a ladies' society was organized in Whitewater.[101] In January, 1891, O'Malley opened his parish society in Oshkosh to all persons over sixteen years of age regardless of sex or belief, provided that they took the total abstinence pledge. By the time the national union held its convention in August, 1891, Wisconsin had six ladies' societies.[102] The Catholic Total Abstinence Society of Medford also opened its roll to people of any religious belief in December, 1894.[103] The state union capitulated to this liberal trend in 1895 by passage of a resolution removing the denominational barrier to membership for all who would sign the constitution.[104] This admittance of non-Catholics was carrying the fraternization with Protestant abstainers to the limits. There is no evidence though of large numbers of non-Catholics joining the Catholic Total Abstinence Union in the state as a result of this open-door policy.

Throughout the union's history the *Catholic Citizen* championed the cause of total abstinence. Its editors took up the cry for high license and for the need of legislative enactments to control the sale of intoxicants.

> The temperance movement is not a matter of moral suasion. Those who think so are always traitors in the camp. It calls for wise and efficient legislative enactments. Liquor selling, if unregulated in our community, would overwhelm the State with evil. It must be regu-

---

[101] P. L. Johnson, "An Experiment in Adult Education," *Salesianum*, XLV (October, 1950), 151.

[102] *Ibid.*, January 24, 1891.

[103] *Catholic Sentinel*, January 3, 1895. According to this account, Catholics and non-Catholics met for a lecture by Father O'Malley, about 600 persons took the pledge, and a society was formed composed of people of various religious beliefs and nationalities. The Protestant minister proposed Father Stephen Duren as president. He was elected and the other offices were filled by Catholics and non-Catholics.

[104] *Catholic Citizen*, July 6, 1895.

lated and the restrictions established must be of no child's play.[105]

Claims were made that the Union's support was influential in obtaining the enactment of high license laws in several localities and in 1884 the state union in convention adopted the following resolution:

> Resolved, That we recognize in the high license law enacted by the recent session of the Wisconsin Legislature a fitting response to a popular demand; that we believe this law ought to be sustained, and further, that every locality should avail itself by popular vote of the highest fee permitted by its provisions.[106]

The *Catholic Citizen* urged Irishmen to become total abstainers and excoriated Irish politicians who did not support high license legislation, Irish saloon-keepers who sold the evil stuff, and Irish drunkards who shamelessly imbibed it.[107] The *Citizen* also lent editorial support to the national union in its opposition to the monks of St. Vincent's monastery at Latrobe, Pennsylvania, who engaged in brewing and selling beer as a means of revenue.[108]

The Irish editor of the *Catholic Sentinel,* on the other hand, who was not a devotee of total abstinence, felt that the attitude of the *Citizen* was extreme. In 1895 he wrote that the Milwaukee paper seemed to exist for two purposes only: to work for the "downfall of the APA and to annihilate the monks of St. Vincent," and he pictured the latter group as easy going, thriving

---

[105] *Ibid.,* February 24, 1883. Willard, who edited the paper with Bray from 1878 to 1882, was one of the founders of the state union. Bray edited the paper alone from 1882 to 1891. During this time, Humphrey Desmond was a contributing editor. Desmond, editor from 1891 into the next century, was also active in the Catholic Total Abstinence movement.

[106] *Ibid.,* June 27, 1885.

[107] An indication of the stand of the *Catholic Citizen* on total abstinence is contained in the following issues: February 24, March 24, 31, June 2, 9, 23, 30, September 8, 1883; September 22, 1888; May 24, 1890; August 25, 1894.

[108] For the position of the Catholic Total Abstinence adherents in relation to the Benedictine monks at Latrobe, Pennsylvania, *cf.* Bland, *op. cit.,* pp. 127-128, 187-188, 204, 215-216.

on their beer, "while the water critics wax thin and pale. Many who differ from them on matters of religion, believe in the virtues of their brew."[109]

Although the advocates of the total abstinence movement in Wisconsin were considered fanatics by some and the movement by its very nature took an extreme and hence a frequently unpopular position on the subject of drinking alcoholic beverages, nevertheless religious and moral as well as cultural and social benefits resulted from its activities. The union always maintained a submissive attitude toward Church authorities, demanded that members be practical Catholics, and urged the observance of Communion days.[110] The agonizing thirst of Christ was offered as motivation for taking the pledge. The organization of local societies within the parish unit under the direction of the pastor promoted closer relations and cooperation between priest and layman. Despite the apparent success of the Catholic Total Abstinence movement, insofar as total membership is concerned, it frequently was not the inveterate drinker who took and kept the pledge, but rather the man who was temperate or who had neither the strong inclination nor the occasion to indulge too freely.

Social and cultural benefits were derived from the annual conventions held by the state union. Irishmen from various locations in the state were motivated by a common purpose, a factor which gave them a sense of unity. The conventions offered opportunities for development of lay leadership among Irishmen, for the exchange of ideas, and for cooperation in administering the affairs of the Union. Moreover, these were advantages of which Irishmen in village and rural parishes might otherwise have been deprived. The functioning of local Catholic Total Abstinence Societies offered many of the same opportunities on a smaller scale. These societies frequently sponsored festivals, bazaars, lectures, literary, musical, and dramatic activities and celebrations of various kinds. An enterprise quite common to parish societies consisted in the organization of a circulating library and provision for a reading

---

[109] *Catholic Sentinel,* November 14, 1895.

[110] When Protestants were admitted to membership it seems that these requirements were still demanded of Catholic members.

room. Where this was done a librarian was elected and listed among the officers. Not infrequently a well organized total abstinence unit was the unifying element within a parish, for it sponsored religious, social, and educational programs with a good deal of enthusiasm.[111]

Less directly connected with parish life were the Irish benevolent societies, such as the Hibernian Benevolent Society and the Knights of St. Patrick, both in Milwaukee, the Emerald Benevolent Society of Kenosha, St. Patrick's Benevolent Society of La Crosse, and St. Joseph's of Waukesha.[112] While the Catholic Total Abstinence Societies were not necessarily Irish in membership, these last named organizations were. Their chief purpose, as their names suggest, was to provide monetary aid to members overcome by sickness or some misfortune which prevented them from earning; also to give aid to the immediate family of a deceased member. A Hibernian Benevolent Society was organized in Milwaukee as early as 1851.[113] It seems to have passed out of existence after 1856, but another was organized in 1866 which functioned successfully until 1887 when the group disbanded.[114]

---

[111] The Catholic Total Abstinence Societies of Watertown and Whitewater are two outstanding examples. They are cited here because sources of information on their activities are readily available. Cf. Meagher, *op. cit.*, pp. 29–30, 33–35, 76–77, 79, for the Watertown society, and Johnson, "An Experiment in Adult Education," *loc. cit.*, pp. 149–158, for the successful functioning of the society in Whitewater. Source material for this article consists of the manuscript Minutes Book (October 4, 1873–November 25, 1894) of St. Patrick's Catholic Total Abstinence Society, Whitewater, Wisconsin. Johnson notes that the society acted as a "sounding-board for lay expression" besides offering social, cultural, and religious benefits to its members.

[112] *Proceedings of the Tenth Annual Convention of the Irish Catholic Benevolent Union Held at Worcester, Massachusetts, September 25 and 26, 1878* (Philadelphia), p. 37.

[113] Milwaukee *Sentinel*, March 17, 1851. The society evidently had been founded before this date, but this notice of its activity is the first evidence of its existence that could be found. Evidence concerning these societies and their activities is limited to newspaper accounts, therefore information concerning them is necessarily limited and frequently incomplete. After 1856 no further indication of a Hibernian Benevolent Society in Milwaukee was found in the newspapers until 1866.

[114] Milwaukee *News*, February 17, 1866; Milwaukee *Sentinel*, February 15, March 2 and 14, 1866; *Catholic Citizen*, December 13, 1919.

By this time the Ancient Order of Hibernians had been organized in Milwaukee and was attracting members to its ranks. A number of the Irish benevolent societies had affiliated with the Irish Catholic Benevolent Union of the United States, which besides its benevolent purpose intended to foster "fraternity and fellowship" among Irishmen and ultimately to become a center of Irish Catholic unity as was the Catholic Central Verein for the Germans.[115]

The Ancient Order of Hibernians, however, more nearly approximated this goal than the Irish Catholic Benevolent Union. This Irish organization is reputed to have been established in Ireland in 1565 for the purpose of defending Irish Catholics against the persecutions of English and Irish Protestants. The organization grew gradually until it spread into England and Scotland. In 1836 Irishmen in New York, with the authorization of the Ancient Order in Ireland, set up a branch of the organization. The New York group also was given permission to establish branches throughout the United States. According to directions from the parent organization, members were to be practical

---

[115] *Proceedings of the Tenth Annual Convention of the ICBU*, p. 37; Milwaukee *Sentinel*, February 9, 1875. The Hibernian Benevolent Society joined the Union in 1875. The Knights of St. Patrick joined in 1877 or 1878. Cf. Milwaukee *Sentinel*, March 20, 1877. La Crosse had a St. Patrick's Mutual Benevolent Society by 1869 and it joined the Union soon after. Cf. St. Paul *Northwestern Chronicle*, November 6, 1869. Naturally, Catholic organizations functioning within the state included various nationalities in their membership. B. J. Blied, "The Story of the Catholic Knights," *The Catholic Knight*, VIII (December, 1952), 17, states that the Catholic Knights of America was introduced into Wisconsin in 1880, but in 1885 the Wisconsin group seceded from the national organization and became the Catholic Knights of Wisconsin. The *Columbia*, June 25, 1885, a German Catholic organ in Milwaukee, found it advisable to report that the Catholic Knights was not an exclusively Irish society, but that it also accepted German Catholics to membership. Blied suggests that considerations of nationality were probably among the causes of the secession. The group of priests and laymen, which set up the independent Wisconsin branch, was about evenly divided between Irish and Germans. The *Catholic Sentinel*, July 21, 1898, reported that C. T. Ragan was representing the English-speaking branch of the Catholic Knights of Chippewa Falls at the annual state convention while Albert Nunkey was representing the German-speaking branch.

Catholics, Irish or of Irish descent, of good moral character, and were not to belong to secret societies contrary to the law of the Catholic Church. The organization's motto was: friendship, unity, and true Christian charity.[116]

The first division of the Ancient Order of Hibernians in Wisconsin was organized at Bay View (now part of Milwaukee) in 1800.[117] By 1886 there were fourteen divisions in Wisconsin with an aggregate membership of about six hundred. Ten years later the order numbered thirty-five divisions with a membership of about two thousand.[118]

The Ancient Order maintained a great deal of secrecy in its proceedings and utilized secret passwords, signs, and ritual. Business carried on with the organization in Ireland was done by means of a secret code. This secrecy and the suspicion that the Order was not aloof from political affiliations caused strained relations between the Hibernians and Catholic Church authorities. At the Cleveland Convention in May, 1884, Bishop Richard Gilmour urged the members to make every effort to place themselves "in harmony with the Church," and thus end the "coldness and hesitancy" that marked the relations between the two.[119]

The Order's relationship to the Church, however, remained an open question for some time, since the hierarchy made no official statement concerning its status. The position of the Order in different dioceses remained subject to the opinion of the respective ordinary. Archbishop Heiss informed Cardinal Gibbons that he

---

[116] Heming, *op. cit.,* p. 1070.

[117] *Ibid.* The state records of the Order prior to 1900 have been lost or destroyed according to James Sheridan, a past state president, interviewed by the writer in Janesville, August 11, 1951.

[118] *Catholic Citizen,* December 18, 1886; July 4, 1896.

[119] St. Paul *Northwestern Chronicle,* May 29, 1884. Archbishop P. A. Feehan of Chicago is credited with having kept the hierarchy from placing the Ancient Order of Hibernians on the list of forbidden societies at the Third Plenary Council of Baltimore in 1884. Blied, *loc. cit.,* p. 16. For a fuller treatment of the Ancient Order of Hibernians and its relationship with the Church cf. Fergus MacDonald, *The Catholic Church and the Secret Societies in the United States* (New York: The United States Catholic Historical Society, 1946), pp. 48-62, 82-91, 111-149.

could find nothing wrong with the Order in Wisconsin and that he did not want the Hibernians in his diocese disturbed. He advised Church authorities against adopting too rigorous a policy toward the organization.[120] In 1890, the *Catholic Citizen* saw evidence of a more favorable relationship with the Church in the large attendance of clergymen at the Wisconsin, Minnesota, and Iowa conventions.[121] Again in 1894 the same publication noted:

> At present the A.O.H. is favorably regarded by very many clergymen of the Catholic Church who understand the order. Bishop Foley of Detroit, has so far endorsed the A.O.H. as to consent to act as its National Chaplain.[122]

Hope was expressed that the hierarchy would see fit to make a definite pronouncement on the status of the society, but this did not materialize. A short time later the *Citizen* expressed the opinion that the A.O.H. needed no episcopal endorsement in view of the fact that it had been formally permitted to establish a chair of Celtic literature in the Catholic University of America in Washington, D. C.[123]

In spite of these attempts to justify the A.O.H., the editor of the *Catholic Citizen* offered suggestions for its improvement. These concerned matters which were constantly being championed by the paper: promotion of the teaching of Irish history in the schools, efforts toward an intellectual and instructive program among its members, and the exclusion of saloon keepers from its ranks.[124]

During the year 1884, probably as a result of Bishop Gilmour's prodding, an attempt was made by the A.O.H. in America to sever connections with the organization in Ireland. This move split the American organization into two factions, one composed of the members affiliated with the American Board, and the other,

---

[120] MacDonald, *op. cit.*, pp. 137, 146.
[121] *Catholic Citizen*, June 21, 1890.
[122] *Ibid.*, September 22, 1894.
[123] *Ibid.*, November 17, 1894.
[124] *Ibid.*, June 21, 1890.

a minority, attached to the Board of Erin.[125] The breach was not healed until 1898, when both groups united as the Ancient Order of Hibernians in America.

A few divisions in Wisconsin were affiliated with the Board of Erin and each faction held its biennial convention separately in 1888 and 1890. By 1892 the two groups in Wisconsin had become reconciled. Naturally, unity increased the order's ability to accomplish its purposes in the state. The insurance feature of the state organization never aroused too great an interest, however, because of the limitations on benefits that could be offered.[126]

The national Ancient Order of Hibernians had approved the organization of Ladies' Auxiliaries in 1894 and auxiliaries were organized in Shullsburg, Darlington, Milwaukee, and La Crosse, in the following year. The 1896 state convention in Wisconsin marked the first at which Ladies' Auxiliaries were represented.[127]

The Ancient Order of Hibernians outgrew and outlived other Irish societies so that it really became the only association established on national lines among the Irish element in America. Socially prominent Irishmen joined its ranks and the order was respected in lay circles. Local divisions sponsored balls, bazaars, and social functions; St. Patrick's Day celebrations were enlivened by parades in which the Hibernians marched in their green uniforms and high hats. Members fulfilled the fraternal aims of the Order by attendance at fellow members' funerals in uniforms, by visits to widows and bereaved families, and by financial aid to worthy causes. Fraternization was also used for political purposes, although the secrecy maintained precludes the possibility of finding direct evidence. In Milwaukee, the order became an organization which had to be reckoned with because of the character and numerical strength of its membership.

---

[125] *Ibid.*, May 22, 1897.
[126] *Ibid.*, July 11, 1896; April 9, 1898; *Catholic Sentinel*, July 9, 1896. The death benefit stood at $150, was raised to $300 in 1896, and again lowered to $150 in 1898. The success of the insurance program of the Catholic Knights of Wisconsin, in which many Irishmen held membership, probably accounts for the lack of interest in the Wisconsin Ancient Order's efforts along insurance lines.
[127] *Catholic Citizen*, July 4, 1896.

Research has not revealed the position taken by the Wisconsin A.O.H. on pertinent questions of the day between 1880 and 1894. At the 1894 state convention, however, as noted elsewhere, their stand on the school question was expressed.[128] They also placed themselves on record at that time in support of temperance, but avoided the issue of total abstinence. Prompted by the labor agitation and strikes that were then taking place, the convention passed a forward-looking resolution with pro-labor proclivities, which advocated study of the economic and social questions of the day, "to the end that we may do our part as intelligent citizens in determining and securing the just and equitable distribution between labor and capital of their joint products."[129]

In April, 1898, when the country was in a fighting mood over the sinking of the *Maine* and war was imminent, the state convention, meeting in Fond du Lac, pledged united support to perpetuate at the risk of life the liberties guaranteed by the constitution, denounced tyranny in every form and every land, and sent greetings and cordial sympathy to the patriots of Cuba. Pro-American sympathy in England at this time and the possibility of a British-American alliance wrung from the convention a denunciation of any attempt to effect an arbitration treaty between the United States and England. They branded any such move as un-American, for England was an "uncompromising foe of republican institutions," any alliance with her would be contrary to the principles of America's past, and "inimical to the cause of freedom the world over."[130] Consonant with the purpose of their organization—to aid Ireland in her cause for freedom—the Wisconsin Hibernians passed resolutions pertinent to the situation then existing in the late 1890's. They urged members to help the

---

[128] *Supra*, pp. 218-219.

[129] *Catholic Sentinel*, July 26, 1894. The entire question of labor trouble and organization in Wisconsin, especially in Milwaukee, would bear investigation. Some correspondence found in the Terence V. Powderly Papers in the Department of Archives and Manuscripts, Catholic University of America, originated in Wisconsin, but appears not to have involved the nationality question. What part, if any, Irishmen as a nationality group played in the labor movement in Wisconsin is unknown and would be difficult to determine.

[130] *Catholic Citizen*, April 9, 1898.

Home Rule party achieve its aims and demanded of Irish representatives in parliament "unity of action and singleness of purpose" so they could present "a united and solid phalanx to the historic enemy of liberty."[131]

This concern for the cause of Home Rule in Ireland on the part of the Ancient Order of Hibernians was merely another example of Irish and Irish-American sympathy for their brethren across the sea. Famine, English oppression, and Irish attempts to combat both evils always aroused considerable agitation among Irishmen and Irish-Americans in the United States, for Irish immigrants and their descendants remained passionately anti-British and loyal to the Irish cause. As a result, Irishmen in the United States not only publicized the plight of Ireland, but generously provided monetary support to Irish political agitation and revolutionary movements.[132]

The Irishmen in Wisconsin were no exception. Daniel O'Connell's Repeal Association in Ireland had its counterpart in Milwaukee where an Irish Repeal Association was organized in March, 1843.[133] The association remained active throughout that year and by October 14 had sent to Daniel O'Connell in Ireland from Wisconsin Territory the sum of 1,219 pounds sterling.[134]

As O'Connell's leadership waned and the great famine gripped the country, Irish Repeal in Wisconsin became a movement for Irish relief. In December of 1846 and the early months of 1847 Irish leaders in Milwaukee and other localities within the state organized relief committees to collect funds. Contributions, although chiefly from Irishmen, came also from other nationalities. Clergymen of various denominations and Bishop Henni contrib-

---

[131] *Ibid.*
[132] Edmund Curtis, *A History of Ireland* (London: Methuen and Company, 1936), p. 370.
[133] Milwaukee *Sentinel*, March 29, 1843. Interestingly, the Irish invited into the Association's ranks others besides Irishmen. Solomon Juneau, mayor of Milwaukee, was elected president and Father Kundig, treasurer. The other officers were Irish: Father Morrissey, vice-president; Richard Murphy and Daniel Fitzsimmons, secretaries.
[134] *Ibid.*, January 27, 1844.

uted and urged others to follow their example. Farmers were asked to contribute foodstuffs and clothing; monetary contributions were used to buy flour and provisions; storage and shipping companies offered free services, including shipment to the East.[135] That Wisconsin contributions reached Ireland was attested to by letter and in the Irish press.[136]

Subsequent famines in Ireland drew a similar response of generosity from Irishmen in Wisconsin. In the spring of 1862 and again in 1863, meetings were held to organize committees for Irish relief, but evidence of the same enthusiasm for collecting which had been mustered in 1847 is lacking.[137] The Civil War probably caused at least some of this lack of interest. Another cause affecting Milwaukee proper, where most of the campaigns were launched on a larger scale than elsewhere in the state, was the loss of Irish leadership and of a goodly number of contributors through the sinking of the *Lady Elgin* less than two years previously.[138] In 1863, however, the Catholics of Wisconsin raised over $4,600 for the suffering poor of Ireland,[139] and the Seventeenth Wisconsin Regiment, which dubbed itself the Irish Brigade, sent $1,302.50 to Archbishop Hughes of New York for the relief of their "distressed fellow countrymen in Ireland."[140]

The collection of funds during the famine in the late 1870's and early 1880's was well organized and carried on throughout

---

[135] *Ibid.*, March 9 and 11, March 1 and 10, 1847. The issue of March 18, 1847, states that the executive committee contracted to buy 300 barrels of flour at $3.75. Supplies were carried free on the SS Oregon, SS Madison, and SS Illinois according to the issues of March 29, May 29, June 3, and July 13, 1847.

[136] *Ibid.*, April 30, 1847, July 12, 1848.

[137] *Ibid.*, April 22, 24, 1862, June 4, 6, 1863.

[138] *Supra*, pp. 54-55.

[139] Milwaukee *Sentinel*, November 24, 1863.

[140] William H. Plunkett, Major of the Seventeenth Wisconsin Volunteers and President of the Regiment Irish Relief Committee, to Archbishop John Hughes, Camp near Lake Providence, Louisiana, April 15, 1863. Copy of the letter given to the writer by the Reverend Henry J. Browne, Archivist, Catholic University of America, Washington, D. C. Original in the Archives of the Archdiocese of New York.

the state.[141] State and municipal officers joined their pleas with those of Irish organizations and the *Catholic Citizen* instituted a "Relief Fund."[142] The German bishops cooperated by having collections taken up within the parishes.[143] In the Milwaukee area the drive for relief received added impetus by the arrival and speech of Charles Stewart Parnell, the great Irish leader, member of Parliament, and president of the National Land League in Ireland.[144]

A short time after Parnell's visit, branches of the National Land League were organized in Milwaukee and among Irish groups throughout the state. Frequently the League received its impetus to organize and encouragement to act from the pastors of Irish parishes.[145] In Milwaukee the League was not organized according to parishes but according to a division of the city into East, South, and West districts.[146] Irish Catholic priests were

---

[141] Milwaukee *Sentinel*, January 16, 25, 30, February 3, 16, 18, 20, March 1, 11, 14, 16, 19, 27, 1880; *Catholic Citizen*, January 31, February 7, 14, March 6, 1880.

[142] *Catholic Citizen*, January 10, 24, 31, February 7, 28, March 6, April 10, 1880. When the Socialists in Milwaukee expressed sympathy for the Irish in a meeting held for that purpose, they proposed socialism and education as a cure for the situation in Ireland. The *Catholic Citizen* censured their stand and warned the Irish to remain aloof from the "Socialistic crowd of German infidels." *Cf.* the issues of January 3 and 10, 1880.

[143] Bishop Heiss had by April collected the sum of $3,400 and according to the report, expected to have the sum of $5,000 when all of the returns were in from his clergy. *Ibid.*, April 10, 1880.

[144] *Ibid.*, January 31, February 21, 28, 1880. Milwaukee *Sentinel*, February 18, 24, 25, 1880. The purpose of the League was to effect a change in the system of rents in Ireland and to force landlords to abandon their highhanded methods of eviction. The money acquired from the League in America was used to help evicted farmers. While the League was in operation, anyone was socially ostracized who dared to rent a farm from which tenants had been evicted. The Land League was outlawed in October, 1881.

[145] J. A. Anderson, *Life and Memoirs of Reverend C. F. X. Goldsmith* (Chippewa Falls, Wisconsin, 1895), pp. 97, 283-301; *Catholic Citizen*, January 21, 1882; Meagher, *op. cit.*, pp. 65-66. The St. Bernard's parish in Watertown had a very active National Land League and later, National League, under the presidency of Dr. Edward Johnson.

[146] Milwaukee *Sentinel*, January 20, 1882.

among the members. Although the League in Ireland was legally outlawed in 1881, the American branches continued their activities. In 1882, the Milwaukee branch admitted both sexes into its membership.[147]

The League in the United States attempted to keep abreast with the movement in Ireland and to keep members informed. Meetings in Wisconsin gnerally consisted of lectures, debates, and musical programs. England received severe condemnation even when the policy of Gladstone and the liberal ministry in England were critically reviewed by Richard Burke; or when the Reverend John Casey spoke on the despotic government of England in its relations with Ireland; when the condition of the American colonies was contrasted with the position of Ireland under British domination; or when the proposition was debated that Ireland had derived more benefit from political agitation than from insurrection.[148] Sentiment usually prevailed that orderly and legal means, not violence, should be employed against England.[149]

Since the National Land League had been outlawed in Ireland in 1881, the necessity of a national organization through which to unite Irish efforts at reform, prompted the Irish to establish the National League. Their objectives—Home Rule, land reform, parliamentary, municipal, and local reform—were to be achieved by parliamentary action. Logically, therefore, the movement fell under Parnell's leadership. In the United States, also, the National Land League gave way to the Irish National League. The aim of the League in the United States was to unite all Irish organizations into support of the cause of Ireland.

In June, 1883, Patrick Egan, former treasurer of the National Land League, and Alexander M. Sullivan, president of the Na-

---

[147] *Catholic Citizen,* January 21, 1882. In Ireland when the Irish leaders had been arrested and members of Parliament were attending sessions, the women took over the League.

[148] *Ibid.,* January 21, 28, February 11, 18, 25, 1882.

[149] *Ibid.,* May 20, 1882. The Michael Davitt Land League of Stevens Point denounced the Phoenix Park Murders, that is, the assassination of Lord Frederick Cavendish, Chief Secretary, and Thomas Burke, Under-Secretary for Ireland, in the city of Dublin, May 6, 1882.

tional League, were welcomed by Irishmen to Milwaukee.[150] This visit and the Philadelphia Convention, which had met in April, 1883, to organize the Irish Nationalists, were important factors in influencing Wisconsin Irishmen to convene in a state convention during the latter part of December, 1883.[151] With Irish nationalism as its moving spirit, the League functioned in Wisconsin throughout the 1880's. From 1884 to 1886, increased stress was placed on monetary contributions to the anti-eviction fund and publicity was given to the donations received.[152] The *Catholic Citizen* recognized the good being accomplished by the Irish National League, but consistently warned against its becoming the tool of politicians. Desmond, the editor, felt that the organization had inspired new leadership among the Irish in the United States, had roused greater intellectual activity, and had been a unifying force. He pointed out that during the decade from 1880 to 1890, Irishmen had risen professionally. Not only had more of them been elected to political office, but on the average they had a higher moral caliber than those preceding them.[153]

With these accomplishments to its credit, the National League

---

[150] *Ibid.*, June 2, 1883.

[151] *Ibid.*, November 3, 24, December 1, 8, 22, 1883. Representation at the convention according to counties was as follows: Ashland 3, Brown 3, Calumet 8, Crawford 1, Dodge 13, Dane 3, Fond du Lac 28, Jefferson 6, Jackson 1, Iowa 2, Kenosha 7, La Crosse 1, Lafayette 8, Manitowoc 11, Marquette 5, Milwaukee 64, Racine 28, Walworth 7, Portage 2, Ozaukee 5, Outagamie 5, Rock 2, Sauk 1, Sheboygan 4, Washington 2, Winnebago 11, Waukesha 29. Officers elected were: president, Patrick Donnelly of Milwaukee; secretaries, T. F. Somers of Milwaukee and John McCrory of Fond du Lac; treasurer, Dr. Edward Johnson of Watertown.

[152] *Ibid.*, January 10, March 14, 1885, January 2, 16, 23, March 20, May 1, June 12, 19, August 7, December 18, 1886, January 15, April 2, June 18, December 3, 1887, February 25, 1888, February 16, July 6, 1889. The issue of March 14, 1885, carried the treasurer's financial report. Contributions, which totaled $2,153.05, had been received from Chilton, Watertown, Willow Springs, Clyman, Meeme, Mauston, Cedarburg, Fox Lake, Waukesha, Richwood, Baraboo, Oshkosh, Fond du Lac, Beaver Dam, Genesee, Appleton, and Milwaukee. Research has also revealed activity in the following places: New Richmond, Darlington, Janesville, Kendall, Edgerton, Elba, Kenosha, Benton, and Hudson.

[153] *Ibid.*, May 24, 1890.

had, by 1890, reached a crucial point in its history. Although its leadership seemed to be of good quality, nevertheless factionalism was, according to the editor, a disease within the organization and the time "may have arrived for closing up the records and writing the obituary."[154] This opinion became paramount when the Parnell-Shea scandal broke, for the *Citizen's* reaction was the same as that of many Irishmen:

> No journal circulating among Irish-Americans has given Parnell, personally, a more cordial support than the *Citizen*. We have never doubted his patriotism or his capacity as a political leader. But the welfare of the Irish race, their respectability as a people, their honor and their place in the esteem of the world, are higher considerations than Mr. Parnell's personality. He can best serve them now by stepping aside.[155]

Irish fund raising in Wisconsin never again reached the high point that it had during the days of the Irish National League. Attempts were made to organize the Irish National Federation in Milwaukee and elsewhere, but despite the fact that politically prominent Irishmen were elected to the offices, enthusiasm was lacking.[156] When John Redmond, member of Parliament and leader of one of the factions into which the followers of Parnell had broken, appeared in Milwaukee, the *Citizen* gave what is probably the best explanation for Irish-American apathy to the state of affairs in Ireland.

> We are not going to tell Mr. Redmond that this great community deplores the present factional situation in

---

[154] *Ibid.*, May 24, 1890.

[155] *Ibid.*, November 22, 1890, January 10, 1891.

[156] *Ibid.*, February 13, 1892, January 11, 1895. The officers were: president, Peter Doyle, former secretary of state of Wisconsin; vice-president, John P Murphy, cashier of the Plankinton Bank; secretary, James T. Bannen, secretary of the National Democratic Convention Committee; treasurer, Patrick Drew, "substantial citizen of Milwaukee." Records of the Irish National Federation of America reveal no participation of Wisconsin Irishmen in the organization's affairs according to Peter J. Sammon, "The History of the Irish National Federation of America" (Master's thesis, Catholic University of America, 1951).

Ireland. Mr. Redmond knows this; for probably he has been told so a dozen times in every American city he has visited. He probably realized before he came to America that Irish faction in Ireland killed fund-gathering in America, and chilled Irish-American interest in Ireland. What he may not as fully realize is the difficulty of ever re-awakening the old Irish-American interest in Irish affairs. It will require a man of the Parnell mould to do so, and he must play his part not before American audiences, but among the lions and the jackals in the arena of the British Parliament.[157]

Societies among Irishmen in Wisconsin were not all founded for benevolent or charitable purposes, and although these had their cultural programs, during the latter half of the nineteenth century independent Irish cultural and intellectual societies were functioning in Milwaukee and other localities. During the middle 1850's a circle of young men who later became prominent in various professions met frequently for discussion.[158] In 1865 the St. Patrick's Literary Association drew together a number of young Irish intellectuals and from 1868 to 1871, the Curran Literary Society, which attracted both men and women was notably active, holding debates and presenting lectures, besides offering social functions.[159] The Irish-American Literary Society and the O'Connell Debating Society functioned during the later 1870's.[160] Janesville,

---

[157] *Ibid.*, January 9, 1896.
[158] *Ibid.*, December 13, 1919.
[159] Milwaukee *Sentinel*, March 7, 20, 1865; *Catholic Citizen*, February 2, 14, 1871, May 1, 1897, December 13, 1919.
[160] Milwaukee *Sentinel*, December 30, 1878, January 12, February 10, 18, March 6, 11, 24, April 1, 15, May 1, 8, 10, October 20, November 10, December 2, 8, 30, 1879; *ibid.*, January 31, 1876; *Catholic Citizen*, December 13, 1919. Among the young Irishmen who were the moving spirit in the first societies and lent prestige to the later societies were: Andrew Mullen, Dr. James Johnson, Edward O'Neill, Jeremiah Quinn, J. J. Lalor, Patrick Donnelly, Thomas G. Shaughnessy, Patrick Turrell, James C. Pollard, John E. Fitzgerald, John F. McDonald, Richard Burke, and others. Among the young women were Josie and Kitty Barry, daughters of Captain Barry, lost on the Lady Elgin; Margaret J. O'Connor (later wife of James C. Pollard), Fannie Davlin, known for her musical ability, Ellen Lynch, and Jennie Murphy.

Watertown, Racine, and other places also had active Irish literary and debating groups.[161] Topics of lectures and debates embraced everything from restriction of Chinese immigration, woman suffrage, and compulsory education, to the advisability of teaching the Irish language in parochial schools, colleges, and universities as a measure conducive to the promotion of the Catholic Faith and the Irish nationality. Guest speakers were frequently invited. The Young Men's Association in Watertown during the 1850's engaged renowned speakers, such as Horace Greeley, Carl Schurz, and George D. Prentice, editor of the Louisville *Journal*.[162] The Catholic Young Men's Literary Association in Janesville also fostered a circulating library besides sponsoring lectures and debates.[163] Young Irish men and women with musical ability were given an opportunity to develop and display their talent through membership in the Irish Musical Society which was popular in Milwaukee during the early 1870's.[164]

Irish sociability and patriotism also found an outlet in military companies which were particularly prolific in Wisconsin just prior to the Civil War.[165] St. Patrick's Day celebrations would not have been complete without the color and thrill which the uniformed military guards provided. After the Civil War the Sheridan Guards were organized in Milwaukee and remained a distinctly Irish military company until it was incorporated into the national guard, thus losing its identity.[166] Irish-American society in Milwaukee was fond of the brilliant military balls sponsored by this group and proud of the record the company maintained in comparison with others in the state.[167]

The activities of all Irish societies—cultural, benevolent, tem-

---

[161] St. Paul *Northwestern Chronicle*, January 23, April 3, 24, 10, May 15, 22, 1869; Milwaukee *Sentinel*, February 23, 1880; Meagher, *op. cit.*, pp. 19, 51-52, 76-77, 85-86; *Catholic Citizen*, January 14, 1885.

[162] Meagher, *op. cit.*, p. 19.

[163] St. Paul *Northwestern Chronicle*, January 23, 1869.

[164] *Catholic Citizen*, May 1, 1897; Milwaukee *Sentinel*, January 29, February 10, June 14, 28, August 9, September 13, 27, October 4, 1872, January 21, 1873.

[165] *Supra*, p. 141, n. 47.

[166] Milwaukee *Sentinel*, June 10, 21, 22, 1869.

[167] Milwaukee *Catholic Citizen*, December 13, 1919.

perance, and social—seemed to reach a climax each year in the elaborate celebration of St. Patrick's Day. Despite March winds and cold weather, military companies, temperance advocates, Hibernians, and benevolent organizations, after attendance at Mass, paraded in distinctive uniform to the tune of Irish airs, carrying banners and flags. These celebrations usually closed with banquets in the evening where food was plentiful, toasts lauding Irish nationalism and American patriotism were numberless, and speeches on the glories of Ireland were interminable. It was great to be an Irishman. Wisconsin's newspapers for weeks after the great day carried accounts of celebrations from practically every locality where Irishmen were found. Even the Boston *Pilot* published letters from Wisconsin Irishmen describing their St. Patrick's Day festivities. These celebrations were carried on so heartily and enthusiastically that the spirit became contagious and irresistible, for non-Irish participation increased with the years. Even St. Francis Seminary became the scene of quite elaborate "doings" on the feast of the Apostle of Ireland.

The functioning of Irish organizations in Wisconsin during the latter half of the nineteenth century lent a unity to Irish-Americans which had not existed prior to the Civil War. It has already been pointed out that the Irish soldiers of Wisconsin had found a common bond by close association in the Irish Regiment and that this had resulted in Irish coordination during the period of Fenian activity.[168] Fenianism had aroused strong nationalistic emotions among Wisconsin Irish-Americans. Likewise, the joint action in the regiment which led to their monetary contribution for Irish relief was carried into civilian life after the war. Combined with strong feelings for Irish nationalism, this successful cooperation in Irish activity had been one of the factors not only in the development of Irish organizations and societies, but also in the cultivation of greater unity among Irishmen in the cities and on a state level.[169] In the rural areas, moreover, organizations

---

[168] *Supra*, pp 142 f.

[169] Irishmen in Milwaukee had met shortly after the climax in Fenian activity had been reached to consider the organization of all Irishmen in a group to be known as the United Irishmen. Dillon O'Brien of St. Paul, who introduced the idea proposed that this body "be composed of men of all parties

and societies could function more smoothly now that settlement had become more permanent and the excessive labor connected with homesteading during the 1840's and 1850's had decreased considerably. Finally, the social nature of the Irishman found outlet in the various types of societies which he helped to organize and which he joined.

It is not easy to characterize the typical Irishman, and one might readily doubt the validity of a national characterization. Nevertheless, the four Irelands, described by one authority who has made a sociological study of the Irish, sum up the characteristics and personality traits which seem necessary to a complete description of "the Irishman."[170] He is a mystic soul, clinging to the old Gaelic traditions, the subject of poets, but at the same time one who, in coping with reality, is likely to lose his temper, loves to argue, harbors deep-seated hatreds and just as deeply-planted loyalties. He would not be an Irishman unless gay, witty, and light-hearted, but also devotedly religious and quite charmingly superstitious. It can truthfully be said of Irishmen, as it has been of other immigrants, that "They change their sky and not their mind who cross the sea."[171] And so the Irish countryman who crossed the sea and settled in Wisconsin retained his Irish character, his customs and traditions, simultaneously adapting himself to American life in the Midwest.

Irishmen and their descendants retained their deep hatred of England and fierce loyalty to the "old sod" while at the same time developing a staunch allegiance to the United States and its institutions, and to the Democratic party. Their political allegiance

---

who, forgetting past differences, would adopt such a course as might be acceptable alike to Fenians and non-Fenians." Irishmen of Milwaukee who sponsored the idea were Mayor Edward O'Neill, Dr. James Johnson, and J. C. Pollard. As so often happened the society did not materialize. Milwaukee *Sentinel,* February 17, 1868; St. Paul *Northwestern Chronicle,* February 22, 1868.

[170] Conrad M. Arensberg, *The Irish Countryman: An Anthropological Study* (New York: Peter Smith, 1950), pp. 13-16.

[171] Anderson, *op. cit.,* p. 248. The Reverend C. F. X. Goldsmith used this phrase in a St. Patrick's Day speech delivered to the St. Patrick's Benevolent Society in La Crosse, March 17, 1872.

was greatly influenced by this traditional hatred for England. There were Irishmen in Wisconsin who spoke only Gaelic, deeming it traitorous to learn the English language. The *Catholic Citizen* urged the teaching of Gaelic and Irish history in the parochial schools. The editors reasoned that the Irish nationality had much to offer America and that Irish history properly taught would offset the harm done to the Irish reputation by "claptrap entertainments" and "stage Irishmen."[172]

This spirit of Irish nationalism was kept alive through the Land Leagues and the Irish-American press which informed its readers of Irish activity at home and abroad. In Wisconsin the most popular Irish-American publications were the Boston *Pilot,* New York *Freeman's Journal,* the New York *Irish World,* the Chippewa Falls *Catholic Sentinel,* Milwaukee *Catholic Citizen,* and the St. Paul *Northwestern Chronicle.*[173]

Settled largely in small rural communities, Irishmen in Wisconsin indulged their light-heartedness and love for a gay time by frequent neighborly get-togethers, weekly dances, and by elaborate celebrations of christenings, weddings, and feast days. These were not merely family, but community affairs. Even the traditional wakes were large social gatherings where good food and a

---

[172] Milwaukee *Catholic Citizen,* September 24, 1887, November 30, December 7, 1889, January 4, 18, February 22, 1890.

[173] Of Irish-American papers published outside of Wisconsin, the Boston *Pilot* was probably the most popular. Subscriptions were received in club lots at various Irish settlements. In 1848 there were already about forty such clubs with one Irishman in each of the forty localities acting as an "agent" for the *Pilot. Cf.* Boston *Pilot,* December 16, 1848. Subsequent issues throughout the years show increases in the number of subscriptions taken by Wisconsin Irishmen. The Milwaukee *Catholic Citizen* grew in circulation until by 1899 it had absorbed four other Catholic papers which were published outside of Wisconsin. Ventures in publishing Irish secular papers in Milwaukee never succeeded very well. During the early 1840's, Daniel Fitzsimmons published a bi-weekly paper, the *Irish Appeal.* An attempt, called the *Irishman,* late in the year 1869 or early in 1870 came to naught. The Milwaukee *Sentinel,* January 12, 1870, noted that the newspaper's office had been robbed and on January 28, 1870, reported that the readers of the *Irishman* could not say "peace to its ashes," because it had never shown a spark of fire.

supply of strong drinks intermixed with ghost stories kept alive the spirits of the mourners, where prayers were offered for the deceased, and Irish keeners, with their lamentations and dirges, bewailed the departed one. Underneath the external demonstration there was a great reverence and devotedness to the bereaved family and the memory of the deceased.

Religion played an important part in the lives of Irishmen, for they had brought from their homeland a deep faith and loyalty to the Catholic Church; a faith for which they had fought and suffered. In the early pioneering days when priests were scarce, great sacrifices were made in order to obtain their ministrations. It is told that in 1857 James K. McLaughlin, an early settler in St. Croix County, with his wife and baby daughter, his sister, her husband and baby son, and two other couples with their infants formed a caravan with oxen and traveled to Stillwater, Minnesota, to have their babies baptized. The trip took a week.[174]

The faith of Irishmen impressed Bishop Heiss who cited two instances, not as exceptions, but rather as typical examples. The bishop wrote to his friend Kilian Kleiner the story of an Irishman who, suffering from a lingering illness, instructed his children from his sickbed in the truths of their religion, doing so up to a few days before his death. Consequently, the pastor of the parish found the children very well instructed.[175] Another "prominent, highly educated" Irishman, on meeting the Bishop soon after his return from a trip to Rome, said to him: "Father Bishop, it does me good to look at you because you have seen our Holy Father face to face."[176] Giving up the practice of the Catholic Faith frequently meant, for an Irishman, ostracism from society. Other Irishmen scornfully called such a renegade a turncoat or lefthander.

In Wisconsin much of the Irishmen's activity centered within their parish organization. In Ireland they had frequently looked to

---

[174] Kinney, *op. cit.*

[175] *Salesianum*, XII (October, 1916), 7, Heiss to Kleiner, La Crosse, Wisconsin, July 4, 1869.

[176] *Ibid.* (January, 1917), 4, Heiss to Kleiner, La Crosse, Wisconsin, June 23, 1871.

their priests for leadership, and that trait was not lost in the New World. On the whole Irish priests were leaders in temperance activity, in the organization of many societies, and in providing intellectual and social functions within their parishes.

Rather closely akin to the Irishman's faith was his belief in fairies and spirits of the other world. Sheds or outbuildings were not to be built on the west side of the house, for the fairies made their path there. No man passed Ghost Hollow alone at night. Mothers passed on the stories of the fairies and banshees to their children but warned them that they were not really true stories and therefore not to be believed.[177] Ask any Irish woman if she really believes in fairies and she will emphatically deny their existence, but will not act consistently with that denial. One elderly Irish woman, a pioneer in southern Wisconsin, after agreeing that belief in fairies was superstition and not to be indulged in, quickly added: "One is really never alone, though. When I awaken at night I feel the presence of spirits about me. Well, anyway, our Guardian Angels are always with us."[178]

These Irish characteristics along with the political, religious, social, and cultural contributions which Irishmen have made to society in Wisconsin are intangibles not easily evaluated. For example, it is impossible to isolate some specific political achievement or social reform which has been accomplished solely by Irishmen in the state or because of their direct influence. Irish membership in the Democratic party was certainly a factor in its survival after the Civil War and Irishmen were the Democratic party in localities such as Erin Township, Washington County,

---

[177] Stasia Shea, in interview, September 21, 1951. Arensberg, *op. cit.*, p. 25, discusses the superstition concerning the "west room" as believed and practiced in Luogh, County Clare.

[178] Stasia Shea, in interview, September 21, 1951. Arensberg, *op. cit.*, p. 25, regarding the Irishmen's belief in the "west room" superstition, notes that, although the people denied belief in fairies and fairy paths, they nevertheless practiced it. No outbuilding or shed occupied the space west of the house throughout the locality. Seam O'Faolain, *The Irish: A Character Study* (New York: The Devin-Adair Company, 1949), p. 17, in calling attention to Irish belief in the tales of the Otherworld, relates that a woman of West Cork was asked whether she really believed in the fairies. Her reply was substantially the same as Stasia Shea's: "No, but they're there!"

and Erin, St. Croix County, but who can measure the extent of this influence? The majority of Irishmen in Wisconsin, moreover, were farmers, many of them very successful and progressive, but an evaluation of this contribution likewise is difficult. The same holds for Irish contributions in other occupational areas, including the professions; lists of Wisconsin lawyers, medical men, and teachers contain a goodly number of Celtic names.

As far as religion and the development of the Catholic Church in Wisconsin is concerned, the Irish membership practically equalled the German, but Irish influence is greatly obscured by German dominance on the hierarchical and administrative levels. Insofar as Irish social and cultural organizations achieved their objectives they were an influential factor in the social life of the state. For example, the Catholic Total Abstinence movement in Wisconsin, which received its impetus mainly from Irish clergy and laymen, did much to lessen drunkenness among Irishmen and others. Their success cannot be evaluated statistically, but effects of the movement were felt in parishes and certain localities.

Material effects of the presence of Irishmen in the state are more demonstrable. Many of the Catholic parishes in Wisconsin which can boast of a physical plant consisting of church, school, rectory, and sisters' convent testify to the spiritual aspirations and loyal cooperation of the Irishmen who composed the parish. Material progress in Wisconsin evident in the network of railroads criss-crossing the state and in the locks and dams on the Fox-Wisconsin Rivers, as well as other public works' projects constructed in the early history of the state was dependent greatly upon the Irishmen. These works are in fact monuments to Irish brawn and labor.

Undue emphasis should not be placed upon the role of Irishmen in Wisconsin, but it is probably correct to maintain that among foreign immigrants to Wisconsin, Irishmen led the way in becoming Americanized. They proved to be adaptable to the American way of life without, however, losing entirely their national identity, their customs, culture, and their love for Ireland. It does not seem rash to conclude that both Wisconsin and the Irish have gained in the process.

APPENDIX

TABLE 4

GRANT COUNTY

Townships	1850 Population Total	1850 Population % of Irish-born	1850 Families Total	1850 Families % of Irish-born	1860 Population Total	1860 Population % of Irish-born	1860 Families Total	1860 Families % of Irish-born
Beetown					1,481	3	271	7
Boscobel					665	2	125	5
Cassville					860	3	170	5
Blue River[a]					444	8	78	17
Clifton					961	4	178	8
Ellenboro[b]					801	2	130	7
District No. 24	7,062	4	1,260	7				
Fennimore	325	2	57	5	1,392	2	250	4
Glen Haven					923	4	172	9
Harrison	764	4	133	6	963	4	170	9
Hickory Grove					590	1	120	2
Highland[b]	597	1	103	4				
Jamestown	666	7	118	5	1,403	5	260	7
Lancaster					1,966	3	357	6
Liberty					644	5	125	5
Lima	580	.9	105	3	872	3	163	8
Little Grant					592	6	106	11
Marion					508	.6	94	2
Millville					1,097	10	206	20
Muscoda					677	2	130	3
Paris	391	.8	70	0	682	.1	120	0
Patch Grove					867	11	157	18
Platteville	2,072	3	383	6	2,865	3	554	7
Potosi					2,078	7	396	9
Smelser	729	5	123	4	1,115	3	202	7
Tafton[c]					996	2	182	4
Waterloo					566	5	117	11
Watterstown					723	5	129	12
Wingville	1,044	2	185	4	670	2	123	5
Wyalusing					601	1	122	4

[a] Name changed from Blue River to Castle Rock.
[b] Name changed from Highland to Ellenboro.
[c] In 1860 name changed from Tafton to Bloomington.

TABLE 5
Iowa County

Townships	1850 Population Total	1850 Population % of Irish-born	1850 Families Total	1850 Families % of Irish-born	1860 Population Total	1860 Population % of Irish-born	1860 Families Total	1860 Families % of Irish-born
Arena	402	3	83	10	1,295	12	252	23
Clyde	138	15	30	20	610	15	113	30
Dodgeville	2,117	1	398	3	3,403	2	621	3
Highland	1,184	14	244	22	2,409	11	438	22
Linden	951	1	180	2	1,640	2	285	4
Mifflin	640	2	113	4	1,220	1	206	2
Mineral Point	2,584	6	495	10	3,565	6	656	12
Pulaski	181	1	34	3	1,000	6	205	9
Ridgeway	706	10	148	15	1,983	11	351	21
Waldwick	421	12	82	22	1,198	11	210	26
Wyoming	206	0	39	0	623	4	101	12

Appendix

TABLE 6
LAFAYETTE COUNTY

	1850				1860			
	Population		Families		Population		Families	
Townships	Total	% of Irish-born	Total	% of Irish-born	Total	% of Irish-born	Total	% of Irish-born
Argyle	421	2	78	5	1,097	5	204	9
Belmont	325	9	54	15	735	4	118	7
Benton	2,227	21	424	30	2,091	17	375	34
Center*	701	6	108	12	1,913	11	347	21
Elk Grove	624	9	98	17	1,316	12	230	23
Fayette	753	4	135	7	985	8	173	17
Gratiot	504	5	81	14	1,006	9	174	21
Kendall	333	11	53	23	1,131	21	194	45
Monticello	198	5	36	8	459	5	72	8
New Diggings	1,752	29	331	43	1,689	24	314	49
Shullsburg	1,678	23	321	34	2,491	20	468	39
Wayne	336	0	50	0	673	.3	139	.7
White Oak Springs	453	7	73	8	513	10	81	21
Willow Springs	615	20	120	34	838	19	170	44
Wiota	721	10	124	13	1,197	6	214	13

*In 1869 name changed from Center to Darlington.

TABLE 7
MILWAUKEE COUNTY

	1850				1860			
	Population		Families		Population		Families	
Townships	Total	% of Irish-born	Total	% of Irish-born	Total	% of Irish-born	Total	% of Irish-born
Franklin	1,178	23	208	42	1,773	12	313	25
Granville	1,716	11	304	21	2,663	7	480	17
Greenfield	1,995	13	351	21	2,490	7	462	16
Lake	1,484	4	258	6	2,133	2	391	5
Milwaukee	1,349	2	255	2	2,574	.4	532	1
Milwaukee (City)	20,061	15	4,083	18	45,246	10	9,041	16
Oak Creek	1,260	12	228	21	2,222	8	424	17
Wauwautosa	2,048	17	348	21	3,415	5	594	10

TABLE 8
Kenosha County

Townships	1850 Population Total	1850 Pop % Irish-born	1850 Families Total	1850 Fam % Irish-born	1860 Population Total	1860 Pop % Irish-born	1860 Families Total	1860 Fam % Irish-born
Brighton	879	19	160	31	1,238	10	210	27
Bristol	1,123	5	195	10	1,392	8	233	14
Kenosha (City)	3,455	15	614	22	3,970	12	754	21
Paris	956	7	161	13	1,374	7	181	17
Pleasant Prairie	956	20	166	37	1,399	11	233	25
Pike*	680	5	111	8				
Randall					659	6	117	10
Salem	1,123	5	198	15	1,472	9	268	19
Somers*					1,277	4	219	9
Southport	373	7	67	13				
Wheatland	1,194	4	202	6	1,095	3	203	4

*In 1851 name changed from Pike to Somers.

TABLE 9
Racine County

Townships	1850 Population Total	1850 Pop % Irish-born	1850 Families Total	1850 Fam % Irish-born	1860 Population Total	1860 Pop % Irish-born	1860 Families Total	1860 Fam % Irish-born
Burlington	1,629	5	302	7	2,263	3	231	13
Caledonia	1,090	6	203	10	2,438	6	471	11
Dover	839	15	155	24	1,108	13	195	30
Mount Pleasant	1,086	2	195	3	1,818	5	342	8
Norway	751	7	146	9	971	3	187	7
Racine	780	6	144	7				
Racine (City)	5,107	6	904	11	7,822	8	1,529	14
Raymond	1,021	7	184	11	1,274	5	244	11
Rochester	1,662	4	303	7	933	3	179	5
Waterford					1,450	3	270	6
Yorkville	998	5	177	7	1,283	4	235	8

TABLE 10
WAUKESHA COUNTY

Townships	1850 Population Total	1850 Population % of Irish-born	1850 Families Total	1850 Families % of Irish-born	1860 Population Total	1860 Population % of Irish-born	1860 Families Total	1860 Families % of Irish-born
Brookfield	1,938	20	313	18	2,104	5	405	11
Delafield	1,134	6	201	8	1,343	5	252	10
Eagle	816	3	154	5	1,280	6	237	11
Genesee	1,289	10	235	17	1,628	7	300	16
Lisbon	1,036	11	197	16	1,426	9	261	17
Menomonee	1,340	12	247	23	2,267	8	406	19
Merton	966	14	196	23	1,475	12	282	23
Mukwanago	1,094	9	194	15	1,373	9	267	17
Muskego	1,111	18	193	34	1,384	15	251	34
New Berlin	1,293	10	248	21	1,903	6	359	16
Oconomowoc	1,216	6	236	13	2,201	9	418	17
Ottawa	793	7	151	13	1,072	4	168	15
Pewaukee	1,106	4	194	5	1,553	6	288	13
Summit	924	3	166	4	1,151	2	194	3
Vernon	889	2	157	3	1,145	4	213	8
Waukesha	2,313	9	403	12	3,529	9	661	18

TABLE 11
JEFFERSON COUNTY

Townships	1850 Population Total	1850 Population % of Irish-born	1850 Families Total	1850 Families % of Irish-born	1860 Population Total	1860 Population % of Irish-born	1860 Families Total	1860 Families % of Irish-born
Aztalan	597	1	112	2	998	1	184	2
Cold Spring	568	1	108	4	726	5	144	12
Concord	725	5	141	6	1,442	4	287	7
Farmington	736	2	154	3	2,010	3	398	5
Hebron	640	.3	121	0	1,068	2	226	4
Ixonia	1,109	7	215	7	1,809	3	341	7
Jefferson	1,060	.3	211	.9	3,375	4	670	5
Koskonong	1,144	6	219	8	2,023	7	384	11
Lake Mills	882	4	171	5	1,529	3	291	7
Milford	728	5	144	9	1,981	11	382	25
Oakland	806	2	151	2	1,195	2	204	4
Palmyra	783	2	153	3	1,579	2	301	5
Sullivan	872	3	167	4	1,602	3	294	7
Sumner					477	3	91	2
Waterloo	807	4	154	5	1,565	3	294	6
Watertown	1,327	23	250	40	1,734	9	326	17
Watertown (City)	1,451	15	296	21	3,303	9	1,122	17

Appendix

TABLE 12
WALWORTH COUNTY

Townships	1850 Population Total	1850 Population % of Irish-born	1850 Families Total	1850 Families % of Irish-born	1860 Population Total	1860 Population % of Irish-born	1860 Families Total	1860 Families % of Irish-born
Bloomfield	879	3	151	6	1,146	3	211	6
Darien	1,013	3	170	4	1,590	8	308	16
Delavan	1,268	5	240	5	2,433	9	446	16
East Troy	1,318	3	237	5	1,717	10	204	33
Elk Horn Village	42	2	10	0	1,081	8	211	15
Geneva	1,557	2	287	3	2,287	8	423	17
Hudson[a]	1,189	8	210	13	1,338	7	240	18
Lafayette	1,048	2	175	2	1,122	9	207	17
Linn	630	7	121	15	1,008	14	172	26
La Grange	1,049	.9	180	2	1,255	4	208	8
Richmond	744	5	137	8	1,016	9	177	19
Sharon	1,169	2	207	2	1,681	3	336	4
Spring Prairie	1,418	3	246	2	1,311	4	248	6
Sugar Creek	1,227	2	231	2	1,139	10	189	17
Troy	1,094	10	195	14	1,238	13	215	24
Walworth	987	3	172	5	1,403	4	264	6
Whitewater[b]	1,229	4	218	8	1,005	11	170	24
Whitewater (City)					2,732	10	540	18

[a] After 1870 name changed from Hudson to Lyons.
[b] The 1850 totals include the village of Whitewater.

TABLE 13
Dane County

Townships	1850 Population Total	1850 Population % of Irish-born	1850 Families Total	1850 Families % of Irish-born	1860 Population Total	1860 Population % of Irish-born	1860 Families Total	1860 Families % of Irish-born
Albion	817	.4	155	1	1,152	2	228	4
Berry	296	0	48	0	673	0	131	0
Black Earth[a]					701	2	81	9
Blooming Grove	291	7	60	10	710	6	121	11
Blue Mounds	341	.6	61	0	809	3	149	7
Bristol	461	8	91	10	1,254	.8	216	1
Burke					1,025	8	175	13
Christiana	1,054	.2	231	0	1,424	.9	250	3
Cottage Grove	785	10	153	17	1,303	10	225	23
Cross Plains	334	4	63	10	1,125	11	213	18
Dane	294	3	56	5	952	2	159	5
Deerfield	639	4	132	5	952	5	158	11
Dunkirk	852	.7	163	1	1,760	5	339	11
Dunn	330	3	66	6	1,055	10	173	24
Farmersville[a]	209	0	44	0				
Fitchburg[b]					1,177	15	210	30
Greenfield[b]	598	13	103	20				
Madison	346	7	63	11	852	12	140	25
Madison (City)	1,525	10	243	12	6,611	14	1,344	24
Mazomanie					976	11	202	21
Medina	497	0	98	0	1,068	5	200	10
Middleton	313	5	60	7	1,315	5	257	8
Montrose	377	8	71	10	856	7	156	8
Oregon	638	2	120	3	1,259	6	225	12
Perry	118	0	25	0	837	2	152	3
Pleasant Springs	732	1	152	3	1,135	2	191	2
Primrose	336	0	62	0	889	1	159	3
Roxbury	265	1	56	4	1,234	4	224	7
Rutland	759	0	155	0	1,181	2	219	5
Springdale	329	2	72	4	943	5	166	13
Springfield	279	0	54	0	1,207	3	232	4
Sun Prairie	496	6	101	11	1,159	11	215	17
Vermont					925	8	179	14
Verona	381	0	70	0	1,221	5	197	8
Vienna	258	2	53	0	748	3	128	4
Westport	179	31	44	23	1,095	20	198	37
Windsor	883	3	161	2	1,021	2	189	4
York	628	1	135	2	1,028	7	197	13

[a] In 1851 name changed from Farmersville to Black Earth.
[b] In 1853 name changed from Greenfield to Fitchburg.

TABLE 14
GREEN COUNTY

Townships	1850 Population Total	1850 Population % of Irish-born	1850 Families Total	1850 Families % of Irish-born	1860 Population Total	1860 Population % of Irish-born	1860 Families Total	1860 Families % of Irish-born
Adams	275	4	43	9	840	11	152	23
Albany	546	6	107	8	1,385	4	245	9
Brooklyn	531	4	101	5	1,061	6	184	8
Cadiz	459	1	79	1	920	1	150	3
Clarno	714	2	119	2	1,372	2	242	5
Decatur	558	.7	102	3	1,618	10	317	21
Exeter	450	8	84	15	1,040	9	187	19
Jefferson	692	.1	117	.9	1,466	3	264	6
Jordan	391	0	68	0	869	2	152	8
Monroe	1,146	.8	206	4	3,110	5	577	11
Mount Pleasant	579	3	106	5	1,240	6	213	13
New Glarus	311	0	65	0	960	.1	190	.5
Spring Grove	703	.1	115	0	1,053	.4	189	1
Sylvester	712	1	122	.8	1,132	3	200	4
Washington	307	.3	61	2	838	5	147	11
York	191	0	40	0	904	2	155	4

TABLE 15
Rock County

Townships	1850 Population Total	1850 Population % of Irish-born	1850 Families Total	1850 Families % of Irish-born	1860 Population Total	1860 Population % of Irish-born	1860 Families Total	1860 Families % of Irish-born
Avon	579	4	108	9	908	4	171	8
Beloit	2,732	3	455	5	775	5	131	8
Beloit (City)					4,098	10	732	19
Bradford	699	4	121	2	1,245	5	205	7
Center	625	5	119	7	1,123	9	217	17
Clinton	1,214	4	228	7	1,554	7	288	15
Fulton	828	5	159	3	1,890	8	372	15
Harmony	840	6	135	4	1,128	6	213	11
Janesville	3,437	9	601	15	905	11	180	19
Janesville (City)					7,703	16	1,463	27
Johnstown	1,271	3	244	3	1,402	7	239	9
LaPrairie	335	6	56	7	849	3	144	3
Lima	839	6	168	8	1,151	6	224	10
Magnolia	630	2	118	3	1,120	9	202	17
Milton	1,032	4	192	4	1,774	9	345	14
Newark	855	.8	165	2	1,136	3	207	8
Plymouth	581	5	110	5	1,231	9	225	22
Porter	882	2	171	5	1,269	13	246	23
Rock	546	5	90	9	1,106	11	200	25
Spring Valley	756	.3	148	.7	1,265	3	240	6
Turtle	1,105	2	172	3	1,412	3	258	5
Union	1,050	.5	197	.5	1,646	3	334	7

TABLE 16
WASHINGTON COUNTY

Townships	1850 Population Total	1850 Population % of Irish-born	1850 Families Total	1850 Families % of Irish-born	1860 Population Total	1860 Population % of Irish-born	1860 Population Total	1860 Population % of Irish-born
Addison	1,144	4	237	6	2,046	.6	349	1
Barton					1,242	1	239	3
Erin	840	40	159	83	1,445	30	237	76
Farmington	504	8	98	18	1,718	6	320	14
Germantown	1,714	3	323	5	2,344	2	412	5
Hartford	1,050	12	207	14	2,510	7	453	15
Jackson	1,038	7	196	13	1,891	6	356	6
Kewaskum*					1,056	3	209	8
North Bend*	672	4	130	7				
Polk	1,260	2	247	5	2,457	1	454	2
Richfield	1,134	12	217	24	1,920	7	325	21
Trenton	504	9	105	14	1,744	5	337	10
Wayne	672	16	136	20	1,630	7	303	13
West Bend	672	2	141	3	1,619	2	302	3

*In 1851 name changed from North Bend to Kewaskum.

TABLE 17
OZAUKEE COUNTY

Townships	1850 Population Total	1850 Population % of Irish-born	1850 Families Total	1850 Families % of Irish-born	1860 Population Total	1860 Population % of Irish-born	1860 Families Total	1860 Families % of Irish-born
Belgium	1,134	1	208	5	2,223	0	413	0
Cedarburg	1,218	27	236	47	2,235	12	394	28
Fredonia	671	5	143	8	1,785	3	322	8
Grafton	709	6	155	17	1,782	4	340	11
Mequon	2,100	6	409	10	3,368	3	609	4
Port Washington	1,606	6	299	8	2,565	3	480	6
Saukville	840	14	158	25	1,724	10	310	23

TABLE 18
Dodge County

Townships	1850 Population Total	1850 Population % of Irish-born	1850 Families Total	1850 Families % of Irish-born	1860 Population Total	1860 Population % of Irish-born	1860 Families Total	1860 Families % of Irish-born
Ashippun	1,017	8	208	17	1,634	8	302	21
Beaver Dam	484	4	82	2	1,425	4	244	8
Beaver Dam (City)	1,015	2	192	3	2,765	6	507	13
Burnett	726	.6	116	.9	1,034	2	163	4
Calamus	413	1	86	1	938	4	172	7
Chester	829	2	153	3	1,803	9	309	15
Clyman	735	13	131	27	1,461	15	245	37
Elba	727	10	139	17	1,640	20	305	37
Emmett	1,247	22	246	36	1,267	16	237	38
Fairfield*	1,143	2	208	1				
Fox Lake					1,461	20	264	39
Herman	918	1	180	2	2,008	2	401	3
Hubbard	874	.8	175	2	2,810	6	516	11
Hustisford	635	2	124	4	1,519	3	273	6
Lebanon	1,030	2	192	3	1,673	2	292	5
Leroy	397	3	86	2	1,107	1	242	3
Lomira	653	2	132	3	1,781	3	303	7
Lowell	834	8	168	6	2,034	5	383	14
Oak Grove*					2,023	5	354	9
Portland	513	12	105	16	1,313	14	247	26
Rubicon	827	5	170	9	1,675	4	327	9
Shields	590	34	126	63	1,110	23	200	55
Theresa	764	3	151	5	2,433	1	439	3
Trenton	997	10	184	16	1,895	14	344	24
Waushara	856	9	166	15				
Westford					628	5	114	8
Williamstown	914	3	174	6	2,199	1	418	3

*In 1852 name changed from Fairfield to Oak Grove.

TABLE 19
COLUMBIA COUNTY

Townships	1850 Population Total	1850 Population % of Irish-born	1850 Families Total	1850 Families % of Irish-born	1860 Population Total	1860 Population % of Irish-born	1860 Families Total	1860 Families % of Irish-born
rlington					769	2	141	5
aledonia					936	3	175	6
olumbus	960	7	125	8	2,068	5	411	10
ourtland[a]					1,219	1	203	3
ekorra	661	1	132	2	1,214	2	242	5
ort Winnebago[b]	1,674	29	283	34	747	23	139	40
ountain Prairie	546	2	110	0	1,079	5	222	7
ampden	489	0	95	0	938	2	163	3
ossuth[c]	394	.3	77	0				
eeds[c]					1,111	.6	206	1
ewiston					1,039	10	183	19
odi	317	.6	64	2	1,384	3	266	6
owville	323	7	72	7	854	8	160	15
arcellon	468	5	94	6	921	7	162	12
ewport					1,020	4	201	9
tsego	412	7	93	6	1,068	6	194	12
acific					297	7	66	9
ortage (City)[b]					2,879	13	556	26
ort Hope	413	8	81	11				
ortage Prairie[a]	603	.6	113	3				
andolph	616	1	113	2	1,165	2	208	3
ott	433	2	91	4	815	2	145	4
ringvale	471	3	87	5	832	2	145	4
est Point	197	0	36	0	743	4	152	7
yocena	588	3	84	7	1,331	5	256	10

[a] In 1852 name changed from Portage Prairie to Courtland.
[b] 1850 totals include the village of Fort Winnebago. The village of Fort Winnebago became the city of Portage.
[c] In 1852 name changed from Kossuth to Leeds.

TABLE 20
FOND DU LAC COUNTY

	1850				1860			
	Population		Families		Population		Families	
Townships	Total	% of Irish-born	Total	% of Irish-born	Total	% of Irish-born	Total	% of Irish-born
Alto	608	2	107	3	1,266	3	238	3
Ashford	628	4	125	7	1,721	3	305	8
Auburn	248	3	52	6	1,180	4	234	8
Byron	835	9	150	13	1,366	8	248	16
Calumet	1,764	.6	376	0	1,454	0	255	0
Ceresco*	356	.1	61	0				
Eden	840	18	162	27	1,271	13	230	30
Eldorado	504	7	87	10	1,180	11	215	21
Empire					809	13	144	25
Fond du Lac	2,014	4	392	5	1,221	19	231	18
Fond du Lac (City)					5,450	9	1,019	17
Forest	1,256	11	279	13	1,231	9	227	18
Friendship	412	16	83	19	637	10	118	25
Lamartine	588	3	112	5	1,151	3	229	6
Marshfield					1,403	0	239	0
Metomen	720	6	99	10	1,611	4	315	8
Oakfield	769	3	131	5	1,146	5	215	8
Osceola					881	21	164	41
Ripon*					1,070	6	193	12
Ripon (City)					2,025	6	418	9
Rosendale	672	2	134	1	1,176	3	211	6
Springvale	588	4	101	2	1,296	8	237	12
Taycheedah	786	8	144	10	1,494	7	263	16
Waupun	880	.8	146	2	2,118	7	414	13

*In 1850 name changed from Ceresco to Ripon.

Appendix

TABLE 21
Kewaunee County

Townships	1860 Population Total	% of Irish-born	1860 Families Total	% of Irish-born
Ahnapee	1,152	1	270	1
Carlton	731	.5	262	.8
Casco	941	6	230	10
Coryville	240	9	54	15
Franklin	573	17	132	30
Kewaunee	799	5	196	8
Montpelier	160	8	42	12
Pierce	260	10	71	13
Red River	674	.7	154	.6

TABLE 22
Calumet County

Townships	1850 Population Total	% of Irish-born	1850 Families Total	% of Irish-born	1860 Population Total	% of Irish-born	1860 Families Total	% of Irish-born
District No. 36	1,734	2	383	3				
Illion					300	0	56	0
Brothertown					1,367	3	244	7
Charlestown					932	5	180	7
Chilton					1,125	13	213	25
Harrison					813	2	151	7
New Holstein					1,126	1	213	2
Rantoul					378	24	65	40
Stockbridge					1,430	4	239	9
Woodville					424	5	76	9

TABLE 23
MANITOWOC COUNTY

Townships	1850 Population Total	1850 Population % of Irish-born	1850 Families Total	1850 Families % of Irish-born	1860 Population Total	1860 Population % of Irish-born	1860 Families Total	1860 Families % of Irish-born
Buchanan[a]					1,130	10	227	20
Cato					1,242	9	237	21
Centerville	210	0	42	0	1,131	1	223	2
Cooperstown	84	6	15	13	1,222	8	235	15
Eaton					802	6	154	14
Franklin					774	26	148	53
Gibson					904	1	183	2
Kossuth					1,708	4	324	7
Manitowoc	756	5	152	5	611	3	122	7
Manitowoc (City)					3,055	5	640	7
Manitowoc Rapids	966	8	190	11	1,392	5	253	9
Maple Grove					656	20	130	40
Meeme	210	8	49	14	1,114	8	210	15
Mishicot					1,258	.7	244	.8
Newton	552	7	113	8	1,390	4	263	9
Rockland					584	4	101	7
Rowley[b]					280	5	55	15
Schleswig					699	5	148	9
Two Rivers	924	3	165	2	2,460	.6	222	2
Two Rivers (Village)					1,337	3	282	6

[a] In 1861 name changed from Buchanan to Liberty.
[b] In 1861 name changed from Rowley to Two Creeks.

TABLE 24

Door County

Townships	1860 Population Total	% of Irish-born	Families Total	% of Irish-born
Brussells	953	2	164	5
Chambers Island	46	0	8	0
Clay Banks	56	0	14	0
Forestville	85	11	23	22
Gibraltar	439	4	89	7
Liberty Grove	120	0	29	0
Nasewaupee	196	3	47	17
Sevastopol	199	7	44	11
Sturgeon Bay	222	2	56	2
Washington	632	20	121	30

TABLE 25
SHEBOYGAN COUNTY

Townships	1850 Population Total	1850 Population % of Irish-born	1850 Families Total	1850 Families % of Irish-born	1860 Population Total	1860 Population % of Irish-born	1860 Families Total	1860 Families % of Irish-born
Abbott[a]	250	17	56	20	1,507	10	286	21
Greenbush	252	4	54	2	1,650	7	305	14
Herman					1,928	0	357	0
Holland					2,233	3	434	5
Lima, Lyndon, Howard, Scott, Olio	1,931	7	398	14				
Lima					1,792	4	337	8
Lyndon					1,489	5	282	12
Mitchell					942	25	183	55
Mosel					977	.4	185	1
Plymouth	1,063	3	242	5	2,106	3	403	7
Rhine					1,359	1	351	2
Russell					556	13	96	26
Scott					1,214	5	224	10
Sheboygan[b]	2,517	3	535	4	947	4	174	7
Sheboygan (City)					4,258	3	870	5
Sheboygan Falls	1,092	4	228	6	2,808	.9	541	2
Wilson and Holland	1,392	3	190	7				
Wilson					1,105	0	216	0

[a] In 1865 name changed from Abbott to Sherman.
[b] The 1850 totals include the city of Sheboygan.

TABLE 26
Outagamie County

Townships	1860 Population Total	% of Irish-born	Families Total	% of Irish-born
Bovina	214	2	42	5
Buchanan	334	12	70	23
Center	384	17	77	39
Dale	668	1	139	2
Ellington	727	6	155	15
Embarrass*	248	4	46	7
Freedom	690	15	137	27
Grand Chute	772	9	148	18
Appleton (City)	2,345	6	403	9
Greenville	1,244	8	235	16
Hortonia	649	5	134	9
Kaukauna	1,001	9	200	18
Liberty	176	2	40	5
Osborn	135	11	29	14

*In 1861 name changed from Embarrass to Maple Creek.

TABLE 27
WINNEBAGO COUNTY

Townships	1850 Population Total	1850 Population % of Irish-born	1850 Families Total	1850 Families % of Irish-born	1860 Population Total	1860 Population % of Irish-born	1860 Families Total	1860 Families % of Irish-born
Algoma	702	4	129	5	699	2	125	3
Black Wolf					693	4	131	8
Bloomingdale[a]	909	3	167	3				
Clayton	402	6	80	9	1,104	4	202	10
Menasha					1,816	11	364	20
Neenah	1,413	13	256	11	1,612	4	323	7
Nekimi	868	7	173	9	1,102	5	206	9
Nepeuskun	403	2	73	3	987	7	183	12
Omro[a]					2,012	2	390	4
Orihula[b]					233	.9	52	2
Oshkosh[c]					761	6	120	11
Oshkosh (City)					6,086	5	1,271	9
Poygan					613	13	103	33
Rushford	514	1	93	1	1,650	2	313	4
Utica	669	1	117	2	1,201	3	202	9
Vinland	672	3	125	4	962	4	159	7
Winchester					855	.5	193	1
Winnebago[c]	1,618	5	306	8				
Winneconne	1,948	4	387	9	1,184	3	224	7

[a] In 1852 name changed from Bloomingdale to Omro.
[b] In 1861 name changed from Orihula to Wolf River.
[c] In 1852 name changed from Winnebago to Oshkosh.

TABLE 28
BROWN COUNTY

Townships	1850 Population Total	1850 Population % of Irish-born	1850 Families Total	1850 Families % of Irish-born	1860 Population Total	1860 Population % of Irish-born	1860 Families Total	1860 Families % of Irish-born
Bellevue					439	.2	80	0
De Pere	798	7	150	11	768	8	154	15
Eaton					151	8	32	19
Ellington[a]	64	20	14	36				
Fort Howard					694	10	138	19
Glenmore					251	39	50	62
Grand Chute[a]	619	3	118	4				
Green Bay	1,923	5	325	6	889	.8	182	2
Green Bay (City)					2,275	6	427	11
Greenville[a]	98	13	27	7				
Holland					650	39	149	68
Hortona[a]	192	7	40	10				
Howard	567	9	79	4	591	2	97	3
Humboldt					640	9	120	2
Kaukaulin[a]	704	10	126	10				
Lansing[a]	209	13	41	20				
Lawrence	256	.8	47	2	613	2	111	5
Marinette[b]	243	8	30	7				
Morrison					401	19	80	43
New Denmark					424	9	84	8
Pittsfield	198	8	21	24	130	0	28	0
Preble					560	3	104	5
Rockland					419	28	73	48
Scott					1,053	1	177	3
Suamico	172	13	14	21	384	5	70	13
Washington[c]	171	5	129	0				
Wrightstown					463	10	88	20

[a] In 1851 to Outagamie County.
[b] In 1851 to Oconto County.
[c] In 1851 to Door County.

TABLE 29
WAUPACA COUNTY

Townships	1860 Population Total	% of Irish-born	Families Total	% of Irish-born
Bear Creek	204	10	42	17
Caledonia	396	4	86	10
Dayton	733	.8	150	3
Farmington	582	2	115	3
Iola	465	.9	100	2
Lebanon	329	41	74	72
Lind	850	2	164	5
Little Wolf	249	12	52	27
Matteson	91	7	17	12
Mukwa	961	6	200	14
Royalton	462	3	99	4
St. Lawrence	516	6	112	9
Scandinavia	653	0	137	0
Union	89	3	21	5
Waupaca	944	3	209	5
Weyauwega	1,327	2	295	3

TABLE 30
Waushara County

Townships	1860 Population Total	% of Irish-born	Families Total	% of Irish-born
Aurora	719	8	146	18
Bloomfield	516	.6	100	1
Coloma	348	1	66	2
Dakota	479	2	104	4
Deerfield	188	2	33	3
Hancock	370	1	82	4
Leon	678	4	150	8
Marion	520	6	109	10
Mount Morris	491	4	107	8
Oasis	474	2	87	3
Plainfield	837	0	160	0
Poysippi	384	16	89	24
Richford	459	2	88	2
Rose	104	5	24	4
Saxeville	618	6	121	11
Springwater	443	3	83	4
Warren	424	13	82	29
Wautoma	718	2	156	3

TABLE 31
MARQUETTE COUNTY

	1850				1860			
Townships	Population		Families		Population		Families	
	Total	% of Irish-born	Total	% of Irish-born	Total	% of Irish-born	Total	% of Irish-born
Albany*	494	1	93	2				
Berlin*	1,061	5	204	7				
Brooklyn*	505	2	105	3				
Buffalo	565	7	117	16	817	10	154	20
Crystal Lake					586	1	111	3
Douglas					659	16	121	34
Green Lake*	725	.7	141	1				
Harris					493	9	104	16
Indian Lands	2,864	6	637	9				
Kingston*	536	7	106	8				
Mackford*	521	2	102	3				
Marquette*	246	2	50	6				
Mecan					711	1	126	2
Middletown*	359	1	68	3				
Montello					767	19	151	36
Moundville					406	3	86	7
Neshkoro					498	14	97	25
Newton					596	.8	114	3
Oxford					625	1	119	3
Packwaukee					627	3	137	8
Pleasant Valley*	766	1	155	1				
Shields					642	12	124	25
Springfield					310	2	67	6
Westfield					496	12	106	18

*In 1858 to Green Lake County.

TABLE 32
GREEN LAKE COUNTY

Townships	1860 Population Total	Population % of Irish-born	Families Total	Families % of Irish-born
Berlin	1,501	8	300	13
Brooklyn	962	2	198	5
Dayton	703	2	123	5
Forsyth	823	6	168	9
Green Lake	1,242	1	224	2
Kingston	813	3	162	4
Mackford	1,598	3	296	5
Manchester	1,048	1	194	2
Marquette	476	7	95	18
Princeton	1,489	5	295	7
St. Marie	630	12	117	22
Seneca	409	15	74	35

TABLE 33

CRAWFORD COUNTY

Townships	1850				1860			
	Population		Families		Population		Families	
	Total	% of Irish-born	Total	% of Irish-born	Total	% of Irish-born	Total	% of Irish-born
Bad Ax	629	1	50	6				
Black River	462	3	216	1				
Clayton					827	8	155	16
Eastman					798	15	160	24
Freeman					779	8	153	9
Haney					462	4	84	8
Lynxville*					262	4	61	5
Marietta					680	5	133	12
Prairie du Chien	1,407	3	305	4	2,398	11	461	19
Hazel Green	1,840	8	363	13	2,543	6	454	10
Scott					331	9	62	21
Seneca					229	11	49	20
Utica					625	7	109	13
Wauzeka					677	9	135	16

*In 1867 Lynxville merged in Seneca.

TABLE 34
RICHLAND COUNTY

Townships	1850 Population Total	1850 Population % of Irish-born	1850 Families Total	1850 Families % of Irish-born	1860 Population Total	1860 Population % of Irish-born	1860 Families Total	1860 Families % of Irish-born
Akan	903	.3	178	.6	341	7	68	21
Bloom					526	4	97	1
Buena Vista					963	.7	201	1
Dayton					494	5	91	5
Eagle					719	3	128	0
Forest					565	.7	119	3
Henrietta					431	12	79	23
Ithaca					952	1	184	3
Marshall					529	6	100	11
Orion					597	.5	107	.9
Richland					1,075	1	219	1
Richwood					776	1	153	3
Rockbridge					546	3	104	6
Sylvan					361	2	71	3
Westford					409	6	72	14
Willow					448	4	93	8

TABLE 35
Sauk County

Townships	1850 Population Total	1850 Population % of Irish-born	1850 Families Total	1850 Families % of Irish-born	1860 Population Total	1860 Population % of Irish-born	1860 Families Total	1860 Families % of Irish-born
Adams	482	.6	93	0				
Baraboo	707	10	84	17	2,187	3	435	7
Bear Creek					611	16	121	31
Brooklyn	429	1	79	1				
Dellona					610	11	113	37
Eagle[a]	336	3	65	6				
Excelsior					787	2	153	5
Fairfield[b]					593	2	145	3
Flora[b]	39	0	43	0				
Franklin					559	5	105	10
Freedom[a]					526	1	98	2
Greenfield					668	3	134	5
Honey Creek	349	.6	71	1	1,050	3	195	7
Ironton					943	6	184	13
Kingston[c]	435	1	85	0	953	2	174	3
Lyons	68	0	15	0				
Manchester	94	6	15	13				
Marston[d]					468	7	90	8
Merrimac					734	6	144	10
New Buffalo[e]	224	2	46	0	1,181	1	243	2
Prairie du Sac	798	0	123	0	1,878	1	379	2
Reedsburg					1,181	2	231	2
Spring Green					835	4	145	7
Troy					811	3	154	5
Washington					708	3	140	8
Westfield	210	2	42	2	718	5	140	10
Winfield					591	19	118	37
Woodlawn					417	2	87	6

[a] In 1851 name changed from Eagle to Freedom.
[b] In 1853 name changed from Flora to Fairfield.
[c] In 1861 name changed from Kingston to Sumpter.
[d] In 1861 name changed from Marston to La Valle.
[e] After 1870 name changed from New Buffalo to Delton.

TABLE 36
ADAMS COUNTY

Townships	1850 Population Total	1850 Population % of Irish-born	1850 Families Total	1850 Families % of Irish-born	1860 Population Total	1860 Population % of Irish-born	1860 Families Total	1860 Families % of Irish-born
Adams	187	12	31	23	470	4	92	11
Brownville[a]					57	2	11	0
Chester					378	7	75	12
Dell Prairie					652	4	129	9
Easton					349	3	74	5
Grand Marsh[b]					432	6	79	9
Jackson					528	2	105	5
Leola					155	2	29	3
Monroe					363	1	69	4
Newark Valley[c]					121	1	26	0
New Haven					616	9	117	19
Preston					292	4	54	7
Quincy					247	7	43	14
Richfield					265	0	63	0
Rome					134	8	28	18
Springville					616	2	106	6
Strongs Prairie					605	1	114	2
White Creek					214	0	42	0

[a] In 1861 name changed from Brownville to Big Flats.
[b] In 1861 name changed from Grand Marsh to Lincoln.
[c] In 1865 Newark Valley merged in Adams, Quincy, and Strongs Prairie.

TABLE 37
LA CROSSE COUNTY

Townships	1860 Population Total	% of Irish-born	Families Total	% of Irish-born
Bangor	787	5	140	10
Barre	1,099	4	206	8
Buchanan*	546	3	100	3
Burns	505	3	87	3
Campbell	918	8	182	9
Farmington	908	2	168	3
Greenfield	701	1	138	3
Holland	615	1	114	3
Jackson	788	4	129	5
La Crosse (City)	3,860	6	759	11
Neshonoc	619	5	113	4
Onalaska	840	5	159	7

*In 1862 name changed from Buchanan to Washington.

TABLE 38
Juneau County

Townships	1860 Population Total	1860 Population % of Irish-born	1860 Families Total	1860 Families % of Irish-born
Armenia	261	2	48	6
Clearfield	215	12	41	15
Fountain	345	3	65	6
Germantown	680	7	127	13
Kildare	552	18	104	38
Lemonweir	1,322	11	262	20
Lisbon	987	6	182	8
Lindina	1,385	4	158	14
Lyndon	448	24	87	47
Marion	282	5	48	13
Necedah	592	8	114	14
Orange	233	.9	45	2
Plymouth	517	12	90	20
Seven Mile Creek	578	35	107	69
Summit	382	8	70	14
Wonewoc	477	8	108	16

TABLE 39
Monroe County

Townships	1860 Population Total	% of Irish-born	Families Total	% of Irish-born
Adrian	340	3	69	6
Angelo	447	2	96	3
Clifton	202	6	48	10
Eaton	116	2	25	4
Glendale	327	5	63	14
Greenfield	611	8	134	13
Jefferson	339	0	69	0
Lafayette	342	6	76	9
Leon	799	2	159	3
Leroy*	246	5	54	6
Little Falls	397	7	88	10
Portland	227	1	47	2
Ridgeville	489	3	98	7
Sheldon	343	6	68	13
Sparta	1,899	2	380	4
Tomah	641	11	144	19
Wellington	245	4	53	8
Wilton	400	5	86	9

TABLE 40
Buffalo County

Townships	1860 Population Total	% of Irish-born	Families Total	% of Irish-born
Alma	263	0	75	0
Belvidere	368	0	77	0
Buffalo	804	.7	188	1
Cross	306	1	58	3
Eagle Mills	187	0	38	0
Gilmanton	203	.5	48	0
Glencoe	277	9	66	15
Maxville	335	4	69	9
Naples	377	5	90	11
Nelson	282	1	80	1
Waumandee	467	3	97	7

TABLE 41
PIERCE COUNTY

Townships	1860 Population Total	% of Irish-born	Families Total	% of Irish-born
Clifton	445	.7	95	1
Diamond Bluff	157	7	37	16
El Paso	93	10	19	21
Hartland	158	10	29	21
Isabelle	92	0	19	0
Martell	534	1	110	.9
Oak Grove	370	5	82	7
Perry*	158	6	29	14
Pleasant Valley	388	11	89	17
Prescott (Village)	1,031	5	215	9
River Falls	412	10	147	10
Trenton	119	9	26	12
Trimbelle	403	2	83	4

*In 1864 name changed from Perry to Ellsworth.

TABLE 42
PEPIN COUNTY

Townships	1860 Population Total	% of Irish-born	Families Total	% of Irish-born
Albany	104	0	22	0
Bear Creek*	427	1	90	3
Frankfort	251	.4	48	2
Lima	175	3	36	6
Pepin	867	5	171	8
Stockholm	209	1	48	4
Waubeek	359	8	62	13

*In 1860 name changed from Bear Creek to Durand.

TABLE 43
VERNON COUNTY

Townships	1860 Population Total	% of Irish-born	1860 Families Total	% of Irish-born
Bergen	349	.6	82	1
Christiana	675	2	141	4
Clinton	335	6	77	10
Coon	382	0	87	0
Forest	263	0	52	0
Franklin	918	7	193	12
Greenwood	442	10	81	20
Hamburg	756	2	164	4
Harmony	386	0	81	0
Hillsboro	535	2	113	4
Jefferson	925	.3	186	1
Kickapoo	825	1	160	4
Liberty	201	.5	88	1
Stark	304	.7	58	2
Sterling	550	1	116	4
Union	193	0	38	0
Viroqua	1,573	.3	315	1
Webster	440	0	88	0
Wheatland	734	4	174	7
Whitestown	221	2	50	6

TABLE 44
TREMPEALEAU COUNTY

Townships	1860 Population Total	% of Irish-born	1860 Families Total	% of Irish-born
Arcadia	247	4	50	10
Caledonia	337	1	68	1
Gale	789	7	169	14
Preston	266	2	54	4
Sumner	130	2	27	7
Trempealeau	791	4	166	7

TABLE 45
St. Croix County

Townships	1850 Population Total	1850 Population % of Irish-born	1850 Families Total	1850 Families % of Irish-born	1860 Population Total	1860 Population % of Irish-born	1860 Families Total	1860 Families % of Irish-born
Buenavista	258	5	74	5				
Cylon					227	10	43	21
Eau Galle					160	0	31	0
Erin					373	46	76	87
Falls St. Croix	168	8	38	5				
Hammond					320	5	61	10
Hudson					1,970	8	76	20
Malone*					358	3	67	4
Mouth St. Croix	111	2	40	3				
Osceola	87	1	29	3				
Pleasant Valley					240	8	40	11
Richmond					251	6	45	13
Rush River					240	5	49	10
Somerset					319	4	65	5
St. Joseph					188	18	32	34
Star Prairie					280	7	56	13
Troy					436	4	81	9
Warren					80	2	11	9

*In 1864 name changed from Malone to Kinnickinick.

TABLE 46
Oconto County

Townships	1860 Population Total	% of Irish-born	Families Total	% of Irish-born
Little Suamico	163	2	29	0
Marinette	474	9	64	8
Oconto	1,375	8	240	12
Pensaukee	364	4	65	8
Peshtigo	564	4	100	8
Stiles	652	10	99	13

TABLE 47
Wood County

Townships	1860 Population Total	% of Irish-born	Families Total	% of Irish-born
Centralia	484	6	80	11
Dexter	256	3	43	5
Grand Rapids	1,000	5	178	12
Hemlock	119	.8	23	4
Rudolph	256	9	45	24
Saratoga	310	13	51	25

TABLE 48
Marathon County

Townships	1850 Population Total	1850 Population % of Irish-born	1850 Families Total	1850 Families % of Irish-born	1860 Population Total	1860 Population % of Irish-born	1860 Families Total	1860 Families % of Irish-born
Berlin					554	0	112	0
Jenny					168	1	48	2
Knowlton					115	6	22	9
Marathon					174	0	39	0
Mosinee					334	12	63	25
Stettin					240	0	59	0
Texas					161	10	32	13
Wausau	508	4	76	1	543	5	187	3
Weston					214	7	47	13

TABLE 49
Portage County

Townships	1850 Population Total	1850 Population % of Irish-born	1850 Families Total	1850 Families % of Irish-born	1860 Population Total	1860 Population % of Irish-born	1860 Families Total	1860 Families % of Irish-born
Almond					491	2	91	5
Amherst					600	1	118	.8
Belmont					465	4	89	8
Buena Vista					428	4	81	6
Eau Pleine					181	4	33	15
Grand Rapids*	341	4	49	6				
Hull					229	14	46	26
Lanark					435	10	84	19
Linwood					274	3	58	5
New Hope					484	0	101	0
Pine Grove					298	2	63	3
Plover	450	4	82	9	895	1	174	2
Sharon					454	10	83	22
Stevens Point	416	3	73	4	1,676	8	339	14
Stockton					592	3	113	6

*In 1856 to Wood County.

TABLE 50
JACKSON COUNTY

Townships	1860 Population Total	% of Irish-born	1860 Families Total	% of Irish-born
Albion	1,245	3	251	4
Alma	699	2	149	2
Hixton	397	2	89	4
Irving	439	4	91	5
Manchester	259	6	51	10
Melrose	671	.4	139	1
Northfield	81	0	16	0
Springfield	379	2	82	5

TABLE 51
EAU CLAIRE COUNTY

Townships	1860 Population Total	% of Irish-born	1860 Families Total	% of Irish-born
Bridge Creek	480	1	91	1
Brunswick	288	5	61	7
Half Moon	279	15	56	29
Eau Claire	636	6	126	7
North Eau Claire	308	19	81	27
Pleasant Valley	118	8	34	9

TABLE 52
CLARK COUNTY

Townships	1860 Population Total	1860 Population % of Irish-born	1860 Families Total	1860 Families % of Irish-born
Levis	93	1	20	5
Pine Valley	488	2	106	5
Weston	210	1	57	2

TABLE 53
CHIPPEWA COUNTY

Townships	1850 Population Total	1850 Population % of Irish-born	1850 Families Total	1850 Families % of Irish-born	1860 Population Total	1860 Population % of Irish-born	1860 Families Total	1860 Families % of Irish-born
	615	9	94	5				
Anson					80	3	11	9
Bloomer					200	3	38	5
Chippewa Falls					753	7	106	13
Eagle Point					545	4	113	6
Lafayette					158	8	47	13
Wheaton					159	4	34	6

TABLE 54
DUNN COUNTY

Townships	1860 Population Total	% of Irish-born	1860 Families Total	% of Irish-born
Dunn	447	5	94	7
Eau Galle	362	11	62	10
Menominee	955	8	132	8
Peru	140	0	27	0
Rock Creek	147	0	30	0
Spring Brook	653	2	125	2

TABLE 55
POLK COUNTY

Townships	1860 Population Total	% of Irish-born	1860 Families Total	% of Irish-born
Alden	157	0	24	0
Farmington	337	5	82	12
Osceola	479	4	96	9
Sterling	73	3	17	6
St. Croix Falls	354	12	75	24

TABLE 56
Barron (Dallas) County

Townships	1860 Population Total	% of Irish-born	Families Total	% of Irish-born
	13	0	5	0

TABLE 57
Douglas County

Townships	1860 Population Total	% of Irish-born	Families Total	% of Irish-born
Nemadji	6	83	4	75
Pokegema	272	5	75	10
Superior	534	6	152	8

TABLE 58
BAYFIELD (LA POINTE) COUNTY

Townships	1850 Population Total	1850 Population % of Irish-born	1850 Families Total	1850 Families % of Irish-born	1860 Population Total	1860 Population % of Irish-born	1860 Families Total	1860 Families % of Irish-born
Fond du Lac (Village)	16	0	4	0				
La Pointe (Village)	473	0	82	0				
Bayfield					357	4	86	5

TABLE 59
ASHLAND COUNTY

Townships	1860 Population Total	1860 Population % of Irish-born	1860 Families Total	1860 Families % of Irish-born
Bay Port	196	1	51	0
La Pointe	319	3	71	6

TABLE 60
BURNETT COUNTY

Townships	1860 Population Total	% of Irish-born	Families Total	% of Irish-born
	12	0	4	0

TABLE 61
SHAWANO COUNTY

Townships	1860 Population Total	% of Irish-born	Families Total	% of Irish-born
Belle Plaine	198	2	36	0
Hartland	21	0	4	0
Keshena	43	0	9	0
Matteson	190	2	37	3
Richmond	220	0	38	0
Shawano	71	0	15	0
Waukechon	86	0	16	0

BIBLIOGRAPHY

I. Manuscript Sources

Archives of the archdiocese of Baltimore:
  Letters written to James Cardinal Gibbons.
Catholic University of America, Department of Archives and Manuscripts:
  John O'Mahony Correspondence in Fenian Papers.
Archives of the Diocese of La Crosse:
  Circular sent by John M. Henni to Diocesan Clergy.
  Priests of La Crosse Diocese to Michael Heiss.
Library of the State Historical Society of Wisconsin, Manuscript Division:
  Wendell A. Anderson Papers.
  Correspondence of Wisconsin Volunteers, 1861-1865, VI.
  Charles H. Eldredge Papers.
  Executive Records, Immigration.
  N. P. Haugen Papers.
  Elisha W. Keyes Papers.
  John S. Roeseler Papers.
  Peter L. Scanlan Papers.
  John H. Tweedy Papers.
  Ellis B. Usher Papers.
  William F. Vilas Papers.
National Archives:
  Manuscripts of the Seventh, Eighth, and Ninth United States Census.
  Owen, D. F. Original map of the Lead Region accompanying the manuscript, "Geological Survey of the Wisconsin Lead Mining Region."
Archives of St. Rose Convent, La Crosse, Wisconsin:
  Schoeberle, Sister M. Bonaventure. "Our Missions." Unpublished manuscript.
Parish Records of St. Patrick's Church, Loreto, Wisconsin:
  Duren, Stephen. "History and Record of Noteworthy Events of St. Patrick's Church, Marble Ridge, Sauk County, Wisconsin." Unpublished manuscript, 1891.

II. Printed Sources

Annual Report of the Emigration Commissioner of the State of Wisconsin for the Year 1853. Madison: Beriah Brown, 1854.
Biennial Report of the Board of Immigration of the State of Wisconsin. Milwaukee, 1885.
Blue Book of the State of Wisconsin. Madison, 1862, 1875, 1876, 1885, 1891.

Chandler, R. W. "Map of the United States' Lead Mines on the Upper Mississippi River, 1829," *Collections of the State Historical Society of Wisconsin,* XI (1888), 400.

Heiss, Michael. Letters to Kilian Kleiner, *Salesianum,* X (October, 1914), 16-26; XII (October, 1916), 1-9; (January, 1917), 1-7; XIII (July, 1918), 28-34.

———. Letters to the Ludwig-missionsverein, *Salesianum,* XXXIX (July, 1944), 117-118; XL (October, 1945), 77-80.

Inama, Adelbert. "Letters of the Reverend Adelbert Inama, O.Praem.," *Wisconsin Magazine of History,* XII (September, 1928), 58-96.

Journal of the Assembly of the State of Wisconsin. 1852.

Kemper, Jackson. "A Trip through Wisconsin in 1838," *Wisconsin Magazine of History,* VIII (June, 1925), 423-445.

Mazzuchelli, Samuel S. *Memoirs Historical and Edifying of a Missionary Apostolic.* Translated by Sister M. Benedicta Kennedy. Chicago: W. F. Hall Printing Company, 1915.

Paulhuber, Francis X. Letter to the Ludwig-missionsverein, *Salesianum,* XXXIX (October, 1944), 171-177.

Proceedings of the Second General Convention of the Catholic Total Abstinence Union of America. 1872-1899.

Proceedings of the Tenth Annual Convention of the Irish Catholic Benevolent Union Held at Worcester, Massachusetts, September 25 and 26, 1878.

Quaife, Milo M. (ed.). *Collections of the State Historical Society of Wisconsin:* Vol. XXVII, *The Convention of 1846;* Vol. XXVIII, *The Struggle over Ratification;* Vol. XXIX, *The Attainment of Statehood.* Madison, 1919-1928.

Salzmann, Joseph. Letter to Ludwig-missionsverein, *Salesianum,* XLII (January, 1947), 19-25.

Thwaites, Rueben G. "The Territorial Census for 1836," *Collections of the State Historical Society of Wisconsin,* XIII (1895), 257-270.

Urbanek, Anthony. "Letter to Vincent E. Milde, Archbishop of Vienna," *Wisconsin Magazine of History,* X (September, 1926), 82-94.

III. NEWSPAPERS

Appleton *Crescent.*
Baraboo *Republic.*
Boston *Pilot.*
Chippewa Falls *Catholic Sentinel.*
Fond du Lac *Commonwealth.*
Janesville *Gazette.*
Madison *Argus.*
Madison *Capitol.*
Madison *Enquirer.*
Madison *Wisconsin Argus.*

Madison *Wisconsin State Journal.*
Manitowoc *Pilot.*
Milwaukee *Catholic Citizen.*
Milwaukee *Columbia* (German).
Milwaukee *Courier.*
Milwaukee *Daily Wisconsin.*
Milwaukee *News.*
Milwaukee *Sentinel.*
New York *Freeman's Journal.*
Oshkosh *Democrat.*
Racine *Advocate.*
St. Paul *Northwestern Chronicle.*
Watertown *Democrat.*
Waukesha *Democrat.*
Waukesha *Plaindealer.*

IV. Unpublished Dissertations

Deutsch, Herman J. "Political Forces in Wisconsin 1871-1881." Unpublished Ph.D. dissertation, University of Wisconsin, 1929.

Engberg, George B. "Labor in the Lake States Lumber Industry, 1830-1930." Unpublished Ph.D. dissertation, University of Minnesota, 1949.

Fitzpatrick, Franklin E. "The Irish Immigration into New York from 1865-1880." Unpublished Master's thesis, Catholic University of America, 1948.

Overmoehle, Sister M. Hedwigis. "The Anti-Clerical Activities of the Forty-Eighters in Wisconsin 1848-1860." Unpublished Ph.D. dissertation, St. Louis University, 1941.

Read, Mary J. "A Population Study of the Driftless Hill Land during the Pioneer Period, 1832-1860." Unpublished Ph.D. dissertation, University of Wisconsin, 1941.

Sammon, Peter J. "The History of the Irish National Federation of America." Unpublished Master's thesis, Catholic University of America, 1951.

V. Books

Adams, William Forbes. *Ireland and Irish Emigration to the New World from 1815 to the Famine.* New Haven, 1932.

Aikens, Andrew J. and Proctor, Louis A. *Men of Progress for Wisconsin.* Milwaukee, 1896.

Anderson, J. A. *Life and Memoirs of Reverend C. F. X. Goldsmith.* Milwaukee, 1895.

Arensberg, Conrad M. *The Irish Countryman.* New York: Peter Smith, 1950.

Barry, Colman J. *The Catholic Church and German Americans.* Milwaukee: The Bruce Publishing Company, 1953.

Bingham, Helen M. *History of Green County, Wisconsin.* Milwaukee, 1877.
Biographical History of Clark and Jackson Counties, Wisconsin. Chicago: The Lewis Publishing Co., 1891.
Biographical Review of Dane County, Wisconsin. Chicago: Biographical Review Publishing Co., 1893.
Bland, Sister Joan. *Hibernian Crusade: The Story of the Catholic Total Abstinence Union of America.* Washington: The Catholic University of America Press, 1951.
Blied, Benjamin. *Catholics and the Civil War.* Milwaukee, 1945.
Buchen, Gustave W. *Historic Sheboygan County,* Sheboygan, 1944.
Buck, James S. *Pioneer History of Milwaukee from the First American Settlement in 1833.* 4 vols. Milwaukee, 1876-1886.
Buck, Solon J. *The Granger Movement.* Cambridge: Harvard University Press, 1933.
Cairnes, John E. *Political Essays.* London, 1873.
Campbell, Henry C., et al. (eds.). *Wisconsin in Three Centuries.* 4 vols. Chicago: S. J. Clarke Publishing Co., 1924.
Current, Richard N. *Pine Logs and Politics; A Life of Philetus Sawyer, 1816-1900.* Madison: State Historical Society of Wisconsin, 1950.
Curtis, Edmund. *A History of Ireland.* London: Methuen and Company, 1936.
Curtiss-Wedge, Franklin and Pierce, E. D. (eds.). *History of Trempealeau County, Wisconsin.* Chicago: H. C. Cooper, Jr. and Co., 1917.
Cassidy, Frederic. *The Place-Names of Dane County, Wisconsin.* Greensboro, North Carolina: American Dialect Society, 1947.
Commemorative Biographical Record of the Upper Wisconsin Counties. Chicago: J. H. Beers Co., 1895.
Commemorative Biographical Record of the West Shore of Green Bay, Wisconsin. Chicago: J. H. Beers Co., 1896.
D'Arcy, William. *The Fenian Movement in the United States: 1858-1886.* Washington, D. C.: Catholic University of America Press, 1947.
Davie, Maurice R. *World Immigration with Special Reference to the United States.* New York: The Macmillan Co., 1946.
Day, Genevieve E. C. *Hudson in the Early Days.* Hudson, Wisconsin, 1932.
DeBow, J. D. B., *Statistical View of the United States: Compendium of the Seventh Census of 1850,* XX.
Department of the Interior, Census Office. *Report on Population of the United States at the Eleventh Census: 1890.* Washington: Government Printing Office, 1895.
Desmond, Humphrey. *The A. P. A. Movement.* Washington: The New Century Press, 1912.
Diamond Jubilee Souvenir and History of Notre Dame Church, Chippewa Falls, Wisconsin, 1856-1931. Chippewa Falls, Wisconsin, 1931.
Dunbar, Rose. *History of St. Paul's Church.* Mineral Point, Wisconsin, 1942.
Ellis, John Tracy. *The Life of James Cardinal Gibbons.* 2 vols. Milwaukee: The Bruce Publishing Company, 1952.

The Emigrants' Manual. Edinburgh, 1851.
Evans, Mary Ellen. *The Seed and the Glory.* New York: McMullen Books, Inc., 1950.
Falge, Louis (ed.). *History of Manitowoc County, Wisconsin.* Chicago: Goodspeed Historical Association, n.d.
Forrester, George (ed.). *Historical and Biographical Album of the Chippewa Valley, Wisconsin.* 2 vols. Chicago: A. Warner, 1891-92.
Freeman, S. *The Emigrants' Handbook and Guide.* Milwaukee, 1851.
Fries, Robert F. *Empire in Pine: The Story of Lumbering in Wisconsin, 1830-1900.* Madison: State Historical Society of Wisconsin, 1951.
Gately, Sister Mary Josephine. *The Sisters of Mercy, Historical Sketches, 1831-1931.* New York: The Macmillan Company, 1931.
Garrison, G. P. *Westward Extension, 1841-1850,* Vol. XVII of *The American Nation: A History.* Edited by A. B. Hart. 28 vols. New York: Harper, 1904-1918.
Gregory, John. *Industrial Resources of Wisconsin.* Milwaukee, 1853.
Gregory, John G. (ed.). *Southwestern Wisconsin: A History of Old Milwaukee County.* 4 vols. Chicago: The S. J. Clarke Publishing Co., 1932.
———. (ed.). *Southwestern Wisconsin: A History of Old Crawford County.* Chicago: The S. J. Clarke Publishing Co., 1932.
Gregory, J. G. and Cunningham, Thomas J. (eds.). *West Central Wisconsin: A History.* Indianapolis: S. J. Clarke Publishing Co., 1933.
Grinnell, J. B. *The Home of the Badgers, or a Sketch of the Early History of Wisconsin.* Milwaukee, 1855.
Guernsey, Orrin and Willard, Josiah F. *History of Rock County and Transactions of the Rock County Agricultural Society and Mechanics' Institute.* Janesville, Wisconsin, 1856.
Hansen, Marcus Lee. *The Atlantic Migration, 1607-1860.* Cambridge: Harvard University Press, 1940.
———. *The Immigrant in American History.* Cambridge: Harvard University Press, 1940.
Hawkins, S. N. *The Hawkins Settlement, St. Croix County, Wisconsin, June 4, 1885.* 1914.
Heming, Harry (ed.). *The Catholic Church in Wisconsin.* Milwaukee, 1895-1898.
Henthorne, Sister Mary Evangela. *The Irish Catholic Colonization Association of the United States.* Champaign, Illinois, 1932.
Hicks, J. D. *The Populist Revolt.* Minneapolis: University of Minnesota Press, 1931.
History of Crawford and Richland Counties. Springfield, Illinois: Union Publishing Co., 1884.
History of Dodge County, Wisconsin. Chicago: Western Historical Co., 1880.
History of Iowa County, Wisconsin. Chicago: Western Historical Co., 1881.
History of Lafayette County, Wisconsin. Chicago: Western Historical Co., 1881.

History of Milwaukee, Wisconsin, from Pre-historic Times to the Present Date. Chicago: Western Historical Co., 1881.
History of Northern Wisconsin. Chicago: The Western Historical Co., 1881.
History of St. Patrick's Church, Janesville, Wisconsin. Janesville, Wisconsin, 1925.
History of Sauk County, Wisconsin. Chicago: Western Historical Co., 1880.
History of Washington and Ozaukee Counties, Wisconsin. Chicago: Western Historical Co., 1881.
The History of Waukesha County, Wisconsin. Chicago: Western Historical Co., 1880.
Holmes, Frederick L. *Old World Wisconsin.* Eau Claire, Wisconsin: E. M. Hale and Co., 1944.
———. (ed.). *Wisconsin: Stability, Progress, Beauty.* 5 vols. Chicago: The Lewis Publishing Co., 1946.
Hubbell, H. S. *History of Dodge County.* 2 vols. Chicago: The S. J. Clarke Publishing Co., 1913.
Hunt, J. W. *Wisconsin Gazetteer containing the Names, Location and Advantages of the Counties, Cities, Towns, Villages, Post Offices, and Settlements, together with a Description of the Lakes, Water Courses, Prairies, and Public Localities, in the State of Wisconsin.* Madison: Beriah Brown, 1853.
Jamieson, Raymond. *A Brief History of St. Mathew's Church at Shullsburg.* Shullsburg, Wisconsin, 1925.
Johnson, Peter Leo. *Stuffed Saddlebags, The Life of Martin Kundig, Priest, 1805-1879.* Milwaukee: Bruce Publishing Co., 1942.
———. *Daughters of Charity in Milwaukee.* Milwaukee, 1946.
——— and Lavies, John G. *Early Catholic Church Property in the Archdiocese of Milwaukee, Wisconsin,* Milwaukee, 1941.
Kelly, Sister Mary Gilbert. *Catholic Immigrant Colonization Projects in the United States,* 1815-1860. New York: The United States Catholic Historical Society, 1939.
Kessinger, Lawrence. *History of Buffalo County, Wisconsin.* Alma, Wisconsin, 1888.
LaFollette, Robert M. *LaFollette's Autobiography.* Madison, 1913.
Lapham, Increase A. *Statistics: Exhibiting the History, Climate and Productions of the State of Wisconsin.* Madison, Wisconsin, 1870.
Lawson, Publius V. (ed.). *History of Winnebago County, Wisconsin, Its Cities, Towns, Resources, People.* Chicago: C. F. Cooper and Co., 1908.
Love, William De Loss. *Wisconsin in the War of the Rebellion: History of All Regiments and Batteries the State Has Sent to the Field.* Chicago: Church and Goodman, 1866.
Ludwig, Sister M. Mileta. *A Chapter of Franciscan History.* New York: Bookman Associates, 1949.
Madison, *Dane County and Surrounding Towns: Being a History and Guide.* Madison, 1877.

MacDonald, Fergus. *The Catholic Church and the Secret Societies in the United States.* New York, 1946.
McGee, Thomas D'Arcy. *Irish Settlers in North America.* Boston, 1852.
McLeod, Donald. *History of Wiskonsan, From Its First Discovery to the Present Period.* Buffalo, 1846.
Meagher, George T. *A Century at St. Bernard's.* Milwaukee: Sentinel Bindery and Printing Co., 1946.
Moynihan, James H. *The Life of Archbishop John Ireland.* New York: Harper and Brothers, 1953.
Nevins, Allan. *Grover Cleveland; a Study in Courage.* New York: Dodd, Mead and Co., 1932.
Pahorezki, Sister M. Sevina. *The Social and Political Activities of William James Onahan.* Washington: The Catholic University of America Press, 1942.
Plumb, Ralph G. *Badger Politics, 1836-1930.* Manitowoc: Brandt Printing Co., 1930.
———. *A History of Manitowoc County, Wisconsin.* Manitowoc, Wisconsin, 1904.
Quaife, Milo M. *Lake Michigan.* Indianapolis: The Bobbs-Merrill Co., 1944.
Raney, W. F. *Wisconsin, A Story of Progress.* New York: Prentice-Hall, 1940.
Reilly, Daniel F. *The School Controversy (1891-1893).* Washington: Catholic University of America Press, 1943.
Riegel, Robert E. *America Moves West.* New York: Henry Holt and Co., 1947.
Roemer, Theodore. *Saint Joseph in Appleton; the History of a Parish.* Menasha, Wisconsin: George Banta Publishing Co., 1943.
Scanlan, C. M. *The Lady Elgin Disaster, September 8, 1860.* Milwaukee, 1928.
Scanlan, Peter L. Prairie du Chien: French, British, American, Menasha, Wisconsin: George Banta Publishing Co., 1937.
Schafer, Joseph. *Four Wisconsin Counties, Prairie and Forest.* Madison: State Historical Society of Wisconsin, 1927.
———. *A History of Agriculture in Wisconsin.* Madison: State Historical Society of Wisconsin, 1922.
———. *The Winnebago-Horicon Basin, A Type Study in Western History.* Madison: State Historical Society of Wisconsin, 1937.
———. *The Wisconsin Lead Region.* Madison: State Historical Society of Wisconsin, 1932.
Still, Bayrd. *Milwaukee: The History of a City.* Madison: State Historical Society of Wisconsin, 1938.
Tenney, Horace A. and Atwood, D. *Memorial Record of the Fathers of Wisconsin.* Madison: David Atwood, 1880.
Thomson, Alexander M. *A Political History of Wisconsin.* Milwaukee: C. N. Caspar Co., 1902.

Usher, Ellis B. *The Greenback Movement of 1875-1884 and Wisconsin's Part in It.* Milwaukee, 1911.
Wisconsin, A Guide to the Badger State. Compiled by Workers of the Writers' Program of the Work Projects Administration in the State of Wisconsin. New York: Duell, Sloan and Pearce, 1941.
Wittke, Carl. *We Who Built America.* New York: Prentice-Hall, 1940.
Zillier, Carl. *History of Sheboygan County, Wisconsin, Past and Present.* Chicago: The S. J. Clarke Publishing Co., 1912.

VI. ARTICLES

Blegen, T. C. "The Competition of the Northwestern States for Immigrants," *Wisconsin Magazine of History,* III (September, 1919), 3-29.
Blied, B. J. "The Story of the Catholic Knights," *The Catholic Knight,* VIII (September, 1952), 24-25; (December, 1952), 16-18.
Browne, Henry J. "Archbishop Hughes and Western Colonization," *Catholic Historical Review,* XXXVI (October, 1950), 257-285.
Bruncken, Ernst. "Political Activity of Wisconsin Germans 1854-1860," *Proceedings of the State Historical Society of Wisconsin,* XVI (1902), 190-211.
———. "Germans in Wisconsin Politics until the Rise of the Republican Party," *Parkman Club Papers.* Milwaukee, 1896.
Desmond, Humphrey J. "Early Irish Settlers in Milwaukee," *Wisconsin Magazine of History,* XIII (June, 1930), 365-374.
Deutsch, Herman. "Carpenter and the Senatorial Election of 1875 in Wisconsin," *Wisconsin Magazine of History,* XVI (September, 1932), 26-46.
———. "Disintegrating Forces in Wisconsin Politics of the Early Seventies," *Wisconsin Magazine of History,* XV (December, 1931), 168-181; (March, 1932), 282-296; (June, 1932), 391-411.
———. "Yankee Teuton Rivalry in Wisconsin Politics in the Seventies," *Wisconsin Magazine of History,* XIV (March, 1931), 262-282; (June, 1931), 403-418.
Dickie, Anna Adams. "Scotch-Irish Presbyterian Settlers in Southern Wisconsin," *Wisconsin Magazine of History,* XXXI (March, 1948), 291-304.
Ganfield, Dorothy. "The Influence of Wisconsin on Federal Politics, 1880-1907," *Wisconsin Magazine of History,* XVI (September, 1932), 3-25.
Hantke, Richard W. "Elisha W. Keyes, the Bismarck of Western Politics," *Wisconsin Magazine of History,* XXXI (September, 1947), 29-41.
Johnson, Peter Leo. "The American Odyssey of the Irish Brigidines," *Salesianum,* XXXIX (April, 1944), 61-67.
———. "An Experiment in Adult Education," *Salesianum,* XLV (October, 1950), 149-158.

――――. "Reverend Patrick O'Kelley, First Resident Catholic Pastor of Milwaukee," *Salesianum*, XLV (July, 1950), 108-113.

――――. "Unofficial Beginnings of the Milwaukee Catholic Diocese," *Wisconsin Magazine of History*, XXIII (September, 1939), 3-16.

Kellogg, Louise P. "The Bennett Law in Wisconsin," *Wisconsin Magazine of History*, II (September, 1918), 3-25.

――――."The Story of Wisconsin, 1634-1848," *Wisconsin Magazine of History*, II (March, 1919), 257-265; (June, 1919), 413-430, III (September, 1919), 30-40; (December, 1919), 189-208; (March, 1920), 314-326; (June, 1920), 397-412.

Klopfer, Stephen. "The First Conferences of the Society of St. Vincent de Paul in Milwaukee," *Salesianum*, XXIX (April, 1934), 23-32; (July, 1934), 8-17.

Lawson, A. J. "New London and Surrounding Country," *Collections of the State Historical Society of Wisconsin*, III (1856), 478-488.

Libby, Orin G. "Chronicle of the Helena Shot Tower," *Collections of the State Historical Society of Wisconsin* (1895), 354-374.

――――. "Significance of the Lead and Shot Trade in Early Wisconsin History," *Collections of the State Historical Society of Wisconsin*, XIII (1895), 293-334.

Mason, Vroman. "The Fugitive Slave Law in Wisconsin," *Proceedings of the State Historical Society of Wisconsin* (1895), 117-144.

Meng, John J. "Cahenslyism: The First Phase, 1863-1891," *Catholic Historical Review*, XXXI (January, 1946), 389-413.

――――. "Cahenslyism: The Second Chapter, 1891-1910," *Catholic Historical Review*, XXXII (October, 1946), 302-340.

Morehouse, Frances. "The Irish Migration of the Forties," *American Historical Review*, XXXIII (April, 1928), 579-592.

Moynihan, Humphrey. "Archbishop Ireland," *Acta et Dicta*, VI (October, 1933), 12-35.

Purcell, Richard J. "The Irish Emigrant Society of New York," *Studies*, XXVII (December, 1938), 583-599.

――――. "The Irish Immigrant, the Famine and the Irish-American," *The Irish Ecclesiastical Record*, Fifth Series, LXIX (October, 1947), 849-869.

Scanlan, Charles. "History of the Irish in Wisconsin," *Journal of the American Irish Historical Society*, XIII (1914), 237-260.

Schafer, Joseph. "Editorial Comment," *Wisconsin Magazine of History*, X (June, 1927), 455-461.

――――. "Origin of Wisconsin's Free School System," *Wisconsin Magazine of History*, IX (September, 1925), 27-46.

――――. "Know-Nothingism in Wisconsin," *Wisconsin Magazine of History*, VIII (September, 1924), 3-21.

――――. "Prohibition in Early Wisconsin," *Wisconsin Magazine of History*, VIII (March, 1925), 281-299.

———. "Church Records in Migration Studies," *Wisconsin Magazine of History*, X (March, 1927), 328-337.

———. "Wisconsin's Farm Loan Law, 1849-1863," *Proceedings of the State Historical Society of Wisconsin* (1920), 156-191.

Smith, Theodore C. "The Free Soil Party in Wisconsin," *Proceedings of the State Historical Society of Wisconsin* (1894), 97-161.

Smith, Alice E. "James Duane Doty: Mephistopheles in Wisconsin," *Wisconsin Magazine of History*, XXXIV (1951), 195-198, 238-240.

Stover, Frances M. "The Schooner That Sank the Lady Elgin," *Wisconsin Magazine of History*, VII (September, 1923), 30-40.

Thwaites, Rueben G. "Notes on Early Lead Mining in the Fever (or Galena) River Region," *Collections of the State Historical Society of Wisconsin*, XIII (1895), 271-292.

Titus, W. A. "Meeme, A Frontier Settlement That Developed Strong Men," *Wisconsin Magazine of History*, IV (March, 1921), 281-286.

Wallace, E. M. "Early Farmers in Exeter," *Wisconsin Magazine of History*, VIII (June, 1925), 415-422.

Whelan, Lincoln F. "Them's They' the Story of Monches, Wisconsin," *Wisconsin Magazine of History*, XXIV (September, 1940), 39-55.

Whyte, William F. "The Bennett Law Campaign in Wisconsin," *Wisconsin Magazine of History*, X (June, 1927), 363-390.

———. "Chronicle of Early Watertown," *Wisconsin Magazine of History*, IV (March, 1921), 287-314.

Wilgus, John A. "The Century Old Lead Region in Early Wisconsin History," *Wisconsin Magazine of History*, X (June, 1927), 401-410.

INDEX

Abbelen, P. M., 214n
Adams County, 95, 100, 108, 283
Adams Township, 46, 69f
Adell, 88
Advocate (Racine), 22
Agnew, Patrick M., 116n
Agriculture, 119f
Ahern, William, 221n
Akan Township, 97
Albion Township, 71, 114
Almond Township, 18
American Board (AOH), 238
American Catholic Clerical Union, 216
American Party, 138n
American Protective Association, 184f
Ancient Order of Hibernians, 225, 236f; on home-rule for Ireland, 241; on labor, 240; and ladies' auxiliaries, 239; organization in Wisconsin, 237; and relationship with Catholic Church, 237f; on school question, 218; on Spanish-American War, 240; on temperance, 240
Anson Township, 116
Appleton, 90, 146, 180, 245n
Arcadia Township, 104
Argyle Township, 46
Armagh (Ettrick), 103
Armstrong family, 67
Ashippun Township, 78
Ashland County, 115, 117, 118, 245n, 297
Askeaton, 92
Augusta (schooner), 54, 55n
Aurora Township, 93

Babcock, Joseph W., 151
Bailey, Patrick, 91n
Baird, Henry S., 128n
Bannen, James T., 246n
Baraboo, 245n
Baraga, Frederick, 198
Barber, Allen, 129n
Barclay family, 67
Barron (Dallas) County, 105, 115, 296
Barry, Garrett, 54, 140
Barry, Josie, 247n
Barry, Kitty, 247n
Barry, Mary Agnes, 222n
Barstow, William A., 137, 138n
Bashford, Coles, 138n
Bayfield (La Pointe) County, 117, 118, 297
Bear Creek, Sauk County, 95, 96, 202n
Bear Creek, Waupaca County, 93
Beaver Creek, 104
Beaver Dam, 76n, 120n, 154, 155, 199, 245n
Beaver Dam Township, 78
Beers, John, 16
Beirne, Andrew, 104n
Beirne, John, 104n
Beirne, Thomas, 104n
Belgians, 111, 112n
Beloit, 61, 62, 67, 109
Beloit College, 9
Beloit Township, 66
Bennett Law, 153, 159n, 168f
Benton, 27, 42, 194, 221n, 245n
Benton Township, 41, 42, 43, 46, 194
Berlin, 86
Beston, John, 58
Billington Township, 112
Birdsal, Sam, 156
Black Earth Township, 71n
Black Hawk War, 9, 70
Black River, 95, 103, 109, 114
Black River Falls, 114
Blaine, James G., 163
Blooming Grove Township, 71n
Board of Erin (AOH), 239
Bonduel, Fleurimont, 198
Booth, Sherman M., 140n
Boston, attack on Catholics in, 18
Boyd, James, 67
Boyles, Edward, 72
Bradley, John, 200n
Bradley, Patrick, 200n
Brady, Bernhard, 104n
Bray, E. A., 179, 211
Brennan, Edward, 17
Brennan, George, 200n, 311
Brennan, John, 174
Brick, James, 92n
Brick, John, 92n

309

Brick, Michael, 92n
Brighton Township, 56
British Emigrant's "Handbook" and Guide to the United States of America, Particularly Illinois, Iowa and Wisconsin, 18
Brookfield Township, 57, 59, 60
Brovold, Eric J., 104n
Brown, James S., 147, 148
Brown County, 13, 14n, 86, 90, 92f, 108, 109, 112, 245n, 275
Bryan, W. J., 186, 187n
Buena Vista Township, 18
Buffalo, New York, 27, 32
Buffalo County, 103, 104f, 108, 287
Buffalo Township, 94
Burke, E. D., 143, 145, 147, 148
Burke, Richard, 244, 247n
Burke Township, 73
Burlington, 195
Burnett County, 105, 117, 298
Burns, John, 42, 92n
Burns, Mary A., 222n
Burns, Timothy, 128n
Burnside family, 67
Burton, Thomas, 98
Byrne, John A., 21, 28
Byron Township, 87

Cady Township, 108
Caffrey, Michael, 106
Cahensly, Peter Paul, 215n
Cahenslyism, 214f
Cahill, Daniel, 104n
Cain family, 71
Cairnes, John Elliott, 6
Calamus Township, 154
Caledonia Township, 56
Calumet County, 86n, 90, 108, 245n, 269
Callahan, John, 105n
Callan, Michael, 16
Campbell, J. S., 231
Camp Randall, 141
Canada, Irish migration into United States from, 12f, 77, 92, 108, 110n, 114
Canadians, in lumbering, 111, 112n, 116
Cance, John, 103, 104n
Cantlon, James, 104n
Cantlon, John, 104n
Cantlon, Richard, 104n
Canton Township, 105
Carmody, Daniel, 143n
Carmody, Patrick, 17

Carmody, Thomas, 17
Carney, J. W., 37n
Carney, Thomas, 96
Carpenter, Matthew, 148, 156
Carroll, James, 92n
Carroll, John, 92n
Carroll College, 9
Casey, James, 101
Casey, John, 106, 244
Casey, Maurice, 104n
Casey, Peter, 98
Cashel, Michael J., 104n
Cass, Lewis, 135n
Castle, Brian J., 165
Catholic Central Verein, 236
Catholic Citizen (Milwaukee), on A. P. A., 185; on Ancient Order of Hibernians, 238; on Bennett Law, 173, 176, 179; on Cahenslyism, 216; on coadjutor question, 213; on Irish in politics, 167f; on Irish-American apathy, 246f; as Irish-American organ, 251; on Irish National League, 245, 246; and Irish Relief fund, 243; on Marquette statue, 184; on nationality question in the Church, 216; on Seminary issue, 207f; on succession to archbishopric of Milwaukee, 176; on teaching Gaelic and Irish history in parochial schools, 238, 251; on temperance, 227, 232f; on Wisconsin Board and German immigration, 38.
Catholic Emigration Society, 24f
Catholic Knights of Wisconsin, 236n
Catholic Sentinel (Chippewa Falls), on A.P.A., 185, 186; on Bennett Law, 179; on influence of Edward Keogh, 189n; as Irish-American organ, 251; on parochial schools, 220; position on election of 1896, 187; on total abstinence movement, 233; on Wisconsin immigration board, 38f
Catholic Telegraph (Cincinnati), 227
Catholic Temperance Association, Dublin, Grant County, 227.
Catholic Total Abstinence in Wisconsin, activities of state union, 231f; beginnings of, 126, 137, 226; Germans and, 229f; and ladies' societies, 231, 232; Samuel Mazzuchelli on, 226; Father

Index

O'Kelley on, 137, 227; organization of state union, 228; social and cultural benefits of, 234. *See also* Catholic Total Abstinence Union of America, *Catholic Citizen, Catholic Sentinel*
Catholic Total Abstinence Society, of Janesville, 227; of Kenosha, 227; of Medford, 232; of Milwaukee, 137; of Watertown, 235n; of Whitewater, 235n
Catholic Total Abstinence Union of America, 228, 231
Catholic Total Abstinence Union of Wisconsin, 197n, 228ff; Convention at Green Bay, 1884, 229
Catholic Young Men's Literary Association of Janesville, 248
Catholics in Wisconsin, 194f; and Bennett Law, 169f, 171, 172f; French, 198; German, 125n, 129n, 158, 198; Indian, 198; Irish, 58, 129n, 158, 194f, 198; and nationality conflict, 195, 203f; Polish, 184n; and Republican strategy against, 159
Cato Township, 89
Caussé, James, 27
Cedarburg, 245n
Cedarburg Township, 11, 82, 84
Centralia Township, 113
Chester Township, 77, 78
Chicago Northwestern Railroad, 63n, 65n, 86
Chilton Township, 90, 245n
Chippewa County, 115f, 294
Chippewa Falls, 115, 156
Chippewa River, 109, 114, 115
Chronicle (Watertown), 14
Citizen (Chicago), 165
Clark County, 110n, 114, 294
Clark, J. M., 138
Clark, John, 228
Clayton Township, 98f
Cleary, James M., 166, 217, 230, 231
Cleary, Matthew, 92n
Cleary, Thomas M., 166
Cleveland, Grover, election of 1888, 163, 165n
Cleveland Township, 113
Clifton Township, 102
Clyde Township, 42
Clyman Township, 77, 156, 245n
Collins, Daniel, 221n
Collins, John, Mount Hope Township, 17

Collins, John, Westport Township, 73
Collins, William, 17, 70
Colonel Cook (schooner), 55n
Colton, James, 200n
Columbia County, 76, 78f, 199, 267
Columbia (Milwaukee), on German dissatisfaction with E. C. Wall, 183
Columbus, 80
Columbus Township, 80
Colwell, Patrick, 92n
Conley, Patrick, 17
Conly, Michael, 96
Connolly, B. P., 99n
Connolly, Michael, 104n
Conroy, John, 92n, 200n
Constitutional Convention in Wisconsin, 130f
Conway, John 4, 200n
Cooperstown Township, 89
Corcoran Guards of Sheboygan, 141n
Corcoran, James, 104n
Corcoran, John B., 104n
Corcoran, Thomas, 17
Costigan, John, 135n
Cottage Grove Township, 72, 73, 224
Cotter, Bishop John, 229
Coughlin, Charles, 92n
Courier (Milwaukee), 14n
Courtney, William, 58
Coyne, Patrick, 17
Cragan, John, 98
Crawford County, 41n, 95, 97f, 108, 245n, 280
Crescent (Appleton), on politics in Fenianism, 146; on Bennett Law, 180
Crocker, Hans, 188
Crogan, Hugh, 104n
Crogan, Peter, 104n
Crogan, Thomas, 104n
Cross Plains, 71n
Cross Plains Township, 71n, 74
Crotty, Michael, 69
Culkin, Thomas, 17
Cull, Henry, 17
Cullity, Daniel, 104n
Cullity, Michael, 104n
Cullity, Thomas, 104n
Cummings, Bridget, 221n
Cummins, John, 98
Curran Literary Society, 247
Cylon Township, 107

Dale family, 67
Daly, James B., 200n

312 *Index*

Daly, John, 152n
Dane County, 40, 41n, 57, 71f, 198n, 199, 245n, 272
Darcey, Henry, 60
D'Arcy, William, 144
Darien Township, 62
Darlington, 239, 245n
Darlington Township, 46
Davlin, Fannie, 247n
Degnan, William E., 220
Delafield Township, 60
Delahunt, Colonel John, 143
Delaney, Thomas, 110n
Dell Prairie Township, 100
Dellona Township, 95, 96
Democratic Bennett Law League, 174, 177f
Democratic Party, 125, 150; and A. P. A., 184f; accused of Catholic alliance, 159f; and Bennett Law, 159n, 168f, 177; decline in Wisconsin, 134n; division on election of 1896, 186; and German-Irish antagonism, 158f; Germans and, 125, 126n, 153n, 181; Irish and, 126f, 129f, 152f, 154, 157, 191, 192f, 250; and Milwaukee politics, 189f; Polish and, 181n, 183; tactics of, 157f
De Pere, 90
Desmond, Humphrey, 170n, 233n, 245
Detroit Western Register, 197
Devaney, Dominick, 23n
Dixon family, 67
Dodge, Henry, 79n, 125n
Dodge County, 76, 77f, 83, 85, 199, 245n, 266
Dodgeville Township, 41, 42n
Doherty, John, 42
Dolan, James, 104n
Dolan, John, 104n
Domschke, Bernard, 126n, 138, 139
Donahoe, Patrick J., 199n, 200n, 214
Donnelly, James, 202n
Donohoe, Patrick, 245n
Donohoe, Patrick, 96, 202n
Doolan, J., 90
Door County, 86n, 90, 271
Door Peninsula, 90, 109
Doran Guards of Outagamie, 141n
Doran, John L., 131, 132, 133, 141
Doty, James Duane, 125n
Dougherty, Cornelius, 9n
Dougherty, John, 70
Dougherty, William, 200n
Dougherty Creek, 70

Douglas, Stephen, 54
Douglas County, 117, 118, 296
Douglas Township, 94
Dover Township, 56
Doyle, James M., 200n, 223
Doyle, Patrick, Irish Diggings, 42n
Doyle, Patrick, Seven Mile Creek, 101
Doyle, Peter, 174, 191
Doyle, Robert, 101n
Downey, Michael, 200n
Dreissiger Liberals, 125n
Drew, Patrick, 246n
Drury, Bartholomew, 110n
Dublin, Wisconsin, 19, 42, 43n, 227
Dufficy, Peter, 104n
Dufficy, Timothy, 104n
Dumphy, Richard, 200n
Dunkirk Township, 71n
Dunn, Barnaby, 98
Dunn, Edward, 17
Dunn, Joseph, 97
Dunn County, 115, 116, 295
Dunn Township, 72
Dunne families, 16
Duren, Stephen, 232n
Dutch, 92
Dutch Reformed Hollanders, 88
Dwenger, Bishop Joseph, 212
Dwyer, Andrew, 96n

Eagle Point Township, 116
Eagle River, 114
Eastman Township, 98
Eau Claire County, 115, 293
Eau Claire River, 115
Eau Claire Township, 115
Eau Galle River, 116
Eau Galle Township, 117
Eden Township, 87
Edgerton, 63n, 245n
Education, beginnings in Milwaukee, 220
Egan, Patrick, 244
Egan, Patrick, Adams Township, Green County, 69n
Elba Township, 77, 83, 154, 245n
Eldorado Township, 87
Eldred and Balcomb's Mill, 111
Eldredge, Charles H., 149
Elk Horn Village, 62
El Paso Township, 105
Elwell, Joseph, 153
Emerald Benevolent Society of Kenosha, 235
Emerald Township, 106, 108

Index

Emerson, Lizzie, 32n
Emigrant's Handbook and Guide, 18
Emigration, *see* Irish
Emmet, Robert, 78
Emmet Township, Dodge County, 77f, 83, 162n, 191n
Emmet Township, Marathon County, 113
Emmett Guards of Dodge, 141n
Empire Township, 87
English, 42, 87n
Episcopalian Seminary, 9, 225
Erin Prairie (Erin) Township, St. Croix County, 106, 107, 108, 187, 219
Erin Township, St. Croix County, 106, 153, 162n, 254
Erin Township, Washington County, 58, 81f, 152, 253
Ettrick Township, 103, 104
Exeter Township, 23, 69, 70f, 224

Fagan, James, 133
Fagan, Thomas, 210, 211n
Fairchild, Governor Lucius, 148
Fall River, Massachusetts, 13
Famine, in Ireland, 3
Farmingon Township, Polk County, 117
Farmington Township, Washington County, 82
Farrell, P. O., 200n
Farwell, Governor Leonard J., 134
Father Matthew Chair, 231
Feehan, Archbishop, P. A., 237n
Fenian Sisterhoods, 143n
Fenians in Wisconsin, location of, 143; organization of, 142f; in politics, 143; attempts to reorganize after 1866, 145n, 149n
Finerty, John F., 165, 166
Finnegan, Bernard, 91n
Finnegan, Hugh, 91n
Finnegan, Patrick, 91n
Finnerty, Thomas, 91n
Fiss, F. J., 231
Fitchburg Township, 71n, 72, 74, 224
Fitzgerald, Garrett M., 132, 188
Fitzgerald, John E., 247n
Fitzgerald, Thomas, 58
Fitzmaurice, W. J., 231
Fitzpatrick, E. J., 210n
Fitzpatrick, Franklin E., 36n
Fitzsimmons, Daniel, 68, 241n, 251n
Flambeau River, 115
Flasch, Kilian, 210n, 212n

Flynn, Jeremiah, 58
Foley, James, 98
Fond du Lac, 61, 65n, 68, 86, 87, 109, 120n, 245n
Fond du Lac County, 86f, 108, 245n, 268
Fond du Lac Guards, 141n
Fond du Lac Township, 87
Forest Township, 87n
Fort Crawford, 98
Fort Howard, 93n
Fortune, Moses B., O.P., 200n
Fort Winnebago, 79f
Fort Winnebago Township, 80
Forty-eighters, 125n, 138, 139, 174n
Foster, Vere, 26
Fox, George, 74
Fox, John, 92n
Fox, Matthew, 74
Fox, Patrick, 92n
Fox, Thomas, 105n
Fox, William H., 74
Fox Lake, 154, 245n
Fox Lake Township, 77, 78
Fox River, 94, 109
Fox River Improvement, 9, 79, 85, 86, 90, 91
Franklin Township, Kewaunee County, 90
Franklin Township, Manitowoc County, 89
Franklin Township, Milwaukee County, 52, 189n, 199
Franklin Township, Vernon County, 101
Freedom Township, 92
Freeman, Samuel, 18
Freeman's Journal (New York), 14n, 16, 25, 251
Free Soilers, 135n, 136
French, 115, 117, 198
French Mountaineers of Brown County, 141n
Fugitive slave case, 54, 140n
Fulton Township, 67

Gaertner, Maximilian, 202n, 203n
Gaffney, Lawrence, 98
Gaffney, Peter, 98
Gale Township, 103
Gallaher, Michael, 58
Gallaher, Patrick, 58
Galloway, William, 67
Gardner, F. B., mill of, 112n
Garrity, Martin, 98
Garrity, Patrick, 98

Garvey, Robert, 99
Garvey, Thomas, 16
Genesee, 245n
Genesee Township, 58
Geneva Township, 62
German American Priests' Society, 216
Germania (Milwaukee), 162
German Protestants, 159f, 163
German Reformed Church, 125n
Germans in Wisconsin, and A.P.A., 185; and Bennett Law, 172, 174f; and coadjutor question, 208f; immigration of, 8, 58, 78n, 84, 87n, 88, 89, 97, 105, 108, 191n; joint political meeting with Irish, 1843, 126f; in lumbering, 111, 112n, 117; and national parishes, 195, 203f; in politics, 125n, 126f, 128, 153n, 158, 183; and school question, 217; and St. Francis Seminary, 206f; and total abstinence, 136, 229f. *See also Dreissiger Liberals,* Forty-eighters
Gibbons, James Cardinal, 208, 212, 215n, 216
Gilmour, Bishop Richard, 237
Glass family, 67
Glencoe Township, 104, 105
Glendale Township, 102
Glenmore Township, 92, 93
Glover, Joshua, 54, 140n
Godfrey, Roley, 67
Goldsmith, C. F. X., 179n
Gorman, Thomas, 42
Goudgeville (Portage), 79, 80n
Gough, Arthur, 38, 110n, 116n, 179n
Grace, Bishop Thomas L., 212
Grady, John, 58
Graham family, 67
Grand Rapids Township, 113
Granger Movement, 150
Grant and Colfax Club, 154
Grant County, 40, 41n, 44, 46, 48, 255
Grant and Wilson Club, 155
Granville Township, 52
Gratiot Grove, 194
Gratiot Township, 46
Gray, E., 200n
Greeley, Horace, 151, 158, 248
Green, William, 101
Greenback Movement, 150, 163
Green Bay, 79, 92, 93; military post, 40, 194
Green Bay Catholic Convention, 183n

Green County, 40, 41n, 46, 57, 69ff, 75n, 198n, 263
Greenfield Township, Milwaukee County, 52, 189n, 195
Greenfield Township, Monroe County, 102
Green Lake County, 86, 94, 199, 279
Greenville Township, 92
Greenwood Township, 101
Gregory, John, 25

Haertl, Herman, 10
Hall, George, 23n
Hamilton, Canada West, 12
Hamilton, William S., 129
Hamilton, Wisconsin, 82
Hammond Township, 108
Hanley, Michael, 17
Hanley, Thomas, 17
Hannon, Mathias, 176n
Hansen, Marcus L., 3
Harmon, John, 104n
Harmony Township, 65
Harriman, Joseph, 200n
Harris family, 67
Harrison, President Benjamin, 164
Hart, Barney, 92n
Hart, Michael, 92n
Hart, Peter, 92n
Harvey Guards of Dodge County, 141n
Haskin, Peter, 96
Havey, James, 101
Havey, Maurice, 101
Hawkins, Lawrence, 106
Hawkins, S. N., 172
Hawkins Settlement, 106
Hayes, John, 92n
Hayes, Patrick, 101
Hazel Green, 219n
Healy, John, 196n, 200n
Heiss, Archbishop Michael, on Bennett Law, 174; death of, 175; arrival in Milwaukee as priest, 198; on Catholicity in Wisconsin, 201; furthers German-Catholic immigration, 203; on nationalities in St. Francis Seminary, 206; in coadjutor question, 208f; appointed coadjutor, 214; and Cahenslyism, 215; and Ancient Order of Hibernians, 238; and Irish Aid, 243n; on faith of Irishmen, 252
Henni, Archbishop John Martin, and alleged Catholic-Democratic al-

Index

liance, 160; in coadjutor question, 175, 208f, 213; editor of Cincinnati *Wahrheitsfreund*, 196; biography of, 197n; first bishop of Milwaukee, 198; furthers German immigration, 203; builds seminary, 206; monetary aid to Ireland, 241
Henrietta Township, 97
Hibernian Benevolent Society, of Milwaukee, 235, 236n; of Watertown, 228n
Hibernians, *See* Ancient Order of
Hickey, Patrick, 96
History of Wiskonsan from Its First Discovery to Its Present Period, 19
Hoard, Governor William, 169n, 175
Hobbes, Martin, 200n
Hobbins, James, 93
Hobbins, Patrick, 92n
Hodnett, John P., 145, 148
Hodnett, Thomas Pope, 228n
Hoff, Peter, 104n
Hogan, James J., 181
Hogan, Michael, 110n, 116n
Holland Township, Brown County, 92, 153
Holland Township, Sheboygan County, 88
Holloway, John, 92n
Horicon, 78
Hoy, Michael, 104n
Hoye, Annie, 221n
Hubbard Township, 78
Hubbell, Judge Levi, 148
Hudson, 106, 107, 245n
Hudson Township, 107
Huebschmann, Francis, 127
Hughes, Archbishop John, on Irish immigration into Wisconsin, 25; and Buffalo Convention, 27
Hughes, Edward, 98
Hughy family, 71
Hull Township, 112
Hunt, John, 104n

Illinois, 12
Immigration, cost of, 31n, 33, 35; English, 42, 78n; hardships of, 31f, 33f; of Polish into Milwaukee, 181n; into the United States, 1; Welsh, 42; into the West, 7; into Wisconsin, 7f, 32f. *See also* Germans, Irish immigration

Inama, Adelbert, 129n, 203
Industrial Resources of Wisconsin, 26
Iowa County, 40, 41, 42, 44, 47, 199, 245n, 256
Ireland, Archbishop John, and Irish colonization plan, 30n; on Bennett Law, 175; and presidential campaign of 1896, 187n; and Cahenslyism, 215n, 216; and Katzer's succession to Milwaukee archdiocese, 216; on the American Clerical Union, 216n; and school question, 217; and Catholic Total Abstinence,, 229f
Irish, in agriculture, 119f; and attitude during Civil War, 140f; and Bennett Law, 172f; characterization of, 250f; and coadjutor question, 208f; contributions of, 253; customs of, 251f; and gold Democrats, 186f; and distribution of school loans, 128; and beginnings in education, 220; and homestead exemption, 130f; immigration of, *see* Irish immigration; and joint political meeting with Germans, 1843, 126f; and labor movement, 240n; and lead mining, 41f, 118f; and loyalty to Catholic Faith, 252f; and lumbering, 109f; and La Follette Reform, 187f; and migration from one locality to another, 54, 56f, 83; and monetary aid to Ireland, 241f; and nationality question in Church, 172, 195, 203ff, 207f; cultural and social organizations of, 247f; military organizations of, 248; and pattern of parish organization, 202f; and pattern of settlement in Wisconsin, 122; in politics before statehood, 126f; in Milwaukee politics, 188f; Protestant, 58, 67, 71, 74, 224f; publications of, 251; and reasons for entering politics, 191f; in railroading, 60, 61, 62, 66, 71, 75f, 78, 80, 100, 101, 102, 103, 120; and St. Patrick Day celebrations, 248f; and school question, 172, 217f; and succession to Archbishopric of Milwaukee, 1890, 175f; and suffrage for foreigners, 130; superstitions of, 253; and tariff question, 135,

163f; and total abstinence, 136f; see also Catholic Total Abstinence in Wisconsin; and unity through organization, 249f; in Wisconsin Seventeenth Regiment, 141f. See also, Ancient Order of Hibernians, Democratic Party, and Republican Party
Irish Aid Society of Boston, 24
Irish-American Literary Society of Milwaukee, 247
Irish Appeal (Milwaukee), 251n
Irish Brigade, 242
Irish Catholic Benevolent Union of the United States, 236
Irish Catholic Colonization Association of the United States, 27, 30
Irish Church Act, 1869, 6
Irish Diggings, 42n, 43
Irish Emigrant Fund, 66
Irish Emigrant Society of New York, 23f
Irish Emigration Aid Society of Madison, 28
Irish Immigrant Aid Convention, 27
Irish immigration, Archbishop John Hughes on, 25; before 1847, 1f; through Canada, 12f, 77, 92, 108, 110n, 114; causes of, 2f, 9f; during the Civil War, 5f; after Civil War, 6f, 119; during famine years, 4ff; fostered by Catholic clergymen, 27; fostered by societies, 23f; into rural areas, 119f; statistics on, 1, 3; into urban areas, 120f; into the West, 8, 24; into Wisconsin, 8, 10f, 12f, 32f, 36f
Irish Land League, 231
Irish Musical Society of Milwaukee, 248
Irish National Emigration Society, 25f
Irish National Federation, 246
Irish National League, 244f
Irish Pioneer Emigration Fund, 26
Irish Repeal Association of Milwaukee. 241
Irish Republic (Chicago), 165n
Irish Ridge, settlement of, 16f, 46
Irish Valley, 104
Irish World (New York), 163, 164, 251
Irishman (Milwaukee), 251n
Iron County, 118
Ironton Township, 18, 97

Irving Township, 114

Jackson, Mother M. Francis, 223
Jackson County, 114, 245n, 293
Jackson Guards of Juneau County, 141n
Jackson Township, 84
James, T. N., 88
Janesville, 26, 61, 62, 65, 66, 67, 68, 72n, 75, 109, 120, 156, 221, 223, 245n
Jefferson, 67
Jefferson County, 57, 63n, 67, 75n, 196, 198n, 245n, 260
Jefferson Township, 68
Jennings, Patrick, 16
Johnson, President Andrew, 144, 145, 146, 147
Johnson, Clara M., 104n
Johnson, Edward, 195n, 245n
Johnson, James, 188, 247n; and plan for Irish immigration, 24n, 250n
Johnson, Peter L., 20n
Johnstown Township, 65
Joyce, Stephen, 93
Jump River, 115
Juneau, 154
Juneau, Solomon, 50, 241n
Juneau County, 96, 100, 101f, 108, 285

Kain, Patrick, 200n
Katzer, Archbishop Frederick X., 183n, 185, 215, 216, 230
Kaukauna, 90f
Keane, Archbishop John, 215n, 229
Keating, Michael, Holland Township, 92n
Keating, Michael, Mount Hope Township, 17
Keating, William, 17
Keegan, M. R., 134
Keenan, George, 74
Keenan, John, 74
Keenan, Thomas, 200n, 204n
Keho's Diggings, 41
Kelley, John T., 165
Kemp and Collins' Diggings, 70
Kemper, Bishop Jackson, 90n
Kendall Township, 46, 245n
Keneally, James, 58
Kennedy, Daniel, 104n
Kennedy, John, 104n
Kennedy, William, 166
Kenney, Lawrence N., 200n
Kenosha (Southport), 9, 33, 49, 50, 56f, 120n, 195, 219, 222, 227, 245n

Index

Kenosha County, 56ff, 196, 245n, 258
Keogh, Edward, 147, 181, 189, 191
Keogh, Morgan, 42
Kern, C. J., 127
Keshena Reservation, 229
Kessinger, Lawrence, 105
Kewaunee County, 86n, 90, 108, 269
Keyes, Elisha, 150, 156, 157, 161
Kildare Township, 95, 101, 102
Killarney, 58, 59
Killoren, Luke, 110n
Kinney, Catharine, 106n
Kinney, John, 58
Kinnickinnic Township, 108
Kinsella, J. J., 200n
Kirkpatrick, Francis, 41n
Kirkpatrick, S., 42n
Kirkpatrick's furnace, 41
Kleiner, Kilian, 252
Knights of St. Patrick, Milwaukee, 235, 236n
Know-Nothingism, 4, 126n, 137f, 179
Koshkonong Township, 67f, 224
Krautbauer, Bishop F. X., 229
Kundig, Martin, and naming of Erin Township, 82n; and early missionary efforts of, 195f, 198f; and elevation of Milwaukee to Catholic diocese, 196f; on coadjutor to Henni, 212; death of, 214; and education, 219, 220; as treasurer of Irish Repeal Association, 241n
Kyles family, 67

La Crosse, 61, 80, 102, 103, 120n, 239
La Crosse and Milwaukee Railroad, 74n
La Crosse County, 100, 101, 102f, 108, 245n, 284
Lady Elgin disaster, 54, 242
Lafayette County, 40, 41, 43, 44, 46, 48, 245n, 257
Lafayette Township, Chippewa County, 116
Lafayette Township, Monroe County, 102
La Follette, Robert M., 151
Lahey, John, 96
Lake Michigan, 108, 109
Lake Winnebago, 93, 109
Lake Township, 189n
Lalor, J. J., 247n
Lanark Township, 112
Land Act of 1870, 6
Lane, Timothy, 104n

Lapham, Increase A., 37
Larkin, James, 104n
Larrabee, Charles H., 132
Lawler, John, 30
Lawlor, Thomas, 91n
Lawrence College, 9
Lebanon Township, 93
Lee family, 67
Lefevre, Bishop Peter P., 195, 227
Leigh, John, 110n, 111
Leland, Frank, 157
Lemonweir Township, 101
Lenehan, Catherine, 99n
Lenehan, James, 98
Leonard, John, 101
Lewiston Township, 80
Liberal Reform in Wisconsin, 151, 158
Liberty Party, 135n
Liberty Township, 89
Lima Township, Rock County, 67, 224
Lima Township, Sheboygan County, 88
Lincoln County, 113
Linden Township, 41, 42
Lisbon Township, 101
Locofocos, 129
Londen family, 67
Loreto, 96, 202n
Loughran, James J., 208n
Louisiana, 12
Lowell Township, 77n
Ludington, Harrison, 152, 161
Lumbering, 108ff
Lutherans, 125n; and Bennett Law, 169f, 172, 174; among German immigrants, 88, 125n; in politics, 182
Lynch, Ellen, 247n
Lynch, General J. M., 28
Lynch, James, 58
Lynch, John, 58
Lynch, Michael, Janesville, 105
Lynch, Michael, Washington County, 59.
Lynch, Robert, 147f
Lyndon, 101
Lyndon Township, Juneau County, 95, 101, 102
Lyndon Township, Sheboygan County, 88
Lynn, John, 71
Lyons Township, 62

McAvoy, Sylvester, 104n

318 *Index*

McCarney family, 67
McCarthy, James, 104n
McCarthy, Maurice J., 75n
McClure, John, 98
McConville, Bernard, 58
McConville Lake, 82
McCord family, 67
McCormack, F. P., O.P., 200n
McCormick, Andrew, 188
McCormick, Patrick, 104n
McCrory, John, 245n
McDermott, Captain Hugh, 141
McDonald, John F., 247n
McDonough, Barney, 105n
McEntee, Owen, 16
McFaul, Michael, 200, 222, 227
McFarland, 71n
McFarlane, Hugh, 128n
McGann, Francis, 200n
McGarry, Edward, 147, 148, 188
McGillindy, Daniel, 104n
McGillindy, Michael, 104n
McGinnity, E. M., 231
McGlynn, Brian, 74
McGowan, J. M., 200n
McGrath of Beaver Dam, 145
McGrath, William, 58
McGuirk, John, 201n
McHugh, Thomas, 128n
McIntyre family, 67
Mack, Dennis, 92n
McKee, David, 20
McKernan family, 16
McKernan, Patrick, 196n, 200
McKinley, James, 114
McKinley, Samuel, 114
McLaughlin, Edward, 174
McLaughlin, James K., 104, 106, 252
McLaughlin, Peter, 195, 196
McLeod, Donald, 19, 43
McMahon, John, 147
McMahon, Hugh, 199n, 201n
MacMillin family, 67
McMulkins, George, 18
McNamara, Daniel, 98
McNamara, Edward, 99
McNamara, James, 106
McNamara, Mayme, 99n
McNamara, Michael, 106
McNamee family, 67
McNamee, Michael, 16, 17
McQueen, Patrick, 92n
McQuillen family, 67
McWhinney, Frank, 67
McWilliams, William, 149n
Madison, 28, 68, 71n, 72, 120n, 155

Madison Township, 71n
Mahoney, Dennis, 104n
Mahoney, John, 104n
Mahoney, Patrick, 78
Maiden Rock Township, 105n
Maine, 12
Mallory, Judge, 147
Malloy Lake, 82
Malone, James, 98
Malone, John, 155n
Maloney, Michael, 98
Manchester Township, 114
Manitowoc, 33, 89, 120n
Manitowoc County, 86n, 89f, 108, 245n, 270
Manitowoc Township, 89
Maple Grove Township, 89
Marathon County, 112f, 292
Marble Ridge, 96
Marietta Township, 99
Marinette County, 109
Marinette Township, 112
Marquette College, 207
Marquette County, 80n, 86n, 94, 245n, 278
Marquette statue, 183f
Marshall Township, 97
Martin, C. K., 145, 147, 148
Massachusetts, 12
Mathew, Theobald, 226
Mauston, 101, 245n
Maxville Township, 104, 105
Mazomanie, 71n
Mazomanie Township, 71n, 72n, 74
Mazzuchelli, Samuel, O.P., 27, 194, 195, 221f, 226
Meagher, T. Francis, 134, 135n
Medina Township, 73, 224
Meehan, John, 92n
Meehan, Patrick, 92n
Meeme, 89, 219, 245n
Meeme Township, 89, 90
Menasha, 90, 156
Menasha Township, 91, 92
Menomonee Township, 58
Menomonie Township, 116, 117
Merton Township, 58, 81
Messmer, Bishop Sebastian G., 230
Metomen Township, 87
Michael Davitt Land League, Stevens Point, 244n
Michigan, 12
Middleton, 71n
Middleton Township, 71n
Milford Township, 68, 77
Milton, 63n, 64, 65

Index

Milton Junction, 63n, 66
Milton Township, 62, 65, 66, 67
Milwaukee, 9, 33, 49, 50f, 72n, 120n, 156, 195, 196, 239, 245n
Milwaukee Badgers of Milwaukee, 141n
Milwaukee and Baraboo Valley Railroad, 73
Milwaukee County, 4n, 49, 50, 54, 56, 57, 196, 198n, 245n, 257
Milwaukee and Mississippi Railroad, 59, 61, 63n, 64, 71n, 75, 80, 86, 98, 101, 193
Milwaukee River, 52
Milwaukee and Rock River Canal, 59
Milwaukee, Watertown and Baraboo Railroad, 68
Milwaukee, Waukesha Railroad, 60
Mineral Point, 9, 44, 47, 49, 61, 194, 199
Mining, lead, 40f
Minnesota, Fond du Lac Railroad, 67, 68
Minnesota Junction, 67, 78
Minocqua, 114
Mississippi River, 61, 103, 108, 109
Missouri, 12
Mitchell, John, 88, 134
Mitchell Township, 88
Monches, 58, 81, 219
Mondovi Township, 105
Monroe, 46, 61, 63n, 69
Monroe County, 101, 102, 286
Montague, Peter, 201n
Montandon, Louis, 72, 73
Montello Township, 94
Montgomery Guards, 141, 156
Mooney, Thomas, 14, 47n, 48
Moor family, 71
Morgan, Patrick, 17
Morgan, Peter, 17
Morissey, John, 17
Morris, James, 201n
Morrison, A. L., 149n
Morrison Township, 92
Morrissey, Thomas, 195, 196, 197n, 198, 200
Mosinee Township, 113
Mountain, William, 58
Mount Hope Township, 16, 46
Mt. Pleasant Township, 195
Mukwa Township, 93
Mukwonago Township, 58
Mulcare, Patrick, 104n
Mulholland, Henry, 90
Mulholland, Peter, 90

Mullen, Andrew, 28, 29, 247n
Mulligan Guards of Kenosha, 141
Mulligan, Owen, 104n
Mulligan, Patrick, 96, 104n
Mulligan, Thomas, 104n
Mulrooney, Darby, 17
Mulrooney, James, 17
Mulrooney, John, 17
Mulrooney, Thomas, 17
Murphy, Arthur, 17
Murphy, D. E., 174
Murphy, Dennis, 41
Murphy, Henry, 98
Murphy, James, Benton, Wisconsin, 42
Murphy, James, Erin Township, Washington County, 58
Murphy, Jennie, 247n
Murphy, John, Clayton Township, 98
Murphy, John, Milwaukee, 246n
Murphy, John, Mount Hope Township, 17
Murphy, Michael, 42
Murphy, Morris, 98
Murphy, Patrick, 201n
Murphy, Philip, 98n
Murphy, Richard, 127, 188, 241n
Murphy Lake, 82
Murray, Miss, 220
Murray, John, 101
Murray, Joseph, 220
Murray, Thomas, 60, 96
Muskego Township, 57

Nagle, Dennis, 90
Nagle, James, 17
Nagle, John, 172, 173, 178, 180, 186, 187, 191
Naples Township, 104
Nashotah, 9, 225
National Immigrant Aid Association, 28f
National Irish Emigration Convention, 28f
National Land League, in America, 244; in Ireland, 243; in Wisconsin, 243
Nativism, 128n, 137f
Necedah Township, 102
Neenah, 90, 91, 156
Neenah Township, 92
Nefficy, Daniel, 104n
Neillsville, 114
Nelson, Nels T., 104n
Nepeuskun Township, 91
Neshkoro Township, 94

Neville, Martin, 110n
New Berlin Township, 57, 58
New Diggings Township, 43, 194, 221n
New Dublin, 82
New Haven Township, 100
Newhall, John, 18
New Jersey, 12
New Lisbon, 102n
New Richmond, 220, 245n
News (Milwaukee), 160; on coadjutor question, 210n, 213n
Newton Township, 89, 90
New York, 8, 12
Nolan, D. W., 228
Nolan, James, 110n, 116n
Norris, John W., 205
Northport, 93
Northwestern Chronicle (St. Paul), 28, 107, 251
Norton, Joseph, 110n
Norwegians, 70, 89, 99, 101n, 104, 105, 112n, 116, 117, 174n, 185n
Nunkey, Albert, 236n

Oak Creek Township, 189n, 195
Oak Grove Township, 77, 78, 84
O'Brien, Dillon, 28, 30, 249n
O'Brien, James, 17
O'Brien, John, 104n
O'Brien, Michael J., 176; on school question, 218
O'Brien, Smith, 134
O'Brien, Timothy, 147n, 188
O'Connell, Daniel, 25, 59, 135n, 241
O'Connell Debating Society of Milwaukee, 247
O'Connellsville, 59
O'Connor, Edward, 200n
O'Connor, J. L., 166, 184, 191
O'Connor, John, 29, 129
O'Connor, M. L., 60
O'Connor, Margaret J., 247n
O'Connor, Patrick, 22
Oconomowoc Township, 60
Oconto County, 86n, 108, 109, 112, 291
Oconto Rifles of Oconto, 141n
O'Farrell, Patrick, 201n
O'Gary, Redmond, 59, 60
Ogden's Mill, 112n
Ohio, 12
O'Keefe, Lawrence, 73
O'Keefe, William, 73
O'Kelley, Patrick, 14n, 137, 195, 199, 227

Olio, 88
O'Malley, James, 228, 230, 232
O'Malley, Martin, 73n
O'Malley, Michael, 73
O'Malley, Thomas, 73n
O'Meara, John, 96
O'Meara, Patrick, 42
Onahan, William J., 28, 29, 30
Oneida County, 113, 114
O'Neil, Alexander, 114
O'Neil, Bartholomew, 143n
O'Neil, Henry, 114
O'Neil, James, 114
O'Neil, John, 104n
O'Neil, Michael, 96
O'Neil, Patrick, 96
O'Neill, Mayor Edward, 28, 29, 188, 247n, 250
Orange Township, 102
O'Reilly, L. P., 231
O'Rourke, J., 141
Osceola Township, Fond du Lac County, 87, 88, 162n
Osceola Township, Polk County, 117, 162n
Osgoodby, George, 165
O'Shaughnessy, Thomas, 17
O'Shea, Patrick, 90
Oshkosh, 65n, 86, 92, 109, 120n, 245n
Oshkosh Township, 92
O'Sullivan, O., 88
Outagamie County, 86n, 90, 92, 245n, 273
Ozaukee County, 11, 14, 76, 82, 85, 108, 109, 196, 198n, 245n, 265

Paine, Byron C., 145
Palmer, H. L., 147.
Parnell, Charles Stewart, 243
Patriot (Madison), on Know-Nothing support of Democratic Party, 137n
Paulhuber, Francis X., 229
Payne, Henry C., 150, 161
Peck, George W., 174n
Pederson, Iver, 104n
Peep O'Day Boys of Racine, 141n
Pennsylvania, 8, 12
Pensaukee Township, 112n
Pentony, Patrick, 133
Pepin County, 100, 103, 105, 108, 288
Pepin Township, 105
Pettit, Patrick, 201n
Pewaukee Township, 58, 60
Philadelphia, Irish Catholics mobbed in, 18

Index

Pierce, Franklin, 135
Pierce County, 103, 105, 117, 288
Pilot (Boston), 5n, 14, 15, 35; attitude toward western emgiration for the Irish, 21n; as Irish organ, 249, 251; on national parishes, 205
Pilot (Manitowoc), on Bennett Law, 173, 178, 180
Pine Bluff, 74
Pine Valley Township, 114
Pio Nono College, 207
Pleasant Prairie Township, 56, 195
Pleasant Springs Township, 71n
Pleasant Valley Township, 105, 106
Plunkett, William H., 242
Plymouth Township, Juneau County, 102
Plymouth Township, Rock County, 67
Polish, 174n, 181n, 183, 184, 190
Polk County, 105, 117, 295
Pollard, James C., 247n, 250n
Pond, Levi E., 169n
Pond, Bill, 169n
Populist Movement, 150
Portage, 79f
Portage Canal, 79, 91, 101, 194
Portage County, 95, 112, 113, 198n, 245n, 292
Porter Township, 67
Portland Township, 77, 154
Power, D. G., 26
Power, Mother Emily, 222
Powers, Richard, 92n
Powers, Thomas L., O.P., 201n
Powers, Will, 92n
Poygan Township, 91
Poysippi Township, 93
Prairie du Chien, 40, 61, 95, 97, 194
Prendergast, Francis, 200n
Prentice, George D., 248
Prentice, Judson, 78n
Prescott, 103, 105, 108
Progressive Movement, 150
Prohibition Movement, 150
"Propellers," 33
Puddle Dock, 70

Quinn, Hugh, 17
Quinn, James, 96, 104n
Quinn, Jeremiah, 142, 143, 174, 190, 247n
Quinn, Patrick, 97
Quinn, William, 200

Racine, 9, 49, 50, 56, 62, 72n, 120n, 195, 199, 248
Racine County, 50n, 56f, 196, 245n, 258, 198n
Ragan, C. T., 236n
Railroads, development in Wisconsin, 61f, 63f, 67f, 69, 71, 75f, 78, 89, 95, 101f, 106; scandal in 1856, 74n, 106
Randall, Governor Alexander W., 54, 140
Rantoul Township, 90
Record (Louisville Catholic), on Bennett Law, 177
Red Cedar River, 115, 116
Redmond, John, 246
Reed, Martin, 73
Rehrl, Caspar, 218n
Reilly, Edward, 104n
Reilly, Thomas Devin, 135n
Religious Congregations of Women, Brigidine Sisterhood, 222; Daughters of Charity of St. Vincent de Paul, 224; Franciscan Sisters of Perpetual Adoration, 224n; Sisters of Mercy, 223; School Sisters of Notre Dame, 224n; Order of St. Dominic, 221
Republican Party, and A.P.A., 184f; and Bennett Law, 159f, 170, 180; in campaigns of 1884, 1888, 163f; attitude of *Catholic Citizen* toward, 180; after Civil War, 150f; formation of, 136n; Germans in, 126n, 138f, 153n; and Irish, 151f, 154f, 158; tactics of, 155, 159f, 167f
Reynolds, John, 28, 29
Reynolds, Thomas, 110n
Rhode Island, 12
Rice, John, 202n
Richland County, 95, 97, 108, 281
Richmond Township, 107, 108
Richwood, 245n
Ring, Patrick, 106
Riordan, George T., 201n
Ripon Township, 86, 87
River Falls Township, 105
Roach, Mathew, 73
Roach, Thomas, 104n
Roche, Henry, 201n
Roche, Richard, 201n
Rochester, 195
Rock County, 27, 57, 62, 63, 65, 66, 67, 196, 198n, 245n, 264
Rockbridge Township, 97

Rockland Township, 92, 93
Rock River, Milwaukee Canal, 59
Rock River Valley, 109
Rock River Valley Railroad, 65n
Rock Township, 67
Roeseler, John S., immigrant study, 46n
Rogan, James, 68
Rogan, Patrick, 68
Rooney, Bartholomew, 116n
Rooney, John, 16, 116n
Rooney, John L., 110n, 116n
Rooney, Patrick, 17
Rooney, William, 96
Roseman, Daniel, 17
Roseman, John, 17
Ruddy family, 72
Rudolph Township, 113
Rusk County, 115
Ryan, Edward G., 130, 140n, 191
Ryan, Hugh, 173
Ryan, James, 98
Ryan, Matthew, 98
Ryan, Patrick, 69n
Ryan, Sam, 146

Sackville-West, Sir Lionel, 164n
Sacred Heart College, Watertown, 221n
St. Bernard's Watertown, 197n; Temperance and Benevolent Society, 228n
St. Croix County, 95, 100, 103, 105f, 117, 153, 195f, 290
St. Croix Falls, 117
St. Croix River, 103, 108, 109, 117
St. Dominic's, Brookfield, 197n
St. Francis', Cedarburg, 197n
St. Francis Seminary, 198, 204, 206f, 249
St. Ignatius', Racine, 197n
St. Joseph Township, 107, 108
St. Joseph's Benevolent Society of Waukesha, 235
St. Louis', Franklin, 197n
St. Marie Township, 94
St. Martin's, Geneva, 197n
St. Mary's, Cascade, 88
St. Mary's, Greenfield, 197n
St. Mary's, Kenosha, 197n
St. Matthias', Oak Creek, 197n
St. Michael's, Granville, 197n
St. Michael's, Ironton, 97
St. Michael's, Mitchell Township, 88
St. Patrick's, Brighton, 197n
St. Patrick's, Sherman Township, 88

St. Patrick's, Yorkville, 197n
St. Patrick's Benevolent Society of La Crosse, 235, 236n
St. Patrick's Literary Association, 247
St. Raphael Society, 215n
St. Stephen's, Mineral Point, 197n
St. Thomas College, Sinsinawa Mound, 221n
Salem Township, Kenosha County, 56, 195
Salem Township, Pierce County, 105n
Salzmann, Joseph, 206
Saratoga Township, 113
Sauk County, 95, 97, 108, 245n, 282
Sauk County Union Guards, 141n
Saukville, 11
Saukville Township, 82
Sawyer, Philetus, 151
Sawyer County, 115, 117
Scandinavians, in lumbering, 111
Scanlan, John, 17
Scanlan, Michael, 165
Scanlan, Peter, 34
Scanlan, Peter L., 98
Schafer, Joseph, 127, 128
Schurz, Carl, 126n, 248
Scofield, Edward, 151
Scotch, 104
Scotch-Irish, 115
Scotch-Irish Presbyterians, 67
Scott, General Winfield, 135
Seawright family, 67
Seebote (Milwaukee), 160
Seneca Township, 99
Sentinel (Milwaukee), on Bennett Law, 176
Setright, James, 92n
Setright, John, 92n
Setright, Michael, 92n
Seven Mile Creek Township, 95, 101, 102
Seventeenth Wisconsin Regiment, 242
Seward, William H., 6
Seymour, S. J., 96
Seymour Township, 46
Sharon Township, 112
Shaughnessy, Thomas G., 247n
Shaw, Thomas, 104n
Shawano County, 86n, 298
Shea, Catherine, 220
Shea, Patrick, 96
Shea, Stasia, 253n
Sheboygan, 33, 88, 120, 156

Index

Sheboygan County, 68n, 87f, 245n, 272
Sheehan, John, 92n
Sheehan, Patrick H., 110n
Sheehy, Leonard P., 104n
Sheehy, Thomas, 104n
Sheridan Guards of Milwaukee, 248
Sherman Township, 88
Shields, Andrew, 58
Shields, General James, 78
Shields, John, 58
Shields, Michael, 58
Shields, Patrick, 106
Shields Township, Dodge County, 77f, 83, 162n, 191n
Shields Township, Marquette County, 94
Shook, Jonas, 69
Shullsburg, 43, 46, 194, 239
Sinsinawa Mound, 221
Skelly, John, 16
Slavan, John H., 28
Slaven, James, 96
Smith, John, Eastman, Wisconsin, 98
Smith, John, Lindina, Wisconsin, 101n
Smith, Joseph, 199n, 201n
Smith, Patrick, 101
Smith, Peter, 101
Smith, R. J., 208n
Socialism, 243n
Society to Promote Western Colonization, Waukesha, 27
Somers, P. J., 174, 182
Somers, T. F., 245n
Southern Wisconsin Railroad, 65n
Southport (Kenosha), 9, 49, 50, 195
Spalding, Bishop John Lancaster, 27, 212
Sparta Township, 102
Springvale Township, 87
Springfield Township, 108
Stack, John, 17
Stacy, William D., 228
Stanton Township, 108
State Historical Society of Wisconsin, 19
Steele family, 67
Stephenson, Isaac, 112, 151
Stevens Point, 112
Stiles Township, 111
Stone, Fred W., 11
Stoughton, 71n
Stroker, Francis, 201n
Suamico Township, 112
Sullivan, Alexander M., 244

Sullivan, Andrew, 128n
Sullivan, John, 58
Sullivan, Richard, 201n
Summers, James, 92n
Summers, Maurice, 92n
Sun (Dodgeville), 176
Sun Prairie, 68, 74
Sun Prairie Township, 72n, 73, 224
Superior, 118
Superior and Bayfield Railroad, 106
Swedes, 105
Sweeney, Edmund, 38
Sweeney Circle of Milwaukee, 143
Swiss, 105

Tallmadge, Nathaniel F., 125n
Taugher family, 90
Taycheedah Township, 87n
Taylor, William, 101, 151
Taylor County, 114
Temperance, 126n, 136f
Thompson, 81
Tiernan, John W., 201n
Tierney, James, 154
Tierney, P. R., 73
Tierney, Peter, 105n
Timlin, John, 96
Timlin, W. H., 178
Tomah Township, 102
Total Abstinence, 136f. *See also* Catholic Total Abstinence in Wisconsin *and* Catholic Total Abstinence Union of America *and* Catholic Total Abstinence Union of Wisconsin
Touhey, J., 165
Tower, Jonas, 18, 97
Townsend, Thomas J., 22
Tracey, Thomas, 221n
Trainor, James, 16, 17
Trainor, Peter, 16, 23n
Trempealeau County, 100, 103, 108, 289
Trempealeau Township, 104
Trenton Township, 77, 78
Trinity parish, Madison, 197n
Troy, man in Kildare Township, Juneau County, 16
Trumpf, G. C., 190
Turrell, Patrick, 247n

Union Guards of Milwaukee, 54
Union Lumber Company, 116
Union Township, 105n
Unionist Movement in politics, 150
United Irishmen, 249n

Index

Urbanek, Anthony, 204
Usher, Ellis B., 186
Vahey, J. W., on Bennett Law, 176
Van Buren, Martin, 135n
Vance family, 67
Van den Broek, Theodore, 198
Vanderpoel, Abram, 133n
Van Steenwyck, G. W., 20
Vermont, 12
Vermont Township, 74
Vernon County, 100, 108, 289
Vilas, Senator William F., 183, 186
Vilas County, 113, 114n

Wahrheitsfreund (Cincinnati), 196, 197
Wall, Edward C., 181, 183, 184, 186
Wall, John, 92n, 104n
Wall, Patrick, 104n
Wall, Thomas, 104n
Wall, Walter, 104n
Wallace family, 71
Walsh, Mathew, 17
Walsh, Patrick, 16
Walworth County, 57, 62, 196, 198n, 245n, 261
Ward, M. J., 231
Warren Township, 93, 107, 108
Washburn, Cadwallader C., 144, 151
Washburn County, 117
Washington County, 14, 58, 76, 81f, 83, 84, 85, 196, 198n, 245n, 265
Washington Island, 90
Waters, Mathias, 105n
Watertown, 61, 68, 77, 109, 120n, 220, 221n, 235n, 245n, 248
Watertown Infantry of Jefferson, 141n
Watertown Township, 68f, 77
Waubeek Township, 105
Waukesha, 27, 57, 245n
Waukesha County, 50, 57, 62, 196, 198n, 245n, 259
Waumandee Township, 104, 105
Waupaca County, 86n, 93, 108, 276
Waupun Township, 87
Waushara County, 86n, 93, 108, 277
Wauwatosa Township, 52
Wauzeka, 95
Wayne Township, 82
Welch, Robert, 98
Wellington Township, 102
Welsh, 42
Welsh, J., 73
Welsh, Michael, 70
Welsh, Peter, 96

Welsh, Thomas, 70
West, William, 6
Westford Township, 97, 154
Weston Township, 114
Westport Township, 71n, 72f, 162n
Whalen, Darby, 104n
Whalen, Thomas, 104n
Wheaton Township, 116
Whelan, John, 58
Whelan, Peter, 58
Whig Party, 125, 129, 135n, 136
White, James S., 156
White, John, 127, 188
Whitesides, William, 16
Whitewater, 62, 120n
Whyte, William F., 78n, 83
Willard, George L., 211, 228, 231
Williams, Fred, 190
Williams, Mary C., 222n
Willow Springs Township, 42, 43, 46, 245n
Wilton Township, 102
Winfield Township, 95, 96
Winnebago County, 86, 90, 91f, 108, 245n, 274
Winneconne Township, 109, 110n
Winnetka, Illinois, 54
Wiota, 69
Wisconsin, Board of Immigration in, 37; Commissioner of Emigration in, 37; Constitutional Convention, 130f; first Catholic diocese in, 197; Emigrant Agency, 20f; early schools in, 220f. *See also* Catholics, Germans, Irish, Irish immigration, Yankees
Wisconsin Historical Collections, 19
Wisconsin River, 95, 109
Wisconsin River Valley, 112
Wisconsin Seventeenth Regiment, 141f
Wolf River, 109
Wolf Tone Circle of Milwaukee, 143
Wood County, 112, 291
Woods, John, 17
Wrightstown Township, 92
Why Ireland Is Poor, 165

Yankees in Wisconsin, 8, 11, 12, 84n, 93
Yellow River, 115
Young Men's Association Watertown, 248
Young Men's Republican Club of Milwaukee, 175

Zeininger, August, 183n

THE IRISH-AMERICANS

An Arno Press Collection

Athearn, Robert G. **THOMAS FRANCIS MEAGHER:** An Irish Revolutionary in America. 1949

Biever, Bruce Francis. **RELIGION, CULTURE AND VALUES:** A Cross-Cultural Analysis of Motivational Factors in Native Irish and American Irish Catholicism. 1976

Bolger, Stephen Garrett. **THE IRISH CHARACTER IN AMERICAN FICTION, 1830-1860.** 1976

Browne, Henry J. **THE CATHOLIC CHURCH AND THE KNIGHTS OF LABOR.** 1949

Buckley, John Patrick. **THE NEW YORK IRISH:** Their View of American Foreign Policy, 1914-1921. 1976

Cochran, Alice Lida. **THE SAGA OF AN IRISH IMMIGRANT FAMILY:** The Descendants of John Mullanphy. 1976

Corbett, James J. **THE ROAR OF THE CROWD.** 1925

Cronin, Harry C. **EUGENE O'NEILL:** Irish and American; A Study in Cultural Context. 1976

Cuddy, Joseph Edward. **IRISH-AMERICAN AND NATIONAL ISOLATIONISM, 1914-1920.** 1976

Curley, James Michael. **I'D DO IT AGAIN:** A Record of All My Uproarious Years. 1957

Deasy, Mary. **THE HOUR OF SPRING.** 1948

Dinneen, Joseph. **WARD EIGHT.** 1936

Doyle, David Noel. **IRISH-AMERICANS, NATIVE RIGHTS AND NATIONAL EMPIRES:** The Structure, Divisions and Attitudes of the Catholic Minority in the Decade of Expansion, 1890-1901. 1976

Dunphy, Jack. **JOHN FURY.** 1946

Fanning, Charles, ed. **MR. DOOLEY AND THE CHICAGO IRISH:** An Anthology. 1976

Farrell, James T. **FATHER AND SON.** 1940

Fleming, Thomas J. **ALL GOOD MEN.** 1961

Funchion, Michael F. **CHICAGO'S IRISH NATIONALISTS, 1881-1890.** 1976

Gudelunas, William A., Jr. and William G. Shade. **BEFORE THE MOLLY MAGUIRES:** The Emergence of the Ethno-Religious Factor in the Politics of the Lower Anthracite Region, 1844-1872. 1976

Henderson, Thomas McLean. **TAMMANY HALL AND THE NEW IMMIGRANTS:** The Progressive Years. 1976

Hueston, Robert Francis. **THE CATHOLIC PRESS AND NATIVISM, 1840-1860.** 1976

Joyce, William Leonard. **EDITORS AND ETHNICITY:** A History of the Irish-American Press, 1848-1883. 1976

Larkin, Emmet. **THE HISTORICAL DIMENSIONS OF IRISH CATHOLICISM.** 1976

Lockhart, Audrey. **SOME ASPECTS OF EMIGRATION FROM IRELAND TO THE NORTH AMERICAN COLONIES BETWEEN 1660-1775.** 1976

Maguire, Edward J., ed. **REVEREND JOHN O'HANLON'S *THE IRISH EMIGRANT'S GUIDE FOR THE UNITED STATES*:** A Critical Edition with Introduction and Commentary. 1976

McCaffrey, Lawrence J., ed. **IRISH NATIONALISM AND THE AMERICAN CONTRIBUTION.** 1976

McDonald, Grace. **HISTORY OF THE IRISH IN WISCONSIN IN THE NINETEENTH CENTURY.** 1954

McManamin, Francis G. **THE AMERICAN YEARS OF JOHN BOYLE O'REILLY, 1870-1890.** 1976

McSorley, Edward. **OUR OWN KIND.** 1946

Moynihan, James H. **THE LIFE OF ARCHBISHOP JOHN IRELAND.** 1953

Niehaus, Earl F. **THE IRISH IN NEW ORLEANS, 1800-1860.** 1965

O'Grady, Joseph Patrick. **IRISH-AMERICANS AND ANGLO-AMERICAN RELATIONS, 1880-1888.** 1976

Rodechko, James Paul. **PATRICK FORD AND HIS SEARCH FOR AMERICA:** A Case Study of Irish-American Journalism, 1870-1913. 1976

Roney, Frank. **IRISH REBEL AND CALIFORNIA LABOR LEADER:** An Autobiography. Edited by Ira B. Cross. 1931

Roohan, James Edmund. **AMERICAN CATHOLICS AND THE SOCIAL QUESTION, 1865-1900.** 1976

Shannon, James. **CATHOLIC COLONIZATION ON THE WESTERN FRONTIER.** 1957

Shaw, Douglas V. **THE MAKING OF AN IMMIGRANT CITY:** Ethnic and Cultural Conflict in Jersey City, New Jersey, 1850-1877. 1976

Sylvester, Harry. **MOON GAFFNEY.** 1947

Tarpey, Marie Veronica. **THE ROLE OF JOSEPH McGARRITY IN THE STRUGGLE FOR IRISH INDEPENDENCE.** 1976

Vinyard, JoEllen McNergney. **THE IRISH ON THE URBAN FRONTIER:** Nineteenth Century Detroit. 1976

Walsh, James P., ed. **THE IRISH: AMERICA'S POLITICAL CLASS.** 1976

Weisz, Howard Ralph. **IRISH-AMERICAN AND ITALIAN-AMERICAN EDUCATIONAL VIEWS AND ACTIVITIES, 1870-1900:** A Comparison. 1976